THE WORLD ATLAS OF
WHISKY

ICHIRO'S CHOICE

1976

Distillery
KAWASAKI

SINGLE GRAIN WHISKY
KAWASAKI

Cask Strength
Non chill-filtered Non coloured
Bottling # **73** / 432

700 ml

THE WORLD ATLAS OF
WHISKY

DAVE BROOM

MITCHELL
BEAZLEY

Dedication

In memory of my beloved mother, Isobel Broom, who sadly didn't live
to see this work completed, but whose constant and loving support
over the years got me to where I am. I hope you'd be proud.

The World Atlas of Whisky
by Dave Broom

First published in Great Britain in 2010 by Mitchell Beazley, an imprint
of Octopus Publishing Group Limited, Endeavour House,
189 Shaftesbury Avenue, London WC2H 8JY
www.octopusbooks.co.uk

An Hachette UK Company, www.hachette.co.uk

Reprinted 2011

Distributed in the United States and Canada by Hachette Book
Group USA, 237 Park Avenue, New York, NY 10017 USA

ISBN: 978 1 84533 577 9

Set in Garamond and Futura
Printed and bound in Hong Kong

Commissioning Editor Hilary Lumsden
Senior Editor Leanne Bryan
Researcher/Copy Editor Susanna Forbes
Proofreader Diona Gregory
Indexer Angie Hipkin
Americanizer Jamie Ambrose
Art Director Pene Parker
Executive Art Editor Juliette Norsworthy
Designer Bounford.com
Picture Research Manager Giulia Hetherington
Picture Researcher Maria Gibbs
Cartographic Researcher Sally Toms
Production Manager Peter Hunt

Cartography
Heritage Editorial, heritage2ed@aol.com
Digital mapping by Encompass Graphics Ltd,
Hove, UK, www.encompass-graphics.co.uk

Acknowledgment
I particularly want to thank Davin de Kergommeaux and Bernhard
Schäfer, who helped significantly in the writing of the Canadian and
Central Europe sections, respectively.

Opposite: **Whisky sleeping** in the vaulted warehouses
at Deanston Distillery, Scotland.

Contents

FOREWORD

If there ever was a time for a comprehensive book on whisky, it's now.
The whisky world is more dynamic than at any other time in recent history.

Why? One reason is that we are in the midst of a whisky boom. More and more people across the globe are beginning to realize the quality, individuality, and value of whisky. Even with the recent increase in whisky prices, whisky's value—especially bourbon—can't be beaten by any other distilled spirit. The whisky industry has responded to increased demand by increasing its output, expanding its capacity, and even building new distilleries.

Another reason is the proliferation of new artisan whisky distillers. Gone are the days when nearly all whisky producers were from Scotland, Ireland, the United States (predominantly Kentucky and Tennessee), and Canada. Japan has proven that its distillers deserve just as much attention and respect by producing whisky that is as good as Scotch whisky.

That's saying a lot! There have never been more Scotch whiskies to choose from—both from the distillery owners themselves, and also from the myriad of independent bottlers. Hundreds, actually. And, thanks to enhancements in distilling and maturation over the past decade or two, the quality of the whisky has never been better.

Additionally, new small craft distillers now make whisky across Europe, throughout the US, and beyond. In the US alone, there are around 60 artisan distillers making whiskey that didn't even exist a decade ago. That's about four times more than established bourbon distillers, and the growth rate of these new distillers is increasing.

What does all this mean to you, the whisky enthusiast? You can look forward to many new whiskies, both from established distillers and the new artisan distillers peppered across the globe, which will continue to proliferate well into the future.

This brings us to *The World Atlas of Whisky*. What I like about it is its comprehensiveness. The book defines whisky, how it's made (from grain to glass), where it's made, and why one whisky tastes different from another. It explains how to best appreciate whisky and gives a great synopsis of the new releases, along with tasting notes to help guide you. The photography accompanying the text is beautiful, even breathtaking at times. It really benefits those who don't have the means to travel to the various distilleries and distilling countries.

Perhaps the most useful and innovative component of the book is the use of "Flavor Camps" when describing the flavor personality of whiskies. While I enjoy the thorough tasting notes provided for the whiskies profiled, the flavor-camp concept is a great resource when trying to capture the general flavor profile of a given whisky. This is a useful guide for all whisky enthusiasts, but I think it will be especially helpful for those just beginning to explore the somewhat daunting and overwhelming array of whiskies to choose from.

Most importantly, *The World Atlas of Whisky* captures the essence of what's happening right now. Dave Broom is one of the very few whisky writers with the ability to do this in such a comprehensive manner. He is one of the most respected independent authorities on whisky worldwide. And justly deserved, I might add. I am particularly captivated by Dave's engaging writing style and colorful tasting notes. It's understandable why his writing is in such demand.

Thanks to Dave, this book is both informative and entertaining to read—regardless of where you are in your whisky journey. His knowledge, passion, and integrity show in everything he writes. *Slainte*!

John Hansell
Publisher and editor,
Malt Advocate magazine

A grain of truth. All single-malt whisky starts with barley.

Opposite: Every glass tells a story. Whisky is the most complex spirit of all.

INTRODUCTION

Whisky is, not for the first time in its convoluted life, at a decision point. The drink that dominated the spirits market for most of the twentieth century is facing a consumer who is now more demanding, more marketing-literate, and, some would argue, more cynical. How can whisky prosper in a world which demands instant gratification? Can a drink that needs to be matured for years before it can even be called whisky (and which needs to spend longer in gentle congress with oak to gain its true character) ever fit with a mind-set that demands things to be faster, quicker, louder?

If you'd asked that question a decade ago then there would have been some doubts as to whether it could. Yet whisky has not just survived the pressures of the recent past, it is growing once more. Although many drinkers have embraced the thrills of the accelerated twenty-first-century culture, there are some who have stepped off, slowed down, and begun to appreciate flavor and craftsmanship. In a chaotic world, whisky gives them a breathing space. They are its future. The whiskies which they will be drinking have changed as well. This used to be a simple category. There was Scotch, dominated by blends; there was bourbon, and a little Irish. These days, blended

Scotch is still the dominant style—and a look at the extraordinary success of blends among new young drinkers in markets such as Brazil, China, Russia, Mexico, and South Africa will quickly silence those who wrote the category's obituary a few years ago. In these new markets, whisky is a signifier of success.

Single-malt Scotch has elevated itself from being the drink of Scottish poets and landowners to become a premium spirit with worldwide relevance and maniacal followers who obsess about every detail of its production and provenance. Bourbon (and rye) has also experienced a renaissance, with exciting innovations and a new top-end quality gloss. Irish whiskey has gone from being a single brand to a rich and varied category, while the whisky-drinkers of the world have in recent years been astounded by the quality and character of the whiskies from Japan, which are finally appearing on the global markets. All of these whiskies have their own style.

In addition, the past decade has seen an explosion of new distillers in almost every country you care to mention. From Tasmania to Taiwan, Brittany to Belgium, Sweden to Colorado, new, mostly small-scale distillers are making their take on whisky and, in doing so, they have increased the range of flavors and forced us to question what whisky is. I believe that we are living in the most exciting period in whisky's long evolution.

The writing of this book has underlined the oft-overlooked fact that whisky-making is a creative act—whisky itself is a natural product made from cereal, yeast, water, and oak. There are none of the added tannins, acidification, micro-oxygenation, or spinning cones that are common in the more commercial realms of winemaking, often regarded as an intrinsically natural process. Don't be fooled by the look of a distillery, all pipes and copper; whisky comes from the earth, from the air, and from the soul of the people who craft it.

If whisky is to grow, it needs to address these new drinkers honestly. That means it needs to *be* honest. It means dismantling the absurd rules that have grown on its back like a weighty carapace, slowing its ability to react: notions like you can only appreciate it if you are 35+, if you are male, that it can only be drunk after dinner, or with or without water. Drink whisky in whatever way you want. It is made to be enjoyed. Celebrate its flavor and diversity. Welcome to whisky world.

The often-forgotten element in whisky-making around the world: people, here at the Murree distillery in Rawalpindi, Pakistan.

HOW THIS BOOK WORKS

With such a wealth of information available, this book includes a number of text and visual devices to enable the reader to get the most out of reading about all the whisky-producing countries, regions, and distilleries. These include: maps, tasting notes with flavor ratings, and details about the individual distilleries themselves. Below is a guide to how these work.

MAPS

Main Key A number of methods are used to show where each distillery is located. In the case of distilleries that have the same name as the nearest place, only the distillery name is given (e.g. Lagavulin). Where there is room and scale allows, the nearest place is shown using a white dot. Where scale or space are an issue, the place-name is given after the distillery name using a comma: Jim Beam, Clermont.

Elevation/Topography Key This relates to all maps and is included on those maps where it is felt that the scale allows for clear definition of the topography.

Regions Within each country, the distilleries are ordered by region, apart from the USA, where Kentucky and Tennessee appear separately from other US distilleries. This is because the distinctly different production process used to make these whiskeys results in its own subcategory.

Distilleries All distilleries that have been written about appear on the maps. Where there are a large number of other distilleries of note—for example, the new whisky-producers in Europe or the craft distilleries in the USA—these are also included on the map, although there may be no reference to them in the text.

Grain Distilleries, Maltings, & Other Whisky-related Features Where feasible and useful, distinctions have been made to clarify what sort of distillery is specified as well as the inclusion of a number of maltings.

DISTILLERY PAGES

Details Every distillery page gives details of the nearest village, town, or city, and (where available) a website or page related to that particular site for those featured in the tasting notes. On pages where there is more than one distillery, the details are divided by "/".

Visits Where the distillery is open for visits, details are included, which are correct at the time of writing. If you are thinking of visiting a distillery, it is always best to get in contact in advance to check current opening details. If you are making an appointment or plan on taking a specific tour, never underestimate the time allowed for winding roads, sheep on the road, etc.!

Sourcing Rare Malts Please note that, although many distilleries are not able to open to the public, their products are available. For these, the best way to find out more is to make contact with a specialist whisky retailer, or refer to specialist whisky websites.

Mothballed This term defines those distilleries that have been taken out of production but which may be brought back into production at some date in the future. At the time of writing, the information given as to which plants are mothballed is as accurate as possible.

New/Planned There are a huge number of new distilleries opening and in the process of being built globally. The aim for this atlas is to be as comprehensive as possible, but there might be cases where we have not had the opportunity to include new distilleries on the maps.

TASTING NOTES

Selection I have chosen a selection of whiskies that best illustrate the breadth of each distillery's offering, looking at new spirit, young, teenage, and older releases where appropriate.

Order They have been ordered in a similar fashion for each country so as to allow easy comparison. The ordering follows one of two approaches: either by age, or, if more than one brand name is produced at a single distillery, in alphabetical order.

Age Definitions Normally the age statement forms part of the name of the whisky. The term "NAS" refers to those with no age statement on the label.

Independent Bottlings Where possible, I have tasted whiskies from the distillery's owner, but on some occasions when these have not been available I have tasted examples from independent bottlers.

Cask Samples Where possible I have tasted bottled products, but on some occasions when these have not been available, the distiller has kindly supplied a cask sample. These are marked as such.

ABV/Proof Whisky strength is written as a percentage of alcohol by volume (abv), i.e. 40%, apart from US whiskeys, where US proof is also indicated (80°/40%). The proof of any whisky is simply double its abv.

Japan For its more specialist bottlings, Japan includes the year when the whisky was laid down, its series, and often a cask number, too.

Flavor Camps Every tasting note includes what we have called a Flavor Camp. Please *see* pp. 26–7 for the full explanation of what these are. There is also a comprehensive listing of all the whiskies in their appropriate Flavor Camps on pp. 308–9. If you like one particular whisky style, this will give you an idea of a broad selection of other whiskies you might also like to try.

Where Next? Working alongside the Flavor Camp rating, this feature is designed to be used as a quick cross-reference to what other whisky/ies you might like to try. In general, it appears with all tasting notes except "new makes" and "cask samples," neither of which are commercially available. There might be some exceptions to this rule, e.g. in entries where there are no bottled products, or for older cask samples.

TERMINOLOGY

Glossary There's lots of fun language associated with whisky and much of it changes around the world. If there's ever a term you are not sure about, check the Glossary on p. 311.

Whisky/Whiskey I have used the spelling "whisky" throughout the book because this is the legally recognized spelling to describe the whiskies from everywhere in the world except for Ireland and the USA. In those two exceptions the spelling whiskey has been used.

WHAT IS WHISKY?

This is an atlas. That means that there are maps, which is handy since it tells you where the distilleries are. However, that physical location is only a small element within a whisky's story. The map will tell you how to get to the distillery and what is nearby. It won't tell you everything you need to know about the whisky itself.

For this atlas to work, it also had to create a map of flavors; so you could see which whiskies are similar, which are different and which challenge the conventional wisdom of the existence of broad, regional styles. In doing so, we arrive in a world where the distiller and the site itself become the prime driving forces in the creation of flavor. In this way our flavor map allows us to discover why each distillery in, say, Scotland (or Kentucky), which effectively operates in the same way as its neighbor, makes a spirit unique to that specific site.

To begin our quest to find the heart of whisky, the book outlines what the shared production processes are for the four main styles of whisky—single malt, grain whisky, traditional Irish pot still, and bourbon—looking at the main decision points available to the distiller which enable him or her to create that unique distillery character.

There isn't a separate history section because the story of each distillery adds its own voice to that map. By looking at flavor, we can see how whisky has evolved over time. In nineteenth-century Scotland, for example, although the motivation for making a specific style may initially have been driven by location (such as the use of peat), as the century progressed, the demands of the market and the development of blends also impacted on the flavors of whiskies being produced. Looking at single-malt Scotch from this angle suggests that, instead of regional styles being dominant, whisky taste has evolved in a series of "flavor ages" which have, in simple terms, gone from heavy to light.

Each distillery is therefore examined not just as a producer of a brand, but as a living entity with its own story to tell—and the people who make it are here to help tell it. It was also important that the spirit itself was tasted from birth onwards if the book was to look at the singularity of each distillery. If this is a map that takes us through the world of whisky, then its starting point has to be when the spirit is born. You cannot talk about distillery character if all you are looking at is the result of that actual distillery character's complex interaction with oak.

By tasting the new make and then the whisky at older increments, we can tease out how the flavors created in the distillery evolve: watch green fruits as they ripen and then dry; see grass turn to hay; observe sulfur drifting off to reveal purity behind; and note any oak influence.

The mature spirits are then grouped into Flavor Camps so that you can easily see similarities and differences (often one distillery will occupy more than one camp as its whisky matures); this also offers other potential routes through the great whisky maze.

Whisky-making is a living, evolving creative art, driven by people who want to accentuate their distinctiveness, and it is this multiplicity of individual personalities that are the waypoints on our map.

Continuity and consistency: two of the bywords of quality whisky-making.

A WHISKY WORLD

What's whisky? That's easy. It's a spirit that's been made by mashing a cereal, fermenting it into a beer, distilling that, and then aging the result. That much, at least, the world agrees on—apart from some Indian distillers who make what they call "whisky" from molasses. It might be an extreme example (and you won't find their "whiskies" in here), but it does illustrate a fundamental point about this spirit: as soon as you think you have a universally shared principle, exceptions spring up.

Let's assume, though, that the wood-aged, distilled cereal base holds true. That gives plenty of scope for distillers. Do they use one cereal or a mix? What yeast will they use? How long will the fermentation last? How will it be distilled—in a column or a pot? And what size and shape? And to what strength? What type of cask will it be aged in and for how long? Where is the warehouse?

On first glance, the creation of a whisky style may seem like a triumph of technology, but in truth it lies at the interface between science, economics, creativity, and landscape.

Why do all these whisky styles—single-malt Scotch, traditional Irish pot still, bourbon, etc.—taste so different? Because of how the distiller reacted to his location and economics.

Bourbon is made from corn and rye because that is what distillers planted (or found) in Kentucky: they created a flavor. Malt whisky is made from barley because it was the hardiest grain in the north of Scotland: it created a flavor. Unmalted barley was used in Ireland because it cut distillers' tax bills: it created a flavor. Column stills were installed in the Lowlands of Scotland because of the volumes of whisky that were needed: it created a flavor. Sour-mashing helped bourbon distillers get over issues with hard, limestone water: it created a flavor. Tennessee's early distillers ironed out inconsistencies in spirit quality by filtering the spirit through charcoal: it created a flavor.

The Scottish middle class drank huge amounts of sherry so there were empty barrels on the quaysides: it created a flavor. The coopers in America wanting to guarantee their jobs insisted that only new barrels could be used to age straight whiskey: it created a flavor. All of these were decisions made because of either where the distiller was or the financial environment in which he found himself.

It's the same issue faced by the new whisky distillers around the world. How, given all the knowledge, do I create a style which I can call my own? The Swedes use juniper and local oak; the Tasmanians use their own peat; Japanese distillers turn to Japanese oak … all impact on flavor. There is also a cultural imperative driving all whisky distillers, new or old. How does this whisky express me, my creativity, my culture, and my location?

At some point they wanted to make something extraordinary, and once they had made it they had to find ways to recapture this evanescence, this weird amalgam of ever-changing aromas and tastes, every single time. It is a form of creativity which, as Shinji Fukuyo of Suntory says, is more about being an artisan than an artist.

Asking six distillers to make a whisky is like asking six guitarists to play the same song. Each of them will take the theme and then improvise upon it. Buddy Guy will play it differently from Skip Spence, whose version will be nothing like Eric Clapton's, whose will be miles away from Jimmy Page's—but it will be the same song. Each distillery plays similar variations on a theme.

What is whisky? Anything you want it to be; but the following pages illustrate some ground rules.

Fields of potential: Speyside remains one of Scotland's main producers of malting barley.

MALT PRODUCTION

While the world's single-malt distilleries follow the same process, each one will have its own particular take on how this is done. It is this individual approach, specific to each distillery, that gives each single malt its distillery character: its DNA. The distiller makes decisions throughout the process; the key decisions are as shown in this diagram.

1 BARLEY

All Scotch malt is made from malted barley, water, and yeast. While distillers prefer to use Scottish barley, there is no legal requirement to do so, which is wise, given the vagaries of the Scottish climate. Most distillers believe that the variety does not have an impact on flavor, although some do feel that a strain called Golden Promise does impart a different mouth-feel to their spirit.

WATER

Distillers need lots of pure, cold water in order to make whisky, which is why finding a ready supply is of vital importance. Most distillers use spring water, but loch sources and even town supplies are also used. While there might be a slight impact on fermentation efficiency, it is not believed that water is a major contributory factor to a whisky's final flavor.

2 MALTING

A grain of barley is like a small packet of starch. Malting is basically fooling the barley into thinking that it is time to start growing by steeping it in water and then allowing it to germinate in cool, damp conditions. Enzymes are triggered which will convert this starch into sugar, and it's sugar that the distiller needs. To insure that he gets access to this, he must stop the germination process by drying the barley.

This leads to his first decision:

3 KILNING Option 1

Drying the malted barley over hot air stops germination but will not impart any flavor.

KILNING Option 2: PEATING

The second option is to dry the barley over a peat fire. This will give a smoky aroma to the final spirit. Peat is semi-carbonized vegetation which, when burned, gives off a fragrant smoke. The oils (phenols) in the smoke stick to the surface of the barley. Many mainland whiskies contain a small amount, but the most overtly smoky malts are those from the islands where peat has always been a traditional fuel, both for home and whisky production.

CHILL-FILTRATION?

This will prevent a whisky from going cloudy but it can reduce mouth-feel.

CARAMEL ADJUSTMENT?

The addition of spirit caramel helps standardize color.

STRENGTH?

Legally whisky must be a minimum of 40% abv or 80° proof, but "cask strength" is becoming more popular.

BOTTLING

The whisky is finally ready for bottling, but there are still some final decisions to make.

MATURATION: TIME

It takes time to mature whisky. Logically, the longer a whisky spends in a cask, the more influence the oak will have on the spirit. Eventually it will dominate the whisky, rendering it impossible to tell which distillery it came from. A very active cask will produce this effect more quickly than one that has been filled many times (and which may give a neutral effect). The age statement on a bottle simply tells how long the youngest whisky has spent in wood. It does not indicate how active (or otherwise) the cask has been. Old does not automatically equal good.

MATURATION: CASK TYPE Option 4: CASK FINISHING

Distillers can give the flavor of their whisky a final twist by "finishing" it. This involves taking a whisky aged (normally in ex-bourbon or refill casks) and giving it a short period of secondary aging in a very active cask that has previously held sherry, port, Madeira, wine, etc., imbuing the whisky with some of the cask's character.

CASK TYPE Option 1: EX-BOURBON

These casks are made from American oak, a species which is high in compounds which give aromas reminiscent of vanilla, *crème brûlée*, pine, eucalypt, spice, and coconut.

CASK TYPE Option 2: EX-SHERRY

These casks are made from European oak, which imparts aromas of dried fruit, clove, incense, walnuts. European oak is also richer in color and higher in mouth-drying tannin.

CASK TYPE Option 3: REFILL

Whisky distillers can use casks many times, and the more they are used, the less effect the species of oak has on the whisky. These "refill" casks are important in allowing distillery character to be shown. In practice, most distillers use a mix of all three options because this adds complexity to the palette of flavors.

8 MATURATION

The new-make spirit is then reduced to 63.5% abv and placed in oak casks to mature. These casks have usually previously been filled with either bourbon or sherry. Three processes take place here.

1. **Removal:** The cask helps to remove the aggressive new-spirit character.
2. **Addition:** The flavor compounds in the cask are extracted by the spirit.
3. **Interaction:** The flavors from the wood and the spirit meld together to increase complexity.

Time, the freshness of the cask, and the type of oak all have a part to play.

4 MILLING

The malt is taken to the distillery, where it is ground into a rough flour called grist.

5 MASHING

The grist is then mixed with hot water (at 146.3°F/63.5°C) in a large vessel called a mash tun. As soon as the hot water strikes the grist, the conversion from starch to sugar takes place. The sweet liquor, known as "worts," is then drained through the perforated bottom of the mash tun. The process is repeated an additional two times in order to extract as much of the sugar as possible. The final "water" is then retained as the first water of the next mash.

MASHING Option 1: CLEAR WORT

If a distiller pumps the wort slowly from the mash tun he obtains what is known as clear worts. This tends to produce a spirit with no great cereal character.

MASHING Option 2: CLOUDY WORT

If a distiller wants to produce a malty spirit with a dry, nutty, cereal character he will pump the worts quickly and pull some solids through from the mash tun.

6 FERMENTATION

The worts are then cooled and pumped into a fermenting vessel known as a washback. These can be made from either wood or stainless steel. Yeast is added and fermentation begins.

FERMENTATION Option 1: SHORT

In fermentation, yeast eats sugar and converts it into alcohol (wash). This process is completed in 48 hours. If a distiller takes this "short" option, his final spirit will have a more pronounced malty character.

FERMENTATION Option 2: LONG

A long fermentation (over 55 hours) allows esterification to take place. This produces lighter, more complex, and fruity flavors.

YEAST

Because the same type of yeast is used throughout the Scotch whisky industry, it is not considered to have an impact on flavor. Japanese distillers, however, will use different strains to produce desired flavors in their malt whiskies.

COPPER

Copper is hugely important in creating whisky's flavor. Because copper holds on to heavy elements, distillers can either prolong or restrict the length of the "conversation" between the alcohol vapor and the copper to create a desired character.

7 DISTILLATION A

The wash has a strength of 8% abv. This is then distilled twice in copper pot stills. The first distillation in a "wash still" produces "low wines" of 23% abv, which is then redistilled in a "spirit still." This time the distillate is divided into three: foreshots, heart, and feints. Only the heart is retained for maturation. The foreshots and feints are recycled with the next batch of low wines.

DISTILLATION Option 1: LONG CONVERSATION

The longer the conversation between alcohol vapor and copper, the lighter the final spirit will be. This means tall stills are more likely to produce light spirit than small ones. Also, running a still slowly can extend the conversation.

DISTILLATION Option 2: SHORT CONVERSATION

Conversely, the shorter the conversation, the heavier the resulting spirit will be. Small stills or quick distillation tend to give this characteristic.

DISTILLATION B: CONDENSING

The alcoholic vapor is turned back into liquid by passing it through a condensing system containing cold water. Once again, the distiller has options that will impact on flavor.

CONDENSING
Option 1: SHELL AND TUBE

This is a tall cylinder containing a mass of small copper pipes filled with cold water. When the alcohol vapor hits the cold pipes, it turns back to liquid. Because there is a large area of copper, shell-and-tube condensers help to "lighten" a spirit.

CONDENSING
Option 2: WORM TUBS

This, the traditional method of condensing, involves a long copper pipe coiled in a tank of cold water. Because there is less copper at play here, worm tubs tend to produce a heavier spirit.

CUT POINTS Option 1: EARLY

As a spirit is distilled, its aromas change. The first to appear are light and delicate. If a distiller wants to make a fragrant whisky, he will cut off spirit early.

CUT POINTS Option 2: LATE

As distillation continues, the aromas deepen becoming more oily and rich: smokiness is one of these. A distiller who wants to make a heavy spirit will therefore cut late.

DISTILLATION C: CUT POINTS

When the condensed spirit from the second distillation arrives in the spirit safe, the stillman must divide it into three: foreshots, heart, and feints. The point where he cuts from foreshots into spirit and from spirit to feints will also have an effect on flavor.

GRAIN PRODUCTION

Though often overlooked as a whisky style (and rarely seen bottled), grain whisky does make up the bulk of the whisky produced in Scotland, and it performs an extremely vital function within blends. Its production is every bit as complex as any other type of whisky, as shown on this page.

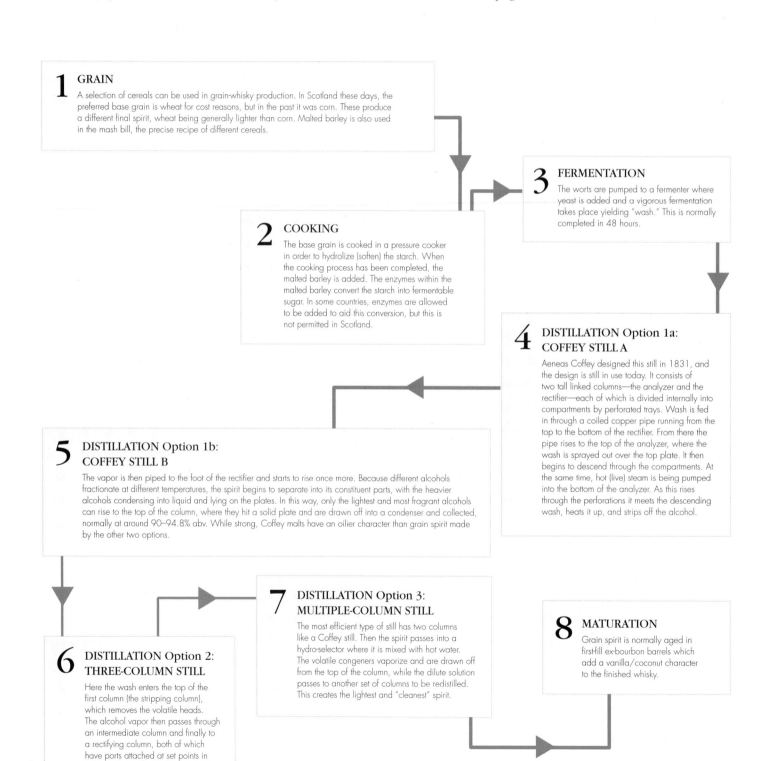

1 GRAIN
A selection of cereals can be used in grain-whisky production. In Scotland these days, the preferred base grain is wheat for cost reasons, but in the past it was corn. These produce a different final spirit, wheat being generally lighter than corn. Malted barley is also used in the mash bill, the precise recipe of different cereals.

2 COOKING
The base grain is cooked in a pressure cooker in order to hydrolize (soften) the starch. When the cooking process has been completed, the malted barley is added. The enzymes within the malted barley convert the starch into fermentable sugar. In some countries, enzymes are allowed to be added to aid this conversion, but this is not permitted in Scotland.

3 FERMENTATION
The worts are pumped to a fermenter where yeast is added and a vigorous fermentation takes place yielding "wash." This is normally completed in 48 hours.

4 DISTILLATION Option 1a: COFFEY STILL A
Aeneas Coffey designed this still in 1831, and the design is still in use today. It consists of two tall linked columns—the analyzer and the rectifier—each of which is divided internally into compartments by perforated trays. Wash is fed in through a coiled copper pipe running from the top to the bottom of the rectifier. From there the pipe rises to the top of the analyzer, where the wash is sprayed out over the top plate. It then begins to descend through the compartments. At the same time, hot (live) steam is being pumped into the bottom of the analyzer. As this rises through the perforations it meets the descending wash, heats it up, and strips off the alcohol.

5 DISTILLATION Option 1b: COFFEY STILL B
The vapor is then piped to the foot of the rectifier and starts to rise once more. Because different alcohols fractionate at different temperatures, the spirit begins to separate into its constituent parts, with the heavier alcohols condensing into liquid and lying on the plates. In this way, only the lightest and most fragrant alcohols can rise to the top of the column, where they hit a solid plate and are drawn off into a condenser and collected, normally at around 90–94.8% abv. While strong, Coffey malts have an oilier character than grain spirit made by the other two options.

6 DISTILLATION Option 2: THREE-COLUMN STILL
Here the wash enters the top of the first column (the stripping column), which removes the volatile heads. The alcohol vapor then passes through an intermediate column and finally to a rectifying column, both of which have ports attached at set points in order to draw off specific congeners. This tends to make a lighter style.

7 DISTILLATION Option 3: MULTIPLE-COLUMN STILL
The most efficient type of still has two columns like a Coffey still. Then the spirit passes into a hydro-selector where it is mixed with hot water. The volatile congeners vaporize and are drawn off from the top of the column, while the dilute solution passes to another set of columns to be redistilled. This creates the lightest and "cleanest" spirit.

8 MATURATION
Grain spirit is normally aged in first-fill ex-bourbon barrels which add a vanilla/coconut character to the finished whisky.

IRISH POT-STILL PRODUCTION

There are three distillers operational in Ireland at the moment, each of which approaches whiskey-making in a different way. Bushmills follows a similar model to single-malt production with the exception of using triple rather than double distillation. Cooley uses double-distilled single-malt production, plus for one brand, peated barley. This diagram outlines a style unique to Ireland: traditional Irish pot-still whiskey, as used by Irish Distillers Ltd.

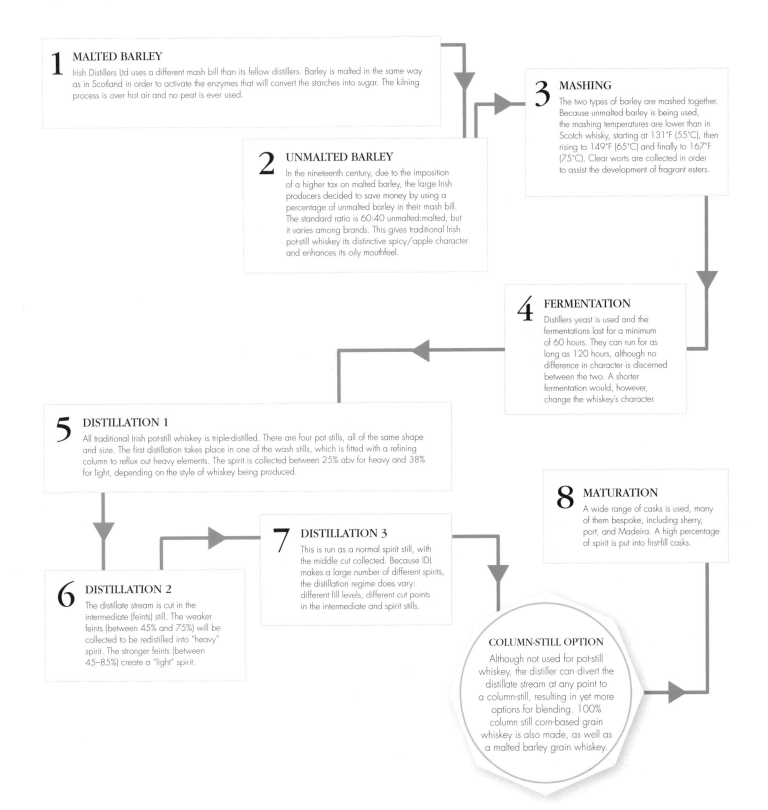

1 MALTED BARLEY
Irish Distillers Ltd uses a different mash bill than its fellow distillers. Barley is malted in the same way as in Scotland in order to activate the enzymes that will convert the starches into sugar. The kilning process is over hot air and no peat is ever used.

2 UNMALTED BARLEY
In the nineteenth century, due to the imposition of a higher tax on malted barley, the large Irish producers decided to save money by using a percentage of unmalted barley in their mash bill. The standard ratio is 60:40 unmalted:malted, but it varies among brands. This gives traditional Irish pot-still whiskey its distinctive spicy/apple character and enhances its oily mouthfeel.

3 MASHING
The two types of barley are mashed together. Because unmalted barley is being used, the mashing temperatures are lower than in Scotch whisky, starting at 131°F (55°C), then rising to 149°F (65°C) and finally to 167°F (75°C). Clear worts are collected in order to assist the development of fragrant esters.

4 FERMENTATION
Distillers yeast is used and the fermentations last for a minimum of 60 hours. They can run for as long as 120 hours, although no difference in character is discerned between the two. A shorter fermentation would, however, change the whiskey's character.

5 DISTILLATION 1
All traditional Irish pot-still whiskey is triple-distilled. There are four pot stills, all of the same shape and size. The first distillation takes place in one of the wash stills, which is fitted with a refining column to reflux out heavy elements. The spirit is collected between 25% abv for heavy and 38% for light, depending on the style of whiskey being produced.

6 DISTILLATION 2
The distillate stream is cut in the intermediate (feints) still. The weaker feints (between 45% and 75%) will be collected to be redistilled into "heavy" spirit. The stronger feints (between 45–85%) create a "light" spirit.

7 DISTILLATION 3
This is run as a normal spirit still, with the middle cut collected. Because IDL makes a large number of different spirits, the distillation regime does vary: different fill levels, different cut points in the intermediate and spirit stills.

8 MATURATION
A wide range of casks is used, many of them bespoke, including sherry, port, and Madeira. A high percentage of spirit is put into first-fill casks.

COLUMN-STILL OPTION
Although not used for pot-still whiskey, the distiller can divert the distillate stream at any point to a column-still, resulting in yet more options for blending. 100% column still corn-based grain whiskey is also made, as well as a malted barley grain whiskey.

KENTUCKY & TENNESSEE PRODUCTION

Bourbon distillers are faced with an equally large number of decision points in the creation of their own individual style. With a relatively small number of distilleries making a wide number of different styles and brands, they express their individuality by looking at the ratio of the cereals used, the types of yeast, the amount of sour mash used, the distillation strength, the barrel strength, and where in the warehouse the barrel is located.

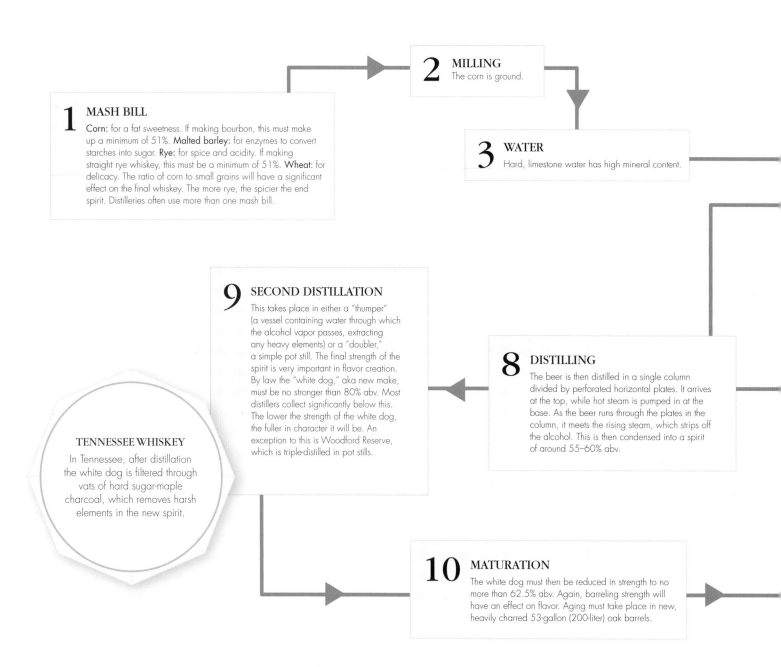

2 MILLING
The corn is ground.

1 MASH BILL
Corn: for a fat sweetness. If making bourbon, this must make up a minimum of 51%. **Malted barley:** for enzymes to convert starches into sugar. **Rye:** for spice and acidity. If making straight rye whiskey, this must be a minimum of 51%. **Wheat:** for delicacy. The ratio of corn to small grains will have a significant effect on the final whiskey. The more rye, the spicier the end spirit. Distilleries often use more than one mash bill.

3 WATER
Hard, limestone water has high mineral content.

9 SECOND DISTILLATION
This takes place in either a "thumper" (a vessel containing water through which the alcohol vapor passes, extracting any heavy elements) or a "doubler," a simple pot still. The final strength of the spirit is very important in flavor creation. By law the "white dog," aka new make, must be no stronger than 80% abv. Most distillers collect significantly below this. The lower the strength of the white dog, the fuller in character it will be. An exception to this is Woodford Reserve, which is triple-distilled in pot stills.

8 DISTILLING
The beer is then distilled in a single column divided by perforated horizontal plates. It arrives at the top, while hot steam is pumped in at the base. As the beer runs through the plates in the column, it meets the rising steam, which strips off the alcohol. This is then condensed into a spirit of around 55–60% abv.

TENNESSEE WHISKEY
In Tennessee, after distillation the white dog is filtered through vats of hard sugar-maple charcoal, which removes harsh elements in the new spirit.

10 MATURATION
The white dog must then be reduced in strength to no more than 62.5% abv. Again, barreling strength will have an effect on flavor. Aging must take place in new, heavily charred 53-gallon (200-liter) oak barrels.

4 COOKING

A Corn is cooked first to hydrolize its starch. Either open cookers or pressure cookers are used. When cooked, the mix is cooled and …

B … rye/wheat is added at lower temperature and cooked. The mix is cooled once more. Then …

C … malted barley is added to convert the starch to sugar.

5 BACKSET/SOUR MASH/SETBACK

This is the acidic spent liquid at the end of distillation that is then added to the fermenter. It adjusts the pH of the fermentation and prevents bacterial infection. The amount of sour you use affects the percentage of sugars in the mash, so for a fresher bourbon, you use less sour. Every bourbon is sour-mashed.

6 YEAST

Each distillery will have its own strain or strains of proprietary yeast. These are jealously guarded because the character of the yeast has a significant effect on the flavor of the final spirit, and helps to promote specific congeners (aka flavoring elements).

7 FERMENTING

Generally, this will take up to three days, at the end of which the distiller has a beer of around 5–6% abv.

11 WAREHOUSING

The warehousing has an additional effect on the spirit's character. The hotter the temperature in the warehouse, the more intense the interaction between the spirit and the oak. Conversely, the cooler the environment, the slower this process will be. This means that the location of the warehouse, the number of floors, and what they are made out of (brick, metal, wood) is important in flavor creation. Equally, the location of the barrel within those warehouses will have an impact. Some distillers rotate barrels to get an even maturation; some "scatter" their barrels across different warehouses; others set aside warehouses or floors within warehouses for specific brands. By law, maturation must be for a minimum of two years.

The start of the Lincoln County Process: making charcoal at Jack Daniel's.

TERROIR

It is widely accepted that a multiplicity of external, geological, and geographical influences—soil, climate, angle of slope, etc.—have a direct influence on the flavor of a wine. You can, for example, draw on this principle to set out broad regional differences between wines. This notion of *terroir* is a more awkward proposition when it comes to whisky. In general, the cereals used will not be grown on the property, and it is widely held that while water has a small influence, in assisting with fermentation, it is not a major driver in terms of flavor creation.

Lagavulin on Islay is one distillery whose spirit seems to distill its surroundings.

Where does this leave the idea of a regional whisky *terroir*? Scotland, for example, is divided into whisky-making regions: Lowland, Highland, Speyside, Islay, etc. But what do these legally delimited names mean? In geographical terms, the Lowlands are divided from the Highlands by a geological fault, but the whisky boundary follows one that was created in the nineteenth century to deal with different levels of taxation. Even if you accept this, are we really to assume that every whisky north of Glasgow tastes the same because it is in the Highlands? I think not.

Is Speyside any easier? Not really. Again, its boundaries are political, rather than being dictated by the watershed of the Spey River. That aside, do all of Speyside's whiskies taste the same? No. While there could be an argument for a regional *terroir* on Islay, thanks to the use of (mostly) local peat, Islay's whiskies do not have to be smoky. It is an individual choice taken by distillers—and two produce mostly unpeated.

Saying that there is regional *terroir* in Scotch whisky (any whisky) is a bit like saying that all French red wines taste the same. What a close examination of whisky's flavors reveals is that each distiller has tried to create a unique character in his whisky: in other words, that he

The most overt link between Scotland's earth and its whisky is in the use of peat.

has been an active participant in the creation of flavor. Where does that leave *terroir*? Is whisky simply a man-made construct forged out of the alchemy between copper and vapor, liquid and oak?

Actually, once the regional *terroir* argument is laid to one side, you are left with a far more complex issue, one which talks about the importance of each site. Intriguingly, the more you talk to distillers and ask them how their whisky's character is created, the more they talk about fermentation times and reflux and oxidation and still shapes and copper conversation … but then they shrug and say, "To be honest, we don't know."

In other words, there is something which happens at each distillery that helps to set it apart. It could be the ambient temperature of the fermentation room; it will certainly be the conditions in the warehouses. A classic example of site-specificity was the Malt Mill distillery, a direct replica of Laphroaig, which operated at Lagavulin (*see* p.160). It made peaty whisky but it never made Laphroaig. In other words, while you can set up a still to make grassy or fruity or peaty whisky, you can never dictate the specific flavors the distillery will produce. That's akin to the type of *terroir* you encounter in Burgundy, and again, it exists across the world of whisky.

The one element of *terroir* that is always overlooked is the human element. There is a cultural *terroir* at work here: the founding distiller's approach being dictated by his own personal preferences, by the smells he inhales every day, by his use (consciously or not) of elements within his landscape. These whiskies taste this way because of the people who first crafted them.

FLAVOR

How then do we make sense of it all? Through flavor. By sticking our noses into the glass and inhaling. Every time we nose a whisky a picture appears, an olfactory hallucination which offers clues about the character of the whisky. The picture is, if you like, a map in itself, telling you about distillation, oak, and time. As fragrance specialist Givaudan's Dr. Roman Kaiser writes in his *Meaningful Scents Around the World*, "The sense of smell gives us a sense of other living beings."

We smell our way through our lives. Aromas help us make sense of the world, but we use them without consciously realizing this. Kaiser argues that there was a deliberate relegation of the sense of smell in the eighteenth and nineteenth centuries, when philosophers and scientists argued that sight was the superior sense, whereas smell was "a primitive, brutish ability associated with savagery and even madness." It is also the case that we simply forget to smell things consciously as we get older. We know what a flower smells like, so why differentiate between a daffodil and a freesia? The fact that so many of the pictures that appear in our minds when we concentrate on a glass of whisky come from our childhood shows that, at some point in our lives, we did take the trouble to inhale.

Flavor—by which I mean aroma and taste—is ultimately how we differentiate between whiskies. We might be tempted by the pack, or find the price attractive (or repellent); we might be led astray by the region, but the prime reason for buying a shot or a bottle of whisky is because we like the flavor. It appeals to us, it speaks to us, it hits a trigger in us.

But what does the picture mean? That aroma of vanilla, *crème brûlée*, coconut (1970s' suntan oil), and pine says that the whisky has been matured in an American oak cask. Those pictures of dried fruit and cloves? They suggest that an ex-sherry cask has been used. The images of spring meadows—all green grass and blossom— speak of long, slow distillation with lots of time for the vapor to talk to the copper. That aroma that brings toasted meat to mind? Short conversation, maybe the use of worm tubs. Is there an intense yet ordered aroma? The whisky could well be Japanese.

Pick up a glass of bourbon and taste it. Does it suddenly get spicier and more acidic towards the back of the tongue? That's rye kicking in; the more spice, the more rye is likely to be in the mash bill. Get that oiliness in the Irish whiskey? Unmalted barley. The sootiness in that whiskey from Tennessee? Charcoal-mellowing. Each of these flavors is natural. It has been created in the distillery, or comes from the cask, or in the case of the leathery, fungal "rancid" richness of older examples, from a long interaction between the two.

Having trouble? Shut your eyes and think of what season the whisky reminds you of. Not only will the aromas suddenly snap into focus, but they will give you a clue about how best to enjoy the whisky. A spring-like whisky? Have it cold, maybe with ice before a meal. Rich and autumnal? After dinner and slowly.

No other spirit has such a complex array of flavors. No other spirit spans the aroma spectrum from whisper-light to heavily peated and all points in between. Don't look at a whisky as being a brand; look at it as a flavor package. If you understand flavor, you understand whisky. Now, let's explore.

Olfactory hallucinations: a whisky's character is expressed through the pictures in the noser's mind.

Opposite: A kaleidoscope of aromas is contained within whisky—from spice and fruit to honey, smoke, and nuts. These anchor it to the real world and speak of our own memories.

HOW TO TASTE

We all know how to taste. If I were to put a plate of food in front of you, you would have an immediate (and strongly held) opinion about it. Were I to put a glass of whisky in front of most of you, however, you would find that the words to describe the aromas and taste wouldn't come as easily. Why? It's not that you can't taste whisky; it's simply that no one has taken the time to explain the language of whisky—to make it simple to understand.

Whisky is currently in the same position that wine was 20 years ago: there is a latent desire to try, but the consumer doesn't have the language with which to describe what he or she wants. Instead of helping, words have become a barrier. To "understand" malt whisky, it is thought, you have to become part of a secret society, be given the codes. That's no way to encourage new drinkers. How, then, to talk without getting tangled up in adjectives, ensnared by nouns, mired in overcomplicated technical details? The answer is to keep things simple. We don't so much need a new language as to start talking in more simple terms about flavor: where it comes from, what it means.

Each of the entries in this book includes tasting notes for a representative selection of whiskies which have then been subdivided into Flavor Camps. This will allow you to compare and contrast whiskies of similar type, and also to see how a distiller can shift a whisky from one camp to another through maturation and/or the use of different wood types. Find a whisky you already know and find another you've never encountered before in the same camp. Now compare the two. What is similar and what are the differences? You don't have to overcomplicate matters by using fancy descriptors: simple terms like "fruity" or "light" or "smoky" are enough. Now find another whisky and repeat. And repeat. And repeat!

Right: Raymond Armstrong, center, makes sure his Bladnoch whisky is maturing properly.

Using the right glasses is crucial in assessing whiskies.

FLAVOR CAMPS

The process of tasting is simple. Take a small measure of the whisky in a glass. Look at the color, certainly, but more importantly, get your nose in the glass. What aromas are you picking up? What pictures are in your head? Which of the following Flavor Camps does the whisky belong to? Now taste. You'll detect many of the aromas you've already noticed, but concentrate on how the whisky behaves in your mouth. What does it feel like? Thick, tongue-coating? Mouth-filling, light? Is it sweet, or dry, or fresh? It should be like a piece of music or a story with a beginning, middle, and end. Now, add some water— just a splash—and repeat.

Fragrant & Floral
The aromas found in these whiskies bring to mind fresh-cut flowers, fruit blossom, cut grass, light green fruit (apple, pear, melon). On the palate they are light, slightly sweet, and often have a fresh acidity. They are ideal as aperitifs, or treat them like white wine: pop the bottle in the fridge and served chilled in wine glasses.

Malty & Dry
These whiskies are drier on the nose. Crisp, cookie-like, sometimes dusty, with aromas that remind you of flour, breakfast cereal, and nuts. The palate is also dry but is normally balanced by sweet oak. Again, these are good aperitifs or breakfast whiskies.

Fruity & Spicy
The fruit we're talking about here is ripe orchard fruit such as peach, apricot, maybe even something more exotic like mango. These whiskies will also show the vanilla, coconut, custard-like aromas of American oak. The spiciness is found on the finish and tends to be sweet, like cinnamon or nutmeg. With a little more weight, these are versatile drams that can be enjoyed at any time.

Rich & Round
There is fruit here too, but now it is dried: raisins, figs, dates, white raisins. This shows the use of European-oak ex-sherry casks. You might detect a slightly drier feel; that's the tannin from the oak. These are deep whiskies, sometimes sweet, sometimes meaty. Best after dinner.

Smoky & Peaty
The smoke comes from burning peat when the malt is being dried. This imparts a whole range of different aromas: soot, lapsang souchong tea, tar, kippers, smoked bacon, burning heather, wood smoke. Often sightly oily in texture, all peaty whiskies must have a balancing "sweet spot." Young peaty whiskies are a great wake-up as aperitifs; try them mixed with soda. Older richer examples are for later in the evening.

KENTUCKY, TENNESSEE & CANADIAN WHISKIES
Soft Corn
The main cereal used in these whiskies, corn creates a sweet nose and a fat, buttery, and juicy quality on the palate.

Every bottle of whisky, such as these at Yamazaki in Japan, contains a whisky with its own individual, distinct character. Grouping them into Flavor Camps makes life easier.

Sweet Wheat
Wheat is occasionally used by bourbon distillers in place of rye. This affects flavor by adding a gentle, mellow sweetness to the bourbon.

Rich & Oaky

All bourbon must be aged in new-oak barrels, which is where the whiskey picks up all those rich, vanilla-accented aromas, along with coconut, pine, cherry, sweet spice. This richness of extract is increasingly powerful the longer the bourbon remains in cask, leading to flavors like tobacco and leather.

Spicy Rye

Rye can often be picked up on the nose in the shape of intense, slightly perfumed, and sometimes slightly dusty aromas—or as an aroma akin to freshly baked rye bread. It appears late in the palate, however, after the fat corn has had its say. It adds an acidic, spiced zestiness that wakes the palate up.

THE SINGLE-MALT WHISKY FLAVOR MAP

The Flavor Map™ was created to help consumers baffled by the volume of Scotch single malt on the market. Each whisky is an individual. We cannot rely on a regional definition as a guarantee of flavor. We can't leave it to retailers or bars; both tend to arrange whiskies alphabetically or by region. So how can we agree on a term to describe that individual?

Part of my job is to teach people—consumers, bartenders, and retailers—about how to taste whisky. I used to find that it was very easy to slip into complex language but considerably more difficult to try and explain flavor in a simple way.

One day I was discussing this issue of simplifying the language to allow people to make a considered choice with Jim Beveridge, master blender at Diageo. His response was to draw two lines on a piece of paper. "This is what we use in the lab," he said. "It allows us to plot the different components in a blend and also to compare Johnnie Walker with other blends." I have since found out that this method is used not just by whisky blenders, but also throughout the spirits and perfume industries. Jim, his colleague Maureen Robinson, and I then sat down to try and produce a consumer-friendly version of the Blenders' Chart.

And here it is. This Flavor Map™ is simple to use. The vertical axis starts at the "Delicate" end with whiskies that are clean and pure. The more complex the whisky, the higher up the line it sits. As soon as any smoke is discernible, then the whisky moves across the central line. The smokier it is, the higher up the line it is positioned.

The horizontal axis moves from "Light" to "Rich," starting with the lightest and most fragrant flavors; as you head towards the center, you move through grassiness, malt, soft fruit, and honey. As soon as you cross the central line heading towards "Rich," the influence of the cask becomes more important: American oak's vanilla and spice to begin with, before the dried fruit of ex-sherry casks becomes the dominant character towards the right-hand side.

It is important to underline that this map is not saying that any whisky is better than any other. It simply says what the dominant flavor characteristic is. There is no one good place to be, nor is there an area where whiskies could be seen to be inferior. It is a generic tool for single-malt Scotch whisky. And you won't find every whisky on the market on this map, either—there just wouldn't be room. Instead, we have selected a large number of the most popular examples, many of which you will find within the pages of this book.

We keep the Flavor Map™ under review to take account of new expressions and changing styles. We hope it gives you an idea of similarities between whiskies—and differences. If you don't like peatiness, then be wary of going too high up the smoky line. If you see a brand you know and like, then this allows you to find an alternative you could explore. Enjoy using it.

The Flavor Map™ is the result of a joint collaboration between Dave Broom and Diageo Scotland Limited. The map features brands of single-malt Scotch whisky, some owned by Diageo Scotland Ltd, and some owned by others. The latter may be registered trademarks of third parties. Copyright © 2010.

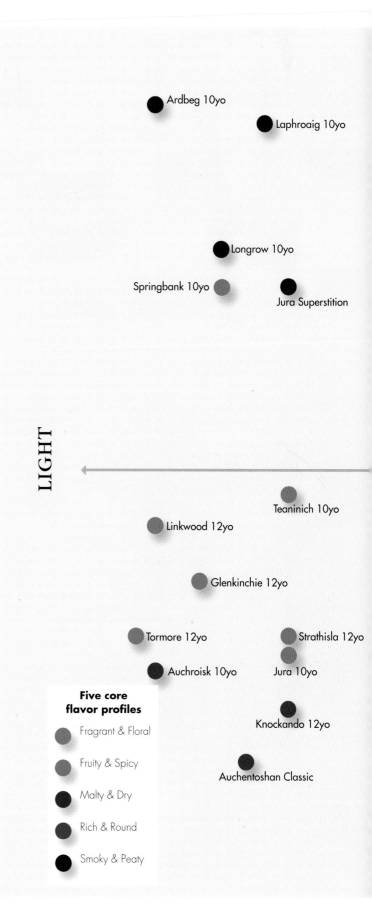

SMOKY

Laphroaig Quarter Cask

Ardbeg Uigedail

Lagavulin 12yo

Lagavulin 16yo

Laphroaig 15yo

Lagavulin Distillers Edition

Caol Ila 12yo

Caol Ila 18yo

Bowmore 12yo

Talisker 10yo

Talisker 18yo

Talisker 25yo

Ardmore Traditional Cask

Brora 30yo

Highland Park 15yo

Highland Park 12yo

Highland Park 18yo

Bowmore Legend

BenRiach 16yo

The Singleton of Glen Ord 18yo

Old Pulteney 12yo

Oban Distillers Edition

Cragganmore Distillers Edition

Oban 14yo

Cragganmore 12yo

Dalwhinnie Distillers Edition

Mortlach 16yo

Bruichladdich 15yo

Benrinnes 15yo

Singleton of Glendullan 12yo

RICH

Dalwhinnie 15yo

Singleton of Dufftown 12yo

Glenmorangie 18yo

Cardhu 12yo

Clynelish 14yo

Clynelish Distillers Edition

Macallan 12yo

Glenfarclas 15yo

Glen Elgin 12yo

Glenmorangie Original

Royal Lochnagar 12yo

Dalmore 12yo

Scapa 16yo

Macallan Fine Oak 10yo

Longmorn16yo

Glenmorangie Lasanta

Balvenie Double Wood

Bruichladdich 10yo

Glenrothes Special Reserve

Glenkinchie Distillers Edition

Cardhu Special Cask Reserve

Macallan Fine Oak 12yo

The Glenlivet 12yo

Glenfiddich 18yo

Glenfiddich Solera

Aberlour 15yo

Glenfiddich 12yo

Balvenie Signature

Aberlour 10yo

Bunnahabhain 12yo

Aberlour a'bunadh

The Glenlivet 18yo

Auchentoshan Three Wood

Auchentoshan 12yo

The Glenlivet 15yo

DELICATE

SCOTLAND

Scotland dominates the whisky world. It has even given its name to the style. Once, in Tunisia, tired of trying to explain where *Ecosse* was, I blurted out "Whisky!" and everyone immediately understood that this foreigner was from "Scotch-land." Scotch is both a style of whisky but also a signifier for a country. It's a country, however, whose geography forces you to take detours—going round the heads of lochs, not over a bridge; sailing to islands rather than flying; walking into remote hills because there is no road. It is a discursive landscape, a property shared by its whiskies. Scotland is also wildly contradictory. In 1919, the critic G. Gregory Smith argued that Scottish literature (and, by extension, the Scottish psyche) was defined by a "zigzag of contradictions," which he called "the Caledonian antisyzygy." Whisky shares that too.

Previous page: Enigmatic and lonely, but two of the elements of whisky-making are here—peat and water.

Scotland's whiskies distill the aromas of their land: the coconut of hot gorse, wet seaweed lying on hot sand, the delicacy of "gean blossom" (wild cherry). Then there's the perfumed headiness of heather, the oiliness of bog myrtle, cut grass, and the myriad aromas of peat: smokehouses and bonfires on the beach, oyster shells and brine. Then there are aromas from overseas: tea and coffee, sherry, raisin, cumin, cinnamon, and nutmeg. There are chemical reasons for all of these, but there are also many cultural reasons.

Every malt-whisky distillery does the same thing. They malt, they grind, they mash, they ferment, they distill twice (occasionally three times), and then they age in oak casks. There are 96 distilleries doing this as I write, and there are over 100 different results.

In the definition "single-malt whisky," the most important word is SINGLE. Why does one distillery do the same as its neighbor but get a different result? In the following pages we'll try to pick out some clues, starting with the new spirit. You cannot understand a whisky fully by looking only at the end product. With that you are inhaling the story of 12 years or more of interplay between the spirit, wood,

and air. The reference point has been lost. If you want to find the uniqueness of each single malt you have to go to the source: the clear spring of knowledge that flows into the spirit safe, that flows from the whisky-maker's mouth. Only by trying to understand each whisky's DNA can you go on this journey of flavor.

Don't expect absolute answers; don't rely on figures and charts. That singularity could be the microclimate of warehouses, maybe the type of warehouses, or the atmospheric pressure in the mashhouse, the shape and the size of the stills, the nature of the fermentation. Yes, the following pages contain talk of reflux and purifiers and wort density, of setting temperatures and oxidation, but ultimately every distiller agrees that no matter how much knowledge they amass, the distillery does its own thing. Whether they are on an island, in pasture lands, or up a mountain, they shrug and say "Flavor? To be honest, I don't know. It's just something about the place." It's Scotland.

The remote and wildly beautiful landscapes of Scotland contain many hidden whisky secrets.

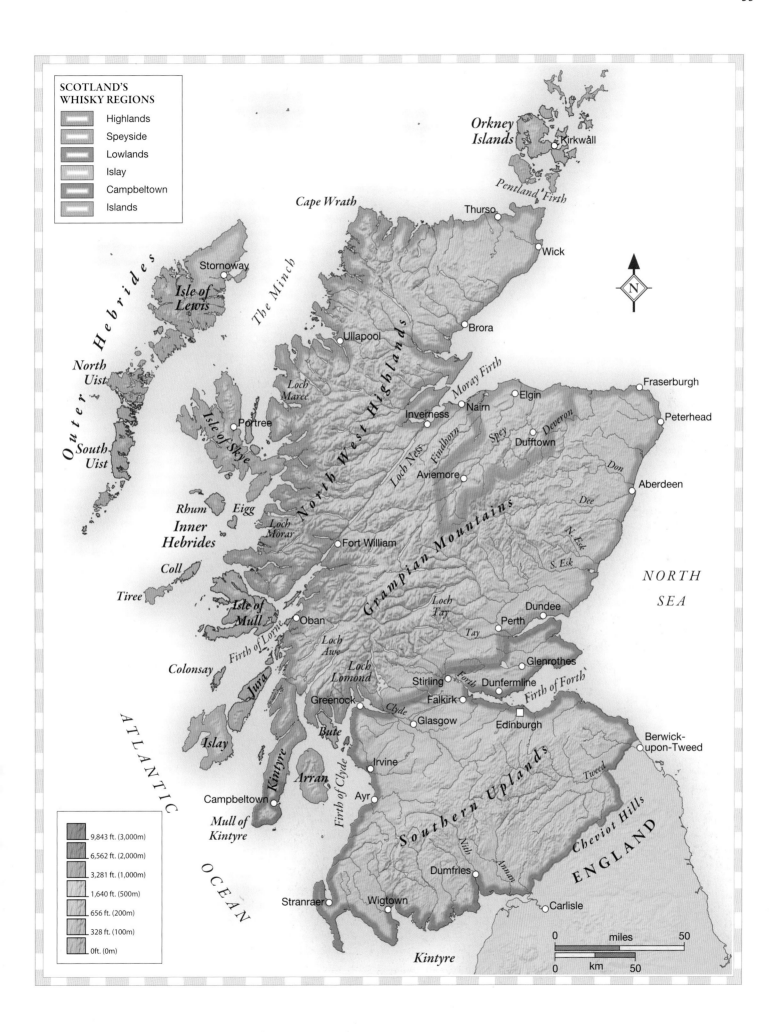

SCOTLAND'S
WHISKY REGIONS

Highlands
Speyside
Lowlands
Islay
Campbeltown
Islands

9,843 ft. (3,000m)
6,562 ft. (2,000m)
3,281 ft. (1,000m)
1,640 ft. (500m)
656 ft. (200m)
328 ft. (100m)
0ft. (0m)

Orkney Islands
Pentland Firth
Kirkwall

Cape Wrath
Thurso
Wick

The Minch
Stornoway
Isle of Lewis
Outer Hebrides

Ullapool
Brora

N

North Uist

Moray Firth
Elgin
Fraserburgh
Inverness Nairn
Peterhead
Portree
Isle of Skye
South Uist
Loch Maree
North West Highlands
Spey *Deveron*
Dufftown

Loch Ness *Findhorn*
Aviemore
Don
Aberdeen
Rhum *Eigg*
Inner Hebrides
Loch Mórar
Dee
Grampian Mountains
N. Esk
Fort William
S. Esk

Coll
NORTH SEA

Tiree
Loch Tay
Dundee
Isle of Mull
Oban
Perth
Tay
Firth of Lorne
Loch Awe
Colonsay
Loch Lomond
Glenrothes
Jura
Stirling *Forth* Dunfermline *Firth of Forth*
Greenock Falkirk
Bute
Clyde Glasgow
Edinburgh
Islay
Kintyre
Arran
Irvine Berwick-upon-Tweed

Campbeltown
Firth of Clyde
Ayr
Southern Uplands
Tweed
Mull of Kintyre

ATLANTIC OCEAN
Cheviot Hills
Nith
Dumfries
Annan
ENGLAND

Stranraer Wigtown
Carlisle

0   miles   50

0   km   50

Kintyre

Scotland's elemental landscape—here, on Skye—is reflected in its whiskies.

SPEYSIDE

What is Speyside? It is a legally delimited region, but all that tells you is what (or where) Speyside isn't. It has long been the heartland of malt-whisky production and because of this it is easy to assume that its makes all fall within the same group. It's not so. There is no single Speyside style, just as there is no uniform Speyside landscape.

Opposite: Seemingly impassable mountains offered moonshiners a safe haven and smugglers secret routes.

How can one compare the rough lands of the Braes and Glenlivet with the fertile flatlands of the Laich O'Moray, or the distilleries that cluster around Ben Rinnes with those of Keith or Dufftown? How, when you delve deeper, can you even assume there is some commonality in the makes from Dufftown, the self-proclaimed capital of whisky-making?

The "clusters" found in the following pages show the geographical proximity of distilleries, but are explorations of the different individualities existing within them. Speyside is about distillers finding their style, of testing new ideas, of remaining true to tradition. It is about modernity and the belief in the microclimate that sets one site apart from the next.

Strathspey (if it was even called that by its inhabitants) was a place of farm distillers, who, with the ban on home distilling in 1781, then the prohibition on exporting below the Highland Line in 1783, and the restriction of the number (and size) of stills in each parish, found legal distilling virtually impossible. It was considerably cheaper to produce whisky illicitly, yet at the same time demand was rising in the Lowlands—the result of poor-quality whisky being made in that region itself. Moonshining was endemic in the late eighteenth and early nineteenth centuries, before changes in the law in 1816 and, more significantly, in 1823, removed the restrictions, encouraging commercial distilling to take place.

How did this affect Speyside's flavors? From 1823 onwards you can observe it being pulled in two directions: between the old ways and the new; between the heavy makes of the sma' still and the lightness achievable from larger stills—and by the end of the century desired by the blenders. Maybe this shift towards the light by some of those original distillers was as much a mental response—a liberation—while others held on to their tradition. The result is an interplay of light versus dark, the fragrant and sunlit against the chthonic, earthy malts whose character speaks of the hiding places, dank, crepuscular *bothies* (huts) and caves. In Speyside we still meet them both.

You can imagine a Speyside distiller looking across at Ben Rinnes, mulling over the options and coming to similar conclusions as Thomas Hardy's narrator in *The Return of The Native*: "To recline on a stump of thorn … to know that everything around and underneath had been from prehistoric times as unaltered as the stars overhead, gave ballast to the mind adrift on change and harassed by the irrepressible New."

Speyside is all about diversity, not commonality. Speyside's journey—and therefore the journey of Scotch malt whisky, too— has been, as we shall see, this development of site-specific individuality. Speyside doesn't exist; its distilleries do.

A land of mountain, plain, and river, Speyside is as varied as the flavors of its whiskies.

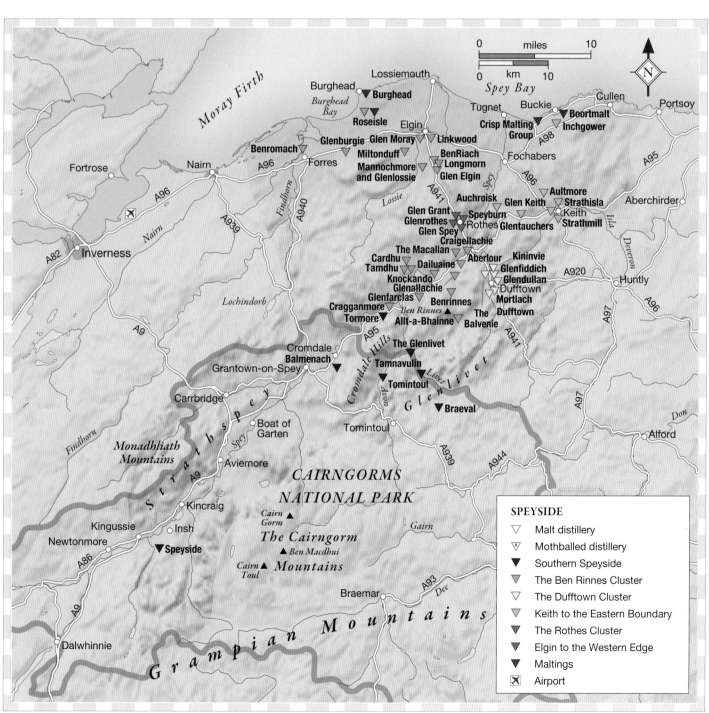

	miles			10
0	km			10

N

Moray Firth

Lossiemouth
Spey Bay

Burghead · ▼ **Burghead**

Burghead Bay

Tugnet · Buckie · Cullen · Portsoy

▼ **Roseisle**

Elgin · **Crisp Malting Group** · ▼ **Boortmalt**

▽ **Glenburgie** · **Glen Moray** ▽ **Linkwood** · **Inchgower**

Benromach ▽ · Forres · ▽ **Miltonduff** · ▽ **BenRiach** · Fochabers

Fortrose · Nairn · **Mannochmore and Glenlossie** · ▽ **Longmorn**

Glen Elgin ▽

Lossie · **Auchroisk** ▽ · ▽ **Aultmore**

Glen Keith ▽ **Strathisla** · Aberchirder

▽ **Glen Grant** · **Speyburn** · **Keith**

Glenrothes · Rothes · **Glentauchers** · ▽ **Strathmill**

Inverness · **Glen Spey** ▽

Craigellachie ▽

The Macallan ▽ · **Kininvie** ▽

Cardhu ▽ · **Dailuaine** · **Aberlour** · **Glenfiddich** ▽

Tamdhu ▽ · ▽ **Glendullan**

Knockando ▽ · **Dufftown** ▽

Glenallachie ▽ · **Mortlach** ▽

Lochindorb · **Glenfarclas** ▽ · **Benrinnes** ▽ · **Dufftown**

Cragganmore ▽ · *Ben Rinnes* ▲ · **The Balvenie** ▽

Tormore ▽ · **Allt-a-Bhainne** ▽

Cromdale Hills

Cromdale · **The Glenlivet** ▽

Balmenach ▼ · **Tamnavulin** ▽

Grantown-on-Spey

Carrbridge · *Livet* · **Tomintoul** ▼ · *Glenlivet*

Boat of Garten · Tomintoul · **Braeval** ▼

Findhorn

Monadhliath Mountains · Aviemore

Kincraig

Kingussie · Insh · A939 · A944 · Alford

Newtonmore

▼ **Speyside**

CAIRNGORMS NATIONAL PARK

Cairn Gorm ▲

The Cairngorm · *Gairn*

▲ *Ben Macdhui* · *Mountains*

Cairn Toul ▲

Braemar · *Dee*

G r a m p i a n   M o u n t a i n s

Dalwhinnie

SPEYSIDE

▽	Malt distillery
▽	Mothballed distillery
▼	Southern Speyside
▼	The Ben Rinnes Cluster
▽	The Dufftown Cluster
▼	Keith to the Eastern Boundary
▼	The Rothes Cluster
▼	Elgin to the Western Edge
▼	Maltings
✕	Airport

SOUTHERN SPEYSIDE

Our journey starts here, in the southern parts of Speyside, once the haunts of moonshiners and smugglers and also where the modern Scotch whisky industry was born. Here are to be found whiskies from every point of our Flavor Map—yes, even peaty. Speyside is not so much a unified single style as a cross section of single-malt Scotch.

The River Avon snakes its way past Tomintoul in southern Speyside.

Speyside

AVIEMORE • WWW.SPEYSIDEDISTILLERY.CO.UK

It seems almost arrogant that the newest distillery in Speyside should take the name of the region itself. However, its owners could claim (with some legitimacy) that there was a distillery of that name in the same town of Kingussie at the end of the nineteenth century—although it only ran until 1911.

The building that now bears the Speyside name has only been operating since 1991, having been painstakingly planned and built by George Christie over a period of three decades. Christie had previously been the owner of the Strathmore/North of Scotland grain distillery in Clackmannanshire—a plant that produced "patent still malt" from column stills (*see* p.16).

Speyside takes a more conventional approach to its whisky-making. Two small stills, obtained from the old Lochside distillery, make what is a light, honeyed malt. "The stills were too big," says manager Andy Shand, "so we had to lop a foot off the top and reweld them in order to make them fit."

Small stills can tend to make a heavy spirit, thanks to a shorter conversation between the alcohol vapor and the lightening properties of copper, so Shand has to have a light touch in order to create his light, new-make spirit. "We're very traditional," he says. "The fermentation is 60 hours long to build up esters and distillation is slow-paced. A lot of big firms fall into the trap of changing the setup and running too fast in order to make more spirit, and then lose their character. We're also

manual. Whisky-making today is too sanitized, too industrial. It's not left to people to do their own thing."

While new, it's easy to believe that the Speyside approach, with its reliance on intuition, links the distillery with the early days of the region's story—not just because of the fact that it was built, slowly, by hand, but also that the architecture and the materials root it in the landscape. The Speyside distillery could have been there for centuries, and in some ways it has: the skills and attitude contained within its dry-stone walls are nothing if not timeless.

Barrels ready for repair: the destination for future Speyside whisky.

SPEYSIDE TASTING NOTES

NEW MAKE

Nose: Very fragrant and intense with sour plum, green apple notes.
Palate: As nose suggests: light and sweet. Fizzy with a green melon lift towards the back.
Finish: Lightly floral.

3YO CASK SAMPLE

Nose: Gold. Lots of nuttiness and a slight earthy note. Toasty, charred oak. Dried apple/apple juice, burlap, and graham crackers.
Palate: Plenty of fresh wood, pancake batter, and a malty crispness. Fruit slightly hidden.
Finish: Softens.
Conclusion: In the additive stage of maturation. The spirit is absorbing rather than giving out.

Flavor Camp: **Fruity & Spicy**

12YO 40%

Nose: Pale straw. Distinctly earthy. Wheat chaff, geranium leaf. In time a herbal note akin to wild garlic and sorrel.
Palate: Spicier than the nose suggests; drier, too; the dusty earthiness carries through.
Finish: Light and short.
Conclusion: A refill cask hasn't woken up the spirit yet.

Flavor Camp: **Malty & Dry**
Where Next? Auchroisk 10yo

15YO 43%

Nose: Rich gold. Some sweetness and some coconut alongside apple peel, light, candied florals, and angelica.
Palate: Plenty of sweet oak. Delicate fruits and a hit of cut flower. Oak gives a crisper structure.
Finish: Clean and sweet.
Conclusion: Clear resemblance to new make. An easygoing and understanding malt.

Flavor Camp: **Fragrant & Floral**
Where Next? Bladnoch 8yo

Balmenach

CROMDALE • WWW.INVERHOUSE.COM/DISTILLERIES-BALMENACH.PHP

If the Speyside Distillery is this simulacrum of an old site, then the next stop is the real deal. Not that it shouts about it. Indeed, its location a mile outside the village of Cromdale gives a clue to its origins. Old distilleries, the ones that sprang up from illicit sites at the start of the nineteenth century, were on farms or sites of black *bothies* or huts: places away from the beaten track.

Close to the wild Cromdale hills, Balmenach is a classic old-style distillery.

In the late eighteenth and early nineteenth centuries, small-still distilling was effectively banned, with the result that a rural population that relied on it for its income was criminalized. In those days, making whisky involved subterfuge. Being hidden in the Cromdale Hills gave Balmenach's moonshining founder, James MacGregor, a positive advantage.

Speyside the region may exist in a legal sense, but it is far from being a single entity. Instead, it is a contrast between the old and the new, the dark and the light. Balmenach, with its small stills, wooden washbacks, and worm tubs, belongs to the former style, and it is these pieces of equipement that help give it its heavy, brooding power.

In simple terms, "light" is achieved through lots of copper contact in the still: the longer the conversation between vapor and copper, the lighter the spirit will be, so condensers, higher distillation temperatures, and cutting higher in the run all help produce a light character.

Using the ancient condensing technique of a copper pipe immersed in a bath of water (i.e. a "worm tub") results in less conversation between vapor and copper—hence a heavier style, and one which, at new-make stage, will normally have a sulfury note. It's important to stress that this sulfur acts as a marker for background complexities and is not in the mature spirit.

"We have worm tubs at Balmenach, anCnoc [Knockdhu], Old Pulteney, and Speyburn," says Stuart Harvey, master blender at Inver House, Balmenach's owner. "We don't pick up a lot of copper during the process but preserve the sulfur compounds produced during fermentation. This results in the cooked vegetables, meaty, struck-match character you find in these new makes.

"During maturation, the sulfur compounds interact with the char layer of the cask," he adds. "This produces the toffee and butter-scotch aromas and flavors in the mature whisky. Once the different sulfur compounds mature, the rest of the new-make character can shine through. The heavier the sulfur compounds, the longer it will take to mature."

Balmenach is in this last camp. Meaty when new, rich and heavy when mature—and perfectly built for long-term maturation in ex-sherry casks. Sadly, though, it's rarely seen. Inver House has chosen to keep this distillery hidden as far as single-malt bottlings go, but search among the independent bottlers for a taste of the old ways.

BALMENACH TASTING NOTES

NEW MAKE

Nose: Robust and deep with meaty, leathery notes. There are notes of mutton stock and ripe apple. Here is evidence of the guts and depth given by the traditional worm tubs coming into play. This power will remain with the spirit as it matures.
Palate: Very heavy and dense in the mouth with an exotic sweetness. It is this sweetness that balances Balmenach: mature in a sherry cask and the meatiness is enhanced; use a refill or ex-bourbon and it is this more aromatic aspect that comes to the fore.
Finish: Long. A little smoke.

1979, BERRY BROS & RUDD BOTTLING
56.3%, BOTTLED 2010

Nose: Full gold. Full and very sweet, with lots of heavy chocolate, toffee, and cacao cream before moving into stewed Assam tea. Weighty. Wet earth. With water, there's milk chocolate and creamy toffee, damp earth, and a shoe-shop note.
Palate: Spicy start with good intensity. Burning leaves (seems to be a touch of smoke). Heavy mid-palate where stewed orchard fruits rest. With water, becomes more savory.
Finish: Firm and long. Lightly drying. Dried apple peel—then after ten minutes, dried honey.
Conclusion: The sweet nature of American oak cask cannot hide Balmenach's bear-like qualities.

Flavor Camp: Fruity & Spicy
Where Next? Deanston 28yo, Old Pulteney 30yo

1993, GORDON & MACPHAIL BOTTLING 43%

Nose: Light gold. Dry leather/new leather belt, suggesting it's still at the early stages of interaction with the oak. Hard toffee and graham crackers, freshly varnished wood; with water, earthiness.
Palate: Thicker than the nose suggests. Chewy. Just a hint of cereal, then a charred smokiness, beech leaves, green tobacco leaf. With water, a previously hidden growly note adds further depth.
Finish: Wood.
Conclusion: Still coming together but the distillery character is there.

Flavor Camp: Fruity & Spicy
Where Next? The Glenlivet 1972

Tamnavulin & Tormore

TAMNAVULIN • BALLINDALLOCH / TORMORE • CROMDALE

While Balmenach has retained a belief in the old ways, this next pair of stills shows that while it is wrong to believe that there is a unified Speyside style, it is possible to argue that there is a shared flavor among distilleries built across Scotland in the 1960s, a period when rising demand for Scotch in the USA led to a rash of new buildings. It seems beyond coincidence that all of these produce whiskies that are light and quite often malty.

The large Tamnavulin plant, built on the side of the Livet River in 1965 by Invergordon Distillers (now part of Whyte & Mackay), is a perfect example. Its six stills give a high-toned, quite simple new make which, when followed through its evolution in cask, shows itself to be a whisky that is happy to do the blender's bidding: one where the cask rather than the whisky takes center stage.

This has its own dangers ... it's easy to lose Tamnavulin in an oak forest. "You have to be careful not to overdress it," says Whyte & Mackay's master blender Richard Paterson. "It's very good in American oak, light sherry, even in tired wood, but heavy clothes will weigh it down."

Tormore, part of the Chivas Brothers portfolio, shares this 1960s' iteration. Located eight miles northwest of Balmenach, it couldn't be more different from its neighbor. While the latter seeks refuge in the Cromdale moorland, the massive Tormore sits boldly beside the A96 highway looking like a modernist homage to a Victorian hydropathic hotel. It was designed by Sir Albert Richardson, president of the Royal Academy, who, for all his qualities as an architect, had clearly never built a distillery when he was commissioned by Long John Distillers in 1959. Its sheer size is a manifestation of the confidence of blenders at that time and its eight stills have always produced the light, dry style which the 1960s' North American market demanded: no peat in the malt, quick mashing, and short fermentations to get a cereal note, plus condensers to help lighten the spirit.

TAMNAVULIN TASTING NOTES

NEW MAKE

Nose: Clean and dry with some dusty cereal notes. Grappa-like.
Palate: Light, with notes of violet and lily. Crisp and bone-dry.
Finish: Nutty, short.

12YO 40%

Nose: Pale in color. Very light. Toasted rice. Some vanilla, then felt.
Palate: Light and dry. Slightly rubbery with barley/malt crunchiness, lemon.
Finish: Quick.
Conclusion: A straight line from the new make. Lightness personified.

Flavor Camp **Malty & Dry**
Where Next? Knockando 12yo, Auchentoshan Classic

1973 CASK SAMPLE

Nose: Greenish rim. Clean sherried notes, roasted nut, brown banana skin, and nut oil. Light dried flower.
Palate: Sweet and light-bodied. Has a nutty middle palate with subtle sweetness. Balanced.
Finish: Clean and medium.
Conclusion: Here a sherry cask has picked up the maltiness and made it nutty while also adding sweetness.

Flavor Camp **Rich & Round**

1966 CASK SAMPLE

Nose: Mahogany in color. Rich and mature. Cracked old leather. Plum and prune with a heavy sweetness. Akin to Brandy de Jerez.
Palate: Light grip. Brazil nut and a fairly dense mid-palate. Dried herbs.
Finish: Nuts.
Conclusion: Maybe a little overdressed, but a demonstration of how malty whiskies need oak.

Flavor Camp **Rich & Round**

TORMORE TASTING NOTES

NEW MAKE

Nose: Full, with fresh corn tones and a slight farmyard (cow breath) note.
Palate: Pure and sweet, with very light fruit.
Finish: Dusty, then light citrus fruit.

12YO 40%

Nose: Slightly hard nose, then some oak shavings. Dry and nutty.
Palate: Tobacco leaf, dry spiciness (coriander powder) with a herbal/heathery note. With water, increasingly bourbon-like.
Finish: Crisp and nutty.
Conclusion: Active oak giving considerable support.

Flavor Camp: **Fruity & Spicy**
Where Next? Glen Moray 12yo, Glen Garioch 12yo

1996, GORDON & MACPHAIL BOTTLING 43%

Nose: Pale. Light maltiness and crab apple. Hint of flowers behind. Quite firm.
Palate: Apple pie. Gorse. Orange-blossom water. When diluted, it remains fresh with an added grassiness and a little oiliness.
Finish: Short and slightly bitter.
Conclusion: Has the distillery's very angular focus.

Flavor Camp: **Fragrant & Floral**
Where Next? Miltonduff 18yo, Hakushu 18yo

Tomintoul & Braeval

TOMINTOUL • BALLINDALLOCH • WWW.TOMINTOULDISTILLERY.CO.UK / BRAEVAL • BALLINDALLOCH

Two other 1960s' plants conform to the lighter template. The first, Tomintoul, was built in 1965 on the banks of the Avon River by whisky-broking firms W. & S. Strong and Haig & MacLeod, and is now part of Angus Dundee's stable. Why build here, though? Probably due to the water supply: three springs feed the plant. Or maybe the original owners tapped into the fact that there's an old whisky-making pedigree here; a cave behind a nearby waterfall was once home to an illicit still.

Tomintoul is sold as "The Gentle Dram," which, while accurate, seems to imply a slightly bland nature that would be doing the malt a disservice. This is malty, but "maltiness" is a broad category, stretching from the anorexic and bone-dry to an almost burnt richness.

Tomintoul sits in the middle, its cereal-like center reminiscent of a warm mash tun and the sweet breath of cattle in the barn. There's an intensity to the new make that opens into soft fruit, which in turn acts as a counterpoint to the crispness of the cereal. There's enough there to cope with long-term aging in active casks. "I liken it to a truffle," says Angus Dundee's blender, Lorne MacKillop. "Its flavor never dominates, but still permeates a dish."

A smoky expression (using local peat) is also produced which gives our first example of how the location of the peat bog is key in the creation of specific aromas. Because of its composition, mainland peat gives a smoky effect more akin to wood smoke rather than the heathery, marine, or tarry notes from peat cut on the islands.

The illicit era is also the backdrop to Scotland's joint-highest distillery, Braeval, built in 1973 in the remote Braes of Glenlivet. This hidden, flagon-shaped valley is bounded by the Ladder Hills and stoppered at its entrance by the Bochel Hill. Scattered around are ruins of old *shielings* (shelters), evidence of the seasonal cattle migration; *braes* is dialect for high pasture. By the time the valley was settled in the eighteenth century, it was producing whisky, although it wasn't until 1972 that the Braes got its first legal distillery. Braeval, too, conforms to the "late Speyside" style of light. There's lots of copper in the system but the make is heavier than you'd expect, with a geranium note.

TOMINTOUL TASTING NOTES

NEW MAKE
Nose: Light cereal, oatmeal, sweet underneath. Touch of mash tun. Appetizing and sweet.
Palate: Focused, high-toned, and sweet, with a clean, green character in the center. Quite intense.
Finish: Malty.

10YO 40%
Nose: Copper. Crisp and slightly malty. Hazelnut, mixed peel. Ovaltine with water. Seems young.
Palate: Sweet, with white raisin, licorice tones. Very smooth.
Finish: Ripe and sweet.
Conclusion: Sherried components lend a dried-fruit softness.

Flavor Camp: **Malty & Dry**
Where Next? Auchentoshan Classic

14YO 46%, NO CARAMEL, NON-CHILL-FILTERED
Nose: Pale straw. Very light and clean with a floral (daffodil/freesia) and white-fruit lift. Delicate oak and a touch of flour/just-baked white bread.
Palate: Immediate floral lift with some pear juice. A fuller feel than the 10yo, with a knob of melting butter in the center. Grows in the mouth.
Finish: Sweet and long.
Conclusion: Here's where Tomintoul's hidden qualities begin to emerge.

Flavor Camp: **Fragrant & Floral**
Where Next? Linkwood 12yo

33YO 43%
Nose: More European oak influence. Oxidized and nutty with some white mushroom, hard toffee, dried black fruit, and that malted-milk character seen in the 10yo.
Palate: Tongue-clinging. Resinous with some sesame notes, sweet malt, and then a development of the white fruit seen in the 14yo.
Finish: Balanced and long.
Conclusion: Mature and elegant and indentifiably Tomintoul.

Flavor Camp: **Rich & Round**
Where Next? Aberlour 25yo

BRAEVAL TASTING NOTES

NEW MAKE
Nose: An estery start with a background heavy yeast-like character; just a whiff of sulfur.
Palate: Soft, with good weight, then lifted to the back.
Finish: Dark grains.

8YO 40%
Nose: Nutty. Pistachio with some apple wood, the roasted cereal note now softened and giving an extra layer. Lighter than you'd think from the *clearic* (new make). Winter russet apples.
Palate: Scented and lifted. Some jasmine and lavender. Delicate.
Finish: Clean and quite simple.
Conclusion: Freshness is enhanced.

Flavor Camp: **Fragrant & Floral**
Where Next? Tomintoul 14yo, Speyburn 10yo

The Glenlivet

BALLINDALLOCH • WWW.GLENLIVET.COM • OPEN TO VISITORS • APR–OCT, MON–SUN

Contrary to popular belief, there were plenty of legal distilleries operating before the date most people believe ushered in legal whisky distilling. The passing of the 1823 Excise Act was, however, the signal for the emergence of what we now recognize as today's Scotch whisky industry. The new legislation was aimed at stamping out illicit distilling by encouraging conditions for capital to be released into small-scale production facilities in the Highlands.

What is also overlooked is that this piece of legislation also expanded the options for distillers and, in doing so, changed whisky's flavors. There's a telling paragraph on this point in Michael Moss and John Hume's rigorously researched history of the Scotch whisky industry: "The new regulations [in 1823] allowed each distiller to choose his own methods of working; the strength of the wash, the size and design of the still, and the quality and the flavor of his whisky."

That's what was at the back of George Smith's mind when he was leaned upon by his landlord to take out one of the new licenses. This was not surprising, given that his landlord was the Duke of Gordon, who had helped initiate the change in the law by saying in the House of Lords that landowners would stop turning a blind eye to illicit distillation.

Smith had been moonshining since 1817 at the Upper Drumin farm high in the wilds of Glenlivet: one of many such operations in this hard-to-police area. Although his neighbors resented his new legal status—and Smith had little option but to go legit—it is what he did next which is intriguing.

He could have taken the same route as the MacGregors of Balmenach and stayed heavy. Smith and his sons, however, seem to have been liberated not just from the illegal ways of old, but from the old flavors. Smith moved into the light, embracing the possibilities of a new style. No more *bothies* and smoke-filled caves, but technology, capital, and, by the middle of the nineteenth century, proto-branding. Despite his being the only legal distillery in Glenlivet, it was Smith's style of whisky that became the shorthand for a specific flavor, and because every other distiller appended the appellation onto their name, Smith's distillery was permitted to call itself THE Glenlivet.

The old Drumin distillery closed in 1858, when Smith built a larger plant nearby at Minmore where the current distillery still stands. Considerably expanded since those days, in 2009–10 it has been given its most dramatic facelift yet. A new mash tun, eight new wooden washbacks, and a further three pairs of stills (making seven pairs in total), all with the same pinched waist of Smith's 1858 design, can make up to 2,641,721 gallons (ten million liters) a year. "The new Briggs mash tun has a monitor and viewing glass to check wort clarity; we don't want anything cloudy to give heavy cereal," says

The quality of its wood management has enabled The Glenlivet to become one of the world's top-selling single malts.

Alan Winchester, The Glenlivet's master distiller. "Then we give it a 48-hour ferment, while those stills give good copper contact to get fruity, floral esters which will then undergo further esterification in the cask."

According to nineteenth-century records, Smith aimed for a pineapple character in his whisky. Today, for me, it is apples that are the defining character, along with a gentle floral note when young. It has guts, however, The Glenlivet, building in finesse as it matures—especially in refill casks (*see* pp.14–15).

High in the cool air of Minmore, The Glenlivet's warehouses have their own microclimate.

Equally important, though, is the design of the new stillhouse. Glenlivet was for many years a gray, industrial-looking unit on a hill. Now with its panoramic window and dressed stone it has become part of the landscape once more, looking back as it does to the Braes and ahead to Ben Rinnes.

THE GLENLIVET TASTING NOTES

NEW MAKE
Nose: Medium-weight. Clean, with some floral notes, a little banana, ripe apple, and a touch of iris.
Palate: Soft, gentle fruits. Light, appley. Fresh zucchini.
Finish: Crisp and clean.

12YO 40%
Nose: Light gold. Scented, with lots of apple (fruit and blossom), jasmine tea, and a touch of toffee.
Palate: Delicate start, then sudden lift of chocolate. Apples flood into flowers, honey, poached pear.
Finish: Clean and soft.
Conclusion: Light and aromatic.

Flavor Camp: Fragrant & Floral
Where Next? Glenkinchie 12yo, anCnoc 16yo

15YO 40%
Nose: Coppery gold. Intensely spiced: sandalwood rosewood, turmeric, cardamom. Rose petal.
Palate: Apples first. Flower stall. Gentle, light; grippy oak.
Finish: The spices return. Cinnamon and ginger.
Conclusion: French oak usage has upped the spiciness.

Flavor Camp: Fruity & Spicy
Where Next? Balblair 1975, Glenmorangie 18yo

18YO 40%
Nose: Full gold. Baked apple, light-brown sugar, antique shop, lilac. Light aniseed.
Palate: Richer than the 12yo with more sherry cask. Cedar, almond blossom, amontillado, and dried orange peel.
Finish: Apple and allspice.
Conclusion: Richer and more evolved, with a good line back to new make.

Flavor Camp: Rich & Round
Where Next? Auchentoshan 21yo

1972 CELLAR COLLECTION 52.3%
Nose: Light amber. Whisky *rancio*. Cigar box, caramelized fruit sugars, light tangerine, *crème brûlée*, spruce, cinnamon.
Palate: There's a touch of smoke in here. Quite heathery as well as leathery (suede). Sweet oak, barbecued pineapple. Relaxed.
Finish: Light smoke and fruit.
Conclusion: A further step into the fusion of wood and spirit.

Flavor Camp: Fruity & Spicy
Where Next? Balmenach 1993, Old Pulteney 30yo

THE BEN RINNES CLUSTER

Ben Rinnes is Scotland's whisky mountain—there's even a toposcope on its summit showing all the distilleries that can be seen from there. In its shadow, the play between the old, traditional ways and the modern, lighter aesthetic reaches its fullest expression. Here, distilleries that make heavy, meaty styles sit alongside those where flowers are the order of the day.

Cardhu (background) looks down to the riverside buildings of Knockando.

Cragganmore

BALLINDALLOCH • WWW.DISCOVERING-DISTILLERIES.COM/CRAGGANMORE • OPEN TO VISITORS • MAY–OCT, MON–FRI

Ben Rinnes is the nexus of Speyside. The most northerly outlier of the Cairngorm massif, it dominates the central part of the region. From its summit, the landscape of the area can be discerned: south to the Cromdales and Glenlivet, north to Rothes and Elgin, east into Dufftown and Keith. The cluster of distilleries that fall within its immediate shadow are further evidence of Speyside's development of its triple-faceted style.

One of the issues facing the post-1823 distiller was how to get his wares to market. Mountain tracks may have been a distinct advantage in the smuggling days, but poor communication with the new markets was a hindrance to many of the new start-ups, and by the 1860s distilleries were struggling.

Their fortunes were to change in 1869 with the building of the Strathspey Railway which linked Dufftown with Boat of Garten and the line to Perth with the central belt. The first distiller within the Ben Rinnes cluster to take advantage of this was John Smith, who built his Cragganmore distillery next to Ballindalloch station in 1869.

John Smith was a large man. In some ways, his size has diminished him, with all the attention paid to his girth detracting from his genius as an innovative distiller. He was related to George Smith of The

Glenlivet (in all probability his illegitimate son) and he was manager there, as well as at Dailuaine and Macallan before heading south to Clydesdale (Wishaw). He then returned to Speyside, briefly holding the lease on Glenfarclas before finally taking the lease on a piece of land beside the Spey to build his distillery.

Although there are now computers in the stillhouse, Smith's approach to whisky-making remains intact. The reason he built here was practical, but inside, it is his creativity as a distiller that is striking. He'd already worked at a diverse selection of other people's stills: Glenlivet in its journey to light, Macallan and Glenfarclas (heavier), the triple-distilled Clydesdale. This was his chance to make his own whisky.

Cragganmore starts normally enough: lightly peated malt that's milled, mashed, and given a long fermentation in wooden washbacks. It is in the stillhouse, however, that Smith's genius is most apparent.

Although hidden from sight, and somewhat off the beaten track, Cragganmore was one of the first distilleries to take advantage of the railway.

A slow evolution in barrel will be one of the factors that adds further layers to this complex single malt.

The wash stills, the first stop, are large with a sharply angled lyne arm leading into a worm tub. Meanwhile, the next vessels, the spirit stills, have a flat top with a long, gently sloping lyne arm stuck onto the side. The key word here is reflux: the process of alcohol vapor condensing inside the body of the still and being redistilled (*see* pp.14–15).

The question is what style of spirit was Smith trying to make? The longer you look, the more confusing and contradictory it seems. The wash stills are huge, suggesting lots of reflux and therefore a light spirit, but the lyne arm is steeply angled downwards, which stops that conversation being too prolonged. The fact that it then leads into a cold worm tub suggests the end result would be heavy. The spirit still is even more confusing. The alcohol vapor pings off the flat top and is refluxed into the roiling mass of low wines. Because the lyne arm is offset from the top, only certain flavors will come across. The long, gentle declination of that lyne arm means there's a longer copper conversation taking place. It all points to extending the copper conversation—until you factor in the small still and cold worms!

The answer? Smith was a master of distillation who wanted to make as complex a spirit as he could. Cragganmore may be confusing, but it is also inspiring. Guys like Smith were not uneducated men simply boiling up beer; they were innovators, experimenters, pioneers.

The guess these days is that Smith's Cragganmore would have been complex and on the lighter side of heavy, or that he even made two styles. "I'm not sure in 1869 that they knew that sulfur disappeared after ten years in cask, so they might have tried to avoid it," says current manager Shane Healy. "The whole process lends itself to producing sulfury in winter and predominantly grassy in summer."

Not that Healy wants that. Today, Cragganmore is making a sulfury/meaty new spirit all year round, so he needs to stop the copper conversation: no air rests and cold worms (which is why, in the warmer summer months, the spirit can get grassy).

Smith's spirit still, however, continues to do its work. Hidden behind that sulfur in the new make is the glimmering of the complex, mature character, all autumn fruit and flashes of late sun through the leaves in Ballindalloch's dark woods.

CRAGGANMORE TASTING NOTES

NEW MAKE
Nose: Concentrated. Meaty (lamb stock). Sulfur. Sweet citrus and fruits behind. Hint of nut.
Palate: Big and strong, with some smoke, then the meat/sulfur tone comes through. Huge and dense. Thick, oily, and old-style. Has weight and suppleness.
Finish: Black fruits and sulfur.

8YO REFILL WOOD, CASK SAMPLE
Nose: Integrated and fruity. Touch of roast meat/roasting pan. Lots of mint, autumn leaves, and moss, even some pineapple and bramble. Sulfur with water.
Palate: Ripe and silky. Character has emerged. Complex and heavy. Fruit-led with backing of wood.
Finish: Closes down. Touch of peat.
Conclusion: The mature character is already emerging.

Flavor Camp: Fruity & Spicy

12YO 40%
Nose: Complex mix of ripe autumn fruit, cassis, some leather, heavy honey, chestnut. Light smoke.
Palate: Full-bodied and fruity. Stewed soft fruits, touches of walnut. Deep. Silky feel. Opened.
Finish: Light smoke.
Conclusion: Sulfur has totally gone and the meat has merged into a rich general fruitiness.

Flavor Camp: Rich & Round
Where Next? Glendronach 12yo, Glengoyne 17yo

1997 MANAGER'S CHOICE 59.7%
Nose: Pale. Light maltiness and crab apple. Hint of flowers behind. Quite firm.
Palate: Light gold. Oiliness, but then begins to lift and becomes light and estery: pineapple, strawberry with honeyed quality. In time coriander, honey.
Finish: Big and toffee-like.
Conclusion: Needs time in the glass to build up in power.

Flavor Camp: Rich & Round
Where Next? Macallan Sherry 10yo, Yamazaki 18yo

Knockando

KNOCKANDO • WWW.MALTS.COM/INDEX.PHP/EN_GB/OUR-WHISKIES/KNOCKANDO/INTRODUCTION

The contrast between Cragganmore and Knockando could not be more extreme. Whereas the former is hidden away in a leafy glen, the latter sits proudly, blond-stoned, beside what used to be the Strathspey railway line and is now the Speyside Way long-distance hiking path. There is an airiness to the layout that somehow reflects this light-bodied malt whose character is reminiscent of motes of dust on a sunlit afternoon.

Knockando is firmly in the light camp. In fact, it is one of the precursors of the skeletal crew which came onto the scene in the 1960s. Here, cloudy wort and short ferments give an overriding malty new-make character (*see* pp.14–15). As a result, the oak touch needs to be whisper-light, just sufficient to provide some sweetness to that dusty palate.

Like John Smith, its original owner, John Thompson, built Knockando on this site to take full advantage of the railway, but things had moved on since Smith's day. By the time Knockando was built, in 1890, blends were in the ascendency, and therefore the blender was in charge of dictating what styles were needed. If the early distillers made, to a great extent, what they wanted—whisky as extension of personality and inclination—by the end of the nineteenth century a more hard-nosed pragmatism was taking over. Distilleries were producing what the blenders wanted, and the blenders in turn had to be cogniscent of what the drinking public craved. What these distilleries from Speyside's last wave of nineteenth-century building show is the widening of the Scotch

The pale buildings of Knockando sit beside the Spey River.

whisky template, the need for an ever-greater range of flavors with which to fashion blends.

Knockando became part of Gilbey's in 1904, one of the London-based blender's portfolio of Speysiders, all of which were on the delicate side. It was eventually to become a major player within J&B, one of the most fragile drams on the market, blended to suit the lighter American Prohibition-time palate.

KNOCKANDO TASTING NOTES

NEW MAKE

Nose: Mashy and clean with hazelnut. With water, becomes dusty: sofa stuffing, felt.
Palate: Light and tight with some lemon. Very dusty. Simple.
Finish: Short, dry.

8YO REFILL WOOD, CASK SAMPLE

Nose: The new-make character is still there: dust and mouse. Old flour. Bone-dry.
Palate: Powdered wheat cereal. There seems to be sweetness but it is well hidden. Crisp and dry.
Finish: Malty.
Conclusion: A dry, nutty character that needs light, sweet wood to bring it to life.

Flavor Camp: Malty & Dry

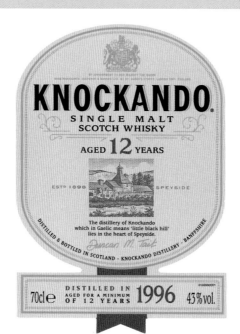

12YO 43%

Nose: Light and more nutty. Dry straw (the dust has gone). Hints of esters behind a soft, if light, vanilla note.
Palate: Light and fluffy with some milk chocolate, lemon. With water, a dry, malty character. Very light.
Finish: Short and dry.
Conclusion: A little longer in cask has filled out the center a little.

Flavor Camp: Malty & Dry
Where Next? Tamnavulin 12yo

Tamdhu

KNOCKANDO • WWW.EDRINGTONGROUP.COM/BRANDS/TAMDHU.ASP

A few yards along the old railway track sits Tamdhu, which follows a similar model to Knockando insofar as it was built in 1896 by a consortium of blenders, who sold it a year later to Highland Distillers (now Edrington). Its dark-stone courtyard and grand buildings combine to give it a somewhat forlorn air, although it is the size of the structures that hide Tamdhu's greatest claim to fame: the site of the last operational Saladin maltings in Scotch whisky.

Up until the invention of the Saladin malting method, a distillery's capacity was restricted by the size of its malting floors. This new method—chamber-sized baths with fans underneath filled with germinating barley turned by an Archimedes screw—allowed huge amounts of malt to be made (each of Tamdhu's ten boxes can hold 22 tons), thus increasing production and bringing about a centralization of malting. As well as being self-sufficient in malt, Tamdhu provided the unpeated malt both for Highland Park and for all of Glenrothes' requirements.

The maltings tend to take attention away from the distillery itself which, since 1972, has been a six-still operation. It has always played a background role in Edrington's offerings, providing fillings for blends, among them Dunhill, whose executives would have entertained their clients in the elegant bar overlooking the Spey; the 1960s' décor is a wistful reminder of those boom times. Today, the old Knockando station, which has been renamed Tamdhu, acts as the reception center.

Its selfless character is apparent in the estery new make, but older expressions have more of a malty character. "As a non-core brand, it probably has changed over time," says Edrington's master blender, Gordon Motion. "A lot of that mature character probably changed as

Wooden washbacks are believed to add to Tamdhu's character.

we became more knowledgeable about casks and introduced a robust wood policy back in the 1990s. We haven't changed the character to suit blending requirements, but rather used the casks to make the changes. I like a range of characters to play with, so would be against two of our distilleries producing a very similar spirit."

The blenders pull the strings. At the time of writing, Tamdhu has been closed again to bring stock into balance.

TAMDHU TASTING NOTES

NEW MAKE
Nose: Clean and light with estery notes and flowers. Fragrant and lifted.
Palate: Perfumed and direct. Hyacinth and freesia, touch of cucumber.
Finish: Clean and swift.

10YO 40%
Nose: Light gold. Yeasty/bready, almost bread-and-butter. More malty than the new make.
Palate: Medium-bodied. Nutty. Light and pretty crisp. Touch of lemon.
Finish: Crisp cereal.
Conclusion: Clean and dry but a difference here from the current new-make style.

Flavor Camp: **Malty & Dry**
Where Next? Aultmore 12yo

18YO 43%
Nose: Bigger and more sherried, quite plump raisins. Like most light whiskies, it picks up cask influence easily.
Palate: Sherried character to the fore. Huge and raisined with a cereal dryness underneath. Balanced.
Finish: Clean and drying. Cookie tones.
Conclusion: Plenty of cask, with distillery character just holding on.

Flavor Camp: **Rich & Round**
Where Next? Arran 1996

32YO CASK SAMPLE
Nose: Open. Nutty and slightly smoky. A previously unseen honeyed note has emerged along with cinnamon.
Palate: Very spicy, with ripe, integrated, soft/dried fruit.
Finish: Light and clean.
Conclusion: Sweet and balanced. Here, a slow maturation has benefited this light spirit well.

Flavor Camp: **Fruity & Spicy**
Where Next? Macallan Fine Oak 25yo, Balmenach 1993

Cardhu

KNOCKANDO • WWW.DISCOVERING-DISTILLERIES.COM/CARDHU • OPEN ALL YEAR • SEE WEB FOR DAYS & DETAILS

One major omission from the standard history of whisky distilling in Scotland has been the role played by women. Seduced by Sir Edwin Landseer's romantic depiction of the illicit distiller—a Highland chieftain, foot on stag, relaxing in his heather-roofed *bothy*—we forget about the careworn crone beside him. It's probably his wife. And she's the distiller.

When their husbands were out in the fields tending the beasts (rather than hunting stags), the women would have been at home working on an endless succession of duties, including distilling. Such was the case at Cardhu. It may have been John Cumming who took the reins of Cardow Farm on Mannoch Hill above the Spey in 1811, but evidence suggests that it was his wife, Helen, who made the whisky—illegally to begin with.

Cardow Farm acted as an early warning station for the moonshiners further south in Glenlivet. Stand at George Smith's original site at Minmore and a great bowl of land is laid out in front of you. There, high on a hill, is Cardhu distillery. According to legend, the *gaugers* (taxmen) would arrive at Cardow Farm and Helen Cumming would invite them in for a wee cup of tea and a scone. As they were being entertained, a red flag would be hoisted up a flagpole, warning the Livet moonshiners that the law was on its way.

In 1824, however, the Cummings took out one of the new licenses (conceivably the first to do so), but this change in legality made no difference to the way the distillery was run; the female hand remained on the tiller. After Helen's death, her daughter-in-law, Elizabeth, took charge of the plant, rebuilding it before, in 1893, selling it to long-time client John Walker & Sons (on the agreement that the family would operate the distilllery). In 1897, it was expanded again under its new owner, while a futher expansion in 1960 saw two more stills added to the original quartet.

Cardhu today is grassy and precise, a keenly focused new make whose orange and chocolate tones emerge later in life. It is, in other words, light, thereby not conforming to the loose theory that the older the distillery, the heavier the style tends to be. "To the best of my knowledge the grassiness isn't a new development," says Douglas Murray, Diageo's master distiller and blender (aka "The Guru"). What we do know is that the character is the result of a

Originally installed by Elizabeth Cumming, Cardhu's stills help create its fresh character.

specific type of fermentation and distillation regime with the extra copper given by condensers taking it away from fruity (à la Glen Elgin) and more into the grassy camp.

Yet, when whisky's first great chronicler, Alfred Barnard, visited in the late 1880s, he found something quite different. Enjoying the "well-known hospitality of Mrs. Cumming," Barnard saw the old farm distillery with buildings that were "straggling and primitive" as well as Helen's brand-new site: "a handsome pile." Unusually for him, he actually comments on the whisky itself: "[It is] of the thickest and richest description and admirably suited for blending purposes."

In other words, it was an old-style, robust Speysider. The question is, when did it go light? Maybe under Walker's ownership as part

A large site with long-established links to Johnnie Walker, Cardhu is a perfect illustration of the rise of blended Scotch.

of the general shift to a lighter character at the turn of the twentieth century. Conceivably it was happening when Barnard was visiting. This is when Helen sold her old stills, mill, and waterwheel to William Grant, who was building his Glenfiddich distillery. Glenfiddich's stills are small. Cardhu's today are large. Maybe that's when the lighter make started. While that's just conjecture, what is clear is that if Ben Rinnes is the focal point, then Cardhu is where this cluster starts to turn and embrace the new.

CARDHU TASTING NOTES

NEW MAKE

Nose: Green fruit pastille, wet grass, turmeric powder, violet, laurel.
Palate: Light and needle-fresh. Tight with some white flour, blueberry.
Finish: Light citrus fruit.

8YO REFILL WOOD, CASK SAMPLE

Nose: Has softened from new-make stage. Mown grass, perfumed soap, and light cereal (the flour). Violet and then mandarin orange.
Palate: More green grass with lots of light aromatics bunched up behind. Has surprising weight. The wood has added a white chocolate effect.
Finish: Still citric.
Conclusion: Beginning to blossom.

Flavor Camp: Fragrant & Floral

12YO 40%

Nose: The grassiness is now drying (maybe from the attentions of the wood). Hay and some wood oil. A developing mix of orange, milk chocolate, and stawberry. Light cedar and mint with water.
Palate: Medium-bodied. The grassiness is now crisp leaving the sweetness to be given by wood interaction and a developing orange note.
Finish: Short, spicy, and chocolate-tinged.
Conclusion: It will continue to develop but, as with most light spirits, has reached a balanced integration relatively early.

Flavor Camp: Fragrant & Floral
Where Next? Strathisla 12yo

Glenfarclas

BALLINDALLOCH • WWW.GLENFARCLAS.CO.UK • OPEN ALL YEAR • OCT–JUN, MON–FRI; JULY–SEPT, MON–SAT

The dichotomy between heavy and light, old and new, which pervades the whole of Speyside is at its most noticeable in the shadow of Ben Rinnes. Three miles to the south of Cardhu, hard on the lower slopes of the mountain, is Glenfarclas, whose heavily sweet, brooding new make immediately identifies it as a member of the former camp.

There is a feeling of permanence, of the past solidifying in your mouth when you taste it. Just as whisky has been pulled in many directions by commercial necessity, so Glenfarclas has stayed rooted. Yet a glance at its stills, the biggest in Speyside, would lead you to believe that here is a distillery making a lighter style. The secret to its new make's depth lies in the blazing fires beneath the stills themselves.

"We tried steam in 1981," says George Grant, whose family has owned the distillery for six generations, "but we pulled it out after three weeks and went straight back to direct fire. Steam might be cheaper, but here it just made the spirit flat. We want a spirit that has weight to it. We want to age it 50 years."

And where it is aged makes a difference. All of Glenfarclas is matured in "dunnage" warehouses: low, slate-roofed, earth-floored buildings. These days distilleries often tanker new spirit off-site to palletized or rack warehousing in different parts of Scotland. If a whisky's character is about the accretion of small details, then could even this slight change in temperature have an effect? Grant believes so.

"There's a huge difference in temperature inside palletized warehouses, which are effectively tin sheds, and that is bound to affect the maturation cycle. Here, our losses are 0.05% a year. I've seen some in palletized sites where it's as high as 5%; the industry average is 2%. Here, the whisky is oxidizing slowly, not evaporating, and that makes a difference." Inside these warehouses on the foothills of "The Ben," surrounded by a piercing wind, is what is regarded as a microclimate. It is site-specificity at work, and there's an almost Burgundian approach to whisky-making: knowing your plot, accepting what it gives you.

The wood type has a significant contribution to the Glenfarclas style; it's predominantly first-fill sherry cask (from José-Miguel Martin) with no first-fill bourbon. It's not just that Glenfarclas can cope with sherry casks; it *needs* sherry casks. Rather than eventually falling into the woodpile, it absorbs the oak's power and binds it in.

There are few families in Scotch with this lineage of distilling, giving the Grants an almost psychic link with place. "We have continuity," says Grant. "We don't have to answer to anyone so we can do it our way, and because we have been doing it for

Situated on the flanks of Ben Rinnes, there has been whisky made on the Glenfarclas site since the eighteenth century.

six generations we're better placed than most. You either have your money in the bank or your money in stock. We have both. This is our 22nd recession! We've learned only to make what we can afford and we never borrow money to make it."

And is this one of the few remnants of an older Speyside? "We don't even call ourselves Speyside!" laughs Grant. "We say that we are a Highland malt. This whole 'Speyside' idea is new [which is true: the region was known both as Strathspey and Glenlivet in the past] and it does confuse people. The Spey runs a long way." He pauses. "Right enough, 'Highland' is even more impossible to define. We are just Glenfarclas. I have a painting from 1791 showing a distillery on this site. We've been here legally for 175 years. People know what Glenfarclas is."

Ex-sherry casks are a major part of Glenfarclas's distinctive flavor profile.

GLENFARCLAS TASTING NOTES

NEW MAKE

Nose: Big, heavy, and fruity. Quite earthy and deep. Powerful with a touch of peat smoke.
Palate: Dry start, quite closed and tight, with that earthy note continuing. Ripe and dense. Old-style.
Finish: Hint of fruit. Brooding.

10YO 40%

Nose: Sherried (amontillado *pasada*); toasted almond, chestnut. Ripe fruits, mulberry but also smoky edge: autumn bonfire. Sweetens into English sherry trifle, larch.
Palate: Clean and quite crisp with good heat in the middle palate. Ripe and full. Damson jam. Still has the earthiness of the new make and that intriguing burnt note. Water sweetens it considerably.
Finish: Thick and long. Length, grip, and power.
Conclusion: Immediate acquisition of cask influences, but this has more to give.

Flavor Camp: **Rich & Round**
Where Next? Edradour 1997

15YO 46%

Nose: Amber. Deep and rich, with date and dried fruit. Still has the edginess of youth but picking up complexity. The earthiness is lightening as things begin to sweeten up: chestnut purée, cedar, hazelnuts on a campfire, fruitcake.
Palate: Tight grip and not so much opening as bulging. Glenfarclas just amasses weight as it matures. Woods. More grip than the 10yo but the spirit is so big that it simply shrugs it aside.
Finish: Powerful and long.
Conclusion: A sense of ever-growing power.

Flavor Camp: **Rich & Round**
Where Next? Benrinnes 15yo, Mortlach 16yo

30YO 43%

Nose: Mahogany. Lots of dark chocolate and espresso. Still edgy. Now raisiny, but also molasses and prune and old leather. In time, there's leaf mulch (a development of the earlier earthiness). Even a meaty touch.
Palate: Woodsy and mysterious. Dense and crepuscular. Bolivar cigar and sweet dark fruits. Some tannic grip.
Finish: Coffee.
Conclusion: There might be big cask influence here, but even after three decades in an active cask the distillery is holding its own.

Flavor Camp: **Rich & Round**
Where Next? Ben Nevis 25yo

Dailuaine

DAILUAINE • ABERLOUR

Despite Dailuaine being one of the most-spotted distilleries in Speyside, few know that's what they have seen. Heading towards Aberlour from Glenfarclas, there will usually be clouds of steam billowing from a hidden valley on the river-side of the road. These are rising from Dailuaine's dark grains plant, where the pot ale and draff from Diageo's central Speyside sites is processed into cattle feed.

Dailuaine itself is an interesting mix of old and new. An 1852 distillery, it was rebuilt in 1884 and was for a time the largest malt distillery in Speyside, featuring a kiln which Alfred Barnard described as having a roof, "of the steepest pitch in Scotland … [which] gives the malt a delicate aroma without having to use coke to prevent the flavor being too pronounced." This was further refined with the installation of the first distillery pagoda in Scotland: clear evidence that Dailuaine was trying to go light(er) in terms of smokiness to meet *fin-de-siècle* market demands.

Once the largest distillery in Speyside, Dailuaine continues to make a big, beefy dram.

For all of that, today Dailuaine remains in the heavy, old-style camp, though it is sweeter at heart with less of the meaty pungency of other members of that club.

While other Diageo plants such as Cragganmore, Mortlach, and Benrinnes find this character relatively easy to make, thanks to worm tubs (*see* pp.14–15), Dailuaine has to work against type to get this sulfury new make from its condensers. As we've seen, sulfuriness is down to a lack of copper interaction, but condensers are packed full of the metal. Solution here? Stainless-steel condensers.

It seems only appropriate that this old distillery, which has always been at the forefront of innovation, should find a creative solution to maintain it within the crepuscular world of the older whisky.

Also in the valley bottom, beside the old railway, is Imperial, whose checkered history speaks volumes about the uncertainties of the Scotch whisky industry. Built in 1897, it had to wait until the 1950s for its longest uninterrupted period of production before being mothballed in 1983. It's still closed, an immense irritation to many who love its American cream soda/floral style.

DAILUAINE TASTING NOTES

NEW MAKE
Nose: Light meatiness, leathery. Some cereal and a partially hidden sweetness.
Palate: Big. Meaty. Sweet and thick, almost toffee-like. Heavy.
Finish: Long, with that hint of sweetness.

8YO REFILL WOOD, CASK SAMPLE
Nose: The meat has receded, leaving that sweetness to dominate. Light leather, black fruits, old apples.
Palate: Big and heavy, with damson and mulberry cut with leather. Rich and full.
Finish: The meatiness only shows now.
Conclusion: A heavy, rich, sweet spirit. A powerhouse.

Flavor Camp: Rich & Round

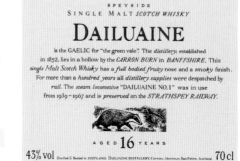

16YO, FLORA & FAUNA 43%
Nose: Red amber. Deep, earthy, sherried. Funky, with a light sulfur lift. Highly concentrated. Olde English marmalade. It remains slightly meaty with molasses, rum and raisin, clove tones.
Palate: Huge and very sweet. Almost PX/Brandy de Jerez-like. Walnuts and chestnuts. An assault on the tongue.
Finish: Gripping, then slowly sweetens.
Conclusion: Sherry casks are needed to tame this beast. Distillery character still strong despite the attentions of oak.

Flavor Camp: Rich & Round
Where Next? Glenfarclas 15yo, Mortlach 16yo

Benrinnes & Allt-a-Bhainne

BENRINNES • ABERLOUR / ALLT-A-BHAINNE • DUFFTOWN

Finally, after skirting round "The Ben," it's time to start climbing its slopes. The granitic outcrop known as Ben Rinnes is alive with springs, home to mountain hares, snow buntings, ptarmigan, and deer. Its lower reaches are thickened with peat, its summits a scrabble of pink granite. It's only a mile from the green Spey Valley, close to towns, but you are in the wild. It certainly spooked chronicler Alfred Barnard, a man best-suited for travel at sea level: "… no more weird or desolate place could be chosen," he wrote of its location.

This weirdness is a fair descriptor of the Benrinnes approach to whisky-making. One sniff of the new make and you are confronted with the Stygian qualities that define so many of Speyside's oldest sites. This is meaty stuff, with sulfur—a strange mix of the savory and a little sweetness. That meatiness is its defining feature: a feral mix of tanned hides and cauldrons.

The character comes from its partial triple distillation. There are two sets of three stills, each working as a trio. The spirit from the wash still is split into "heads" and "tails." The former, high in strength, goes to one receiver, the latter, weaker, is redistilled in the intermediate still with the foreshots and feints from its previous run. The middle cut is collected and mixed with the "heads" from the wash still and the foreshots and feints from the previous run of the spirit still. Outside, chilled worm tubs help to cut down any copper contact. The sulfur comes from the worms, the meatiness from that intermediate still.

It is hard to think of a greater contrast to "The Ben" than the distillery on the mountain's eastern flanks. Built by Seagram in 1975, Allt-a-Bhainne and its slender stills with upward-angled lyne arms yield a whisky with a delicacy typical of its era and its owner's house style.

BENRINNES TASTING NOTES

NEW MAKE
Nose: Dense. Hoof glue. Gravy. Lea & Perrins. Big meatiness.
Palate: Big and bruised. Heavy and full-bodied with some smoke. Good weight. Dry and powerful.
Finish: Sulfury.

8YO REFILL WOOD, CASK SAMPLE
Nose: Beef stock cubes, steak gravy. Very earthy and rooty.
Palate: Thick and concentrated, with a tamarind-like sweetness in the center. Licorice and chocolate.
Finish: Meaty/sulfury.
Conclusion: A big bruiser; needs time to open to full maturity.

Flavor Camp: **Rich & Round**

15YO, FLORA & FAUNA 43%
Nose: Red amber. Meaty. Toffee and still stock-cube dry meatiness. More time adds dried cep liquor. With water, a smoky heathery lift.
Palate: Robust. Roasted meat and a fair grip of tannin. Long and ripe, but the water helps to loosen the tannic grip, as does the inherent richness of the spirit. Hints of emerging leatheriness.
Finish: Bitter chocolate and coffee.
Conclusion: Now begining to enter a mature stage.

Flavor Camp: **Rich & Round**
Where Next? Glenfarclas 21yo, Macallan 18yo Sherry

High on the slopes of The Ben, where Barnard feared to tread.

23YO 58.8%
Nose: Deep mahogany. Prune (Armagnac-like) with a light steak note behind. This interplay between muscularity and rippling sweetness continues all the way through. Bergamot, tomato paste, touch of allspice, and a slightly carbonized *jus* note, caramel apple, roast chestnut, coffee, earthiness.
Palate: Big, powerful and assertive but not astringent since the concentrated sweetness remains. Raisin (PX) and lots of date. The feral beast has been semi-tamed. Softens as it slowly moves across the tongue. Water lightens the grip and adds a slight smoked character. Beefy in all senses.
Finish: Molasses.
Conclusion: Even after 23 years in a first-fill sherry cask, it is identifiably Benrinnes.

Flavor Camp: **Rich & Round**
Where Next? Macallan 25yo, Ben Nevis 25yo

ALLT-A-BHAINNE TASTING NOTES

NEW MAKE PEATED MALT
Nose: Very light smoke to start with. Plain, very clean, light base spirit with wisps of slightly grassy smoke coming across. Bonfire.
Palate: The smoke hits with full effect here. Wood smoke. Dry.
Finish: Drying.

1991 62.3%
Nose: Grassy and estery. Cooperage aromas. Oak. Light and clean. Quite simple.
Palate: Perfumed and floral note. Lots of freshly charred oak. Hint of barley sugar. High-toned and estery.
Finish: Clean and short.
Conclusion: Very much on the house style of the lighter side of Speyside.

Flavor Camp: **Fragrant & Floral**
Where Next: Glenburgie 12yo, Glen Grant 10yo

Casks awaiting repair or rejuvenation at the Speyside Cooperage.

Aberlour & Glenallachie

ABERLOUR • WWW.ABERLOUR.COM • OPEN ALL YEAR • NOV–MAR, MON–FRI; APR–OCT, MON–SUN / GLENALLACHIE • ABERLOUR

Turning your back on the mountain and heading towards the Spey and the town of Aberlour, the whisky-traveler first comes across Glenallachie. Although its location, out of sight from the road and away from the railway, suggests that this started life as an illicit site, it's another of The Ben's modern plants. Built in 1967 by Charles Mackinlay, it's a classic 1960s' distillery, made specifically to provide light (and in this case, cereal-accented) spirit for the growing North American market. That maltiness is on the sweeter side of the scale, along with a latent fruity note.

The influence of Ben Rinnes itself may yet have an influence, however. One reason why the Benrinnes distillery makes a meaty spirit is because of the very cold water that flows from the mountain into its worms. Glenallachie also draws its water from the mountain, but here the cold temperature can cause problems with achieving character.

"These big, Jura-like stills are made to make light [new make]," (*see* pp.14–15) says Alan Winchester, distilleries manager at owner Chivas Brothers. "But it can go sulfury if the process water gets too cold. The key to keeping the style is running things a wee bit warmer."

The mountain has finally relinquished its grip by the time you reach the neat little town of Aberlour. The tendency of distillers to secrete their plants up side alleys, however, seems still to be in force. The town's eponymous (and large) plant is some distance from the main road, with only a rather smart Victorian gatehouse as evidence of its existence.

There has been a legal distillery in Aberlour since the 1820s, when two local farmers, John and George Graham, tried out their luck with one of the new licenses. The plant we see today was, however, originally built in 1879 by James Fleming, and it is he who is considered its true founder. It's unlikely he would recognize the plant today since it was rebuilt in the 1970s, and like Glenallachie is a good example of the open-spaced, clean, and efficient design prevalent at the time.

It's more intriguing to wonder if Fleming would recognize the make. Because he was building at the start of the lightening process of the 1880s, it's quite possible that he would. "The key for me in the new make is currant and a little green apple," says

Winchester, previously a manager here. "There's also an absence of cereal." Certainly, while Aberlour fits into the fruitier side of the Chivas Brothers house style, it is Winchester's currant leaf which gives Aberlour an intriguing, almost herbal fragrance as it matures. The fruitiness, meanwhile, adds mid-palate softness, and there's sufficient weight to the spirit to allow it to sit happily in a sherry cask.

"The local" for workers, managers, and visitors to Aberlour, The Mash Tun is one of Speyside's finest pubs.

One of Scotland's hidden distilleries, Glenallachie is a classic 1960s' site.

A flavor akin to malt (rather than cereal) in the new make is possibly the start of the whisky's signature mature note of toffee. While it might not be as beefy as some of the Ben's drams, neither is it as light as others. Instead, this supple character seems to bridge the stylistic gap between heavy and delicate. "What intrigues me," Winchester adds, "is how it is so close to Glenallachie in terms of location, yet the make is so different. We'll never know all the answers."

ABERLOUR TASTING NOTES

NEW MAKE
Nose: Sweet with currant leaf, some heavy florals, malt, and, with water, some burlap.
Palate: Clean, with citrus-fruit flesh, behind which you will find apple. Has presence.
Finish: Herbal.

10YO 40%
Nose: Copper. Intense malt note. Fruity, rounded, with oak overlay. With water, becomes scented.
Palate: A positive nutty start, pecan pie. Toffee-like richness, then scented leaf quality seen on new make.
Finish: Assam tea, mint.
Conclusion: The oak adds volume and heft.

> **Flavor Camp: Rich & Round**
> **Where Next?** Ardmore 1977, Macduff 1984

16YO 43%
Nose: Amber. The oak has taken it deep. Scent has gone, but growing toffee. Dried fruit, polish.
Palate: More wet earth. Dense and thick with fruit paste and chestnut. Sweet.
Finish: Roasted nut.
Conclusion: The cask has taken it into a thicker dimension.

> **Flavor Camp: Rich & Round**
> **Where Next?** Macallan Sherry Oak 10yo

1990 43%
Nose: Gold. Fresh with some lavender, and sage. Light citrus fruit. Creamy vanilla notes with water. Hint of smoke?
Palate: More dried fruits from sherry oak in the mouth. Lightly toffee-like. Water brings out the esteriness. Lightly curranty.
Finish: Clean and short. Some malt.
Conclusion: Balanced and medium-bodied.

> **Flavor Camp: Rich & Round**
> **Where Next?** Balvenie Madeira Cask

25YO 51.1%
Nose: Deep amber. Redwood. The fragrance of the 10yo has returned along with the chestnut of the 16yo (though now it is purée). Humidor. Amontillado sherry.
Palate: Lots of minty chocolate. Ripe mulberry and just a little leather. A light curranty note. Rich and sweet.
Finish: Long, slightly nutty, a touch of treacle.
Conclusion: The oak adds volume and heft.

> **Flavor Camp: Rich & Round**
> **Where Next?** Dalmore 1981, Tomintoul 33yo

A'BUNADH 60.5%
Nose: Deep amber in color, this is heavily sherried. Roasted almond with a little pimento and walnut oil. Resin and a light oil of cloves and allspice. Notes of fruitcake. Hot. With water there are hints of tamarind.
Palate: Rich and slightly hot. Black cherry then the lift of grasses takes over, followed by some vetiver and cigar.
Finish: Long and peppery.
Conclusion: Aberlour's cask strength—an uncut expression that's typically soft, but dangerous.

> **Flavor Camp: Rich & Round**
> **Where Next?** GlenDronach 12yo, Jura 16yo

GLENALLACHIE TASTING NOTES

NEW MAKE
Nose: Light and sweet. Mashed corn. This is aromatic and light.
Palate: Clean and precise. Soft and sweet.
Finish: Dry and clean.

18YO 57.1%
Nose: Amber. Clean and sherried, with notes of fireworks, plum jam, raisins, light chicory, marmalade. Rich and expressive with Brazil nuts.
Palate: Ripe and slightly dry, with plenty of mature, leathery notes. Nutty. Shows hints of its light, floral character with water.
Finish: Long, sweet, and balanced.
Conclusion: The cask in charge but lending a degree of sophistication.

> **Flavor Camp: Rich & Round**
> **Where Next?** Arran 1996, Glenrothes 1991

ABERLOUR®
ESTᴰ 1879

ABERLOUR
DISTILLERY
SCOTLAND

HIGHLAND
SPEYSIDE
AGED MALT

HIGHLAND SINGLE MALT
SCOTCH WHISKY

Matured in a combination of hand-selected Traditional and Sherry oak casks for a minimum of ten years, this expression represents the very essence of Aberlour character.

As a classic Speyside malt, this Ten Year Old Aberlour achieves a remarkable harmony marrying subtle aromas of spice with hints of autumn fruits, giving it a soft and long finish.

10 YEARS OLD

70 cl e 40% vol 40°GL   DISTILLED & BOTTLED IN SCOTLAND
ABERLOUR DISTILLERY COMPANY LTD
700 ml 40% alc./vol.   ABERLOUR SPEYSIDE AB38 9PJ

ABERLOUR®
ESTᴰ 1879

ABERLOUR
DISTILLERY
SCOTLAND

HIGHLAND
SPEYSIDE
AGED MALT

St. Drostan's Well

HIGHLAND SINGLE MALT
SCOTCH WHISKY

AGED **16** YEARS

70 cl e   43% vol.
DISTILLED & BOTTLED IN SCOTLAND
ABERLOUR DISTILLERY COMPANY LTD.
ABERLOUR SPEYSIDE AB38 9PJ

The Macallan

CRAIGELLACHIE • WWW.THEMACALLAN.COM • OPEN TO VISITORS • SEPT–EASTER, MON–FRI; EASTER–AUG, MON–SAT

Maybe it's the way in which its HQ, Easter Elchies house, looks down from its ridge over the Spey, but The Macallan Distillery has always had a slightly aloof air to it. Though its approach links directly with the older distilleries in this cluster—the earliest ones (The Macallan was founded in 1824) making the heaviest whiskies theory—the manner in which it has sold its whisky has always seen it exist slightly off-center from the rest of the industry. One suspects it doesn't mind that much.

This connection with the old ways is manifested most clearly in the stillhouse (or to be precise, one of the two stillhouses; a second one, silent since the 1970s, was resurrected in 2008), where tiny spirit stills hunker over their condensers like dwarves counting their treasure. Direct fire on the spirit side adds guts, while the small neck means there's little chance for reflux, necessitating a tight spirit cut. The Macallan sits there as new make: oily, malty, deep, but importantly, sweet. It's opinionated, making it clear from day one that this is not a spirit that will be pushed around by oak.

Oak at The Macallan means bespoke ex-sherry casks, whose construction, purchase, and management is overseen by master of wood George Espie. As has been traditional in Jerez for centuries, a mix of European oak (*Quercus robur*), with its aromas of clove and dried fruit and higher tannin, and American (*Quercus alba*), all vanilla and coconut, is used, giving whisky-maker Bob Dalgarno two very different streams of flavor to play with, and many variations within those.

"You need both wood types," says Dalgarno. "American oak gives sweetness and softness, but I need the richness of European, too." He looks along a line of samples of the same age, from the same cask type, each of different hue, with which he has to make a bottling of 12yo with the same character as the last. "We know we have variation," he says.

"We just have to know how to manage it. For us, the unexpected is expected." What was unexpected to many Macallan devotees was the launch of Fine Oak, a parallel range aged predominantly in American oak. Its arrival drove some apoplectic with rage. The fact was, Macallan had been filled into American oak for years, but its reputation had been built on being a 100 percent "sherried" (i.e. European oak) single malt.

Fine Oak does not diminish Macallan's character; instead, it takes it in a different direction, revealing more of the cereal and soft, fruity notes. In Sherry Oak the key is how the oiliness of the new make is used both as a facilitator of the flavors seeping from the oak and a barrier to aggressive tannins, preventing them from grabbing the palate like a ferret with a rabbit. The oil makes old Macallan smooth, not grippy.

The final controversy has been the whisky's recent repositioning of itself as a luxury brand. Ken Grier, director of malts at owner Edrington, is quick to dismiss accusations that luxury simply means conspicuous consumption of expensive goods. "What we're finding is that people are interested in the stories behind the brands. Luxury is about the stories, it's about bespoke; it's not bling. It also means you must invest, and I believe that we spend more on our whisky than anyone. There is a danger that it seems contrived, but it all comes back to the story and the provenance, and that means Bob Dalgarno and George Espie. We have no 'divine right' to a drinker. We're actually quite humble!"

Secreted away in The Macallan's many warehouses are ex-sherry casks, the contents of which whisky-maker Bob Dalgarno turns into one of this iconic distillery's many releases.

MACALLAN TASTING NOTES

NEW MAKE

Nose: Clean. Some green fruit. Quite fat/oily, malty. Light sulfur

Palate: Fat and oily and tongue-coating. Heavy. Green olive. Unyielding.

Finish: Rich and long.

10YO SHERRY OAK 40%

Nose: Amber. Immediate sherry-cask notes: white raisin and chestnut, fruitcake, all backed with that fatness of spirit. Ripe but still young.

Palate: Oily and clinging with date, sweet toffee. Gentle.

Finish: Light molasses, then malt.

Conclusion: The oils have immediately bound to the European oak.

Flavor Camp: Rich & Round

Where Next? Aberlour 16yo, Cragganmore 1997, Singleton of Glen Ord 12yo

10YO FINE OAK 43%

Nose: Gold. Light and clean. Fresh with sappy/ pine notes. Touch of apple and vanilla and sweet cereal.

Palate: Light but still has that oiliness. *Crème brûlée*/melted butter, dried banana.

Finish: Gentle but crisp.

Conclusion: More maltiness apparent here.

Flavor Camp: Fruity & Spicy

Where Next? Bruichladdich 2002, Scapa 16yo

15YO FINE OAK 43%

Nose: Gold. Orange peel and ripe melon, mango, vanilla bean. Hot sawdust, hazelnut, and wax polish.

Palate: Nutty oak, cooked orchard fruits, black banana. Caramel toffee, bracken, malt, and dark chocolate.

Finish: Complex and fruity.

Conclusion: The distillery character and "Fine Oak" casks in balance.

Flavor Camp: Fruity & Spicy

Where Next? Glenmorangie 18yo, Glencadam 15yo

18YO SHERRY OAK 43%

Nose: Dark amber. fruitcake, plum pudding, rich moist cake, walnut, and gingerbread, then a touch of molasses and dried berries.

Palate: Rich and mouth-filling. Chewy. Raisin and fig. Very ripe and oily/rich.

Finish: A singed note adding to the complexity.

Conclusion: Balance struck between the bold distillery character and rich oak.

Flavor Camp: Rich & Round

Where Next? Dalmore 1981, Glenfarclas 15yo

18YO FINE OAK 43%

Nose: Full gold. Hint of the cereal to the fore but now the richness of the mid-palate is developing. There's some burning wood.

Palate: Fat and buttery (rather than oily). Gentle and lifted with a little mashed banana and some sweet raisin.

Finish: Ripe soft fruit.

Conclusion: Still coming together. A slower-maturing style.

Flavor Camp: Fruity & Spicy

Where Next? Longmorn 16yo, Dalwhinnie 15yo

25YO SHERRY OAK 43%

Nose: Rich amber. Full-on Brandy de Jerez notes: dark, sweet fruit, toasted almond, dried herbs. Almost fruit-compote sweetness, the sweetness of the spirit now in its fullest expression, along with resin from the oak.

Palate: Very sweet. Into red-wine notes. Fine grip, mulberry, cassis, smoke, earthy, then a full hit of raisin.

Finish: Long and rich.

Conclusion: The sherry oak seems to link to the oil and play variations on that theme.

Flavor Camp: Rich & Round

Where Next? Glendronach 1989, Benromach 1981

25YO FINE OAK 43%

Nose: Rich gold. The cereal from the new make is still here. Ripe, sweet, with more candied fruit.

Palate: Clean and quite crisp. The malt is more obvious, along with a hint of spruce.

Finish: White raisins.

Conclusion: If Sherry Oak equals an uptake of oil, then Fine Oak is an improvisation on cereal and fruit.

Flavor Camp: Fruity & Spicy

Where Next? Tamdhu 32yo, Aberfeldy 21yo

Craigellachie

CRAIGELLACHIE • SPEYSIDE COOPERAGE • WWW.SPEYSIDECOOPERAGE.CO.UK • OPEN ALL YEAR • MON–FRI

There is an element of resolution in this struggle between the old and the new, the light and the heavy, when we reach the final member of this, the largest of the Speyside clusters. Craigellachie looks both ways. It is a railway distillery, a late Victorian arrival, but it is one that has also retained older, traditional whisky-making ways. One of a number of distilleries built in the 1890s by a consortium of blenders and brokers, it was located here purely because of Craigellachie's transport links. This was the major rail junction in the days of the whisky trains, and by 1863 it was the station that linked Dufftown, Keith, Elgin, and Rothes with the Strathspey Railway.

If it took whisky out, it also brought raw materials and visitors to the area: the imposing Craigellachie Hotel was built in 1893 as a railway hotel. One of the blenders who had a stake in Craigellachie from the outset was Sir Peter Mackie, owner of White Horse Scotch Whisky and Lagavulin, and it was he who bought Craigellachie outright in 1915. While the distillery has been extended and enlarged (the stillhouse has one of Scottish Malt Distillers' standard "car-dealer showroom" panoramic windows dating from the 1960s), it is the retention of older features that creates Craigellachie's singularity.

Nose the new make and there are the sulfury notes which have followed us across our Speyside journey—an aroma indicative of the use of worm tubs. Instead of the meatiness seen elsewhere, however, there's a waxiness (Snuffed candles? Sealing wax? Waxed fruit?) on the nose that then coats the tongue. Everything suggests that this is a weighty whisky, but one which is hiding another aspect of its personality. It's not so much shy as sly.

This is a sulfury new make with undertones of waxed fruit. "We use a sulfuring process in the malting stage," explains Keith Geddes, assistant master blender at present owner John Dewar & Sons. This

Located in the middle of the village, Craigellachie became another of Speyside's many distilleries to be found close to the railway.

SPEYSIDE COOPERAGE

Located on a hill above Craigellachie, next to a field of Highland cows, is a field filled with ziggurats of whisky casks. This is the Speyside Cooperage, which has been operating on this site since 1947. Now owned by French cooper Francois Frères, over 100,000 casks are either repaired, recharred, or coopered from scratch here. There's also a visitors' center that allows people a rare insight into what remains a little-known yet vital craft.

is then enhanced in Craigellachie's large stills (allowing reflux) with a long spirit run ("just a trickle") that directs the vapor into those worm tubs (*see* pp.14–15). "Copper removes sulfur," says Geddes, "and Craigellachie's worm tubs have less available copper. The sulfury new-make character is always there and is a Craigellachie signature. We couldn't replicate this on any of our other sites because they're all shell-and-tube sites. We could get sulfur if we wanted from them but it wouldn't be the same."

As ever with sulfury sites, the question is what lies beneath. "We could push it further if we wanted," says Geddes, "and take it into meaty territory, but we are looking for balance." That gravy-like depth in Dailuaine and Benrinnes isn't here. As it matures, Craigellachie moves into a world of exotic fruit, with the waxy feel on the tongue adding an extra textural element which seems to enhance the very light smoke in older bottlings.

It's not a common style. Clynelish (p.138) is the other classic example of a waxy whisky, while Deanston (p.110) and older Aberfeldy (p.115) also have it in evidence. Blenders love it—it's a heavier Clynelish in some ways. "Craigellachie adds weight to a blend," says Geddes. "Because it helps to promote the fruity and the floral, it's a great platform on which to build."

Wooden washbacks are just one of many traditional touches that help to maintain Craigellachie's singular character.

Craigellachie is the perfect point at which to leave the Ben Rinnes cluster, a group of distilleries in which the entire history of Scotch can be seen. It would be easy to think that the spirit's journey has been one in which it has moved inexorably towards the big and the modern and the light, but this cluster shows that, throughout Scotland, the past is alive, the old ways have been retained, and the link with the land—whether physical or emotional—has resulted in a collection of whiskies for which the uniqueness of site is the major factor in the creation of character.

CRAIGELLACHIE TASTING NOTES

NEW MAKE

Nose: Waxy. Vegetable. Radish. Boiled potato/starch. Light smoke.
Palate: Nutty and sweet with heavy beeswax and some sulfur notes. Heavy and full.
Finish: Deep and long. The vegetable returns.

14YO 40%

Nose: Pale gold. Waxed fruit. Quince. Fleshy, then apricot alongside light smoke and sealing wax and red currant. With water there's wet reed, squash ball, and olive oil.
Palate: Light coconut before the feel takes over. Unctuous and glycerine-like. Jellied fresh fruits. Sweet yet solid.
Finish: Quince and then flour.
Conclusion: A blender's dream. A textural single malt.

Flavor Camp: **Fruity & Spicy**
Where Next? Clynelish 14yo, Scapa 16yo

1994, GORDON & MACPHAIL BOTTLING 46%

Nose: Gold in color. Typically oily/waxy nose. Old saddle soap and soft tropical hints with an added jag of citrus fruit.
Palate: Like eating waxed fruit. Rounded and palate-clinging. A little more estery with water, and a gentle honeyed/syrupy quality towards the finish.
Finish: Lightly spiced, with touches of sweet, dried tropical fruit.
Conclusion: Balanced and expanding. Expressive.

Flavor Camp: **Fruity & Spicy**
Where Next? Old Pulteney 17yo

THE DUFFTOWN CLUSTER

The self-proclaimed whisky capital of Speyside with its six distilleries on its fringes, Dufftown is little older than its first distillery, having been constructed in 1817 when James Duff built it as an improved town. Home to the world's biggest-selling single malt brand and conceivably the world's biggest single malt (in terms of weight), this is a fine place to test the notion of *terroir*.

Steam rises into chill winter air over the pagodas of Balvenie.

Glenfiddich

DUFFTOWN • WWW.GLENFIDDICH.COM • OPEN ALL YEAR • MON–SUN

As the world's best-selling single malt and the first distillery to open its doors (in 1969), it would be easy for first-time visitors to Glenfiddich to expect a somewhat clichéd recreation of whisky-making, but instead they get the opposite. This is a huge (35 acres) working site with its own cooperage, coppersmith, bottling line (all Glenfiddich is bottled on site), warehousing ... and three distilleries. Glenfiddich is both a modern single-malt brand, but also a distillery where, despite the scale, a traditional ethos of self-sufficiency has been retained.

Built by William Grant in 1886 and still owned by his descendants, the first spirit ran from its small stills (themselves bought from Cardhu) on Christmas Day the following year. You can't help but feel that, even in those early days, the founder had an eye on marketing.

Glenfiddich is about lightness of character, but walking into the stillhouse you'd think it would produce a similar style to Macallan. The stills are tiny, and science tells us small stills tend to produce a heavy, often sulfury new make (*see* pp.14–15). Nose Glenfiddich, however, and it's all grass, green apple, and pear. "We cut at high strength, which is how we get this estery, clean spirit," says William Grant's master blender, Brian Kinsman. "If we ran any deeper and cut later, it would be much heavier and potentially sulfury."

So is this a case of a distillery running against type? "Not as far as we can tell," says Kinsman. "Glenfiddich, from our records, has always been light. The stills have always been that shape, and as demand grew we just built more of them." If they'd stuck at four stills and tried to cope with increased sales, they'd have had to widen the cut in order to get more liquid—and changed the style. Building new stills was the only option in order to retain character. The fact that there are 28 stills in two stillhouses shows how big that demand is.

This lack of sulfur is also advantageous, Kinsman says, "because you don't have to overcome something before you start getting additive maturation." Even at three years of age, Glenfiddich is picking up wood notes: oak shavings in refill; ripe pineapple and creamy vanilla in first-fill bourbon; marmalade and white raisins in first-fill European ... all cut with that green freshness.

A significant improvement in wood management and a rejigging of the wood mix has resulted in a much more coherent range. Whereas in the past Glenfiddich had a somewhat frustrating randomness about it, now there's a thread given by European oak which is increased slowly with each age expression (bar the 21yo rum finish). As age takes hold, so the green apples of youth ripen, the cut grass dries, and a chocolate note slowly develops. For a light whisky, it manages to hold its own—even at 40 and 50 years. "The new make is light on the nose but it matures incredibly well," says Kinsman. "I think that freshness and intensity belie how much complexity is in there." For me, it seems to ride on a wave of oak, buoyed up by it but always remaining identifiably Glenfiddich.

The integration of oak and spirit is best personified by the pioneering establishing in 1998 of a *solera* vat for the 15yo. This Jerezano technique of fractional blending involves removing only

A large and complex distillery, Glenfiddich distills, matures, and bottles on site ...

... **and is one** of the last distilleries to have its own cooperage.

50% of the vat's contents for each bottling. This is then replaced with a mix composed of 70% from refill bourbon, 20% from European oak, and 10% in virgin oak. *Solera* blending not only adds depth (some whiskies have been there since 1998), but it also imparts a different, softer mouthfeel. A similar technique is employed with the 40yo, whose never-emptied vat contains remnants from the 1920s.

It is this general amenability that holds the key to Glenfiddich's long-term aging ability—and, one might guess, is the secret of its commercial success as well.

GLENFIDDICH TASTING NOTES

NEW MAKE

Nose: Crisp, clean, grassy, green apple, and in time ripe pineapple. Very pure and fresh.
Palate: All pears, grass, and esters. Light cereal in background.
Finish: Light and fresh.

12YO 40%

Nose: The aroma is led by vanilla, then red apple, and a little white raisin in the background adding sweetness. With water, some milk chocolate.
Palate: Sweet with plenty of vanilla, then a little fruitcake batter and mixed fruit. Gentle and smooth.
Finish: Buttery, but grassy.
Conclusion: The green notes of new make have now deepened and ripened. Some European oak has added depth.

Flavor Camp: **Fragrant & Floral**
Where Next? Glenlivet 12yo, anCnoc 16yo

15YO 40%

Nose: Ripe and very soft, with a character akin to plum jam and baked apple.
Palate: Soft and silky. Thicker than 12yo with stewed black fruit, coconut notes, and dried grass.
Finish: Ripe and full.
Conclusion: *Solera* adds a richer depth and feel.

Flavor Camp: **Rich & Round**
Where Next? Glencadam 1978, Blair Atholl 12yo

18YO 40%

Nose: More overt sherried notes: raisin and sherry-soaked dried fruit, mulberry, dark chocolate, and hay.
Palate: Concentrated dark fruits, more grip than the 15yo. Cacao, cedar.
Finish: Smooth, long, and still sweet.
Conclusion: The midpoint of the range as the freshness of youth gives way to the dark mysteries of age.

Flavor Camp: **Rich & Round**
Where Next? Jura 16yo, Royal Lochnagar Select Reserve

21YO 40%

Nose: Deep amber. Sweet and oaky, with coffee/cacao and a touch of cedar. Barley sugar and caramel toffee. Some black banana.
Palate: Rich and sweet with good length. Mocha, bitter chocolate, and forest floor. Light tannins.
Finish: Dry oak. Leafy.
Conclusion: Has maturity. This has been given a finishing period in rum cask.

Flavor Camp: **Fruity & Spicy**
Where Next? Balblair 1990, Longmorn 16yo

30YO 40%

Nose: Resinous and thick. Ripe, rich, *rancioed*. Cigar humidor, nuttiness, and a surprisingly energetic lift.
Palate: Very smooth and silky. Flows over the tongue with a slight mossiness. Chocolate and coffee grounds now in charge.
Finish: Fading, but has residual sweetness.
Conclusion: The fruits have now been fully concentrated but that dry grassiness is retained, giving a vestigial freshness.

Flavor Camp: **Rich & Round**
Where Next? Macallan 25yo, Sherry Oak Glen Grant 25yo

40YO 43.5%

Nose: Oily and resinous. Herbs, damp moss. Deep, rich. Whisky *rancio* but grassiness comes back, even at this advanced age. Beeswax. Slightly herbal.
Palate: Big and rounded with elegant chocolate notes: plum, espresso, mulberry. Oak is balanced because of the richness of the spirit. Relaxes to allow spices to come through. Lightly, nutty.
Finish: Herbal and long.
Conclusion: A *solera*-style system used here with some of the original batch, containing whiskies from the 1920s–40s, kept in the vat.

Flavor Camp: **Rich & Round**
Where Next? Dalmore Candela

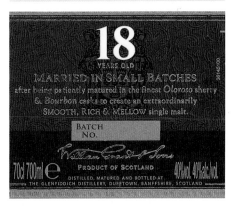

The Balvenie & Kininvie

BALVENIE • DUFFTOWN • WWW.THEBALVENIE.COM • OPEN ALL YEAR • MON–FRI, BOOKING ESSENTIAL / KININVIE • KEITH

The second of the trio of distilleries on William Grant's Dufftown site, Balvenie is no longer the little sister, the overlooked companion, the guarded cult, but a front-line single-malt brand in its own right. It also offers a good test for the notion of a Dufftown *terroir*, or the idea that geography is reflected in spirit or wine. Three distilleries using the same water, identical malt, and virtually the same mashing, fermentation, and distillation regime yet producing three identifiably different malts. "The basic process is the same," says William Grant's master blender Brian Kinsman. "The only difference is the stills."

So where does that leave the importance of location as a contributor to flavor? "It will have some influence," he replies. "The ambient conditions within a plant will have an impact, somehow, on the character. You can tell this because even if you replicate a distillery in a different location, as we have done with Ailsa Bay (*see* p.148), you will not automatically get the same result. You need to change some elements in order to get the closest replication." And, as has been shown many times, that replication, while close, will never be identical. What we are talking about here, therefore, is not a regional (or even subregional) *terroir*, but a site-specific *terroir*. Balvenie, rather than the Dufftown site—or by extension Dufftown. Or Speyside.

Built in 1892, Balvenie has retained its own malting floor, although it produces only a tiny percentage of the distillery's needs. Anyone at Balvenie will tell you that the key to its character is its fat, short-necked stills. These yield a new make that is nutty and malty, but one that also has the sensation of a massing of fruit underneath, a glimpse of potential.

Even at seven years in refill cask, that nutty shell has cracked open, allowing the sweet honeyed fruits to emerge. All through its aging process, this cereal note continues to shift down a gear, giving just a whisper of a dry structure as those fruits grow and expand.

If Glenfiddich is supported by wood, Balvenie seems to absorb oak into itself, integrating the flavors from the oak and adding them to its honey-colored tapestry of taste. Balvenie is never overwhelmed by wood; it's too big and fruity a dram for that.

It is this quality that prompted David Stewart, Grant's former master blender, to choose it as arguably the first "finished" whisky. Since then, the Balvenie range has expanded to include expressions finished in Madeira, rum, and port casks, and there is also a single-barrel range. In many ways, it is the opposite to the slow build of Glenfiddich. Here the whisky simply takes on board the new flavors from different oaks and turns them to its advantage, creating a wider range of flavors but an equally strong identity.

Balvenie was built because demand was outstripping supply for Glenfiddich. It also enabled the Grant family to guarantee the water rights to the site and allowed another variant for the firm's blends. In 1990, the company was faced with the same dilemma, so they repeated the exercise and built Kininvie as a provider of fillings for blends. Its stillhouse lies between Glenfiddich and Balvenie, and stylistically (neatly enough), its quick-maturing style sits pretty much between its siblings.

Balvenie still malts a small percentage of its own barley and dries it in its own kiln.

BALVENIE TASTING NOTES

NEW MAKE

Nose: Heavy. Nutty cereal, but great solid concentration of fruit behind. Very clean and sweet.
Palate: Cereal, robust, ripe. Nutty/muesli. Sweet.
Finish: Nutty and clean.

12YO SIGNATURE 40%

Nose: Fresh-cut oak, clover honey, tarragon, and light nuttiness.
Palate: The fruit is all ripe apricots in syrup. Smooth, with a little flour, custard, and buttercups.
Finish: Sweet and honeyed. Touch of nut.
Conclusion: Here you can see that flipping of nuttiness and fruit.

> **Flavor Camp: Fruity & Spicy**
> **Where Next?** Dalwhinnie 15yo, Ben Nevis 10yo

12YO DOUBLE WOOD 40%

Nose: Sweet but in a mixed-peel way. Beeswax and pollen alongside light Scottish fruitcake. Touch of struck match.
Palate: Fatter than Signature with softer fruit. Chewy and juicy. Light grip from a combination of sherry cask and nuttiness. Cut peels and honey.
Finish: Long and with a little dried fruit.
Conclusion: A balance struck between evolving character and cask.

> **Flavor Camp: Fruity & Spicy**
> **Where Next?** BenRiach 16yo, Longmorn 16yo

17YO MADEIRA CASK 43%

Nose: Deep, rich. Plump, cooked wild fruit (blackberries, elderberries) cut with an earthy, slightly burnt note.
Palate: Sweet with a dusty quality akin to geranium leaf. Ripe and long. Black fruit.
Finish: The singed Madeira quality comes through.
Conclusion: The 17yo is made up of small releases in different casks.

> **Flavor Camp: Rich & Round**
> **Where Next?** Jura 16yo, Singleton of Glendullan, Bushmills 16yo

21YO PORTWOOD 40%

Nose: Full concentration. Cherry, rosehip syrup, planed oak with wood smoke behind.
Palate: Unctuous but honeyed. The fruit seems fresher than the 17yo Madeira: more mixed red and black fruit, with integrated oak. Powerful but sweet.
Finish: Long and sweet.
Conclusion: Though this is growing in weight, there's a clear line to the 12yo.

> **Flavor Camp: Fruity & Spicy**
> **Where Next?** Strathisla 18yo

30YO 47.3%

Nose: Masses of coconut and cooked orange peel. Luscious and soft.
Palate: Gentle, oozing, long, and ripe and ... yes ... honeyed. Ripe, sweet orchard fruit, light oak, and a hint of sweet spice.
Finish: Sweet and full.
Conclusion: Has the languorous length of a slow-matured whisky.

> **Flavor Camp: Fruity & Spicy**
> **Where Next?** Tamdhu 32yo

KININVIE TASTING NOTES

NEW MAKE

Nose: Light and predominantly flowery and perfumed. Estery and clean.
Palate: Hay. Floral, leafy, and crisp. The lightest but also driest of the Dufftown trio.
Finish: Clean and short.

6YO CASK SAMPLE

Nose: Hugely floral. A fresh bouquet with vanilla bean.
Palate: Light, fragrant (hyacinth), lifted, sweet, and effusive.
Finish: Short and sweet.
Conclusion: A quick-maturing style.

> **Flavor Camp: Fragrant & Floral**

Mortlach, Glendullan, & Dufftown

MORTLACH • DUFFTOWN
GLENDULLAN • DUFFTOWN • WWW.MALTS.COM/INDEX.PHP/EN_GB/OUR-WHISKIES/THE-SINGLETON-OF-GLENDULLAN
DUFFTOWN • WWW.MALTS.COM/INDEX.PHP/EN_GB/OUR-WHISKIES/THE-SINGLETON-OF-DUFFTOWN

There's a hidden side to Dufftown's half-dozen malts, one that taps into that older, more mysterious Speyside. It's fittingly found in Mortlach, the name of both the original settlement and the town's oldest distillery, which was built in 1823 by James Findlater, Donald Mackintosh, and Alex Gordon, probably on the site of an older illicit operation.

If you can split Speyside into three—malty, fragrant, and heavy—then here's a member of the last group, perhaps the heaviest of them all. Mortlach's robust, meaty whisky is another which talks of older times, of woods and hollowways, of times when the soul needed serious, belly-filling fortification.

Where does the meaty style come from? "We don't know when it originated," says Diageo's master distiller and blender, Douglas Murray. "We inherited it." Perhaps it came from the illicit days, certainly in its use of worm tubs and a complex distillation regime, which on first glance seems somewhat improvised.

In a similar way to Benrinnes, Mortlach uses partial triple distillation in order to build up the meaty element. Mortlach, Murray says blithely, "is distilled 2.7 times." Everything revolves around what happens in the stillhouse, where a seemingly random collection of stills has been assembled. There are half a dozen of these weird beasts: one triangular, some thin-necked, and a tiny afterthought in the corner which is known as "the Wee Witchie."

The easiest way to try and understand the distillation regime here is to think of Mortlach as having two stillhouses. Two stills work as normal. Then wash stills Numbers 1 and 2 work in tandem. The first 80% of the run is collected as the charge for the Number 2 spirit still. The remaining (weak) 20% is destined for the Wee Witchie. This is charged, run, and all the spirit is collected. The process is repeated twice, with the middle cut only being collected on the third run. It's from the Wee Witchie that Mortlach's meatiness comes, but to get

meaty you also need sulfury, which means no copper. Mortlach, therefore, runs flat out, with condensing done via cold worm tubs.

At its best in European oak (it has the muscle to cope), Mortlach has become a cult single malt, but it is unlikely ever to be a front-line player because its individuality is too highly prized by blenders. This throwback to the old days, to days before Dufftown even existed, lies at the foundation of many famous blends. It is the dark reduction of whisky to some primal essence.

Mortlach, on its steep-sided hill, overlooks Dullan Water and the two distilleries sheltering there. Glendullan itself started in 1897, although the current box plant was built in 1962. This was the site of a raid by troops billeted there in World War II, who, overcome with fumes (or desire), rammed the warehouses with a gun carriage. The "dull" in the name somewhat detracts from the whisky itself, whose aromatic, grapey lift in youth develops into a sloe-berry sweetness by the time it is a 12yo and a member of Diageo's Singleton range.

The glen is also home to Dufftown distillery, one of many former mills that have been converted into distilleries. Built the year before Glendullan, it is another whose destiny has always been inextricably linked with blends. If Mortlach is a representative of an ultra-traditional style, then Dufftown is a shape-shifter. A nutty/malty site in its days as a member of the Bell's estate, these days the new make is in the grassy camp. It, too, is a Singleton brand.

One town, six distilleries and every Flavor Camp (except smoky) covered. Maybe that "Capital-of-Whisky" moniker is justified after all.

In the glen outside Dufftown sit three distilleries, each making its own very distinct whisky.

MORTLACH TASTING NOTES

SPEYSIDE
SINGLE MALT
SCOTCH WHISKY

MORTLACH

was the first of seven *distilleries* in *Dufftown*. In the C10th *farm animals* kept in adjoining byres were fed on *barley* left over from processing. Today *water* from springs in the *CONVAL HILLS* is used to produce this delightful *smooth, fruity single MALT SCOTCH WHISKY*.

AGED **16** YEARS

NEW MAKE

Nose: Dry, sulfury smoke. Powerful, meaty, and heavy. Beef-stock-like density.
Palate: Feral. Old woods, meat stock, fireworks. Muscular.
Finish: Thick and hot.

8YO REFILL WOOD, CASK SAMPLE

Nose: A strange mix: roast beef, citrus peel, eucalyptus; shows there's more than meat stock to Mortlach.
Palate: Peppered steak, meat pie. A little dumb now.
Finish: Tight and compacted.
Conclusion: Still opening.

Flavor Camp: **Rich & Round**

16YO, FLORA & FAUNA 43%

Nose: Massive. Gravy, roasting pan, roast mutton, Fig Newtons, bitter chocolate, even some mint. Biltong/pemmican.
Palate: Firm, grippy, deep. Solidly built, with European oak tannins, chestnut/walnut. The wood adds grip, the spirit gives depth. Solid, but with a savory sweetness underneath.
Finish: Dry. Licorice, meat extracts.
Conclusion: An enormous malt.

Flavor Camp: **Rich & Round**

Where Next? Macallan 18yo, GlenDronach 15yo, Benrinnes 15yo

GLENDULLAN TASTING NOTES

NEW MAKE

Nose: Perfumed, light, and floral (freesia); grape-like blossom. Becomes green-grassy.
Palate: Quite dry then delicate patisserie fruits. Very soft and gentle.
Finish: Light, clean, and quick.

8YO REFILL WOOD, CASK SAMPLE

Nose: Aromatic and lifted. Dessert apple. Sharp and slightly perfumed. Light lemon. Floral/aniseed. Bouquet-like.
Palate: All fresh and delicate. The freesia still there, along with lemon and light acidity.
Finish: Clean and sharp.
Conclusion: Freshness. Impression is that it will be best in a refill cask since it's easily dominated by active oak.

Flavor Camp: **Fragrant & Floral**

12YO, FLORA & FAUNA 43%

Nose: Light and gentle, with some wood influence and a touch of sawdust. Apple continues to show, now with added custard from the wood.
Palate: Delicate, almost transparent to start, then a twang of acidity halfway in bursts it open. Fragrant.
Finish: Lemon.
Conclusion: A slow development from the 8yo with just a little uptake of oak.

Flavor Camp: **Fragrant & Floral**

Where Next? Linkwood

THE SINGLETON OF GLENDULLAN 12YO 40%

Nose: Full gold. Sherried with Moscatel-like sweetness and dusky sloe. Still aromatic, but now the dried fruits are taking charge. Firm wood.
Palate: Light fruit. Black grapes and fruit sugars; then comes a mellow European oak richness. The aromatic intensity is still there, although the acidity has gone.
Finish: Gentle. Sweet, almost jammy.
Conclusion: Still (just) Glendullan but cask now in charge.

Flavor Camp: **Fruity & Spicy**

Where Next? Glenfiddich 15yo, Glenmorangie Lasanta, Fettercairn 16yo

DUFFTOWN TASTING NOTES

NEW MAKE

Nose: Slightly bready, pineapple, estery, touch of wheat chaff.
Palate: Clean, estery fruitiness. High-toned and sharp with some cereal behind.
Finish: Nutty and clean.

8YO REFILL WOOD, CASK SAMPLE

Nose: Very clean. Malty, wheat breakfast cereal, touch of farmyard, malt bin.
Palate: Dry and quite crisp. Nutty, then a sweet hit that sinks very slightly onto the tongue.
Finish: Sesame.
Conclusion: Clean and nutty—a good example of old-style Dufftown.

Flavor Camp: **Malty & Dry**

THE SINGLETON OF DUFFTOWN 12YO 40%

Nose: Sweet and figgy, with a nutshell undertow. Opens into sawn oak, draff, then marshmallow and a touch of apple and fig relish.
Palate: Nut oils. Quite biscuity and rich. Leafy.
Finish: Crisp, short.
Conclusion: European oak taking the (old) dry Dufftown character into a sweeter realm.

Flavor Camp: **Rich & Round**

Where Next? Jura 16yo

1997, MANAGER'S CHOICE
SINGLE CASK, 60.1%

Nose: Light gold. Malt bins, peanut, then a lift of pink grapefruit before nuts and wood come through.
Palate: Lots of cereal, along with that tongue-clinging quality. Almond flakes, chestnut flour. Light and quite simple.
Finish: Dry and nutty.
Conclusion: Like eating a bag of nuts in a carpenter's workshop.

Flavor Camp: **Malty & Dry**

Where Next? Auchentoshan Classic

KEITH TO THE EASTERN BOUNDARY

The importance of the blenders is seen clearly in the distilleries that surround the small town of Keith.
Here are distilleries whose life has been spent in their service.

The Auld Brig at Keith has carried whisky over the River Isla for centuries.

Strathisla

KEITH • WWW.MALTWHISKYDISTILLERIES.COM • OPEN TO VISITORS • APR–OCT, MON–SUN; NOV–DEC, SHOP ONLY, MON–FRI

Although it is unofficially recognized as the prettiest distillery in Scotland, Strathisla's whisky is surprisingly less well-known. In fact, none of the Keith cluster is a front-line single-malt brand. In this part of Speyside, whisky-makers keep their heads down and produce their spirit for blends—no matter how attractive their distilleries may be.

At Strathisla, the blend connection runs deep. This is a malt whisky distillery that is a tourist attraction—people are rightly drawn to its cobbled courtyard, manicured lawns, and waterwheel—but it also subsumes its own individual personality to act as the spiritual home of a blend: in Strathisla's case, Chivas Regal. While this is perfectly common practice, it obscures Strathisla's main claim to fame: as the oldest licensed malt distillery in Scotland.

Some form of alcohol has been made on this site for 700 years. A monastic brewery stood on the site in the thirteenth century, while the Milton distillery (as Strathisla was known until 1953) took out a license in 1786, right at the start of the whisky-smuggling era.

Its spirit, however, doesn't conform to the old/heavy template, although the merest touch of sulfur in the new make suggests that there's some desire on the part of the plant to cleave to these older ways. The key lies in the stillhouse, where the necks of the small stills rise into the rafters. "What's strange about Strathisla is that it's trying to make the light Speyside style, but these small stills can end up giving that wee touch of sulfur and an aroma like pot ale," says Chivas Brothers' distilleries manager, Alan Winchester. "But there's a fruitiness that's sitting behind that."

It takes time for that to come to the fore. Strathisla seems to be made up of three distinct pieces: a mossy-woods note, the soft fruit, and floral

A candidate for Scotland's prettiest distillery, Strathisla has been making whisky since 1786.

top notes. As it matures, so these rise and fall: mossiness when young, fruits and orange when aged. That's great blending material.

STRATHISLA TASTING NOTES

NEW MAKE

Nose: Clean, with sweet mash, damp hay, and moss. Lightly floral, then a little burnt/sulfury note.
Palate: Very pure. Sweet, fine-bodied, with very gentle fruit in the middle.
Finish: Cereal at the end.

12YO 40%

Nose: Copper, sweet oak, plenty of light coconut; green moss, citrus pulp, quince. Singed note at back.
Palate: Sweet vanilla, white chocolate. Very clean, with a cashew-like flavor dry grass and light fruit.
Finish: Toasted. Lightly perfumed.
Conclusion: Strathisla starts its life light and almost fragile—but watch what happens.

Flavor Camp: Fragrant & Floral
Where Next? Cardhu 12yo

18YO 40%

Nose: Copper. Wood-driven, with a toasted nuttiness. The moss has changed to green fern. Now comes more soft white fruit, a hint of honey, deeper florals, and dried apples.
Palate: Rounder than the 12yo with a more solid middle palate. Green plum, then crisp wood.
Finish: Bone-dry and spicy.
Conclusion: In its teens, the fruit begins to build in strength.

Flavor Camp: Fruity & Spicy
Where Next? Glengoyne 10yo, Benromach 25yo

25YO 53.3%

Nose: Bigger (sherry) cask influence. Some *rancio*, dried mushroom, vetiver tones. Deep and sweet, with fruitcake batter.
Palate: Full, soft, and light with some orange peel. Then its full ripeness shows, once again in the middle of the tongue, where it deepens finally into orange-blossom honey. Succulent.
Finish: Long, soft, and clean.
Conclusion: It has finally emerged from the woods.

Flavor Camp: Rich & Round
Where Next? Springbank 18yo

Strathmill

STRATHMILL • KEITH

Keith itself has a long history of mills, most powered by the Isla River, which snakes its way through the town. These grew in importance during the eighteenth century, when the Earl of Findlater built "New Keith." The water was used to run woolen mills, while locally grown cereal crops were also ground here. In 1892, one of these cereal mills was converted into a distillery: Glenisla-Glenlivet. There was considerably more money to be made in whisky than in bread.

Glenisla was soon sold to the gin producer W&A Gilbey, who changed its name to Strathmill, and in time the make became an integral part of J&B. It's worth noting that all of the distilleries within this little cluster provide spirit for lighter-bodied blends.

Strathmill has an intriguing olive-oil note that adds a slick texture to its inherently light character. The oiliness, as in Glenlossie, is the result of a purifier pipe on the lyne arm of the spirit still which increases reflux—a lightening technique which was installed in 1968.

This search for the delicate by using different distillation techniques was also found at the Glen Keith distillery, which was built in 1958 by Seagram. "Glen Keith started as a copy of Bushmills," says Alan Winchester, Chivas Brothers' distilleries manager. "They also had columns there as well as a still that was just known as 'the Irish still.' There was heavy-peated wash, from heavy-peated barley, known in-house as Glen Isla, run through as well." This continued experimentation never paid off and Glen Keith has now been mothballed.

Originally a woolen mill, Strathmill is an important player in J&B.

STRATHMILL TASTING NOTES

NEW MAKE

Nose: Olive oil, corn with butter. Has a discreet substance. Fresh yeast and a hint of red fruit.
Palate: Needle-sharp, quite hot. Evaporates on the tongue. With water, shows its weight and the raspberry leaf emerges.
Finish: Zingy and hot.

8YO REFILL WOOD, CASK SAMPLE

Nose: Rounded and buttery, moving into honey plus a hint of old-fashioned talcum powder and delicate rose. Still hard.
Palate: Grassy and quite clean, with a little violet and that red-fruit acidity seen in new make.
Finish: Clean and still tense.
Conclusion: Light, but that buttery quality gives the weight to cope with aging.

Flavor Camp: Fragrant & Floral

12YO FLORA & FAUNA 43%

Nose: Dry and reminiscent of oatmeal with light-brown sugar. Toasted corn and a hint of honey.
Palate: The honeyed quality comes through strongly. The red fruits have gone and given way to an intense, coriander-seed spiciness.
Finish: Clean and lifted.
Conclusion: Another which develops interestingly—and relatively quickly.

Flavor Camp: Fragrant & Floral
Where Next? Glenturret 10yo, Yamazaki 10yo

Aultmore & Glentauchers

AULTMORE • KEITH / GLENTAUCHERS • KEITH

The Keith cluster's willingness to play a supporting role is repeated at Aultmore. Built in 1896 to take advantage of the blend boom, it has been part of the John Dewar & Sons stable since 1923. Dewar's was one of the first great Scotch blends and has for many years enjoyed most success in the USA, a market that went light in a fairly significant fashion from Prohibition onwards. Little surprise, then, that the Dewar's stable consists of distilleries offering variations of the fragrant and more delicate kind.

One nose of the Aultmore new make and you can see why this fits in with the Dewar's house style. Intense, sweet, and filled with green-grassiness, this would give a lift to any blend. "To get this character we need really clear wort from the lauter tun," says Keith Geddes, assistant master blender at Dewar's. "The stills are small, with downward-angled lyne arms; once it's over the neck, it's over. That gives us a more characterful spirit that's not as estery as Royal Brackla or Aberfeldy, but which can stand up well in a blend and give balance." It's a key point. Light doesn't mean one-dimensional, nor do all "light" whiskies taste the same. Their subtle whisperings are every bit as complex as the big hitters.

Heading west towards Rothes from Keith, you pass by yet another one of those "What's its name again?" distilleries. Unseen as a major malt brand, Glentauchers' six stills have been producing whisky since 1898, originally for James Buchanan's Black & White blend. For a short period at the start of the twentieth century it distilled malt whisky through a column still, a technique the Scotch Whisky Association recently deemed "non-traditional."

Mothballed in 1985, it became part of Allied Distillers, now Chivas Brothers, which, since its purchase in 1989, has removed any peatiness in the barley used and balanced the distillation of its

Keeping an eye on the spirit. Collecting the right flavors in the middle cut is the most important part of a stillman's job.

six stills. "We wanted to bring this into the fruity/floral camp," explains distilleries manager Alan Winchester. His enthusiasm for the spirit is shared by blenders such as Chivas Brothers' Sandy Hyslop, who uses its grassy/floral character in blends such as Ballantine's.

AULTMORE TASTING NOTES

NEW MAKE

Nose: Sweet. Scallion. Grassy.
Palate: Sweet but firm. Full weight. A bit burnt, rounded.
Finish: Strawberry and melon, which again may develop into something interesting.

12YO 40%

Nose: Sweeter than the new make with saltines and lime blossom. Lemon zest. Nuttier with time. A wheat note with water.
Palate: Creamy with dry malt being pushed back. Vanilla. Smooth and lightly scented. Seeds.
Finish: Clean, if short.
Conclusion: While distillery character retains its fresh demeanor, you can play many tunes on Aultmore.

Flavor Camp: Fragrant & Floral
Where Next? Strathisla 12yo, Glenlossie 12yo

16YO DEWAR RATTRAY 57.9%

Nose: Rich and heavily sherried. Fig Newtons, fruitcake, bitter orange, and a light, almost tarry note. Sweeter with water: sweet coffee, some perfume on top.
Palate: Ripe with tomato leaf, black cherry, walnut, and (seemingly) smoke. Good grip balances a silky feel.
Finish: Long and generous.
Conclusion: Heavily influenced by cask, but that floral quality is just discernible on the nose.

Flavor Camp: Rich & Round
Where Next? Royal Lochnagar Select Reserve, Aberlour 16yo

GLENTAUCHERS TASTING NOTES

NEW MAKE

Nose: Grassy, light. An unusual note of chocolate graham crackers, then tea leaf and florals.
Palate: Light and pure. Slightly fizzy, light, and ethereal.
Finish: Clean.

1991 GORDON & MACPHAIL BOTTLING

Nose: Pale gold. Typical of the light and floral distillery character. High-toned, with hyacinth and a little rose. Clean sweet oak. Still delicate.
Palate: Fresh and whisper-light. Little hint of ripe red apple then some lemon verbena.
Finish: Short and light.
Conclusion: A little more substance than the oak, but gently handled so as not to drown this fragile whisky.

Flavor Camp: Fragrant & Floral
Where Next? Bladnoch 8yo, anCnoc 16yo

Auchroisk & Inchgower

AUCHROISK • KEITH / INCHGOWER • BUCKIE

Just as mature spirits can be placed on a flavor wheel or map, so new-make character has an industry-shared list of descriptors. If two distillers were talking about a similar character but one called it "cereal" while the other said "hamster cages," then there could be confusion. If they both agree to call it "nutty/spicy," then things become considerably easier.

That's not to say that all nutty/spicy sites make identical whisky. The final two members of the Keith cluster belong to this new-make family, but are in fact at either ends of the spectrum.

"Nutty/spicy is in fact two camps," says Douglas Murray, Diageo's master distiller and blender, aka The Guru. "If you mash quickly and pull solids through, that's nutty/cereal. If you mash at a higher temperature on the second water, you can take out the cereal note and end up with spicy. In the fermenter, that cloudy wort will give nutty/spicy if you ferment for 45–50 hours. Ferment for longer and the character changes. The danger is that if you

speed up production, cut ferment times, and get cloudy wort, then you lose your character and make nutty/spicy" (*see* pp.14–15).

Auchroisk is a modern, angular, white-rendered distillery on the Keith to Rothes road. Here the new-make style has a heavy, almost burnt nuttiness created by overboiling the wash still and allowing some solids to come over. Once in wood, this singed note dies off and is replaced by sweetness.

Inchgower, on the other hand, is intensely spicy, which may account for the fact that this coastal distillery in Buckie seemingly has a saline edge and a new-make aroma that's akin to tomato sauce. "There are lots of tanks at Inchgower," says Murray, "and lots of tanks in the system pushes that spiciness towards waxiness. Remember all sites do not make one flavor descriptor but a unique mix of flavors and intensity. Small changes give big character variations."

AUCHROISK TASTING NOTES

NEW MAKE

Nose: Burnt. Heavy cereal. Bran flakes. Pot ale.
Palate: Firm, crisp, wheat germ. Quite hard. Beneath there's a nodule of sweetness.
Finish: Dry.

8YO REFILL WOOD CASK SAMPLE

Nose: Cookies, light citrus fruit. Singed grass. Carpet shop, a little rubber.
Palate: Dry but clean. Assam tea. Chalky.
Finish: Still firm.
Conclusion: Is purified but still needs time to sweeten fully.

Flavor Camp: Malty & Dry

10YO, FLORA & FAUNA 43%

Nose: Considerably sweeter with more nuttiness. Sugary, with cashews and macadamia nuts, hints of wild herbs (lemon balm). The burnt note has receded into a roasted depth.
Palate: The suggestion of sweetness in new make and 8yo is now brought out by coconutty, sweet cask influence that has the effect of riding over the wheaty maltiness.
Finish: Still dry.
Conclusion: It's taken a decade of slow maturation in refill to start to reveal its full and pretty, sweet personality.

Flavor Camp: Malty & Dry
Where Next? Speyside 12yo

INCHGOWER TASTING NOTES

NEW MAKE

Nose: High-toned and very intense. Tomato sauce, green malt, cucumber. Slightly saline. Touch of geranium.
Palate: Acidic, nutty. Spritzy, sea-spray feel. Tingling, spicy.
Finish: Salted nuts.

8YO REFILL WOOD, CASK SAMPLE

Nose: Still intense now, with added lemon and lime (almost young/fermenting Semillon). The fruit is restrained, hard, and green. Green jelly.
Palate: Retained that salinity. Light and clean, with the nuttiness taking charge late on.
Finish: Spicy.
Conclusion: A hard nut to crack. Still coming together.

Flavor Camp: Malty & Dry

14YO, FLORA & FAUNA 43%

Nose: Still intensely spicy—and it might be that spice which gives the impression of saltiness. Lemon puffs, vanilla ice cream, and wood smoke.
Palate: The highly focused, spicy distillery character dominates at the start and towards the back, effectively squeezing any sweetness into a small spot in the center of the tongue.
Finish: Energetic and salty.
Conclusion: A one-off with such a powerful distillery character that you doubt whether it will ever be dominated.

Flavor Camp: Fruity & Spicy
Where Next? Old Pulteney 12yo, Glengoyne 10yo

SPEYSIDE
SINGLE MALT
SCOTCH WHISKY

In a striking *hilltop location, visible from ROTHES,* is sited the

AUCHROISK

distillery. The unusual name, *meaning* "FORD *of the* RED STREAM" *in Gaelic,* refers to the MULBEN BURN *from which the distillery draws its cooling water.* However, the principal reason for the *siting of the distillery is* DORIES WELL *an abundant source of soft, pure springwater.* Through the *smoke and nutty sweetness,* comes the *unmistakeable feel of* DORIES silky water, *followed by a dry,* well balanced *finish.*

AGED **10** YEARS

43% vol   Distilled & Bottled in *SCOTLAND*   70cl
AUCHROISK DISTILLERY, Mulben, Keith, Banffshire, *Scotland.*

THE ROTHES CLUSTER

Although it could give Dufftown a run for its money for the title of Speyside's whisky capital, Rothes seems to prefer to draw a veil over its whisky-making activities, yet they range from the world's leading producer of pot stills, through a selection of top-class distilleries, and a dark grains plant which processes all the residue, turning it into cattle feed. All whisky is here.

Slumbering in the crepuscular warehouses at Glen Grant.

Glen Grant

ROTHES • WWW.GLENGRANT.COM • DISTILLERY & GARDEN OPEN • MID-JAN–MID-DEC, MON–SUN

John and James Grant moved to Rothes to establish its first distillery in 1840, after some experience of distilling in Aberlour. John was a gentleman distiller while James was an engineer and politician. The year after the distillery appeared, James proposed to the Elgin and Lossiemouth Harbour Co. that a railway should be built, linking the Lossiemouth port to Elgin, and that it should be extended to Craigellachie via Rothes. Eventually it was, but only thanks to the Grant brothers bankrolling it to the tune of £4,500 ($6,793).

While James was machinating, John was creating not just a distillery but an estate. Distilleries are, by nature, functional, and while their locations may be spectacular or their architecture aesthetically pleasing, they are essentially industrial sites. Glen Grant is an exception, and as such it speaks volumes not just about the remarkable family that ran it until 1978, but the arrival of the gentleman distiller. No other distillery can quite match the extravagances of John Grant and, more significantly, his son, John (aka The Major), who took over in 1872.

Extravagantly moustachioed, seemingly never without a rod or gun, The Major was the epitome of Victorian sensibilities: a big-game hunter, a playboy, interested in engineering and innovation. He was the first man to have a car in the Highlands, the first man there to have an electric light (powered by water turbines in the distillery). Rothes is an unlikely place to find grapes and peaches (even today, a lemon in the local shop is unusual), yet all grew in The Major's stately pleasure dome next to where the Spey did run.

Glen Grant remains a manifestation of The Major's restlessness. It started as a two-stiller, then expanded to four, but one pair included

THE SAD TALE OF CAPERDONICH

In 1898, The Major set up another distillery next to the railway line. Caperdonich promptly closed in 1902 and only reopened in 1965, closing once more in 2003. "Why did it fail?" asks Malcolm. "It had the same water, the same yeast, even the same manager. But they had a different shape of still, though even when they put in the German helmet it still didn't make Glen Grant." The site is now part of the coppersmith Forsyth's workshops.

a large wash still and a small spirit, "Wee Geordie." When a new stillhouse was built in the 1960s, it ran on gas fires while the old stillhouse remained on coal.

Today, there are eight massive, steam-driven stills, the wash ones with a "German helmet" bulge at the base of their bull necks. All of the lyne arms then take a dip into purifying tanks. "The purifiers have been here since The Major," says Dennis Malcolm, Glen Grant's master distiller. "It's clear that he wanted to make a lighter spirit." These days, the new make is whistle-clean, all green grass, apple,

The distillery's water runs beside the woodland paths of "The Major's" famed Victorian garden, a visitor attraction in its own right.

The new and ultra-modern visitors' center features "help yourself" dramming.

and bubblegum. The process started by The Major has been constantly tweaked in order to get to this point. Wee Geordie ("which gave a heavier style") was retired in 1975; coal went, then gas; the final wisps of peat disappeared in 1972; while sherry casks have been replaced primarily with ex-bourbon.

It was its lightness that endeared Glen Grant to the Italian market—this was the biggest-selling single malt for many years, thanks to its dominance there—a link that was finally cemented when Gruppo Campari bought Glen Grant, brand and all, for £170 million ($256 million) in 2006. Since then, millions more have been spent by Malcolm, bringing the distillery and The Major's gardens back to life.

In the tranquil garden—alive with bird song and the smell of privet hedges, brown, foaming water rampaging over the rocks—sipping a dram from The Major's safe in a cliffside cave and looking back into the sun, a golden haze over the garden, you are for a second back in whisky's gentlemanly interlude, with raked paths, peaches in your greenhouses, your Rolls-Royce in the garage.

GLEN GRANT TASTING NOTES

NEW MAKE
Nose: Very clean and sweet. Green apples, flowers, and bubblegum with a hint of yeast behind. Lifted and high-toned.
Palate: Immediate fruity/estery notes of apple and pineapple. Pure and clean.
Finish: Lightly floral.

10YO 40%
Nose: Pale gold. Light and floral, with a vanilla undertone. Estery. The fruit has been ripened and, in the pineapple's case, canned. With water, cupcakes, hyacinth.
Palate: Light, with a sappy quality. Good wood here, giving lots of creaminess while adding a subtle sweet spice.
Finish: Soft with a hint of green grape.
Conclusion: Clean, light, and refreshing.

Flavor Camp: **Fragrant & Floral**
Where Next? Mannochmore 12yo

1992 CELLAR RESERVE 46%
Nose: In similar vein to the 10yo with more wood integration. The freshness and floral notes are retained, but the oak has added vanilla custard and also a toasty, dry quality.
Palate: Clean with light grip. Dry hay. With water it becomes more floral with a touch of sweet spice.
Finish: Crisp and cookie-like.
Conclusion: Flowers are still here but the fruits are in the background as the wood comes forward.

Flavor Camp: **Fragrant & Floral**
Where Next? Tullibardine 2004

25YO GORDON & MACPHAIL BOTTLING 40%
Nose: Classic sherried overtones of light fruitcake, toasted almond, and winter fruit. For the first time a malted-grain note and smoke. Resinous.
Palate: Slightly dumb start, then nuts. Thick but fragrant Moscatel style. Light and delicate, with a faint effervescence.
Finish: Molasses.
Conclusion: A rich, heavily sherried example with only a few hints of the perfume of the distillery character.

Flavor Camp: **Rich & Round**
Where Next? Glenfiddich 30yo, Benromach 1981

Glenrothes

GLENROTHES • ROTHES

In the old Rothes graveyard, its tombstones covered with what look like mourning weeds, stands a grave-watcher's house where, in the eighteenth century, grieving relatives stationed themselves immediately after the body's committal. Here they would remain until the decomposition of their beloved's corpse eliminated any chance of body-snatching taking place. Their morbid vigil, one imagines, would have required regular fortification with illicit hooch brought down from the neigboring hills.

The body-snatching era had long gone by the time the new Glenrothes distillery was established in 1878. The graveyard returned to being a place of peace rather than desecration, the fumes from the distillery triggering the slow growth of the black, crepe-like fungus that festoons the tombs. The siting of the distillery, graveyard apart, is further evidence of how the liberalization of distilling laws in 1823 brought about a physical change to Speyside's distilleries. No longer did they have to be secreted in peat sheds, *shielings,* and remote farms. Now, as distillers moved from the moonlight into daylight, they also moved into the area's towns, although old habits appear to have died hard: all of this whisky town's distilleries still remain a discreet distance from the main street.

Glenrothes, however, almost failed to become a Rothes plant. Soon after its establishment it immediately ran into financial difficulties when the Glasgow Bank went belly-up. It was only saved a year later thanks to a cash injection from the unlikeliest source: the United Free Presbyterian Church of Knockando, which put aside its teetotal beliefs when it saw a sound business opportunity. The congregation would

be surprised by what sits on the site today. Glenrothes has expanded dramatically from its old core. Today there are ten stills (five wash, five spirit) producing its whisky.

A quick mashing cycle creates worts which are pumped into either stainless-steel or wooden washbacks. While debate continues over the benefits of one type over the other, very few distilleries have this halfway house. This suggests to the casual observer that Glenrothes' distillers feel there is no difference in character between the two; that's not necesarily true. "We still make sure that each charge of the wash still is from two wooden to one steel," says manager Sandy Coutts. "Changing over entirely to stainless steel might just have changed the character."

A combination of long (90-hour) and short (55-hour) fermentations also necessitates a slight tweak in order to preserve character. These are set at different temperatures, whether steel or wood, and depend on the length of ferment. "This," says Coutts, "will iron out any differences in flavor."

Glenrothes, a late nineteenth-century distillery, soon transported its A-listed whisky south to the blenders.

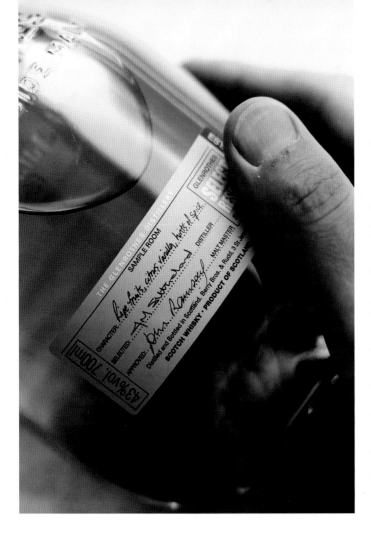

The Glenrothes pack is modeled on old sample-room bottles and each is signed by its whisky-maker.

It's in Glenrothes' cathedral-like stillhouse that Coutts feels the true character is created. Here the stillman sits, framed among the ten pots. All are big, with boil bulbs to increase reflux and a very slow distillation to tease out the rich, soft fruitiness that sits at Glenrothes' heart.

The new make is filled mostly into ex-sherry casks—the distillery itself is owned by that great sherry-lover, the Edrington Group. Until recently most of it went to blends—not just Grouse but Chivas and other top makes. Its hidden location, one feels, wasn't just physical but philosophical. It did its work out of sight, behind the scenes.

Recently, however, it has come into the new world of single malt, thanks to its brand owner, London wine merchant Berry Bros. & Rudd, which has taken its 300 years of expertise in fine wine and applied it to single malt. Glenrothes doesn't conform to the standard approach of age statements but is released in vintages to show different facets of this most elegant of malts.

Glenrothes is a slow whisky, its complexities taking time in the glass, on the nose, and mostly in the mouth to develop. Rich but not heavy, sherried, but never overly so, it plays variations on a theme between oak, fruit, spice, and honey with, in older expressions, a dazzling spice on the back palate. Understated rather than bold, it seems to symbolize its discreet location.

GLENROTHES TASTING NOTES

NEW MAKE

Nose: Clean. Vanilla, Chanel No. 5, white-fleshed fruit, canned pear, touch of cereal, buttery.
Palate: Buttery and fat, but rather than Macallan-like oiliness, there's a lifted spicy quality. Intense.
Finish: Creamy.

SELECT RESERVE NAS, 43%

Nose: Rain-moistened tweed. Cereal/cookie-like. Malty and slightly tense with a little touch of fresh black plum behind. Butter.
Palate: Nutty to start, then a shift into damson giving extra middle-palate weight (which is very Edrington), with that vanilla note seen in the new make adding a softness.
Finish: Long and nutty.
Conclusion: Still in its youth.

Flavor Camp: **Fruity & Spicy**
Where Next? Balvenie Double Wood, Glen Garioch 12yo

1991 43%

Nose: Rich amber. Full and ripe and has lost the hard, cereal shell of the Select Reserve. Here the spice seen on the new make surges forward and dances on the tongue. Moving from fresh fruit to dried fruit in the middle of the palate. Black cherry.
Palate: Smooth and silky, with very full fruit. Still that levitation of spice above and a cereal crispness adding a grounding effect.
Finish: Molasses. Soft and elegant.
Conclusion: Fully integrated with the oak, which allows the richness of the spirit to develop.

Flavor Camp: **Rich & Round**
Where Next? Royal Lochnagar Select Reserve, Glenallachie 18yo

1978 43%

Nose: Dark amber. Ripe and concentrated. Full, dried-fruit effect. Mulberry, oloroso sherry, and a little dried mint and some tobacco leaf.
Palate: Rich and sweet. The cereal is just a back note here as the fat quality seen at the start now takes charge, melding wholly with the wood.
Finish: Long, with a tickle of sweet spice.
Conclusion: It has taken this length of time for its personality to reach its fullest expression.

Flavor Camp: **Rich & Round**
Where Next? Dalmore 1981

Speyburn

ROTHES • WWW.INVERHOUSE.COM/DISTILLERIES-SPEYBURN.PHP

The only sight you get of Speyburn as you drive on the road to (or from) Elgin is a pagoda roof poking out of a tight little glen, giving it the impression of an old, secret, illicit site. In fact, like all of Rothes' distilleries, this one dates from the late nineteenth century, and instead of being hidden from sight, it is located right next to the Rothes-Elgin branch line, built at the instigation of John Grant. This change of angle also makes it seems as if the distillery runs back from the road, only slowly revealing its conglomeration of buildings. From the railway side, however, you'll see a frontage of pagoda-topped distillery, warehouses, and a malting plant. It's our perspective that has changed, not Speyburn's.

The spirit of innovation that Rothes seems to attract was alive here as well. Not only does Speyburn sit opposite the first purpose-built dark-grains plant in Scotland which turns waste grain into animal feed, but it was the first distillery in Scotland to try pneumatic (aka drum) malting on site. Speyburn's drums continued until 1968, two years after the railway stopped carrying freight. With this, Speyburn sank back into relative obscurity.

It's worth discovering. This is another of Inver House's worm-tub sites, making a new spirit that's full of struck match and town gas tones. It behaves, however, like its stablemate anCnoc (Knockdhu), shedding its sulfur early on and revealing its true fruity, fragrant/floral character.

"It's easy drinking," says Inver House's master blender, Stuart Harvey, "but it has more body than anCnoc: that's the difference." The difference in production might be subtle, but the effect is noticeable. "It's impossible to fix precisely what makes each

Being almost wholly obscured from view seems to suit the subtle Speyburn style.

character different," says Harvey. "You can run everything in exactly the same way in an identical distillery and you'll get different characters," he adds. "Whisky is site-specific. You can only make our character at our distilleries."

SPEYBURN TASTING NOTES

NEW MAKE

Nose: Wet leather. Light bran/oat. Touch of Jamaican pot-still rum. Plenty of citrus fruit. Struck match/gassy sulfuriness.
Palate: Big and slightly bready, with some meaty notes, but a delicate quality is hiding. Has depth.
Finish: Freshens.

10YO 40%

Nose: Pale gold. Light and floral, with hard candy and light lemon tones. Clean, fresh, and soft. Stewed rhubarb. Cherry blossom.
Palate: Creamy vanilla, then flowers. Good middle-palate weight yields a succulent feel.
Finish: Lightly acidic.
Conclusion: Another of those where sulfur lifts to reveal esteriness and also palate weight.

Flavor Camp: **Fragrant & Floral**
Where Next? Glenkinchie 12yo, Glencadam 10yo

21YO 58.5%

Nose: Rich sherry notes: cake, nut, and prune. Bitter chocolate and a charred, meaty tone.
Palate: Powerful European-oak punch: orange, sweet spices, molasses, and cookies with some sweet spirit. The charred notes lend an intriguing balance.
Finish: Licorice.
Conclusion: Big cask influence and maybe that meatiness indicate a heavier style being made in the past?

Flavor Camp: **Rich & Round**
Where Next? Tullibardine 1988, Dailuaine 16yo

Glen Spey

GLEN SPEY • ROTHES

At the opposite end of the town from Speyburn is the gated entrance to Glen Spey, the final member of this reticent whisky hub. Rothes may prefer to keep its business to itself, but within these streets the whole whisky-making process takes place. It was no coincidence that Rothes was chosen by early distillers. There are multiple water sources and there was the railway, while it was also on the southern limits of the barley-growing plains and had access to peat. The situation, in other words, was vital.

Each distillery would have had its own maltings (Glen Grant and Speyburn had drum maltings into the 1960s) and local coppersmiths (Forsyth's continues to supply stills to the whole whisky industry), and with Speyburn's dark-grains plant, Rothes was the perfect example of self-sufficiency.

Glen Spey is, like its neighbors, a late nineteenth-century plant, having been established in 1878 when a local grain merchant, James Stuart, saw an opportunity to extend his mill in Rothes to include a distillery. After expanding the distillery footprint and changing its name to Glen Spey, he sold it in 1887 to gin distiller W&A Gilbey, the first of that firm's Speyside interests (in time it also owned Knockando and another old grain mill, under the name of Strathmill).

Still retaining an air of Victorian rectitude, Glen Spey conforms to the light Gilbey/J&B style. Here, as at Strathmill, there's a purifier on the tall, reflux-inducing wash stills which—who knows?—may have appeared after a neighborly visit to Glen Grant. This has the effect of introducing an oily element to the nutty character which manifests itself, to this writer at least, as an almond note.

Rothes at first glance may not seem like a whisky town—but it is.

Typical of the Rothes distilleries, Glen Spey prefers the quiet life out of the public glare.

GLEN SPEY TASTING NOTES

NEW MAKE

Nose: Fat, popcorn/butterscotch-like with sweet fruit behind. Slight saltiness, then green almond/almond oil.
Palate: Clean and green. Light nut/flour. Dry overall. Simple.
Finish: Dry and crisp.

8YO REFILL WOOD, CASK SAMPLE

Nose: Slightly immature but lifted. Toasted wood/roasted malt; peanuts and almonds. White rum. Behind there's baked apple.
Palate: Very intense, then at the halfway point comes hazelnut flour. Light and clean.
Finish: Nutty.
Conclusion: Not yet integrated and a little twiggy.

Flavor Camp: Malty & Dry

12YO, FLORA & FAUNA 43%

Nose: Malty but scented, with a hint of lavender and earthiness. Dusty chalk (school blackboards) and then that signature almond note.
Palate: Peanuts and almond flakes. Clean, with a soft sweet spot in the center. Lilac and iris on the back palate.
Finish: Crisp and clean.
Conclusion: Fully developed into a balanced mix of malt and fragrance.

Flavor Camp: Malty & Dry
Where Next? Inchmurrin 12yo, Auchentoshan Classic

ELGIN TO THE WESTERN EDGE

The Bermuda Triangle of whisky lies just outside Speyside's largest town. Here are cult distilleries whose whiskies are revered by blenders and aficionados, but which seem to have disappeared from the general drinker's consciousness. There are some surprises in store: the epitome of fruitiness, of fragrance—and the heaviest peated spirit in Speyside.

Sandstone cliffs illuminated by low evening sunlight at Burghead.

Glen Elgin
GLEN ELGIN • ELGIN

In what appears to be a Speyside characteristic, even the region's largest conurbation keeps its local distilleries somewhat hidden. Apart from two front-line single-malt brands, Glen Moray and BenRiach, these are stills whose work is done behind the scenes, absorbed into a multiplicity of blends. The result is that they are often overlooked as nothing more than fodder for fillings, whereas the opposite is in fact the case. The reason that the bulk of this cluster's distilleries are little-seen is because blenders prize their idiosyncratic singularities.

Glen Elgin is a classic case. Hidden up a narrow road off the A941 highway, its character is the definition of fruitiness—almost absurdly so, since its fleshy ripeness brings visions of peach juice dribbling down your chin. This seems surprising if you give the distillery no more than a cursory glance. Six small stills plus worm tubs equal sulfury new make, right? No. Here is one of three worm sites owned by Diageo that works against type.

"Provided you run the stills to ensure that the sulfur is removed during distillation, then you can make an intense, light spirit," explains Douglas Murray, Diageo's master distiller and blender. That sulfury new-make character seen elsewhere is avoided here by allowing the vapor a more relaxed relationship with the copper in the still. Equally, the fermentation is important. "In Glen Elgin, the bulk of the character is created before it goes to the still," he continues. This erotically charged fruitiness is generated by a relaxed regime: longer and slightly cooler ferments, and a slow and copper-rich conversation in the still.

Then there are the worms. "Worm sites have increased complexity and give a more intense character," says Murray. "There's actually not that much difference between Cardhu and Glen Elgin in terms of process." There is, however, a huge difference in character: the succulent versus the grassy, the lush versus the sharp.

Old coopering equipment that has seen long service sitting in the warehouses of Glen Elgin.

GLEN ELGIN TASTING NOTES

NEW MAKE
Nose: Ripe. Juicy Fruit chewing gum. Red apple, baked banana, green peach. Silky.
Palate: Light smoke. Clean but ripe and rich. Silky mouth-feel.
Finish: Luscious and long.

8YO REFILL WOOD, CASK SAMPLE
Nose: The fruit has softened and ripened and now ranges from canned to fresh. Lots of canned peach, fresh melon, seemingly creamy. Sweet, plump, and juicy. Light smoke.
Palate: Very sweet and concentrated. Pools in the center of the tongue. Apricot. Very juicy and sweet. Peach nectar.
Finish: Soft and, yes, fruity.
Conclusion: Sweet and rich and almost in need of some control from cask.

Flavor Camp: **Fruity & Spicy**

12YO 43%
Nose: Full gold. The fruit is now sharing the top slot, with a sweet and slightly dusty spiciness. Some nutmeg and cumin. More integrated oak adding some grip to the fresh fruit.
Palate: Soft, tropical fruit to start, then changes suddenly halfway through into those spices, which slowly become fragrant woods.
Finish: Fruity but drying.
Conclusion: The cask has added complexity to the whole package, but distillery character is still clearly visible.

Flavor Camp: **Fruity & Spicy**
Where Next? Balblair 1990, Glenmorangie Original

Longmorn

LONGMORN • ELGIN

Glen Elgin's near neighbor has also tended to keep its own counsel. Longmorn is one of those malts which, like some underground musician, builds a reputation among an obsessive fan base, who then somehow resent the fact that their hero might just be becoming better-known.

Longmorn was established in 1893 by John Duff, who was born in the nearby town of Aberchirder. Duff had previously designed Glenlossie before heading to the Transvaal to try and start the South African whisky industry. When this failed, he headed home to the Lossie to design and build Longmorn, here in the rich farmlands of the Laich O'Moray, near to the peats from the *foggie loans* (peat moss) of the nearby Mannoch Hill.

Duff's business went bust at the end of the nineteenth century and Longmorn passed into the hands of James Grant. Soon, it was elevated to A1 status by blenders.

"Longmorn is a real gem," says Colin Scott, master blender at owner Chivas Brothers. "It is a true friend to a blender because it has the power to influence and the elegance to harmonize the other whiskies in the blend." It's those blenders who were the jealous fans. Even when it became part of the Glenlivet Distilleries group, unlike its stablemates, Glen Grant and The Glenlivet, Longmorn was never promoted to single-malt brand status.

What the blenders are guarding is a soft, rich, complex new make produced in fat, plain stills. It is sweet, it is fruity, it has depth, it has breadth. It is fragrant yet powerful. It is gentle and honeyed in

Longmorn's complex, fruity new make runs into one of the most ornate spirit safes in the industry.

American oak barrels, richer and spicily expansive in hogsheads, darkly rich and powerful in ex-sherry butts. It has the ability to perform a multiplicity of functions.

As a keystone of many blends, it is also one of the foundations of Japanese single malt. The shape of the original stills served as the model for the Yoichi distillery in Japan because it was here that one of the fathers of Japanese whisky, Masataka Taketsuru, first experienced hands-on distilling. Word spreads, but other than an expensively packaged official 16yo, Longmorn remains in the hands of its original fans.

LONGMORN TASTING NOTES

NEW MAKE

Nose: Soft and fruity: almost fruitcake. Ripe banana, pear. Rich and round, with a soft, meat-like note at the back.
Palate: The fruit continues. Ripe and long.
Finish: A little floral touch.

10YO CASK SAMPLE

Nose: Pale gold. The fruit is ripening, but has a slight green-peach character, followed by vanilla and cream.
Palate: The central fruitiness is now rising: apricot and mango, then with water, melted milk chocolate and mace.
Finish: Lightly spiced.
Conclusion: For all the soft power, the impression is that this is still slightly asleep.

Flavor Camp: Fruity & Spicy

16YO 48%

Nose: Old gold. fruitcake. There's still soft fruit, but also a hint of dusty spice, fried banana, citrus fruit. Diluted, there's cream toffee, peach, and plum.
Palate: Thick. Chocolate again. Ripe, tropical fruit, fruit sugars.
Finish: Ginger snaps.
Conclusion: Ripe and complex.

Flavor Camp: Fruity & Spicy
Where Next? Glenmorangie 18yo, BenRiach 16yo

1977 50.7%

Nose: Banana chips, jungle mix; given depth by cereal. Peachy, scented. Chinese tea, stewed fruit, citrus fruit.
Palate: Deep. Rich. Opens into sandalwood, vetiver, damson, and sweet, stewed fruit.
Finish: Full and long. Cinnamon in butter.
Conclusion: Goes into lusciousness. An absorbing whisky.

Flavor Camp: Fruity & Spicy
Where Next? Macallan Fine Oak 25yo

33YO DUNCAN TAYLOR BOTTLING, 49.4%

Nose: Even after over so long this retains the distillery character's fruitiness. Cooked quince, guava with a light crystallized ginger in syrup. A little smoke.
Palate: Gentle, sweet, and fruity. Lies on tongue. The tingling gingeriness/ginseng? adds a lift to the back palate.
Finish: Fruits return, now semi-dried.
Conclusion: The oak is in balance, allowing the distillery character to show its fullest expression.

Flavor Camp: Fruity & Spicy
Where Next? Glenmorangie 25yo, Dalwhinnie 1986

BenRiach

ELGIN • WWW.BENRIACHDISTILLERY.CO.UK

Britain was luxuriating in an economic boom at the end of the nineteenth century. Industrial output was rising and a side effect of this was an increased investment in new distilleries. Boom, inevitably, is followed by bust, and, perhaps triggered by the collapse of blending and broking house Pattison in 1898, the industry began to slither into a decline. Although exports for blends were growing, sales in the domestic market (upon which Scotch was still heavily reliant) began to fall, leaving the stocks out of balance and with the possibility of worse to come as the large plants built at the tail-end of the century came into operation.

Some of those were bailed out by blending firms looking to extend their own estate (and control more of their own requirements). Others closed, considered surplus to requirements. There were 161 distilleries (including grain) open in Scotland in 1899. By 1908, this number had fallen to 132. Many of those that closed were large-scale enterprises built in the last days of wild optimism, silenced before they had had a chance to open their mouths. Caperdonich, built in 1898 as Glen Grant Mark II, closed in 1902; Imperial, built as Dailuaine II in 1897, closed in 1899. Another new plant that had the shortest of lives was BenRiach, the last of the Fogwatt Triangle, which started off as Longmorn's sister plant in 1898 and closed in 1900. It was 65 years before it began to distill whisky again.

In the intervening years, Longmorn used malt from BenRiach's malting floors, but it wasn't until the middle of another boom in whisky sales and buoyant mood among blending firms that spirit began to run from its four stills once more.

It remained in a supporting role, a quiet whisper within blends, adding some spicy fruitiness, perhaps at times adding a heavy peated character when stocks of Islay were running low. While occasionally officially bottled as a single malt, even those releases seemed to indicate a whisky which, while decent, was never as startling as the other two members of this triumvirate: Glen Grant and Longmorn.

When it closed in 2003, it looked at if BenRiach's jinxed life was continuing. This time, however, there was a white knight in the shape of former Burn Stewart managing director Billy Walker. Eyebrows were raised on news of the purchase—and then the whiskies started appearing. Complex, spicy, and, in older examples, showing the dazzling, dancing quality on the palate that is only ever discerned in whiskies of this style which have had a long, relaxed maturation in refill casks. In other words, a revelation to drinkers, if not to blenders.

These days production is flat-out and the world of single malt is very much the focus. "It has taken us five years to get everything

Mashing in at BenRiach: the moment in the early stages when the barley's starches are turned into fermentable sugars.

balanced properly," says manager Stewart Buchanan. "A lot of equipment had been removed," he adds, "so there was plenty to be replaced and then rebalanced. As we had no records of new make before the takeover, we did numerous trials of cut points and we think it's pretty much spot-on.

"What we look for is a perfumed, fruity sweetness; you can even get some of those fruits in the tun room where the smell becomes really appley. I think any whisky-making is about looking after the barley, and because we have a broad cut, we're capturing a good

A quiet supplier of fillings for blends for many years, BenRiach now has the capacity to become a significant single-malt brand.

spread of flavors, from this early sweetness to those cereal notes from later in the run."

It might have been a latecomer on the scene, but BenRiach is breaking free of the blend-oriented focus of this part of Speyside. And who knows? It could be leading some of these quiet but often spectacular performers into a new arena.

BENRIACH TASTING NOTES

NEW MAKE

Nose: Sweet, cake-like, fruity, zucchini, fennel. Lemon, then a sweet, cookie-like note, chalk.
Palate: That highly concentrated, slightly waxy, soft fruitiness leads the way, then comes a dusky/dusty perfumed quality. Chewy.
Finish: Crisp and clean. Malt. Then lots of spice.

CURIOSITAS 10YO PEATED, 40%

Nose: Raffia to start, then dried wood smoke/ charred sticks moving into bitumen and baked fruit behind.
Palate: Hugely smoky, then sweet oak and a lightly fruity palate. Good feel.
Finish: Still smoked, with a light cereal note.
Conclusion: A curiosity indeed. Originally made to provide a peaty component for Chivas Brothers blends.

> **Flavor Camp: Smoky & Peaty**
> **Where Next?** Ardmore Traditional Cask

12YO 40%

Nose: Full gold. Spicy start, with some perfumed/ waxy exotic florals (frangipan), confectioner's sugar, and sawdust. Fresh fruit and more fresh oak with water.
Palate: Remains lightly waxy, with a clinging, fruit-syrup quality. Apricot, banana, and cinnamon.
Finish: A burst of spice, then a quick end.
Conclusion: A slow build, with American oak an ideal partner.

> **Flavor Camp: Fruity & Spicy**
> **Where Next?** Longmorn 10yo, Clynelish 14yo

16YO 40%

Nose: Full gold. Everything has deepened and the spice has receded as the fruit emerges as the dominant partner. Touch of wood smoke. Dried banana and ripe melon. A little nuttiness. Retains an exotic edge.
Palate: More dense and less fresh fruit, more baked/semi-dried. Bigger, chewier, and more intense, with some cumin. With water, sherried notes.
Finish: Dry oak and white raisins.
Conclusion: Flexing its muscles.

> **Flavor Camp: Fruity & Spicy**
> **Where Next?** Balvenie Double Wood

21YO 46%

Nose: Gold. Smoke and damp hay, bay leaf/laurel, autumn leaves, and pear. Melon remains, but the spices have moved to a light dusting in the background.
Palate: Smoky and nutty. Walnut shell. Sage but still with that chewy quality. Oak has moved into sandalwood and camphor. Restrained, with good oak support.
Finish: Ginger and light peat.
Conclusion: Moving into the third stage of its evolution.

> **Flavor Camp: Fruity & Spicy**
> **Where Next?** Balblair 1975, Glenmorangie 18yo

Glenlossie, Mannochmore, & Roseisle

GLENLOSSIE & MANNOCHMORE • ELGIN / ROSEISLE • BURGHEAD

If BenRiach has emerged fully formed from its sequestration, then the next trio appears content to remain hidden from view (although the newest one will find it hard). Glenlossie and Mannochmore share a site; in fact Mannochmore lies inside Glenlossie's bounds, somewhat protected by its considerably older brother. Both are in the lighter end of the flavor spectrum but, importantly, make different variations on that theme.

Glenlossie is a good example of the search for lightness that took place in the late nineteenth century. Built in 1876 by John Duff, a former manager of GlenDronach, its stills have always been equipped with purifiers, which is a clear indication of clever design being utilized to supply this more delicate character.

Reflux is the key here: that prolonged, intentional redistilling of condensing vapors inside the still (*see* pp.14–15). Glenlossie is more than just light, however. A nose of the new make shows an oiliness that adds both aroma to the basic delicate, grassy fragrance and a slickness to the mouthfeel. "If you run the fermentation in such a way as to make things grassy and then increase the reflux, you'll get that added oiliness," says Douglas Murray, Diageo's master distiller and blender. "Oiliness is lots of active copper on a potentially grassy spirit."

It's possible that Glenlossie has been saved by its purifier pipe. Quietly, it certainly has had a fair amount of attention lavished on it, having been extended from four to six stills in 1962. It is quite common for one of the members of a double site to close. It's

ROSEISLE: A MODEL OF VERSATILITY

The Moray coast has long produced barley, so it's little surprise that there are malting plants located here. Diageo alone has two, at Burghhead and Roseisle. From 2009, the latter has also been home to the firm's newest distillery, one that has opened a new chapter in whisky distilling in Scotland. Whereas traditionally, Scottish distilleries have produced one style (there are a few exceptions but they are just that), Roseisle has been set up to produce multiple styles of whisky: light, heavy, malty, and peaty, with the possibility that more distillate streams could also be made if required. While this is hardly new within the world whisky industry—Irish Distillers, Suntory, and Nikka all do the same thing at their plants—it came as a shock to many Scotch producers, who saw it as potentially starting the centralization of production. The fact that William Grant began producing multiple styles at its Aisla Bay plant seems to have bypassed many of Roseisle's critics. Roseisle, Diageo says, has been built to produce flavors of whisky for its blends (the same applies to Aisla Bay).

The stillhouse at Diageo's remarkable Roseisle distillery.

what happened at Clynelish, for example, when Brora disappeared, while Teaninich and Linkwood's old stillhouses are also now no longer producing. Not so here.

In 1971, the six-still Mannochmore was built within the Glenlossie site (along with a dark-grains plant) and started to produce its own variation on the light theme. No oil here; this is all about a sweet, floral freshness when new that develops a fleshy quality when mature. It needs careful handling; the boisterousness of first-fill sherry would obliterate its rather discreet nature.

This makes it all the more surprising that Mannochmore was chosen as the malt to lie beneath the thick, black molasses that made up Loch Dhu, the notorious "black whisky" which (very) briefly appeared on the market in the 1990s. Dismissed out of hand on release, Loch Dhu is now highly collectible. Mannochmore, meanwhile, has drawn the covers over its head once more.

A quiet but a significant player in the whisky world.

NEW MAKE

Nose: Sweet carrot, fennel, flower stems straying into stone fruit. Grappa-like.
Palate: Light and clean. Floral, gentle, and fresh.
Finish: Quick, discreet.

8YO REFILL WOOD, CASK SAMPLE

Nose: A deeper fragrance with a touch of wet earth and jasmine. Vanilla; still some immature grappa-like edginess; slightly chalky.
Palate: Fat and quite broad. Unripe peach, then vanilla and that flower-shop character.
Finish: Still hot.
Conclusion: Seemingly light in aroma but is taking its time to build up momentum. A dark horse.

Flavor Camp: Fragrant & Floral

12YO, FLORA & FAUNA 43%

Nose: Clean. Vine flower with some peach juice developing, along with dessert apple.
Palate: Lightly oily and slightly spicy. A mandarin-like freshness. Very delicate and uncluttered.
Finish: Fresh and slightly citric.
Conclusion: Still light and perfumed.

Flavor Camp: Fragrant & Floral
Where Next? Braeval, Speyside 15yo

18YO SPECIAL RELEASE 54.9%

Nose: Beeswax, nuts, and an intense cinnamon lift. Freshly polished oak dominates at the start but underneath is a soft fruitiness: banana, stewed rhubarb, that characteristic peachiness, and some coconut.
Palate: The lush nature of the nose is confirmed on the palate, along with apricot, orange peel, vanilla, and a light grip from the oak. Good acidity. Sinks onto the mid-palate, where a shift to spiciness takes place before, surprisingly, the fruit reappears along with macaroon hints.
Finish: Soft to start, then a slight oaky grip. Clean and fine.
Conclusion: Here's a whisky which, while light at new-make stage, benefits hugely from the attentions of American oak (on evidence, European oak dominates it).

Flavor Camp: Fruity & Spicy
Where Next? Craigellachie 14yo, Old Pulteney 17yo

NEW MAKE

Nose: Melting butter, quite broad. White currant, wet chamois. Green and oily; canola oil.
Palate: The oil shows on the palate; unripe fruit; sweet cardboard.
Finish: Strawberry (unripe).

8YO REFILL WOOD, CASK SAMPLE

Nose: More floral, with a peachy note. Similar elderflower cordial note to Linkwood, light mint, lime, and pink grapefruit. The fruit is ripening.
Palate: Intense and aromatic with a clinging quality.
Finish: Fresh and light.
Conclusion: At a midpoint in its evolution. Needs time to ripen. Again, the texture is key.

Flavor Camp: Fragrant & Floral

1999, MANAGER'S CHOICE SINGLE CASK 59.3%

Nose: Pale gold. Linseed oil, grapes, jasmine, Amalfi lemons. Very upfront and direct, but don't confuse that with it being immature. There's an intriguing antiseptic note with water, along with toasted marshmallow.
Palate: Peppery, zesty, grassy; the oak delivers a menthol/eucalyptus hit. Lots of lemon. Light and perfumed.
Finish: Clean, fragrant, and lifted.
Conclusion: Another lesser light that's shining brightly.

Flavor Camp: Fragrant & Floral
Where Next? Glentauchers 1991, anCnoc 16yo

Linkwood

LINKWOOD • ELGIN

Speyside's hidden narrative is the pursuit of the light. The distillers who joined in the hunt found themselves in varied places within this new flavor world. Occasionally, some pursued light with such relentless drive that character was close to being sucked out of their whiskies. Others headed down a grassy track, some went dusty with vampiric vigor, still others lay in floral bowers. All were faced with the reality that light whiskies need to be handled with care and discretion: refill casks, a little hint of first fill, but don't overload with oak if you wish to retain that carefully crafted distillery character.

The other issue facing these distillers is that, as new drinkers have come to single malt, so they have pursued bolder flavors. In this way single malt is no different from wine: the new wine-drinker cuts his or her teeth on fruit bombs. In this new market, what space is there for the subtle, the discreet?

What if there were a single malt somewhere that managed to combine a delicacy of aroma with palate weight; that was as fresh as a late spring day but wasn't as wispy as a chiffon dress? Not many single malts manage to achieve this tricky balancing act, but Linkwood does.

According to Douglas Murray, Diageo's distilling and blending guru, this style of whisky is the most testing type to make because it appears to do something that seems to run counter to what whisky is about: it suppresses flavors. Even its new-make definition ("clean") seems to drag it closer to the world of vodka and neutrality rather than to the congener-rich complexities of single malt.

Situated in farmland on the outskirts of Elgin, Linkwood's make is among the most aromatic in Scotch.

Light it may seem, but Linkwood blooms with age.

They're filled low and given a long distillation in order to maximize the time that the vapor can dribble back down the inside of these great copper bellies, stripping away more unwanted characters. Condensers are used to extend this copper interaction, although the old Linkwood distillery, which sits on the other side of the courtyard, has worm tubs. Old Linkwood, however, still shows this spring-like quality. (It was in old Linkwood, incidentally, that much of Diageo's research into copper and worm tub character was tested.)

It's a whisky that is in demand by blenders, offering both texture and top notes to a blend. While it can stand up to sherry casks—that fragrance and feel are retained—it shows at its best in refill casks, allowing the drinker to set out different ages and experience a liquid version of time-lapse photography: as the blossom of youth fruits, falls, and lies on a bed of dried flowers.

Fear not. Linkwood's new make smells like the peach skins, or light apple blossom falling in an orchard. In the mouth it sticks and seems to spin in a ball in the middle of the tongue. It's a conjuring act: you expect one thing and get another.

It starts early in the process with a different grind being given to the malted barley in order to give a thick filter bed in the mash tun. No cereal-producing solids are wanted in the low-gravity wort, which is given a long fermentation. "The whole issue here is to stop characters forming," says Murray.

The stills are rounded and Rubenesque and unusual (although not unique) in the fact that the spirit stills are larger than the wash still.

LINKWOOD TASTING NOTES

NEW MAKE

Nose: Perfumed. Pineapple, peach blossom/peach skin, quince. Some weight.
Palate: Incredibly fresh. Pastries, apple. Lightly oily/chewy in feel.
Finish: Clean and surprisingly long.

8YO REFILL WOOD, CASK SAMPLE

Nose: Straw. Green apple, elderflower, white fruit. Amazingly fresh. With water there's pear.
Palate: Good weight. Apples and gently poached pear, then elderflower cordial. Tongue-coating.
Finish: Fresh, light, and zesty.
Conclusion: An intriguing mix of fragrance and body.

Flavor Camp: **Fragrant & Floral**

12YO, FLORA & FAUNA 43%

Nose: Big, fragrant. Chamomile and jasmine mixed with apple. Quite scented and heavy. Picks up weight as it goes.
Palate: Rounded. The oily character in the center is now adding extra depth, allowing the ripe fruit and touches of grass to revolve around it.
Finish: Tropical fruit and grass.
Conclusion: A perfumed, clean whisky that deepens with age.

Flavor Camp: **Fragrant & Floral**
Where Next? Miltonduff 18yo, Tomintoul 14yo

SPEYSIDE
SINGLE MALT
SCOTCH WHISKY

LINKWOOD

distillery stands on the *River Lossie*, close to *ELGIN* in *Speyside*. The *distillery* has retained its *traditional atmosphere* since its *establishment* in 1821. Great care has always been taken to *safeguard* the character of the *whisky* which has remained the same through the years. Linkwood is one of the FINEST Single Malt Scotch Whiskies available - *full bodied* with a *hint* of *sweetness* and a *slightly smoky aroma.*

YEARS **12** OLD

43% vol   Distilled & Bottled in *SCOTLAND.*
LINKWOOD DISTILLERY
Elgin, Moray, *Scotland.*   70cl

Glen Moray

ELGIN • WWW.GLENMORAY.COM • OPEN ALL YEAR • OCT–APR, MON–FRI; MAY–SEPT, MON–SAT

Hidden beside the Lossie River and surrounded by a housing estate, Glen Moray's low profile (in both senses of the term) is a surprise, given the size of the site. Originally a brewery, this was another distillery built in the late nineteenth-century whisky boom which fell foul of the change in economic circumstances and closed in 1910. However, unlike BenRiach, its silent period was relatively short: it reopened in 1923. The stillhouse, small and compact, seems out of proportion with the rest of the buildings which used to house the distillery's own Saladin maltings.

The fruitiness that is a constant thread through this Elgin grouping reappears here with an added buttery quality that lends the palate a gently soft quality which is married with American oak. If you like fruit salad and ice cream, then Glen Moray is your whisky.

It's the distillery's microclimate which manager Graham Coull zones in on when describing Glen Moray's DNA. "The slightly warmer Moray climate and the location of the distillery in this low level really helps to suck the spirit into the wood, heightening the oak's effects on flavor. In addition, the low-lying dunnage warehouses with a low water table (they've flooded on numerous occasions) create what we feel is a greater mellowing to the product. Add the high proportion of first-fill casks, and you create a whisky with a wonderful sweet/spicy balance."

Some fresh oak barrels have also been tested here. A cask bottled by the Scotch Malt Whisky Society was generous with its flavors, but while the whisky showed an intense *crème brûlée*/butterscotch effect, the deep fruitiness of Glen Moray showed through. The below-the-radar properties extend to the marketing, too. Despite its evident

The flatlands beside the River Lossie are home to this huge whisky-making site.

qualities, Glen Moray was sold as a loss leader by previous owner Glenmorangie; while good for volume, this did little for its image, or for that of the category. Soon after the LVMH takeover of Glenmorangie, Glen Moray was sold to French distiller La Martiniquaise.

GLEN MORAY TASTING NOTES

NEW MAKE
Nose: Very clean and (fresh) fruity, with a buttery note and a touch of slightly spicy cereal.
Palate: A lightly waxy feel, then comes the ripe, pulpy fruits with some dessert apple.
Finish: Clean.

CLASSIC NAS 40%
Nose: Light gold. Like most no-age-statement (NAS) brands, the wood is the dominant partner. Crisp and oaky with that butteriness and a little green fruit. Apple.
Palate: Gentle and creamy. Soft feel.
Finish: Gentle, soft, and clean.
Conclusion: All slightly suppressed. Slightly sleepy.

> **Flavor Camp: Fruity & Spicy**
> **Where Next?** Macallan 10yo Fine Oak, Glencadam 15yo

12YO 40%
Nose: The soft fruit returns. Fruit chews, pear followed by blond tobacco and vanilla. Mint in time.
Palate: Quite bourbon-like, new oak, pine sap. Light apple.
Finish: Spice and the nuts in cream toffee.
Conclusion: First-fill influence adds another soft layer.

> **Flavor Camp: Fruity & Spicy**
> **Where Next?** Bruchladdich 2002, Tormore 12yo

16YO 40%
Nose: Gold. Resinous note often found in older whiskies. Still syrupy sweetness, creamed coconut, suntan oil.
Palate: Wood is fairly grippy, but sufficient of the distillery character seeps in towards the finish to balance.
Finish: Clean and silky.
Conclusion: Amenable.

> **Flavor Camp: Fruity & Spicy**
> **Where Next?** Macallan 18yo Fine Oak, Mannochmore 18yo

30YO 40%
Nose: Mature and autumnal. Spices now come through. Again there's tobacco—this time Dominican Republic cigar—and a touch of light varnish.
Palate: Smoky wood. Hickory. Deck oil.
Finish: Soft and finally fruity.
Conclusion: Big, sweet wood influence here.

> **Flavor Camp: Fruity & Spicy**
> **Where Next?** Old Pulteney 30yo

Miltonduff

MILTONDUFF • ELGIN

By the start of the 1930s, a collection of global circumstances was conspiring against the Scotch whisky industry. Falling demand in the UK, partly triggered by the economic effects of the Great Depression, had dramatically lowered production. The only bright spot was the continuing solidity of exports to Canada. The fact that many (if not most) of the cases of blends headed straight from the warehouses of Canadian importers into bootleggers' trucks and the still-dry American market was of no concern to the Scots. It was also clear that Prohibition was entering its end game, and with the anticipation of a boom in sales in the US, there was considerable positioning behind the scenes.

Sales did not rise immediately after the Repeal of Prohibition in 1933, due to the result of a $5-a-gallon import duty. After this was halved, Canadian distiller Hiram Walker-Gooderham & Worts went on a spending spree, buying its second Scotch distillery, Miltonduff, and the blending firm of George Ballantine, and starting work on the Dumbarton grain distillery which would go on to produce the most "Canadian" of Scotland's grains.

In buying Miltonduff, Hiram Walker had a distillery which, legend has it, was originally the mill for neighboring Pluscarden Abbey and which had been licensed since 1824.

It wasn't unused to innovation, either. "Miltonduff was triple-distilled in the late nineteenth century and for a time it's believed that it was trying to make something akin to Highland Park," says Alan Winchester, Chivas Brothers' distilleries manager. "Hiram Walker changed that, for whatever reason, to what we have now." In 1964 it also added a pair of Lomond stills, producing a malt called Mosstowie.

Winchester's "reason" lies with Ballantine's and the changing North American palate, which during Prohibition, had gone light. The

Miltonduff is alleged to be located on the site of an ancient monastic brewery.

Canadians brought not just capital but a new sensibility to whisky-making. The days of the delicate and gentle, building since the start of the century, had arrived. This is shown when you take a whiff of its floral, green, oily new make with a lifted complexity which, with a light touch when it comes to cask management, blooms.

MILTONDUFF TASTING NOTES

NEW MAKE

Nose: Sweet, with cucumber. Green/oily, with some lime blossom and vine flower.
Palate: Intense but balanced, with a lightly buttery center.
Finish: Crisp. Peanuts.

18YO 51.3%

Nose: Rounded but still that characteristic purity. Chamomile, elderflower. Very fragile and delicate. Blossom-like.
Palate: While there's oak, it is still sweet with slightly heavier florals: hyacinth, rose petal. Precise. It holds well on the tongue.
Finish: Clean, perfumed.
Conclusion: Stick candy.

Flavor Camp: Fragrant & Floral
Where Next? Linkwood 12yo, Speyburn 10yo, Hakushu 18yo, Tormore 1996

1976 57.3%

Nose: Light and scented: heather and cannabis, potpourri, vanilla, coconut, and orchid.
Palate: Rounded and oaky, but retains the intensity of new make. There's a lot going on.
Finish: Clean and light.
Conclusion: The retention of fragrance is the key here.

Flavor Camp: Fragrant & Floral
Where Next? Tomintoul 14yo

Benromach

FORRES • WWW.BENROMACH.COM • OPEN ALL YEAR • OCT–APR, MON–FRI; MAY–SEPT, MON–SAT

Benromach is a conundrum. When independent bottler Gordon & MacPhail bought it in 1994, it was a blank canvas. Closed since 1983, another victim of the Great Crash of the early 1980s, it was a shell. Everything you now see inside—mash tun, wooden washbacks, the stills with their external condensers—is new. The question facing G&M was, do we start from scratch and make a new whisky, or try to replicate what went before? Interestingly, they have managed to do both.

As we've seen, the distilleries of the 1960s and 1970s can be grouped mostly within a similar Flavor Camp. Benromach is different. In the new make you can detect echoes of an older Speyside, when even its lighter whiskies had middle-palate depth and a smoky edge. It's not as heavy as Mortlach, Glenfarclas, or Balmenach, perhaps, but certainly fuller than the super-light brigade. "There has been a gradual lightening of Speyside in the last 40 years as changes were made to raw materials and production processes," says Ewen Mackintosh, whisky supply manager at G&M. "When we set about re-equipping Benromach, we made the decision to create a single malt that was typical of a Speyside whisky found pre-1960s."

The end result, however, was more mysterious. The stills, for example, are a different shape and smaller than the originals, yet, as Mackintosh explains, when they compared new make from the previous and current regimes, there was a shared fingerprint. "The only factors that remain the same are the water source and some of the wood used to build the washbacks," he says. "There is also a little mystery surrounding Scotch whisky which suggests that where the characteristics of a single malt are derived will never be fully explained." In other words, despite changing everything, something about Benromach will always make it Benromach.

It would be wrong to think that this is simply a replica. New Benromach comes in wine finishes, new oak is used, there's an organic variant, a wood-smoke-rich, heavily peated one, and the fat and creamy Origins which uses 100 percent Golden Promise barley. From a period of silence, Benromach is now pretty noisy—or as noisy as the gentlemanly Gordon & MacPhail ever gets.

BENROMACH TASTING NOTES

NEW MAKE

Nose: Very sweet, with banana and maltiness. Medium to full, white mushroom, and light smoke.
Palate: Chewy and quite thick, with a little touch of soft fruitiness.
Finish: Clean, with a little peatiness.

10YO 43%

Nose: Light gold, some cedar notes and fresh oak character. Moves into pineapple and buttery malt, wholewheat bread and banana skin.
Palate: Light grip, mouth-filling. Light, dried apricot on top of that malty core. Has relaxed into an expansive character. Seems slightly oilier than the new make.
Finish: Wood smoke. Length.
Conclusion: Wood has added a new dimension, enhancing the basic richness of the spirit. A new old-style Speysider.

Flavor Camp: Fruity & Spicy
Where Next? Longmorn 10yo, Yamazaki 12yo

25YO 43%

Nose: A similar cedary note to 10yo; hints of leathery maturity. In time, citrus fruit, custard, nuts. Grassy for its age. Freshens with water. Light peatiness.
Palate: Very sweet and direct, giving a line to the 10yo, but this shows the extra spiciness of age. Light, powdered ginger and a stewed-fruit character.
Finish: Grassy and quite dry.
Conclusion: Although the stills have changed since this was made, somehow it remains the same.

Flavor Camp: Fruity & Spicy
Where Next? Auchentoshan 21yo

1981 VINTAGE 43%

Nose: Mahogany. Big, resinous. Black fruit, significant sherried impact. Moving into a sweet/savory character and some wood. Substantial weight and a dried, mulchy undertow. Black banana, Seville orange, and toasted marshmallow.
Palate: Big and intense. Varnish and slightly oily texture. Cookie-like/nutty. In time a tingle of allspice.
Finish: Smoke and dense fruit.
Conclusion: It has the weight to cope with the close attentions of sherry casks.

Flavor Camp: Rich & Round
Where Next? Springbank 15yo

Glenburgie
GLENBURGIE • FORRES

Like Miltonduff, eight miles away, Glenburgie was another of the distilleries into which its original owner, Hiram Walker, installed Lomond stills. Invented by Alastair Cunningham in 1955, the still's design contained movable baffle plates in its thick neck. The continuing belief that this was in order to make a heavier whisky is, however, overly simplistic. Cunningham's brief was to try and widen the range of distillates coming from one still. The adjusting of the plates, as well as the fact that they could be water-cooled or left dry, would, the theory went, produce different types of reflux and thereby allow different flavors to be created.

The trouble was, they didn't work particularly well. When run as wash stills the plates became coated with solids, thereby cutting back on copper availability as well as potentially producing a burnt note in the final spirit. Quietly the Lomonds were retired, scrapped, or cannibalized. Today, there are just two left. Scapa's, with its plates removed, runs as a normal wash still, while Bruichladdich has just installed one called "Ugly Betty" (Lomonds are not the most aesthetically pleasing of designs—more of a copper oil drum than an elegant swan) which ran in the Inverleven distillery.

In some ways, Miltonduff and Glenburgie can be seen as a mirror image of Diageo's Glenlossie and Mannochmore. "We always swapped between those," confirms Chivas Brothers' distilleries manager Alan Winchester, whose firm acquired the first pair when it bought Allied Distillers, "though I'd say Glenburgie was more of what I'd call a sweeter, grassier style."

Today there's no signs of the "Glencraig" Lomonds at Glenburgie, whose slightly brutal open-plan layout shows how far whisky has come since the 1823 revolution. The only suggestion of the distillery's nineteenth-century origins is a tiny stone cellar that sits somewhat incongruously in the middle of the distillery's busy roadway. Its

The sole remaining original building contains some of Glenburgie's most precious stocks.

presence here takes on a symbolic air as we bid farewell to Speyside, this heartland of malt distilling, this land of river, moor, and coastal plain; of boldness and understatement; of tradition and innovation; of origins and future possibilities; whose broad range of aromas, techniques, and philosophies has so influenced the direction of Scotch whisky.

GLENBURGIE TASTING NOTES

NEW MAKE
Nose: Very clean and light, with a touch of grassiness, linseed oil, and sweetness.
Palate: Delicate and fragrant, but also oily on the tongue.
Finish: Nutty and intense.

12YO 59.8%
Nose: Pale gold. Grassy, but being in a fairly active cask allows coconut to become the stronger personality.
Palate: When diluted (it's too hot and intense when neat) this is sweet and gentle. Vanilla bean from the cask. The gentle, tongue-sticking quality adds interest.
Finish: Grassy. Chinese white tea.
Conclusion: Assertive wood matches the intrinsic sweetness of the spirit.

Flavor Camp: Fragrant & Floral
Where Next? anCnoc 12yo, Linkwood 12yo

15YO 58.9%
Nose: Gold. Lots of acetone, almond milk. Light and sweet. Clean.
Palate: The grass has both dried into raffia and added a slight bison-grass-like fragrance, then comes a pleasant agricultural note akin to cowpats.
Finish: Light spice. Clean.
Conclusion: Gentle and attractive.

Flavor Camp: Fragrant & Floral
Where Next? Teaninich 10yo

HIGHLANDS

If Speyside illustrates the absurdity of the belief that two distilleries next to each other should make a similar style, how is it possible to link the malt distilleries that stretch from the housing schemes of northern Glasgow to the Pentland Firth? Legally, in whisky terms the Highlands are everything north of the Highland Line, which isn't Speyside, but even that boundary is a political one, abandoned in 1816, instead of the geological boundary that separates the "Low Land" from the "High Land."

This "High Land" has a powerful appeal. It is what most visitors think Scotland really is: a place of mountain and moor, of lochs, castles, soaring eagles, and stags at bay. In other words, Scotland as cliché. The Highland distilleries and their whiskies reveal a richer, living landscape. These whiskies exist because of the battle between man and his environment; they speak of folk wisdom and technology, of clearance and repopulation, and a stubborn (in Scots, *thrawn*) refusal to conform. They exist because they offer something that is outside the norm, beyond the gravitational pull of Speyside.

In the Highlands it is wise to expect the unexpected. Here we find grass, smoke, wax, tropical fruit, and currants, austerity and voluptuousness. Again, there is no unity, but there are flavor trails which can be followed: the honey that runs from Deanston to Dalwhinnie, the different fruit of the northeast coast, the unexpected blast of peat smoke in the Garioch.

Sometimes it is what *isn't* there which intrigues. Why are the surviving Perthshire distilleries clustered together in such a small area of such a fertile county, and why are they all so wildly different in terms of flavor? Why couldn't the equally rich arable lands of the east coast support whisky-making? Why are there no distilleries in Aberdeen or Inverness?

Even the seemingly coherent mini-region of the northeast coast, where every train station seems to have a distillery next to it, confounds expectations: from the barley fields of the Black Isle just north of the Moray Firth, where Scotland's first whisky "brand" was born and died, to the startling sight of snow-dusted hills on one side of the road and a moored oil rig in the deep firth on the other. In truly paradoxical Highland style, it is a place of both Pictish stones and heavy industry, of creation myths and the birth of geology; oil, and whisky, flowing land and herring fleets, and a succession of distilleries which seem deliberately to try to outdo each other in terms of weird alchemy. As you head ever further north in the ever-changing light of this forgotten coastline, the Caledonian antisyzygy is distilled.

Most of Scotland is "High Land," and this multifaceted area of hill and moor gives a disparate range of whisky styles.

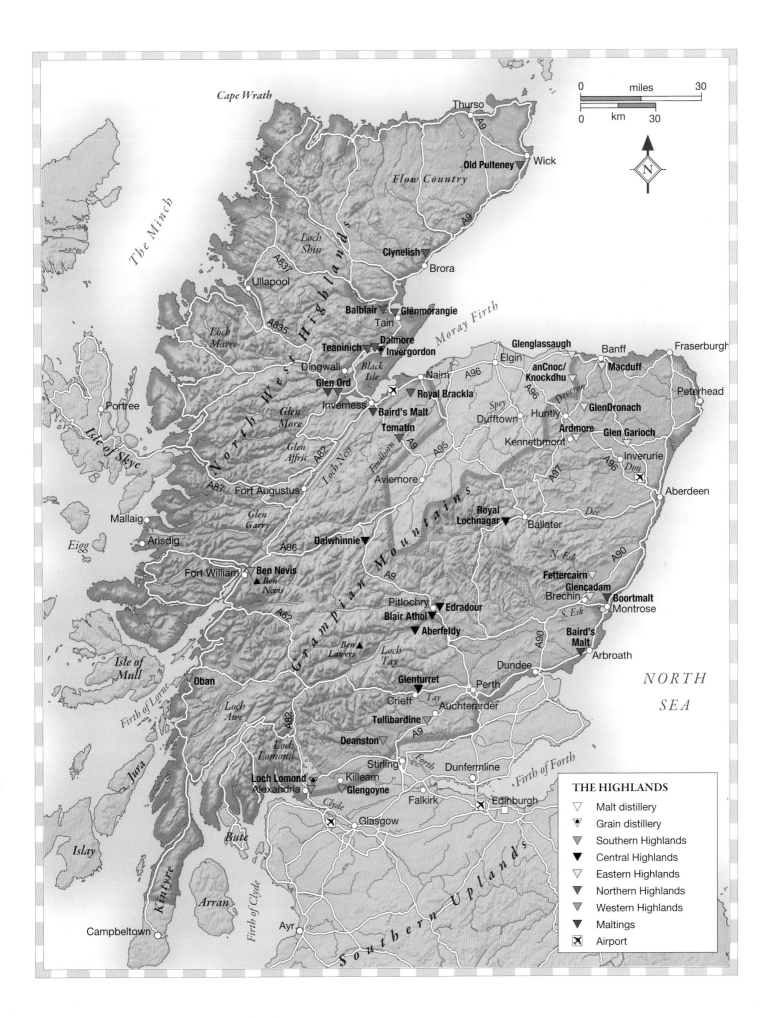

Cape Wrath

Thurso

Flow Country

Old Pulteney Wick

The Minch

Clynelish
Brora

Loch Shin

A837

Ullapool

A835

Loch Maree

Balblair **Glenmorangie**
Tain

Moray Firth

Glenglassaugh Banff Fraserburgh

Teaninich **Dalmore**
Invergordon

Elgin **anCnoc/** **Macduff**
Knockdhu

Dingwall *Black Isle* Nairn A96

Spey Huntly Peterhead

Glen Ord *Deveron*

Inverness

Royal Brackla Dufftown **GlenDronach**

Portree

Glen More **Baird's Malt**

Kennethmont **Ardmore** **Glen Garioch**

Glen Affric **Tomatin**

A95 *Don* Inverurie

Isle of Skye

A82 *Loch Ness*

A87 Fort Augustus *Findhorn* Aviemore

A97 A96 Aberdeen

Glen Garry

Royal *Dee*
Lochnagar Ballater

Mallaig

Arisaig A86

N. Esk A90

Eigg

Dalwhinnie

A9

Glen Fort William ▲*Ben*
Nevis **Ben Nevis**

A82

Fettercairn
Glencadam
Brechin

Boortmalt
Montrose

Pitlochry **Edradour**

Blair Athol

Baird's
Malt
Arbroath

Aberfeldy

Ben ▲
Lawers

Loch Tay

Dundee

Isle of Mull

Oban **Glenturret**

Crieff *Tay* Perth

Firth of Lorne

Loch Awe

A82 Auchterarder

Tullibardine A9

Jura

Loch Lomond

Deanston

Stirling *Forth* Dunfermline

Firth of Forth

Islay

Loch Lomond
Alexandria

Killearn

Glengoyne

Falkirk

Clyde Edinburgh

Isle of Bute

Glasgow

Arran

Firth of Clyde

Campbeltown Ayr

Kintyre

Southern Uplands

NORTH
SEA

THE HIGHLANDS

▽ Malt distillery
◉ Grain distillery
▼ Southern Highlands
▼ Central Highlands
▽ Eastern Highlands
▼ Northern Highlands
▼ Western Highlands
▼ Maltings
✕ Airport

0 miles 30

0 km 30

N

North West Highlands

Grampian Mountains

Raw material. Barley fields in the Highlands with the Cairngorm Mountains beyond.

SOUTHERN HIGHLANDS

Close to the northern suburbs of Glasgow they may be, but the distilleries in this part of Scotland have their own identities. They are less unified in character and more of a collection of intriguing personalities: an old farm site, a little-known distillery where innovation is the byword, Scotland's greenest site, and a resurrected plant.

Ben Lomond dominates the landscape of the Southern Highlands.

Glengoyne

KILLEARN, GLASGOW • WWW.GLENGOYNE.COM • OPEN ALL YEAR • MON–SUN

No matter which way you cut it—defining the Highlands as the "High Land" above the geological fault that runs diagonally across Scotland, or by an arbitrary line drawn by nineteenth-century politicians for tax purposes (the way in which the regions are now legally defined)—Glengoyne is a Highland distillery.

A neat, white-painted farm-style plant, it's wedged into a small valley under the volcanic plug of Dumgoyne, the most westerly end of the Campsie Fells. To the south are green fields, and then the outskirts of Glasgow.

It's an intriguing distillery, small in scale (a perfect place for the whisky newbie to learn about distillation). The new make, however, is light and intense, with grassy notes and a smooth, fruity, middle palate that stretches out slowly during maturation.

For manager Robbie Hughes, the key is the combination of time and copper, starting with fermentation. "The minimum 56-hour fermentation time ensures that most of the energy has been removed from the wash," he says, "and reduces carry-over on the wash still, which can produce a nuttier note."

Distillation is equally prolonged; again, it's time—and copper. "We try and have maximum copper contact," says Hughes. "Slow distillation runs, maximizing the copper contact, and thus increasing the estery notes. We distill very slowly, never overheating the stills. This aids reflux, so many of the heavier compounds won't get the energy to get over the neck and into the middle cut. We also have copper pipes all the way to the spirit safe."

It's this mix of vigor and central fruitiness that allows Glengoyne to enjoy long maturation and gives it a sufficient intensity of

The mash tun at Glengoyne.

character to cope easily with first-fill sherry butts. A distillery that has tended to be overlooked in the past, it's now making a strong case for future inclusion in the top ranks.

GLENGOYNE TASTING NOTES

NEW MAKE

Nose: Very intense and lifted. Grassy (sweet hay), with a light, fruity note.
Palate: Sweet, with a solid mid-palate. Good bite.
Finish: Tight and pent-up. Instant coffee granules. Spicy.

10YO 40%

Nose: Pale gold. Immediate sherried notes. Cookie dough with a little butter, then moorland/green bracken.
Palate: Light, clean, and quite dry before central sweetness comes through. With water, cake-like.
Finish: Tight and drying, becoming spicy.
Conclusion: The assumption from the new make is that this is light, but there's depth within this vibrant character.

Flavor Camp: **Fruity & Spicy**
Where Next? Strathisla 18yo, Royal Lochnagar 12yo

17YO 43%

Nose: Full. Chocolate, cedar, and country-house hotel. Sweet nut which links with cacao. Interesting sweet/savory development. Powerful, with plenty of cask.
Palate: Very ripe, with a positive cask influence. The spices flood through early and a balance is struck between the nuttiness and the sweet extract from the wood.
Finish: Soft and smooth, then a tightening of tannin.
Conclusion: Full integration and the perfect seamless balance between distillery and cask.

Flavor Camp: **Rich & Round**
Where Next? Glencadam 1978 Cragganmore 12yo

21YO 43%

Nose: Even more dense. Mushrooms, a touch of saddle oil, fruitcake, and a hint of allspice. Dried black cherry. Still has that central solidity seen in the new make. Fruitcake batter.
Palate: Earl Grey tea and dried rose petals. Espresso. Sweetness is a little hidden and the maltiness is now malt extract. Water allows some dried raspberry to show.
Finish: Tannic.
Conclusion: The cask is now in charge, but the distillery character continues to evolve underneath.

Flavor Camp: **Rich & Round**
Where Next? Tamnavulin 1963, Ben Nevis 25yo

Loch Lomond

ALEXANDRIA • WWW.LOCHLOMONDDISTILLERY.COM

One of Scotland's most remarkable (and probably its least-known) distilleries lies in Alexandria, near the southern banks of Loch Lomond. This is a strange interzone between the industrial Lowlands and the romantic Highlands, an undecided borderland that's home to housing schemes and golf clubs, mountains and urban sprawl. The distillery reflects this multiple (and slightly confusing) environment. Is it Highland? Lowland? Both? Loch Lomond is a grain and malt distillery on the same site. This is a self-sufficient whisky plant making blends, single malts, and whiskies that have legislators tied up in knots.

The malt distillery has four sets of stills of three different designs: there are the original stills from 1966, a set of standard pots from 1999, plus a new set which are larger replicas of the originals, whose design is intriguing. Often wrongly described as Lomond stills, they are pots with a rectifying column in the neck.

"I like to explain it by saying that since we can take spirit off at different plates, we are lengthening or shortening the neck," says sales and marketing director Gavin Durnin. "This has a direct effect on character." The eight different malt types produced here (including peated) provide the base for single-malt expressions and, with grain from the distillery's other plant, all the components for its High Commissioner blend.

Innovation is key here. Take yeast. Scotch whisky is peculiar in its dependency on the same strains of yeast. Not Loch Lomond. "We've been using wine yeasts for about five years," says Durnin. "The negative side is that they are twice as expensive as distillers yeast, but we feel it brings something to the whisky. The first time I tried the new make, I wondered if it was whisky."

The controversy lies in the production of a malt spirit that is produced in a column still (*see* p.16). The firm claims that it should be a malt whisky, but the Scotch Whisky Association says it's not traditional—despite the fact that this is actually a nineteenth-century technique. Not that Loch Lomond seems to care; it does things its own way.

"We're not beholden to anyone," Durnin explains. "It makes sense that a blender meets its own needs."

It might just be a model for the future.

LOCH LOMOND TASTING NOTES

SINGLE MALT NAS, 40%

Nose: Gold color. Malt bin, geranium, and lemon. With water, vegetal notes and sweet wood phenols.
Palate: A herbal/nutty and slightly oat-like crispness, then a lightly clinging mid-palate. Brass.
Finish: Oily.
Conclusion: Light spirit and fresh oak working together.

Flavor Camp: Malty & Dry
Where Next? Glen Spey 12yo, Auchentoshan Classic

29YO, WM CADENHEAD BOTTLING 54%

Nose: Fluffy and light: marshmallow, floury hamburger buns, confectioner's sugar in an apple cake. Then hardens into green fern, cucumber.
Palate: Malty and sweet to start. Nicely soft.
Finish: Clean and short.
Conclusion: A very slow maturation. Summer-fresh.

Flavor Camp: Fragrant & Floral
Where Next? Glenburgie 15yo

SINGLE MALT 1966 STILLS, NAS, 45%

Nose: Dark gold color. Masses of oak extract. Suntan oil, sauna. Very sweet and bourbon-like. With water, fruit chews and red plum.
Palate: Intense. Wood oils and pine. Touch of fresh oregano. Lemon zest.
Finish: Drying
Conclusion: Clean, light spirit, and active oak.

Flavor Camp: Fruity & Spicy
Where Next? Maker's Mark, Bernheim Wheat, Glen Moray 16yo

INCHMURRIN 12YO 40%

Nose: Very nutty/bran-like. High-toned. Peanuts, cashews, and wheat chaff.
Palate: Light-bodied. Clean spirit with a light juiciness.
Finish: Bright. Cold tea.
Conclusion: Light and clean.

Flavor Camp: Malty & Dry
Where Next? Glen Spey 12yo

Deanston
DEANSTON • STIRLING

Deanston, it must be said, doesn't look like a distillery. Neither should it, really. It was, after all, originally an eighteenth-century mill, which at one time boasted the largest waterwheel in Europe and was home to the development of the Spinning Jenny. The mill was here because of the water. The Teith River was harnessed to provide power, and today 5,283,441 gallons (20 million liters) an hour pass through the distillery turbines, meaning that it is not only self-sufficient in power, but sells off the excess. Green is the word.

Deanston is a relative newcomer, dating from just 1964, when the old mill finally closed. Once owned by Invergordon, it's now part of Burn Stewart, whose general distilleries manager, Ian MacMillan, is based here.

It's also one of Scotland's more surprising sites. The turbines are unusual, for starters, but so, somehow, is the size: the 11-ton open-topped mash tun, the little details like the brass chokers around the necks of the four fat stills, and the upward angle of the lyne arms.

The biggest surprise, for those who haven't tried Deanston recently, is the new make: all snuffed candles and beeswax, the latter easing itself into honey as it matures. It's miles away from the simple, dry style of the recent past.

"That waxiness was the original house style," MacMillan explains, "but during Invergordon's stewardship (1972–90) it got lost, and I made it my task to get it back on track." So how has he achieved this? "By changing things bit by bit, but mainly by reintroducing lower gravities (i.e. less sugar) in the worts to help promote esters. The ferments are longer and we're distilling slowly and giving the stills air rests. I believe in the old-fashioned ways."

In the extraordinary vaulted warehouse lie casks of organic whisky, while all the single-malt bottlings are now at 46 percent and non-chill-filtered. "Chill-filtering means you lose aroma and flavor," says MacMillan. "It's taken 12 years to develop these flavors. Why take them straight out? I want people to taste them!"

Deanston: a surprise at every turn.

DEANSTON TASTING NOTES

NEW MAKE
Nose: Heavy. Snuffed candle/beeswax, and, in time, wild garlic. Wet reeds and a hint of cereal underneath.
Palate: Clean and very thick on the tongue. Tongue-coating. With water, a touch of bran, but mostly it's candle wax.
Finish: Lightly clinging.

10YO CASK SAMPLE
Nose: Gold. Big American oak influence with masses of coconut. The waxiness seems to have gone, but a new honeyed aspect is emerging. Suntan lotion. Light chocolate.
Palate: Big wood influence with masses of sweetness. Very honeyed and gentle. Feel is similar to new make.
Finish: Soft, with light butterscotch.
Conclusion: Flavors show integration between wood and that waxy character, which is now becoming more honeyed.

Flavor Camp: Malty & Dry

12YO 46.3%
Nose: Light gold. Clean and sweet. Corn syrup. Some toffee, canned peach as it opens, along with melting milk chocolate. Sweet cereal in the background along with clementine.
Palate: Very sweet and concentrated. Honeyed, canned rice pudding, and slightly waxy, with a touch of crisp oak towards the finish.
Finish: Tingling and lightly spiced.
Conclusion: Now at 46.3% and non-chill-filtered, it has revealed a softer and juicier heart than the older expression.

Flavor Camp: Fruity & Spicy
Where Next? Aberfeldy 12yo, BenRiach 16yo

28YO CASK SAMPLE
Nose: Gold/amber. Classic mature character. Lots of spices and also a hint of soapiness, then lightly polished furniture—we're almost back to the beeswax of the new make, cut with caramel and pecans.
Palate: Drying. Slightly faded but with a strawberry note (that was also in the 16yo). The waxiness is back. Fragile.
Finish: Tingling, clean, cinnamon.
Conclusion: Deanston's been on a roller-coaster.

Flavor Camp: Fruity & Spicy

Tullibardine

AUCHTERARDER • WWW.TULLIBARDINE.COM • OPEN ALL YEAR • MON–SUN

It's little wonder that Tullibardine was built in Blackford, at the northern edge of the Ochil Hills. This is a site with plentiful supplies of water. Highland Spring water is bottled here, while beer has been brewed since 1488. The first Tullibardine was established in 1798, but the current site was constructed in 1949 during the postwar boom—again on the site of a brewery. Designed by famous distillery architect William Delmé-Evans, it was a tiny operation that was refitted when new owner Brodie Hepburn took over in 1953; the original mash tun and washbacks headed eight miles north to Glenturret.

It ended up with Whyte & Mackay, and in 1994 Tullibardine was mothballed, only to be reopened in 2003 by a consortium of businessmen who had the foresight to engage John Black as manager. Born at Cardhu and with 52 years in the industry, Black has, you feel, seen it all.

"I wanted more of the fruity florals in the spirit," he says. "You can overdo the foreshot run and miss those, so we tweaked it a wee bit." The major investment has, however, come in wood: first-fill bourbon and sherry casks. "This was a blending malt, used young, filled into refill," says Black. "We've no interest in that. We had to make lots of changes." A short ferment provides the cereal background, onto which there's a fragrant overtone in the new make, reminiscent of iris.

Black, however, comes back to water as one of the keys to Tullibardine. "There's lots of water here," he says. "It rains a lot as well, so there's a different microclimate. Even our rack warehouses have earth floors so there's no peaks and troughs in temperature like you get in concrete-floored modern ones. A cask needs to breathe. You'll not notice a modern warehouse effect in a blend,

The gates at Tullibardine were locked for nine years, but the distillery is now happily up and running once more.

but you will in a single malt. Maturation in the old days was slower. The accountants might not have liked it, but it worked, and good wood and vaulted warehouses are the key."

TULLIBARDINE TASTING NOTES

NEW MAKE

Nose: Quite nutty and firm to start. In time, a fragrant, floral note develops. Iris.
Palate: Intense, spicy with this continuing perfumed top note. Light- to medium-bodied, with sweetness in the center.
Finish: Dry. Then very nutty.

2004, AGED OAK 40%

Nose: Straw. Light and floral. Seems lighter than new make. Sugary-sweet with lilac and a buttery cask influence.
Palate: Fragrant. The floral notes head off towards jasmine. Plenty of vanilla extract. Delicate and clean.
Finish: Sweet and short.
Conclusion: Fresh and simple.

Flavor Camp: Fragrant & Floral
Where Next? Glen Grant 1992, Tamnavulin

1988 JOHN BLACK 56%

Nose: Dark amber. Roasted nut (as seen on new make) but still sweet. Dried fruit, canned prune, black fruit. Dunnage floors. Flowers now shifted to violet. Slightly musky.
Palate: Savory with lots of eucalyptus. Heavily perfumed. A significant change.
Finish: Now the nuts emerge.
Conclusion: Good cask, damp warehouse. There's a thread from new make.

Flavor Camp: Rich & Round
Where Next? Springbank 18yo

CENTRAL HIGHLANDS

Clustered around central Perthshire with two outliers, we find distilleries whose stories speak of secrets, smuggling, millers, farmers, royalty, and blenders being drawn back to their family roots. This once was a center of distilling activity, but only these few have survived. The reason? Quality and individuality.

The countryside watered by the River Tay has long been whisky country.

Glenturret

CRIEFF • WWW.THEFAMOUSGROUSE.COM • HOME TO THE FAMOUS GROUSE EXPERIENCE • OPEN ALL YEAR • MON–SUN

With the exception of its two outliers, the Central Highland's distilleries are clustered together in central Perthshire, as if to draw on a sense of mutual support. There would be no surprise if they did. While there are only a half-dozen central Highland stills left today, once Perthshire alone was home to over 70. The majority of those were opened in the post-1823 get-rich-quick boom when farmer-smugglers, in the spirit of Isaiah 2:4, turned away from the illegal and embraced a new lawful and peaceable life.

Many quickly discovered that there was a difference between producing small amounts of variable-quality whisky for back-door sales, and selling larger amounts of consistent quality through the front. Couple this with the economic depression of the 1840s, and most had gone by the mid-nineteenth century.

Two distilleries in this region do, however, give an idea of what these old farm sites might have looked like. The first is Glenturret on the outskirts of Crieff. The mash is a mere one ton, the stills are basic and angular, and the overall impression is of barns and outbuildings being put to secondary use rather than a purpose-built site.

Glenturret is actually an exercise in re-creation. Dismantled in 1929, it lay derelict for three decades. Now part of the Edrington Group, it's home to the Famous Grouse Experience, and as a result is one of Scotland's busiest distilleries.

In some ways, the big bird has deflected attention from the fact that Glenturret makes a delightful dram—although this itself has been re-created. "John Ramsay [Edrington's former master blender] re-engineered Glenturret when we bought it in 1990, adjusting flow rates and cut points and being more consistent in their application," says his successor, Gordon Motion. "The previous style was variable and sometimes contained a butyric [baby-vomit] note, which John was very keen to get rid of." The intensely clean, citric character of the new make shows that it has been a complete success. There's now also a heavily peated variant which is used for Black Grouse.

Re-engineered it may be, but is it still recognizably Glenturret? "We couldn't change the stills, so we can still only make a certain type of whisky," says Motion. "Any distillery is a balance between what you inherit and what it will give you. Then you can tweak within that."

Whisky-making in miniature, Glenturret is one of Perthshire's few remaining farm distilleries.

GLENTURRET TASTING NOTES

NEW MAKE

Nose: Green bitter-orange, curaçao, some sulfur, and corn with a little enamel paint behind.
Palate: Quite nutty and jalapeño-hot. Texture is creamy. Touch of sulfur on the back palate. Lightness and freshness behind, which will emerge in cask.
Finish: Clean.

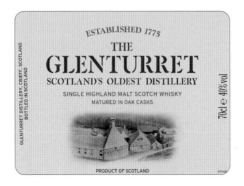

10YO 40%

Nose: Light gold. Sweet. Proving bread; linoleum, orange blossom.
Palate: Floral but quite fat and creamy on the tongue. With water, there are dried flowers, garden twine, and pink rhubarb. Lifted and citric.
Finish: Fragrant and fresh.
Conclusion: Light in aroma, but with enough weight to stand long-term maturing.

Flavor Camp: Fragrant & Floral
Where Next? Bladnoch 8yo, Strathmill 12yo

Aberfeldy

ABERFELDY • HOME TO DEWAR'S WORLD OF WHISKY • WWW.DEWARSWOW.COM • OPEN ALL YEAR • MON–SUN

Perthshire is Scotland caught in two minds, and if you stick to the main roads you'd believe it was a landscape of relaxed, grassy hills. Deviate from that crowded route, however, and you'll find a countryside that is "High Land," a place of 3,000-foot (920-metre) peaks: Ben Lawers, Meall Garbh, Schiehallion. The last was where, in 1774, the Earth's weight was calculated, and as a consequence, where contour lines and modern mapping were invented.

It's an interzone, unsure as to whether it is wilderness or manicured farmland, a place where the past seeps in. Driving along Glen Lyon from Aberfeldy you pass Fortingall, where, hunched and dark in the churchyard, there is a yew tree estimated to be 5,000 years old; follow the glen west and you end up in the peat bogs of Rannoch Moor.

It was into this borderland that John Dewar was born in 1805, on a croft in Shenavail two miles outside Aberfeldy. Apprenticed as a carpenter at age 23, he headed to Perth to join a distant relative's wine-merchant business. By 1846 he had his own business and had begun dealing in whisky. By the end of the century, Dewar's blend was selling over half a million cases worldwide. The firm needed a distillery, and in 1898 they opened one at Aberfeldy.

Why here? John's sons, John Alexander and Tommy, could have built their distillery anywhere. By the end of the nineteenth century, Speyside would have been the most logical place. Instead, they built within sight of their father's humble birthplace, where he walked bare-footed as a child, carrying peats for the fire as payment for his education. They built in Aberfeldy because of an emotional link. The beeswax/honey note is triggered in the long fermentation and

The grand Aberfeldy distillery was built by John Dewar's sons only two miles from their father's humble farmhouse.

concentrated during slow distillation in the tight-necked, onion-shaped stills. Cutting high in the run preserves a delicacy of aroma, seen best in maturation in refill or first-fill American oak, while the waxiness adds a thickness to the palate, allowing long maturation.

It may have been set up to produce a style that suited a blender's requirements, but location speaks of a psychic link to place. Aberfeldy's pragmatic and emotional reasons come together.

ABERFELDY TASTING NOTES

NEW MAKE
Nose: Sweet, with a lightly waxed note, white fruit.
Palate: Clean, focused. Highly sweet, waxy texture.
Finish: Long and slowly drying.

8YO CASK SAMPLE
Nose: Gold. Sweet. Clover honey, malty notes, pear.
Palate: Sweet and silky and surprisingly spicy. Tries to attack but is restrained by a central thick sweetness.
Finish: Lean.
Conclusion: Still evolving.

Flavor Camp: Fruity & Spicy

12YO 40%
Nose: Amber. The honey on the 8yo is much deeper but also more scented. The green pear has gone and a floral tone—the estery notes in new make—emerges with ripe apple. Fresh oak and raspberry jam.
Palate: The oak leads but has also now been bound into the sweetness, developing a butterscotch accent. Rounded. Peach juice.
Finish: Long and sweet.
Conclusion: Firing on all cylinders now.

Flavor Camp: Fruity & Spicy
Where Next: Bruichladdich 16yo, Longmorn 10yo, Glen Elgin 12yo

21YO 40%
Nose: Amber. Medium to heavy with more smoke, Corn syrup, macadamia nut. Supple. Oak is now just a support. Touch of beeswax and coconut cream. With water, heather honey and peat.
Palate: Surprisingly smoky, which adds a fragrant (but also dry) layer on top of the sweet, silky, and lightly minty/waxiness.
Finish: Long and softly spiced. Oak comes through.
Conclusion: Intriguing.

Flavor Camp: Fruity & Spicy
Where Next: Glenmorangie 25yo

Edradour & Blair Athol

EDRADOUR • PITLOCHRY • WWW.EDRADOUR.COM • OPEN ALL YEAR • JAN–FEB, MON–SAT; MAR–DEC, MON–SUN
BLAIR ATHOL • PITLOCHRY • WWW.DISCOVERING-DISTILLERIES.COM/BLAIRATHOL • OPEN ALL YEAR • SEE WEB FOR DAYS & DETAILS

Pitlochry is a prosperous-looking, wide-streeted Victorian town, but in the eighteenth and nineteenth centuries, the center of commerce lay three miles to the north in the village of Moulin. While there is some debate over the meaning of the name, it's close to the Gaelic *muileann* (mill), and where there's a mill, there's usually a distillery. In Moulin's case, there were four. One remains.

Whether Edradour is still Scotland's smallest distillery is a moot point. Any that are smaller are recent builds. The most important element is that it has survived from the Victorian era, and, more significantly, that it is still producing whisky. Want an insight into the old days of Perthshire distilling? The clues are all here.

"Essentially, it's the same kit," says Des McCagherty of Signatory Vintage, which bought Edradour in 2002. "Open-topped rake mash tun, Morton's refrigerator, wooden washbacks, and tiny stills with worm tubs. We've only changed things because we had to: the worm had to be replaced and we've put in a new stainless-steel Morton's refrigerator." The traditional kit produces an oily, sweet new make that is deeply honeyed, with some roasted-cereal notes and a ripe thickness on the palate. This robust character is now going mostly

into traditional wood. "The final thing is that Edradour is now all single malt [rather than going into blends], and we are filling into first- or second-fill wood," says McCagherty. "The bulk of Edradour goes to sherry [casks] and Ballechin [the new heavily peated variant] mainly into first-fill bourbon. Edradour lends itself to a good sherry cask."

It's another of a small but growing band of independent distillers McCagherty thinks are keeping alive techniques that would have died, and distilleries which would have disappeared.

Pitlochry is also home to Diageo's Blair Athol distillery, producing legally since 1798 and part of the Bell's stable since 1933. Bell's was a distiller that ran most of its sites in a similar fashion: cloudy worts, short ferments, condensers, resulting in a nutty/spicy style. Blair Atholl is at the extreme heavy end of this. Controlled carry-over in the wash still creates an agriculturally pungent new make that leads into a richly fruited maturity. Like Edradour, it is at its best in ex-sherry casks.

BLAIR ATHOL TASTING NOTES

NEW MAKE
Nose: Heavy malt-extract character. Cattle feed/dark grains. Seeds and nuts, then carbolic soap.
Palate: Charred and malty. Heavy and powerful.
Finish: Bone-dry.

8YO REFILL WOOD, CASK SAMPLE
Nose: Muesli: black grapes, flaked oats. Rich and broad, the fruit emerging.
Palate: Hot, full-bodied, and slightly earthy. Weighty and still burnt/dry. Powerful potential.
Finish: Dry and long.
Conclusion: This heavyweight needs time and active casks to pull out its hidden secrets.

Flavor Camp: **Malty & Dry**

12YO, FLORA & FAUNA 43%
Nose: Dark amber. Roasted malt, violet. malted loaf, some raisin. Slightly waxy, with light prune. Sweetens with water.
Palate: Heavy and sweet. Dry, malty/nutty depth with raisin on top. The charred note is now integrated into the oak, adding depth and richness. Malted milk with water.
Finish: Bitter chocolate.
Conclusion: European oak gives this big, malty spirit the extra layers it needs to balance out.

Flavor Camp: **Rich & Round**
Where Next? Macallan 15yo Sherry, Fettercairn 33yo, Glenfiddich 15yo, Dailuaine 16yo

BALLECHIN TASTING NOTES

NEW MAKE
Nose: As heavy as Edradour, with a little more cereal and wood smoke (birch logs).
Palate: Immediate smoke, but the deep fruit and oils balance.
Finish: Oily but fruity. A big spirit but balanced.

HIGHLAND
SINGLE MALT
SCOTCH WHISKY

BLAIR ATHOL

distillery, established in 1798, stands on *peaty moorland* in the *foothills* of the GRAMPIAN MOUNTAINS. An ancient source of *water* for the *distillery*, ALLT DOUR BURN ~ 'The Burn of the Otter', flows close by. This *single MALT SCOTCH WHISKY* has a *mellow deep toned* aroma, a *strong fruity* flavour and a *smooth* finish.

AGED **12** YEARS

43% vol   Distilled & Bottled in SCOTLAND.   70cl
BLAIR ATHOL DISTILLERY. Pitlochry, Perthshire, Scotland.

EDRADOUR TASTING NOTES

NEW MAKE
Nose: Heavy. Clean. Honeyed and lightly oily with black fruit, banana skins, meadow hay/hayloft. Barley.
Palate: Sweet start, then linseed oil and curranty fruit. Chewy and muscular. Mouth-coating, with firm cereal support.
Finish: Long. Drying.

1996 OLOROSO FINISH 57%
Nose: Full gold. Hazelnut oil, dry grass, touch of spice. Light earth. Roast nuts. With water, herbs, almonds.
Palate: Nutty start, then the oiliness carries it forward, becoming sweet in the center. Mouth-coating and generous.
Finish: Light aniseed.
Conclusion: Interestingly, a bit akin to Lepanto brandy.

Flavor Camp: **Fruity & Spicy**
Where Next? Dalmore 12yo

1997 57.2%
Nose: Copper. More restrained than the 1996. Lightly stewed fruits. Plum and fruitcake. With water a hint of graphite and pears poached in red wine.
Palate: The honeyed sweetness is in control. Fresh red fruit, dried raspberry, strawberry, chocolate hint.
Finish: Sweet.
Conclusion: Like many Edradours, there's an intriguing vinous quality.

Flavor Camp: **Rich & Round**
Where Next? Dalmore 15yo, Jura 21yo

Royal Lochnagar

BALLATER • WWW.DISCOVERING-DISTILLERIES.COM/ROYALLOCHNAGAR • OPEN ALL YEAR • SEE WEB FOR DAYS & DETAILS

The next central distillery lies in Deeside, an hour north of Moulin, over the high pass of Glenshee. Coming into this landscape of heavy, dark-green forests and neat towns festooned with royal warrants can lull the visitor into believing this is an easily read area of middle-class respectability, but this has always been a hideaway. Its high mountain passes gave grazing and soft passage to the drovers taking their cattle to the central markets—the same routes plied by whisky smugglers heading south from Speyside, or from Deeside's own black *bothies* (huts). Queen Victoria and Prince Albert built Balmoral Castle here because of the isolation; it was here the mourning queen sequestered herself.

The surrounding back country is scattered with fine lodges, and *shielings, bothies,* and old distilleries—a secret, hermetic, landscape in which you can easily lose yourself. Nothing is quite what it seems. The first distillery in Upper Deeside was allegedly burned down by illicit distillers after its owner, James Robertson, himself a moonshiner, set up a legal site beside the river at Crathie.

By 1845, Royal Lochnagar (it was given the accolade by Queen Victoria, who liked a tipple mixed with claret) was built. Given the nature of this part of the world, it is inevitably hidden above the Dee on a mini-plateau, its thick walls made of local granite whose flecks of mica and feldspar make it glisten in the sun after rain.

The tiniest of Diageo's plants, your assumption when looking at Royal Lochnagar's two small stills and its worm tubs is that this is a heavy site. And yet this is a distillery which, rather like Glen Elgin (*see* p.90), works against type, using techniques that hyper-extend the copper conversation.

"We take a relaxed approach here," says manager Donald Renwick, "running our stills only twice a week and giving them an air rest between distillations to allow the copper to rejuvenate. The worm tubs are kept warm—again to increase copper availablity." What should be sulfury is instead grassy, but Lochnagar's inbuilt character means this grass isn't green, but dry, offering a minor echo of its location and in its (yes, inevitably, easily overlooked) middle-palate solidity, the clues to its suitability for long-term maturation. In Upper Deeside, nothing is quite what it seems …

ROYAL LOCHNAGAR TASTING NOTES

NEW MAKE

Nose: Dry hay, light pear, and fruit with just a hint of smoke. Heavy, grassy.
Palate: Fresh and clean with distinct smokiness in a solid center. Dips on the tongue.
Finish: Clean.

8YO REFILL WOOD, CASK SAMPLE

Nose: Picked up some vanilla/white chocolate from the cask. Still the hay/straw character but the fruit is now softening. Light smoke.
Palate: A surprising citric, appley note to start, then comes the sweet straw. Retains good palate richness which is beginning to develop flavor.
Finish: Pear-like. Dry grass again.
Conclusion: Worm tubs have given this grassy malt extra depth.

Flavor Camp: **Fruity & Spicy**

12YO 40%

Nose: Clean. Grass clippings, with a touch of cereal behind. Quite fresh with a crisp nature. In time there's dry hay, hazelnut, light cumin seed, and lemon.
Palate: Sweeter than you expect. Light to medium-bodied, but a balance has been struck between the dryness (malt/hay) and sweet (praline/light fruit) notes. Cinnamon.
Finish: Gentle and clean.
Conclusion: Fresh and appealing.

Flavor Camp: **Fruity & Spicy**
Where Next? Glengoyne 10yo, Yamazaki 12yo

SELECTED RESERVE NAS, 43%

Nose: Big sherried influence. Sweet dried fruit, some rum and raisin, and a little molasses.
Palate: Fruitcake with a light tingle of allspice. The grassiness has gone, but the depth of the spirit allows it to cope with the oak.
Finish: Long and sweet.
Conclusion: A bold expression in which the distillery character plays a secondary role.

Flavor Camp: **Rich & Round**
Where Next? Glenfiddich 18yo, Dailuaine 16yo

Dalwhinnie

DALWHINNIE • WWW.DISCOVERING-DISTILLERIES.COM/DALWHINNIE • OPEN ALL YEAR • SEE WEB FOR DAYS & DETAILS

After the Deeside detour, the final distillery in this central region sits, isolated, on a high plateau between the Cairngorm and the Monadliath mountain ranges. The location, while spectacular, is initially at least surprising. This is an exposed site: the joint-highest distillery in Scotland (an honor it shares with Braeval), situated in the coldest settlement in the UK. The distillery used to have a bunkhouse that served as a billet both for workers unable to get home—because of the weather, naturally—and stranded motorists.

Why build here? The answer lies at what most visitors arriving by road think is the back of the distillery (it's actually the front): the railway line. Here is another late Victorian distillery (it was constructed in 1897) built to take advantage of the blending boom and easy access to the central belt. Whether distilling took place here prior to this is unclear. Certainly its situation as a meeting point of drove roads suggests that plenty of illicit stuff must have passed through over the years.

That honeyed thread that runs through some of these central Highland distilleries reaches its most concentrated expression here. Rich, thick, and sweet, Dalwhinnie's texture, appropriately enough given its location, allows it to be a single malt that takes on a new dimension when frozen. Honey is, however, not immediately apparent when the new make is nosed. Dalwhinnie's secret lies at the road entrance, the large circular wooden tubs containing the worm tubs for its pair of stills (*see* picture, opposite).

The new make, starved of copper contact, ends up leaving those worms as sulfury as car exhaust fumes. It seems a strange way to go about making whisky. Why, with all the technology at its disposal, doesn't Diageo simply make it without the sulfur?

"It's the price you pay at this stage for wanting the real distillery character," says Diageo's distilling and blending guru, Douglas Murray. "If you ran it to take out the sulfur, as we do at Royal Lochnagar, the new make would be grassy or fruity. If you run things to make sulfury [spirit], the building blocks which give that grassy/fruity character don't get together, so you end up with a light and delicate character. Sulfur is simply a marker when it is new. The real character lies underneath."

It lies there for a long time. Dalwhinnie slumbers under this blanket for many years, one reason for the main expression being bottled at 15yo. The other advantage of this longer maturation is that the honeyed note, just discernible in new make, has a chance to concentrate, which begs another question: where does the honey come from?

"I think honey is a halfway house," says Murray. "To simplify things we talk about waxy, or grassy, or fruity in new make, but if you run the distillery in order to make waxiness, but don't push it to the extreme (as we do at Clynelish), you end up with a pleasant, sweet butteriness." Sweetness combined with waxiness can be perceived as beeswax when young and honey when mature, the same character that you pick up at Aberfeldy or Deanston.

And here, in the tundra, surrounded by nothing but moor and mountain, time seems to slow. As the visitor takes deep breaths to calm the city-tuned heart, he is mirroring Dalwhinnie's whisky, with its steady, relaxed thickening, its accretion of density, its real personality.

Dalwhinnie new make flows through worm tubs into the spirit safe.

WORMS V CONDENSER

Although the original method of condensing, these days worm tubs are a rarity. "Shell and tube" condensers were introduced throughout the industry during the twentieth century. While more efficient, they also fundamentally altered character, removing depth. The proof of this was discovered here at Dalwhinnie when the old worms were removed. With them went "Dalwhinnie." They were quickly replaced and Dalwhinnie reappeared.

Scotland's joint-highest distillery, Dalwhinnie is also the coldest settlement in Britain.

DALWHINNIE TASTING NOTES

NEW MAKE

Nose: Pea soup, sauerkraut. Masses of sulfur. Heavy and with some peat smoke. Exhaust fumes.
Palate: Dry and deep, with sweetness underneath. Heavy.
Finish: Sulfur.

8YO REFILL WOOD, CASK SAMPLE

Nose: Leafy notes, some wood, and still some sulfur (broccoli), but also runny honey and hot butter.
Palate: The sensation is of dimly seen potential flavors. A soporific heaviness with glimpses of honey, heather, and soft fruit.
Finish: Dumb and smoky.
Conclusion: Sleeping still. Interesting to compare this at the same age to other sulfury new makes such as Speyburn, anCnoc, and Glenkinchie. Just needs time for its mature character to emerge fully.

Flavor Camp: Fruity & Spicy

15YO 43%

Nose: Mellow, with rich sweetness and lots of American oak/crème brûlée character. Whisper of smoke. Honeyed, with lemon zest. Becomes more pollen-like with water. Good weight.
Palate: Immediate and quite thick start. Smoke is light but noticeable. Good mix of dessert-like sweetness/ Greek yoghurt with acacia honey and crisp wood.
Finish: Long and soft.
Conclusion: Now fully awake, it has shaken off its sulfury overcoat to reveal itself in its honeyed guise.

Flavor Camp: Fruity & Spicy
Where Next? Balvenie Signature

DISTILLER'S EDITION 43%

Nose: Deep gold. Fat and creamy with a new tangerine marmalade note. More fragrant and smooth than the 15yo, with an added nuttier note as well, while the smoke has gone. Dessert apple and sweet pear mixing with the discreet honey.
Palate: Rounded and sweet and the grilled nut has given extra grip and interest to the palate. Orange-blossom honey and almonds.
Finish: Longer and slightly thicker.
Conclusion: Slightly juicier and more interesting. Balanced.

Flavor Camp: Fruity & Spicy
Where Next? Glenmorangie Original, Balvenie Signature

1992, MANAGER'S CHOICE
SINGLE CASK, 50%

Nose: Bright gold. Saddle soap that's gone a bit hard and tacky. Behind that are some heavy florals (think lily), currant leaf, and a touch of sulfur.
Palate: Ripe and fruity; it's reminiscent of the wee packs of breakfast spreads you get in a Scottish B&B, a hint of apricot, some tangerine marmalade, a bee's worth of honey. Light.
Finish: Whipped cream, but short.
Conclusion: A slightly less active cask and the sulfur is still there.

Flavor Camp: Fruity & Spicy
Where Next? Aberfeldy 12yo

1986, 20YO SPECIAL RELEASE 56.8%

Nose: Glowing amber. Rich and ripe. Light moor-burn notes drift in immediately, alongside dry bracken. Then it deepens: cooked autumn fruit, dried peach, heather honey running over hot crumpet, peach tart. With water, the impression is of caramelized fruit sugars and moist light-brown sugar.
Palate: Soft, with light smoke and a previously hidden spiciness. Time seems to slow it, deepen, and sweeten the flavors: spices, bitter orange. Cake-like richness, toffee.
Finish: Generous and long. Ripe fruit.
Conclusion: The depth of character is now revealed.

Flavor Camp: Fruity & Spicy
Where Next? Balblair 1979, Aberfeldy 21yo

EASTERN HIGHLANDS

Fertile it may be, but this is a relatively sparsely populated part of Scotland, distillery-wise. The reasons for this are complex and surprising—as are the whiskies. As ever, though, you can't make broad assumptions about regional style. Even the smokiest example from the Eastern Highlands is also one of the most fragrant.

The River Deveron snakes into the Moray Firth at Macduff.

Glencadam

BRECHIN • WWW.GLENCADAMDISTILLERY.CO.UK

The Eastern Highlands are littered with the memories of failed plants. Brechin's North Port; Glenury-Royal in Stonehaven; all of Aberdeen's distilleries. Our story starts, however, in Montrose, which once boasted three distilleries: Glenesk (aka Hillside), which also made grain whisky and had its own drum maltings; Lochside, another joint malt/grain plant; and Glencadam. When all three shut, it seemed as if the east coast's distilling history had been consigned to the past. Then, in 2003, Glencadam was bought by Angus Dundee. Little-known in the days of being a provider of juice for Ballantine's and Stewart's Cream of the Barley blends, its whiskies have proved to be a revelation.

The fact that Glenesk and Lochside both made grain (and the former had its own maltings) shows how rich in raw materials this part of the country is. Why, then, were distilleries decimated? Some argue that there was a lack of water, although the truth might be more business-led.

Malt whisky is all about individuality. The question at times of stock surplus is, is this whisky individual enough? All the east-coasters were small sites owned by large blending firms, and the brutal reality was that they were surplus to requirements in flavor terms. The grain whisky could be made elsewhere; the make coming from the malt plants was close enough to that coming from larger distilleries. At times of crisis (such as the late 1970s) you trim at the margins of the estate. Whisky is rarely romantic. There's precious little room for sentiment.

Glencadam, however, has survived. Its fragrant, floral style of whisky isn't that far from Linkwood (*see* p.96) with which it shares a clinging quality in the center of the tongue. This lightness of character, Angus Dundee blender Lorne MacKillop believes, comes from the fact that the stills' lyne pipes are at an upward angle, thereby increasing reflux. "It wasn't known as a single malt," he says, "and we wanted to accentuate this floral style, so decided to bottle it unchill-filtered, with no caramel added." The east coast may not be exactly rising but at least it is alive.

GLENCADAM TASTING NOTES

NEW MAKE

Nose: Fragrant/floral, with some *eaux de vie* (poire William), green grape, a little popcorn underneath.
Palate: Very sweet. Green, with a pooling effect in the middle of the tongue. Becomes more floral to the finish.
Finish: Clean and light.

10YO 46%

Nose: Light gold. Delicate, with flowers; then fresh apricot, just-ripe pear, lemon.
Palate: Gentle and smooth. Sweet, with vanilla, nutmeg, then cappuccino. Again, the fruits settle and sit in the center before the floral lift.
Finish: Apple blossom.
Conclusion: Delicate, yet with substance.

Flavor Camp: **Fragrant & Floral**
Where Next? Glenkinchie 12yo, Speyburn 10yo, Linkwood 12yo

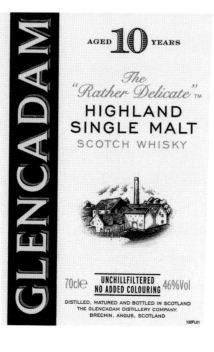

15YO 46%

Nose: Gold. Sweet and slightly restrained, with just a little more dry-leaf character. The flowers are a little heavier, the wood has added a balanced nuttiness.
Palate: Firmer than 10yo, but still tongue-coating. Nuts, a hint of light date, ripe fruit.
Finish: Fruit now pulls free.
Conclusion: Crisp with positive bite, but such sweet concentration the wood doesn't dominate.

Flavor Camp: **Fruity & Spicy**
Where Next? Scapa 16yo, Craigellachie 14yo

1978 46%

Nose: Dark amber. Full and sherried, with some *rancio*. The fruit now heading into late-autumn ripeness. The green apple is now caramel apple. Lots of chocolate, then cigar box/humidor.
Palate: Firm but smooth. Again, rich chestnut and chocolate but still that inherent ripeness. Highland toffee.
Finish: Soft and nutty.
Conclusion: Has held up well for what seems a light spirit.

Flavor Camp: **Rich & Round**
Where Next? Glengoyne 17yo, Glenfiddich 15yo, Hakushu 25yo

Fettercairn

FETTERCAIRN • WWW.WHYTEANDMACKAY.COM • OPEN TO VISITORS • MAY–SEPT, MON–SAT

The Howe of the Mearns is the setting for Lewis Grassic Gibbon's *Scots Quair* trilogy, which recounts the changes in Scotland as it moves from a golden age of agriculture to twentieth-century industrialization. Though written in the twentieth century, it can be seen as a late romantic book that both celebrates a mythical link to the land and meditates on loss: of roots, of faith, of political belief. Its narrative arc covers the same period as the rise of whisky and it is centered on the part of the world where Fettercairn sits.

The distillery sits on the flatlands looking out towards the coast, just outside a pretty town which could have acted as a model for Gibbon's Seggie, but its backdrop is mountainous. It is only a short (if hilly) trek to Royal Lochnagar.

Inside, the setup seems to speak of traditional ways of whisky-making … maybe even with some echoes of the moonshining days when the smugglers descended from Deeside with their wares. There's an open-topped mash tun, stills with soap grinders on the sides—soap was used as a surfactant to reduce frothing in the wash still but did not add flavor—although it's in the dunnage warehouses that a more modern side is revealed.

This acts as one of the experimental sites where Whyte & Mackay master blender Richard Paterson investigates wood, here most notably virgin oak, and for a specific reason: to try to surmount the burnt/vegetable note in younger Fettercairn. "It is a fight," says Paterson. "There were stainless-steel condensers here from 1995 until 2009, which gave that burnt note and made the malt a bit hard. This is a whisky that needs American oak to sweeten it, and that's

The lush lands of The Mearns surround this one-time farm distillery.

why I started using virgin oak—just to give it that sweet start."

Fettercairn, it strikes me, is an awkward delinquent which takes a long time to lose its youthful sulkiness. When it does finally reach maturity, it appears to have learned from its somewhat aggressive past and becomes a whisky to sit down with. Don't dismiss it.

FETTERCAIRN TASTING NOTES

NEW MAKE

Nose: Floury, vegetable, light sulfur, hinting at sweetness.
Palate: Firm, slightly fruity, and with weight. Seems closed.
Finish: Crisp and short.

9YO CASK SAMPLE

Nose: Preserved lemon and turnips. Slightly singed. Lots of cask influence. Vanilla hit and oak shavings.
Palate: Better than the nose with sweet cardboard, some red apple.
Finish: Nuts.
Conclusion: Still absorbing the oak, still resisting. Even now this Fettercairn seems to be refusing to grow up.

Flavor Camp: **Fruity & Spicy**

16YO 40%

Nose: Light amber. Bigger and sweeter, with a coconut/white raisin mix and a little smoke. Better balance.
Palate: Some wood smoke drifts through, along with Assam-like tea notes, some raisin, Brazil nuts.
Finish: Toffee, quite rounded.
Conclusion: It needs sweetness, it needs direction. It's a delinquent whisky.

Flavor Camp: **Rich & Round**
Where Next? Dalmore 15yo, Singleton of Glendullan

21YO CASK SAMPLE

Nose: Light balsamic vinegar tone. Lightly juicy. Touch of pot ale.
Palate: Big European oak tannins. Akin to Manzanilla *pasada*. Almond, then burning grass. Opens with water with a little smoke.
Finish: Firm and tight.
Conclusion: Plenty of cask influence trying to prize open a tough customer.

Flavor Camp: **Rich & Round**
Where Next? Glendronach 12yo

30YO 43.3%

Nose: Amber. Very soft to start, touches of cream, but an earthy, leathery quality develops. Fruits. Smoke.
Palate: Black fruits, fruitcake, cigar. Very leathery.
Finish: Shows slight fragility but balanced.
Conclusion: The teenage rebel has grown up, showing an avuncular nature from a leather armchair.

Flavor Camp: **Rich & Round**
Where Next? Benrinnes 23yo, Tullibardine 1988

30 YEARS OLD
70cle   SINGLE HIGHLAND MALT SCOTCH WHISKY   43.3%vol

Glen Garioch

OLD MELDRUM, NR ABERDEEN • WWW.GLENGARIOCH.COM • OPEN ALL YEAR • MON–FRI

At the tap o' the Garioch, in the lands o' Leith Hall, a skranky black farmer in Earlsfield did dwell ... This ballad, first sung at the start of the agricultural revolution, speaks of the hard lives of seasonally hired workers in the Garioch (pronounced *geerie*), the 150 square miles of fertile land centered around Inverurie and running northwest to Strathbogie, which was "improved" during the late eighteenth/early nineteenth centuries. It's a fecund place, an ancient, feminized landscape dominated by the mother hills of Tap O'Noth and the Mither Tap. Maybe at the end of his servitude to his *skranky* (thin, mean) master, the singer would have tried the whisky made at one of the Garioch's trio of distilleries.

If so, perhaps it would have been the eldest, Glen Garioch. Founded in 1798, by the twentieth century it had been absorbed into the Distillers Company Ltd (DCL, the precursor of Diageo) and was piling on the local peat, along with its neighbor Ardmore, resulting in that unusual style, the smoky Highlander. In 1968, DCL needed increased production of smoky whiskies for its blends but claimed there was insufficient water to expand Glen Garioch, so closed the plant and looked elsewhere— a move that resulted in the reopening of Brora in the Northern Highlands.

Lack of water in this area of springs? Bowmore's owner, Stanley P. Morrison, thought otherwise. He bought Glen Garioch, hired a local water diviner (there's a link to ancient wisdom), and found a new and plentiful water source.

Today, this tiny distillery, whose stillhouse reminds you of a conservatory, makes a peat-free spirit, but the richness of its make remains. These small stills produce a powerful punch. "What I look for in new make is a meaty, tallow character which has gone by the time it's being used in Founder's Reserve, leaving a rich depth," says Iain McCallum, blender at Morrison Bowmore

Glen Garioch's stills sit in a conservatory-stillhouse and produce a richly sweet make.

Distillers. "To me, Glen Garioch is boisterous and robust." It's clearly not in any way *skranky*.

After years of languishing on the sidelines, Glen Garioch has a new pack, new expressions, and there's potential for more to come. "It's almost silently efficient," says McCallum, "one of those undiscovered gems." How true is that of this part of the world?

GLEN GARIOCH TASTING NOTES

NEW MAKE

Nose: Cooked vegetable: cabbage, stewing nettles. Gravy, then whole-grain bread dough. With water, sweet; cow barn.

Palate: Meal-like, sweet, and long. Has a rich weight and a sulfury note.

Finish: Nutty.

FOUNDER'S RESERVE NAS 48%

Nose: Light gold. Sulfur has gone, revealing sandalwood and a lightly herbal/heathery rootiness. Becoming a little honeyed, with the oak comes hints of orange *crème brûlée* and pine sap.

Palate: Dry; a crunchy start. The solidity of the spirit gives good feel now that the wood has done its softening act. With water, butter cookies.

Finish: Long. Friable.

Conclusion: Substantial but sweet.

Flavor Camp: Malty & Dry
Where Next? Auchroisk 10yo

12YO 43%

Nose: Full gold. Toasted cereal. The sweetness carries through here. Fleshy, with a touch of nutmeg and that heathery note.

Palate: Brazil nuts, some pepper. A chunkily fruity, rich mid-palate. With water, showing a light beeswaxy note, then the herbs come back.

Finish: Long and lightly nutty.

Conclusion: Bold and generous.

Flavor Camp: Fruity & Spicy
Where Next? Glenrothes Select Reserve, Tormore 12yo,

Ardmore

KENNETHMONT • WWW.ARDMOREWHISKY.COM

The second of the Garioch distilleries is another that came into existence as major blenders looked to own their production facilities; Dewar's at Aberfeldy, Johnnie Walker with Cardhu, and here, just outside Kennethmont in 1898, the Glasgow-based blender Teacher's built Ardmore. Its size speaks of the way in which blenders had acceded to the landed gentry. Adam Teacher discovered the site when he went to visit Colonel Leith-Hay in Leith Hall (echoes of the *"skranky black farmer"*) and it is named after the Teacher's own country pile on the Firth of Clyde.

The reason for its location was threefold: access to raw materials (locally grown barley and peat from Pitsligo), plentiful water, and the fact that Kennethmont was on the Great North of Scotland Railway, which linked Inverness to Aberdeen. It is a big site, once home to a Saladin maltings plant, and its heavy, industrialized air seems somewhat out of place in this rural setting. Its links with its Victorian past remained until 2001, when the coal fires were finally removed.

Ardmore is a paradoxical whisky that somehow manages to be both heavily peated and fragrant. This bonfire-in-the-apple-orchard character has set it apart and made it prized by blenders. You cannot imagine that such a now-isolated site would have survived if it did not offer something significantly outside the norm.

While its wooden washbacks may give an influence, it's in the stillhouse that Ardmore's secrets are to be found. "The coal fires had to come out because of the law," says manager Alistair Longwell. "The difficult thing for us to do was to retain that coal-fired character, which gives heaviness, when we switched to steam. It took seven months to get the flavor back by adjusting cut points and creating hotspots inside the stills."

Although an unpeated version (Ardlair) is made these days, it's the smoke that sets Ardmore apart. "The rest of the industry moved away from us," says Longwell, "but this was the character that made Teacher's." He pauses. "It's the last bit of Teacher's that's left. It's a labor of love." Here in the farmlands, the paradox carries on a lost tradition.

ARDMORE TASTING NOTES

NEW MAKE

Nose: Wood smoke and light oiliness, with a light, grassy note behind. In time, apple skin, lime, and very light cereal tone.

Palate: Sweet and smoky. Positive weight and oiliness with a touch of citrus fruit and dried flower providing lift. A complex new make with many avenues of potential approach.

Finish: Light smoke. Clean.

TRADITIONAL CASK NAS 46%

Nose: Full gold. Sweet, oaky notes, burning leaves, dried grasses, slightly exotic. Incense, apple purée, grass clippings on a bonfire. New wood.

Palate: Fruitier than new make; the smoke is in check but when it comes, there's a hint of smoked ham, then pepper. Same oily feel, becoming sweeter and more vanilla-led.

Finish: Peppery wood smoke.

Conclusion: Finished in quarter casks, this young whisky shows the fusion of light fruit and smoke that typifies Ardmore.

Flavor Camp: Smoky & Peaty
Where Next? Young Ardbeg, Springbank 10yo, Connemara 12yo, Bruichladdich's Port Charlotte PC8

TRIPLE WOOD A WORK IN PROGRESS 55.7%

Nose: Big, oak-driven, creamy vanilla, cut with wood smoke and fruitcake. Smoke well integrated, then a lime-cordial blast.

Palate: The casks here seem to have pulled out the oily character and accentuated the hints of citrus fruit on the new make.

Finish: Only now does the smoke show itself.

Conclusion: Despite a triple-wood maturation (five years in ex-bourbon, three and a half in quarter, then three in European oak puncheon), it can cope.

25YO 51.4%

Nose: Pale gold. Dry smoke, apple wood, some earth, cedar, nut bowl, heavy peat. Very lifted.

Palate: Classic Ardmore: the top notes now released, the green apple-skin now old fruit, the smoke fully integrated. Seems delicate but the heaviness of the center pulls the complex strands together.

Finish: Long and smoky.

Conclusion: Pale due to it being aged in a refill cask. A clear line to new make.

Flavor Camp: Smoky & Peaty
Where Next? Longrow 14yo

1977, 30 YO OLD MALT CASK BOTTLING, 50%

Nose: Cow breath and sweet hay, with a hint of scented smoke. Lemon. Mature. Becomes fresher and greener in time. Privet.

Palate: Clean, leafy with an acidic energy. Orchard fruit, then hazelnut and light smoke. Balanced.

Finish: Tight and smoky.

Conclusion: Mature and balanced. Although smoky, the fragrance tips it into the fragrant camp.

Flavor Camp: Fragrant & Floral
Where Next? Hakushu 18yo

ARDMORE FOUNDED 1898 HIGHLANDS
HIGHLAND SINGLE MALT
SCOTCH WHISKY | PEATED
TRADITIONAL CASK
MATURED FOR A FINAL PERIOD IN SMALL
19TH CENTURY STYLE 'QUARTER CASKS'
NON-CHILL FILTERED
DISTILLED AND BOTTLED IN SCOTLAND
OUR *TRADITIONAL METHODS* ENSURE A DISTINCTIVE TASTE THAT
IS *FULL AND RICH*, WITH UNIQUE HIGHLAND *PEAT-SMOKE* NOTES
70 cle   ARDMORE DISTILLERY, KENNETHMONT, ABERDEENSHIRE   46% VOL

GlenDronach

FORGUE, BY HUNTLY • WWW.GLENDRONACHDISTILLERY.COM • OPEN ALL YEAR • MON–SUN

The last member of the Garioch trio lies in the village of Forgue and was built in 1826 by a consortium of local farmers. Unusually, in an industry where consolidation has always been the norm, GlenDronach remained in private hands until 1960 when it became part of Teacher's, the blending house that also owned the nearby Ardmore distillery.

Teacher's is a muscular blend, and GlenDronach was a good fit. This is a big spirit whose new make is weighty with a buttery effect that spreads over the tongue. It's built to cope with prolonged aging—and ex-sherry casks.

Though one-time owner Allied tried to make it a single-malt brand like its Garioch neighbors, GlenDronach seemed destined to be a cult until it was bought in 2006 by BenRiach's Billy Walker (*see* p.92). The focus is now on single malt.

Its muscularity, believes manager Alan McConnochie, lies in an adherence to traditional methods, such as a rake system in the mash tun. "It's a funny thing," he says. "We get the same malt as BenRiach, but if you stick your head in the mash tun here, the smell is totally different. They say water doesn't make a difference; I'm not so sure."

Long ferments in wooden washbacks take the wash to a slow distillation. "There's little reflux," says McConnochie. "There's no stress here, none of that running up and down the inside of the still." Neither did he notice a difference when the coal fires were extinguished in 2005.

GlenDronach is a malt of serious mien whose brief show of youthful exuberance in the 12yo version soon deepens, becoming serious as it does, seemingly being drawn back into the heavy earth of its birth.

Deep in color, rich in aroma, GlenDronach's opulent style is made for ex-sherry casks.

The new owner is now giving it five years in ex-bourbon casks before re-racking into oloroso sherry casks and sometimes from there into PX. "People associate GlenDronach with sherry," says McConnochie. "It's a lot harder to overpower it with wood, which is a nice problem to have." The muscularity of the farmlands shows through once more.

GLENDRONACH TASTING NOTES

NEW MAKE
Nose: Heavy but sweet and rich. Slightly earthy fruitiness.
Palate: Robust but at the same time buttery in texture, adding weight and suppleness.
Finish: Very long and fruity. Plum.

12YO 43%
Nose: Deep gold. Sweet and sherried. Tweedy, with a little plum pit and a dusty cereal note.
Palate: Big, rich with dried fruit, already good concentration. Unctuous feel, then damson. Water gives it a sudden spark of lift where grassiness develops.
Finish: Earth and sooty smoke.
Conclusion: Already full and deep with a spark of adolescent cockiness.

Flavor Camp: Rich & Round
Where Next? Glenfiddich 15yo, Cragganmore 12yo, Glenfarclas 12yo

15YO 46%
Nose: Deep amber. Leathery with some cask sulfur adding lift. Concentrated. The plums have now dried into prunes. Menthol, rum, and raisin. Bitter chocolate.
Palate: More grippy than the 12yo, with bruised black fruit. Muscular and deep. Light touch of smoke.
Finish: Concentrated, sweet black fruit.
Conclusion: Getting ever larger and not in any way dominated by wood.

Flavor Camp: Rich & Round
Where Next? Glengoyne 21yo, Glenrothes 1991, Dalmore 15yo, Macallan 18yo Sherry Oak

1989 CASK SAMPLE
Nose: Rich mahogany. Resinous, clove and coffee. Sweet and savory with some tomato paste, prunes, molasses, and tobacco.
Palate: Firm and heavily sherried but the deep fruitiness of the distillery still shows. Coffee and pipe tobacco.
Finish: Lightly bitter.
Conclusion: Even now it's unbowed.

Flavor Camp: Rich & Round

anCnoc, Macduff, & Glenglassaugh

ANCNOC • KNOCK • WWW.ANCNOC.COM / MACDUFF • PORTSOY / WWW.GLENGLASSAUGH.COM • TOURS BY APPOINTMENT

Here's an anomaly. A distillery that can't make up its mind what it is called and which, from a regional overview, seemingly can't decide in which region it belongs. Confused? Knockdhu distillery, in the village of Knock, was built in 1893 by mighty blender John Haig & Co. When it was launched as a single malt, its new owner, Inver House, felt that its name was too close to Knockando, so it became anCnoc.

AnCnoc lies close to the Speyside boundary, but as we have seen, this is a line that follows a parliamentary route rather than one possessing any geographical logic, so Knockdhu is a Highlander. Just to confuse matters further, it produces a whisky which Inver House master blender Stuart Harvey says, "is typical of what most people think of as a 'Speyside.' In fact, it might actually be more 'Speyside' than most Speysides." Those drinkers used to an appley, fragrant, light dram, may be surprised at the new make: a member of the sulfury brigade. The background is intense and citric, and it is this underlying character that is fully expressed in the bottle.

"It's actually slightly heavier than Old Pulteney," says Harvey, "because there's less reflux in the stills, while the worm tubs add that vegetable note to the new make. The biggest change in Scotch whisky's character came when distilleries took out worm tubs and installed condensers. They might be more efficient, but because they strip out sulfur they can also remove underlying weight and complexity." Here the sulfur is a marker for what lies beneath. A heavily peated variant is now being produced, but for the moment it is only used for blending. Just as well, we're confused enough!

The Eastern Highlands peter out on the Moray coastline with a pair of seaside distilleries: Macduff and Glenglassaugh. Macduff seems to suffer from a personality crisis because its make is bottled under a different name, Glen Deveron. A "new" distillery built by a group of Glasgow-based whisky-brokers to tap into the 1960s' blend boom, it lies at the heart of the William Lawson's blend. It is everything a 1960s' distillery should be—highly engineered, lauter tun, condensers, steam-driven stills—which suggests it's going to be light. Yet Macduff has depth.

The lightness here manifests itself as a malty character, or "nutty spicy," as Keith Geddes, assistant master blender at owner John Dewar & Sons, describes it. "We get cloudy wort and use short ferments of under 50 hours to help promote this," he adds. While some nutty/spicy sites head into a dusty delicacy, this is on the heavier side, thanks, he believes, to the condensing system. The wash stills' condensers are vertical, but those on the spirit stills are horizontal, giving what Geddes calls "almost a halfway house between the light character you get from condensers and the heavier style from worms." So, an engineered site? "In a way," he admits. "By the 1960s, people knew what style they needed, so maybe distilleries were engineered to answer these requirements."

Glenglassaugh, in the pretty village of Portsoy, was built in 1878 and ran intermittently until 1986, when owner Highland Distillers mothballed it. Always at the whim of blenders, its still capacity was doubled in the late 1950s to make a lighter style. It is now operational once more under a new owner: Dutch-based energy firm Scaent.

ANCNOC TASTING NOTES

NEW MAKE
Nose: Cabbage/broccoli-like sulfury notes, but with an intense lift of grapefruit and lime.
Palate: Sulfur again. Middle-weight, then comes the citrus peel along with fragrant notes.
Finish: Clean and long. Surprising weight.

16YO 46%
Nose: More obvious oak, but the aromas seem to be growing at the same pace. Apple blossom, cut flower, lime, and a little mint.
Palate: Sweet and slightly fuller, with more oak extract. Green grape; fresh (more Sancerre than absinthe).
Finish: Dusty/chalky before return of green herbs of 12yo.
Conclusion: Freshness is the key here, but allied to a supple feel.

Flavor Camp: Fragrant & Floral
Where Next? The Glenlivet 12yo, Teaninich 10yo, Hakushu 12yo

MACDUFF TASTING NOTES

NEW MAKE
Nose: Green, malty. Peanut oil and fava bean with a heavy cereal note behind.
Palate: Fat and thick, with a whiff of sulfur, then intense cassis tones.
Finish: Dries suddenly.

1984 BERRY BROS & RUDD BOTTLING 57.2%
Nose: Mahogany. Aniseed and malt. The currant leaf has moved into skunk/cannabis.
Palate: A touch paradoxical: it starts quite dry, but then the fat fruit bunches together in the center.
Finish: Very nutty, with a little dusting of white pepper.
Conclusion: Idiosyncratic to the last.

Flavor Camp: Malty & Dry
Where Next? Deanston 12yo

GLENGLASSAUGH TASTING NOTES

SCAENT ERA THE SPIRIT DRINK THAT DARE NOT SPEAK ITS NAME, I.E. NEW MAKE
Nose: Very sweet, fennel, oiliness.
Palate: Clean, sweet. Some cereal, underlying grassiness.
Finish: Clean.

HIGHLAND DISTILLERS ERA
1983 BERRY BROS & RUDD BOTTLING 46%
Nose: Mature. Very heathery, with cereal, light woods, dry, charred note balancing vanilla. Ripe soft fruit. Water makes it more herbal; a hint of birch sap.
Palate: Clover honey, cream, and pure fruit. Water shows light, oily grip with banana, peach, and heather.
Finish: Clean.
Conclusion: Suggests new style is aligned well with the old.

Flavor Camp: Fragrant & Floral
Where Next? Miltonduff 18yo, Glen Grant Cellar 1992

NORTHERN HIGHLANDS

Scotch whisky's forgotten coast stretches from north of Inverness to Wick, and although it is home to one of the biggest malt brands, the majority of its malts remain less well-known. Here, though, you will find some of the country's most idiosyncratic and individual distilleries. This is an area where aroma, flavor, and texture are pushed to the extreme.

Northern lands. Whisky's forgotten coast ends here at Thurso Bay, but the journey continues to the horizon—and Orkney.

Tomatin & Royal Brackla

TOMATIN • INVERNESS • WWW.TOMATIN.COM • OPEN ALL YEAR • MON–SUN / ROYAL BRACKLA • NAIRN

If you want to see a physical manifestation of the changing moods of the Scotch whisky industry, then head to Tomatin. The distillery was built in 1897 with two stills. This number was doubled in 1956. It rose to six in 1958, ten in 1961, 14 in 1974. Then, just as the rest of the industry was closing distilleries in the early 1980s, Tomatin increased to 23 stills in 1986. By then, it had been bought by Takara Shuzo, a Japanese distiller, who needed fillings for blends.

These days there are six pairs of stills. and production, which peaked at 3.2 million gallons (12m liters) per year, is now 528,344 gallons (2m liters). Not that Tomatin is complaining. "There has been a definite improvement over the years," says sales director Stephen Bremner, "due to a change in strategy from producing a malt for blending to a good-quality single malt." This, when you think on it, is a fair reflection of the market as well.

The make is fragrant and intense, with estery fruit and a little spice—the result of long fermentations and distillation in small but long-necked stills, whose condensers sit in the chill air. One of Bremner's improvements has come about as a result of a tightening of wood policy (Tomatin is one of the few distilleries with its own cooperage), with an increase in first-fill bourbon casks and sherry butts.

A similar intensity of character, this time with an added hay-like note, can be found in a distillery on the Moray Coast. Brackla (the Royal prefix was added in 1835) is now part of John Dewar & Sons. "We use a really clear wort here," says Keith Geddes, assistant master blender at the firm. "The spirit run is long as well: the second-longest in the estate after Aberfeldy." Add in big stills with upwardly inclined lyne arms and you've created opportunities for plenty of reflux.

TOMATIN TASTING NOTES

NEW MAKE

Nose: Intense. Fruit *eaux de vie*. Floral.
Palate: Slightly vegetal, suggesting there's some weight to come out, but overall, high-toned and sweet.
Finish: Hot.

1997 CASK SAMPLE, 57.1%

Nose: Pale gold. Light. Daffodil-like. Spring-like, with a powdery quality, then comes an intense mintiness. Lifted and fragrant. Confectioners' sugar and almond.
Palate: Sweet and floral. Hugely fragrant and lifted. Like on the nose, the mint blasts through.
Finish: Balanced and sweet.
Conclusion: Aromatic and developing interesting secondary aromas.

Flavor Camp: **Fragrant & Floral**

1990 CASK SAMPLE, 58.1%

Nose: Gold. Deeper, with earthier notes. The mint is there, but more dried and leading to a herbal quality. Oak leaves. More weight but still fragrance. Hay.
Palate: In character. Menthol cut with marzipan. Some soft, ripe fruit plus an almost hidden funkiness.
Finish: Light and tingling.
Conclusion: As the new make suggested, there's some depth here. Becoming more complex.

Flavor Camp: **Fragrant & Floral**

1980 CASK SAMPLE, 47.4%

Nose: Gold. Herbal once more, but now given a pillowy softness with more integration with the cask (bourbon refill), which itself has added spice. The mintiness is receding and the fresh flowers are now potpourri.
Palate: The cask has added a creamy note. The middle continues to thicken, but still the lifted character adds freshness. With water, there's banana skin, almond.
Finish: Long and sweet.
Conclusion: A clear, slow evolution.

Flavor Camp: **Fruity & Spicy**

ROYAL BRACKLA TASTING NOTES

NEW MAKE

Nose: Fruity/oily with porcelain-like coolness. Cucumber.
Palate: Needle-sharp. Pineapple, green apple, and unripe fruits. Very clean and slightly oily.
Finish: Grassy.

15YO REFILL WOOD, CASK SAMPLE

Nose: Assertive spiciness from the cask. Ripe apple and cinnamon/mace. The cucumber remains.
Palate: Has retained its purity. Light and floral/lilac. Concentrated in the center of the tongue, with a hint of *crème brûlée* as it goes. In time, a hint of Calvados and burnt wood sugars.
Finish: Ripe, with cream toffee, then a fresh, acidic end.
Conclusion: Has developed secondary and tertiary aromas. Needs gentle handling.

Flavor Camp: **Fragrant & Floral**

25YO 43%

Nose: Sandalwood, sweet malt, cherry, spices, and peanut shell. *Crème pâtissière*.
Palate: Sweet fruits: melon, apricot. The sweet vanilla custard takes charge with some nuttiness beneath. Oak is firm.
Finish: Dry and nutty.
Conclusion: A little maltier than new-make style but the sweetness dominates.

Flavor Camp: **Fruity & Spicy**
Where Next? Macallan 18yo Fine Oak

LIMITED **1980** RELEASE
994   07.08.2008
Cask No.   Date Bottled
700ml ℮ 47.4% alc./vol.
DISTILLED AND BOTTLED IN SCOTLAND
BY
THE TOMATIN DISTILLERY C? LT?

Glen Ord & Teaninich

GLEN ORD • MUIR OF ORD, NR INVERNESS • WWW.DISCOVERING-DISTILLERIES.COM/GLENORD • OPEN ALL YEAR • SEE WEB
TEANINICH • ALNESS, ROSS-SHIRE

The Black Isle is neither an island nor, come to think of it, is it black. This promontory, which lies between the Moray and Cromarty Firths, is, however, fertile, and the ideal conditions for cultivating barley helped make it the site of one of the most remarkable early distilleries. Ferintosh was established in the late seventeenth century by landowner Duncan Forbes. As a reward for the support he gave to Protestant King William of Orange in his battle with Catholic King James I, Forbes was granted the privilege of being allowed to distill whisky made from grain grown on his own land duty-free. Eventually he had four distilleries on his estate, netting the family £18,000 ($26,433) in profit per annum (£2m/$2.9m in today's money). Ferintosh, it's believed, accounted for two-thirds of the whisky sold in Scotland by the end of the eighteenth century, before the privilege was withdrawn in 1784.

The sites of the original Ferintosh plants have long gone. Today, its successor is Glen Ord, whose position here has all to do with the quality of the malting barley. This is a self-sufficient plant, malting all of its own requirements, thanks to the drum maltings on site which also supplies malt for six other Diageo sites, including Talisker.

Surrounded by verdant fields, it is only appropriate that Glen Ord makes a green, grassy spirit with a drift of peat running through it. Various attempts have been made to market it as a single malt; the latest finds it joining Diageo's Singleton series and draped in sherry casks.

This grassiness links Glen Ord to the first distillery on the coastal strip that we follow now on the way to Wick. Teaninich is slightly oilier thanks to a mash filter providing an ultra-clean wort, and its bulky stills maximizing copper contact. A weird exoticism pervades its aromatics: Japanese and Chinese green teas, lemongrass, and a perfume akin to bison grass.

While medium-bodied Ord melds amiably into wood, Teaninich stands apart: aloof, rapier-like, cutting through any attempts by wood to tame it. We will find this singularity is a theme that continues as we head north.

GLEN ORD TASTING NOTES

NEW MAKE
Nose: Freshly cut green grass and light smoke. With water, it's just-cut hedges.
Palate: Good weight again, with that grassy/privet note. Like chewing spring leaves, green pea-shoots. With water, some smoke emerges.
Finish: Fermenting white wine.

THE SINGLETON OF GLEN ORD 12YO 40%
Nose: Deep amber. Green-fig jam, fresh date, garden twine, garden bonfire in the distance. Brazil nuts. Sweet and plummy, with a gingerbread note when diluted.
Palate: Fruit compote, light on the palate until the center when smoke and cashew appear. Raisin cake. Vanilla towards the back. Thick.
Finish: Lightly grassy.
Conclusion: The distillery character is (just) there but this is a big, sweet variation on the theme.

> Flavor Camp: **Rich & Round**
> **Where Next:** Macallan 10yo, Aberlour 12yo, Aberlour 16yo, Glenfarclas 10yo

TEANINICH TASTING NOTES

NEW MAKE
Nose: Scented, aromatic, privet hedge, lawnmower, Japanese green tea, and green pineapple.
Palate: Intense and very green and acidic. Softens slightly with water. Has substance.
Finish: Privet. Short and hot.

8YO REFILL WOOD, CASK SAMPLE
Nose: Intense, clean, now Chinese white tea, bison grass, lemongrass. With water, a hint of gum tree.
Palate: Needle-sharp and slightly austere. Daffodils and grass. Wet bamboo. With water, a softer texture.
Finish: Clean and smoothly minty.
Conclusion: Highly individual and "Asian."

> Flavor Camp: **Fragrant & Floral**

10YO, FLORA & FAUNA 43%
Nose: Still has exotic lemongrass but now it's Chinese green tea. The austerity remains, with a little more creaminess than the 8yo. With water, green anise.
Palate: A soft start with herbs and spices. The soft center is guarded but water smooths things considerably.
Finish: Herbal.
Conclusion: Light but complex.

> Flavor Camp: **Fragrant & Floral**
> **Where Next?** Glenburgie 15yo, anCnoc 16yo, Hakushu 12yo

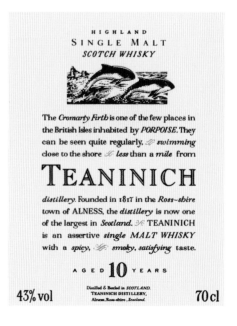

HIGHLAND
SINGLE MALT
SCOTCH WHISKY

The *Cromarty Firth* is one of the few places in the British Isles inhabited by *PORPOISE*. They can be seen quite regularly, *swimming* close to the shore *less* than a *mile* from

TEANINICH

distillery. Founded in 1817 in the *Ross-shire* town of ALNESS, the *distillery* is now one of the largest in *Scotland.* TEANINICH is an assertive *single MALT WHISKY* with a *spicy, smoky, satisfying* taste.

AGED **10** YEARS

Distilled & Bottled in SCOTLAND.
TEANINICH DISTILLERY,
Alness, Ross-shire, Scotland.

43% vol   70cl

Dalmore

ALNESS • WWW.THEDALMORE.COM • OPEN ALL YEAR • MON–FRI

A heightened sense of individuality is the key to all the whiskies from this northeast coast, and Dalmore couldn't be any further from Teaninich's steeliness. This is a whisky that revels in its richness and depth. If Teaninich seems to speak of an eternal cold spring, at Dalmore then, hard on the shores of the Cromarty Firth, it is as if it is autumn all year round. You leave with berry juice filling your mouth.

Dalmore was established in 1839, and the distillation regime seems to have been born out of some manic episode on the part of the founder. Maybe eccentricity is normal in this part of Scotland; Dalmore's stillhouse certainly revels in it.

The wash stills have flat tops and lyne arms sticking out the sides; the spirit stills have water-jacket mufflers around their necks. Both help to promote reflux and only collect specific flavors.

To make matters more complicated, they're all different sizes. Dalmore has two stillhouses. The pair of wash stills in the old stillhouse differ in size to each other; the pair in the new stillhouse match each other in size, but are different from those in the old stillhouse. Result? Different strengths and character of low wines. This similarity in design, but discrepancy between size, is repeated with the spirit stills.

Every distillery redistills the heads and tails (aka feints) from the previous run with the low wines (*see* pp.14–15). At Dalmore, the strength of this charge will vary because the stills are all different shapes and sizes. At any point there might be high-strength feints arriving from the spirit-still side along with high-strength low wines from the wash-still side; equally there might be low-strength feints and low-strength low wines; or high-strength feints and low-strength low wines, etc. That's a myriad of different flavors being combined for redistillation.

In any distillery, the ratio of low wines to feints has a significant effect on the character of the new make. When this ratio varies as wildly as it does at Dalmore, the new make is complex, sweet, and heavy but with citrus fruit tones, a touch of cassis-like fruit, and also some cereal.

"I don't know of any other distillery that does it this way," laughs David Robertson, head of brand at Dalmore. "It's a nightmare to run, but it also offers an almost infinite complexity. One reason why we don't change is because the spirit is so good."

This weight also helps dictate Dalmore's wood policy. This is a spirit that revels in the close attentions of ex-sherry casks, which add structure but also pick up the sweetness and take it deep into mysterious areas. At five years of age it seems to be absorbing wood but keeping its counsel, even at 12 there's a feeling that the forces of darkness are massing behind the oaken gates. Only at 15 years does the sleek Dalmore begin to step out.

In recent years this forgotten giant has been relaunched, propelling itself into the luxury arena with a succession of ultra-aged and ultra-expensive expressions. Sirius, Candela, and Selene all have in excess of half a century in cask and are filled with the exotic, concentrated *rancio* scents of maturity.

"Sometimes I wonder if this weird setup allows Dalmore to have the strength of character to go further," muses Robertson. "While it may lack elegance when young, it can go on to 40 or 50 years."

Althought a similarly weighty whisky doesn't appear again on this coastline, we will find that the weirdness will continue.

Dalmore is right on the shore of the Cromarty Firth.

Dalmore's stills are not only some of the weirdest in the Scotch industry; the way they operate is enough to give a normal person a nervous breakdown.

DALMORE TASTING NOTES

NEW MAKE

Nose: Sweet black fruit with a squeeze of orange juice/kumquat. Curranty.
Palate: Ripe and heavy, with underlying cereal.
Finish: Freshens into citrus-fruit tones.

12YO 40%

Nose: Quite restrained and crisp to start. This is more malt-driven. Some dried fruit.
Palate: Clean, then lots of fruitcake, orange peel, and currant leaf.
Finish: Long and fruity.
Conclusion: Already sweetening, but still finding its way.

Flavor Camp: Fruity & Spicy
Where Next? Edradour 1996 Oloroso Finish

15YO 40%

Nose: Sweet, with a heavy sherry influence. Jammy, with wild fruit (the leaf has gone into fruit). Substantial and weighty.
Palate: Soft and gentle. Dried fruit, orange pekoe tea.
Finish: Kumquat.
Conclusion: A mix of bold sherry casks; the distillery and the wood have achieved an equilibrium at this age.

Flavor Camp: Rich & Round
Where Next? Glenrothes 1991, Singleton of Dufftown 12yo

1981 MATUSALEM 44%

Nose: Round and rich with mulberry, coffee, a touch of cheese-like *rancio*, walnut. Seville orange.
Palate: Long, soft, and powerful. Robusto cigar, leaf mulch, espresso.
Finish: Long, with a light grip.
Conclusion: Has grown in intensity and power, thanks to serious attention from intense, sweet-sherry cask.

Flavor Camp: Rich & Round
Where Next? Aberlour 25yo, The Macallan 18yo Sherry Oak

CANDELA 50YO 50%

Nose: Mahogany. Oily, funky. Huge and intense. Lots of mushroom/truffle-like whisky *rancio*. Touch of soy.
Palate: Of similar intensity. Sweet, but with a fresh and surprising acidity before a mid-palate sweetness. Finishes with an explosion of cumin, fenugreek, and turmeric. Tight and lean.
Finish: Long, lingering. Cep.
Conclusion: A venerable whisky but with remarkable freshness—and a remarkable price.

Flavor Camp: Rich & Round
Where Next? Glenfiddich 40yo

Glenmorangie

TAIN • WWW.GLENMORANGIE.COM • OPEN ALL YEAR • SEPT–MAY, MON–SAT; JUN–AUG, MON–SUN

In a field outside the village of Hilton of Cadboll stands a re-creation by sculptor Barry Grove of the largest Pictish carved stone ever found. Around its twining animals, bosses, and knotwork is a scroll of stylized birds, each of which sits slightly off-center from its partner on the opposite side. "The Picts liked assymetry," says Grove, "out of which they achieved balance."

The bottom panel of the stone is the source of Glenmorangie's signet trademark: a whirling maze of linked patterns that seems both to link it to this locus, and also to replicate the assymetric whorls you see when water is added to whisky (aka vyscimetry). This is echoed in the water bubbling through the sandy base of Glenmorangie's Tarlogie Springs.

This hard water, rich in magnesium and calcium, might have an effect on lenmorangie's character. "If all of Glenmorangie's flavors equal 100%, then the water might be 5%—at max," says Dr. Bill Lumsden, head of distilling and whisky creation at Glenmorangie.

Originally a brewery, Glenmorangie's "Old Red" sandstone buildings cascade down the hill to the Dornoch Firth, a practical gravity-fed nineteenth-century design, allowing barley to enter at the top of the hill and emerge, transformed, into clear spirit at the bottom.

The start of the Glenmorangie process is contained within functional stainless-steel tuns and washbacks, but just as with any distillery, you have to find the line of flavor and try and tease it apart—just like tracing one of the strands on the Cadboll Stone.

The first part of teasing apart Glenmorangie's knots takes place in the stillhouse, where tall, slender stills stand like supermodels, their necks arcing dismissively into condensers. There's masses of copper at play here in the tallest stills in the industry.

The spirit cut starts very high-toned, filled with nail polish and cucumber, then it freshens to citrus fruit, banana, melon, fennel, and soft fruit. Aromatic, lifted, and clean, there's also a discreet cereal note adding a crisp undercurrent and preventing things getting too lush and fruity—all the result of Lumsden's narrowing of the cut when he was manager here.

Constructed out of the local "Old Red" sandstone, Glenmorangie was originally the site of Tain's brewery.

The flavor line then runs to the warehouses. While all distillers these days appreciate the importance of oak, with Lumsden it's an obsession. He only uses casks twice, and the make-up is mostly American oak. In one dank, earth-floored warehouse he explains why he keeps all the second-fill casks in this environment: "There's much more cask-driven oxidation in second fill. You get a greater range of complexities, and this environment is perfect for that to take place."

Original (as the 10yo has been renamed) is 100 percent American oak: an assemblage of first-fill ("giving the coconut and vanilla"), and these dunnage-aged second-fills ("giving those honey and minty characters"). While the Glenmorangie character is slowly interacting, becoming sweetly fruited, there's a third element in the mix: a portion of whisky aged in Glenmorangie's bespoke casks made from slow-growth, air-dried American oak. These expensive babies are seen in full light in Astar—"Original on steroids," as Lumsden puts it: all popcorn, eucalyptus, and *crème brûlée*.

Lumsden was a pioneer of finishing, the technique of giving whisky a second period of maturation in an active cask. When it works well, it gives a new twist to the line of flavor, but it can easily be overdone. "The wood makes the whisky, but wood can ruin whisky as well," he says. As ever, balance is key. In many ways Glenmorangie

Bespoke casks resting in one of Glenmorangie's many warehouses. The firm is one of the leading researchers into wood management.

operates like that Pictish scrollwork: an asymmetrical balance in which distillery character and cask play off each other. The wood gently squeezes the fruits, the juices run, oak reveals itself but always underneath runs the original character, like a Pictish pattern leading you back to the start.

GLENMORANGIE TASTING NOTES

NEW MAKE

Nose: Intense. Floral. Crystallized fruit. Citrus fruit and banana, fennel.
Palate: Sweet and intense with pure fruit. Flowers, with a light nuttiness behind. Chalk and cotton candy.
Finish: Clean.

THE ORIGINAL 10YO, 40%

Nose: Pale gold. Soft fruit, sweet sawdust, white peach, nettle, light mint, vanilla, banana split, coconut ice cream, mango, tangerine.
Palate: Light oak touches. Vanilla and cream, then cinnamon. Light touch of passion-fruit.
Finish: Minty and cool.
Conclusion: Oak is providing a very subtle and aromatically harmonious support.

> **Flavor Camp: Fruity & Spicy**
> **Where Next?** Glen Elgin 12yo, Aberfeldy 12yo

18YO 43%

Nose: *Crème brûlée*, light chocolate, eucalyptus, pine resin, raspberry, honey, crème caramel, and jasmine.
Palate: Dried fruit, mint. Ripe and palate-thickening, with light plum and hard toffee.
Finish: Allspice and long pepper.
Conclusion: Age has added a deeper layer of flavor; wood is integrated but still the distillery character shines through.

> **Flavor Camp: Fruity & Spicy**
> **Where Next?** Longmorn 16yo, Glen Moray 16yo, Yamazaki 18yo, Macallan 15yo Fine Oak

25YO 43%

Nose: Mature, deep, and sweet. Honeycomb, wax, and citrus peel with some marzipan, nut, and cigar wrapper. Red fruit cut with herbs and peach pit. Hint of clove. Those passion-fruits reappear. Luscious toffee. Sweet orange peel.
Palate: Mouth-coating. Honey. Nutmeg, red pepper flakes. Starts sweet, then deepens in the center with a light oak structure. Orange *crème brûlée*, strawberry, orange-blossom water. Complex.
Finish: Toffee, raspberry leaf, and spiced honey. Hot toddy.
Conclusion: Layered.

> **Flavor Camp: Fruity & Spicy**
> **Where Next?** Longmorn 1977, Aberfeldy 21yo, Balvenie 30yo

Balblair

EDDERTON, TAIN • WWW.BALBLAIR.COM

As you move north of Tain, the black-earthed fields that have accompanied you since Dingwall become squeezed between mountain and shore. The light, constantly changing, glancing off the firth, throws shadows across worn-down, heather-covered hills. These are Balblair's surroundings. Known as "The Parish of the Peats," the evidence is there in the encroaching heather moor. There's been a distillery in the village of Edderton since 1798, but production shifted here, next to the railway, in 1872.

Small and solid, there's a feeling of permanence about Balblair that is reflected in the whisky-making philosophy at work inside. As at Glenmorangie (which employs 20 people), staffing levels at Balblair are high by today's standards where sometimes you can walk around a distillery without seeing a soul. "We've got nine working here," says assistant manager Graeme Bowie. "I prefer the manual way of making whisky. I can see why people have moved to automation, but surely a distillery is at the heart of a community? For me, the traditional way is best."

Traditional is an appropriate word here. This is one of those cuddly old distilleries, a collection of rooms and low lintels, a place of energy, heat, and building in of aromas. "You can run a distillery like a modern brewery," says Stuart Harvey, master blender at Balblair's

owner, Inver House, "but it can become too sterile. Then you lose the character, which is exactly what you want."

The washbacks are wooden, but it's the stills where the Balblair DNA lurks. Bowie explains: "In Balblair you get that natural spiciness coming through. There's a deep bed in the mash tun and a bright wash, therefore we're encouraging floral/citric esters, but also want depth and fruit." That's where the stills come into play. Short and squat, like inverted mushrooms, there are three in the stillhouse but only two are in use.

"It's the only one of our sites with condensers," says Harvey. "Yet these stills make a complex and full-bodied spirit. We burst the yeast cells in the distillation, which is where fruit comes from: it is the

Tracking progress. Balblair sits right next to the railway line which links the northeast coast with Inverness.

equivalent of *battonage* in Burgundy, and these short, fat stills will capture it. We want a meaty/sulfury spirit, so that when you put it in cask it will react with the wood and produce butterscotch and toffee."

This heavier new make takes longer to interact with wood. Although you could describe both Balbair and Glenmorangie as "fruity," they are different types of fruit: Glenmorangie is light, carried along on a wave of oak, while Balblair is fuller and richer, needing time.

It certainly was patient insofar as becoming a front-line malt. This was another make that was earmarked for use by blenders and whose rebranding (a modernistic bottle complete with Pictish symbol, vintage rather than age-statement releases) was revelatory to malt consumers. The fruit and toffee are always present, but as it matures, the exotic,

Traditional "dunnage" warehouses are considered to have a significant impact on the charactoer of Balblair's whiskies.

heady spices come increasingly to the fore. A slow developer, it also behaves slowly in the mouth. Another very different style.

"There is this individuality to these northern malts," says Harvey. "I think they are more unique identities than the whiskies from Speyside which, to be honest, is a bit of a maze." It chimes with the comments of author (and whisky-lover) Neil M. Gunn, who was born locally. Speaking of Old Pulteney, he could "recognize some of the strong characteristics of the northern temperament" in it. It's a phrase that could apply to any one of the whiskies from this northeastern coast.

BALBLAIR TASTING NOTES

NEW MAKE

Nose: Vegetable (cabbage) sulfur with fruity, hot, weighty notes; dry leather. With water, creamy.
Palate: Little nut but dominated by spice and fruit.
Finish: Spicy.

2000 CASK SAMPLE

Nose: Pale gold. Clean, sweet, and spicy with prickles of ginger and mace alongside light coconut and marshmallow. Very sweet. With water, talcum powder and lemon.
Palate: Hugely spicy start. Light and dancing on the tongue. Unripe fruit underneath. Sweet and softening. Lots of distillery character.
Finish: Zingy. Massed spiciness.
Conclusion: Though it needs a little more time for the fruits to soften, the full Balblair spiciness is on show.

Flavor Camp: Fruity & Spicy

1990 43%

Nose: Full gold. Tropical fruit and light cereal. Luscious with some just-ripe apricot, sandalwood. Fragrant.
Palate: More oak interaction allowing a thicker feel as well as more grip. Vanilla bean and masses of sweet spice. Fruits are now baked and there's less citrus fruit. With water, *crème brûlée*, rose petal.
Finish: Fenugreek. Dry oak.
Conclusion: The cask is melding with the fruit, softening them, and, with the light cereal, adding grip and a toasty background.

Flavor Camp: Fruity & Spicy

Where Next? Longmorn 1977, Glen Elgin 12yo, Miyagikyo 1990

1975 46%

Nose: Rich amber. Deep, slightly resinous, and complex. The spice is in charge: cardamom, coriander seed, butter. The leathery note of age with heavy jasmine. A little smoky. Varnish with water.

Palate: Big and smoky. Resin, molasses, cardamom, and ginger; almost Japanese in its intensity. Best neat. Light cigar, lead, and antique-shop notes.
Finish: Still the spice. Cedar and rose dust.
Conclusion: The key here is following the spice and seeing how it interplays with the fruit.

Flavor Camp: Fruity & Spicy

Where Next? BenRiach 21yo, Glenmorangie 18yo, Tamdhu 32yo

BALBLAIR
Established in 1790
VINTAGE
19 75
Highland Single Malt
Scotch Whisky
70cl.e 46%vol.

Clynelish

BRORA • WWW.DISCOVERING-DISTILLERIES.COM/CLYNELISH • OPEN TO VISITORS • APR–OCT, MON–FRI

Caithness is sliced by broad valleys (*straths*) that run far into its interior. Man's footprints are hard to discern; there are a few piles of stones, some lines in the turf indicating old field workings. Yet until 1809 this was once pasture. On the road to Brora you pass Dunrobin Castle, the seat of the Duke and Duchess of Sutherland. It was they and their estate manager, Patrick Sellar, who cleared this land, replacing families with sheep and game, forcing their tenants onto the coast, housing them in crofts with insufficient land to cultivate crops for their own needs. Some went to sea, hunting the herring; others were put to work in the duke's new coal mine at Brora, in the parish of Clyne.

Coal transformed Brora. There were a brick works, a tile works, a tweed mill, salt panning—and, in 1819, a distillery that could use the grain the crofters grew, the coal they dug, and make the duke a handsome profit. By the end of the century, Clynelish's whisky was the most expensive on the market and on allocation. This popularity (it became part of the Johnnie Walker stable) resulted in a new distillery being constructed in 1967.

The old plant was given a reprieve in 1969, however. A dry period on Islay had stopped production and Distillers Company Ltd needed supplies of heavily peated malt. Now renamed Brora, Old Clynelish's two pots were fired up once more. This heavy, peated phase lasted until 1972, when, with Islay up and running, peating levels dropped off. They continued to fluctuate for the rest of Brora's late renaissance until it closed in 1983.

Brora is (usually) smoky, oily, and peppery with an undertone of grass. Clynelish, meanwhile, moved in a different direction. Its new make smells like a just-snuffed candle and wet oilskins. Here, the effusive, upfront aromatics of its neighbors have been subsumed in favor of texture. That waxiness is quite deliberate and created in the feints and foreshots receiver, where a natural precipitation of oils builds up over the year. In most distilleries this is removed, but not here.

From its panoramic stillhouse window, you can look out to the old Brora, lichen-festooned and decaying—the industrial equivalent of the ruined *sheilings* (cottages) in the *straths*.

CLYNELISH TASTING NOTES

NEW MAKE

Nose: Sealing wax, sour orange. Very clean. Snuffed candle and wet oilskins.
Palate: Distinctly waxy feel with a clinging quality. Mouthfilling. Broadens and deepens. This is about texture rather than flavor at this stage.
Finish: Long.

8YO REFILL WOOD, CASK SAMPLE

Nose: The heavy wax on the nose seems to have gone, revealing apricot jam, pine, sweet citrus peel, and then with water, a scented candle re-emerges.
Palate: Clean and soft. Still that textural quality now with more sweet fruit, cocoa, and masses of orange. Some oak.
Finish: The wax returns.
Conclusion: Has opened already, but will continue to develop.

Flavor Camp: **Fruity & Spicy**

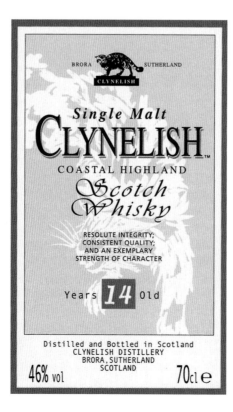

14YO 46%

Nose: The snuffed-candle (orange-scented) notes remain. Oily and clean, with some scented grass and sealing wax. Open and fresh. Ginger. With water, coastal freshness.
Palate: Good feel. More about sensation than specific flavors. In time, a waxy lift that's slightly floral, slightly citric. Hint of brininess.
Finish: Long and gentle.
Conclusion: Small change aromatically from 8yo, more a slow oak integration and a deepening of flavor.

Flavor Camp: **Fruity & Spicy**
Where Next? Craigellachie 14yo, Old Pulteney

1997, MANAGER'S CHOICE SINGLE CASK, 58.8%

Nose: Bright gold. Aromatic and slightly herbal: sage and marjoram with lifted citric notes: kumquat plus lemon; then ripe summer fruit: apple, quince.
Palate: Very spicy start alongside soft and gentle fruit and a touch of the sea. Water allows buttery oak to show alongside *crème brûlée*.
Finish: Long and smooth, with citrus–fruit tones.
Conclusion: A really waxy example, with the quince note which seems to be part of the style as well.

Flavor Camp: **Fruity & Spicy**
Where Next? Old Pulteney 12yo

Old Pulteney

WICK • WWW.OLDPULTENEY.COM • OPEN ALL YEAR • MON–FRI; EASTER–SEPT, MON–SAT

The town of Wick, where the most northerly mainland distillery is to be found, is effectively on an island separated from the rest of Scotland by the expanse of the Flow Country, a dun and tawny expanse of black pools, peat bog, and reed. Location is about more than just a place on the map; it is a psychological state. It's not unsurprising that, when it comes to whisky, Wick has its own approach. Whisky is here because of Wick, and Wick is here because of the herring.

Fish called the men into existence. The distillery, in turn, took its name from Pulteneytown, built by Thomas Telford, an urban distillery at the center of its community, producing spirits for a thirsty town. Pulteneytown is named in honor of Sir William Pulteney MP, who, at the end of the eighteenth century, had lobbied for the creation of new fishing ports in the remote north. The new harbor his vision built could hold larger crafts, which in turn landed more fish. In the nineteenth century, Wick was like the Klondike, with men hunting the "silver darlings" instead of gold.

They needed whisky. Enter James Henderson, gentleman distiller, who had been making whisky at his family seat at Stemster. Henderson moved production to the boom town.

Other distillers in this era took the opportunity to change their distilling kit. Not Henderson. His stills, Alfred Barnard wrote in 1886, were "of the oldest pattern known, similar to the old smuggler's kettle." A wash still sported an exaggerated boil bulb and flat top; the spirit still had a purifier, and its looping lyne arm looked like a stylized Pictish animal. Both sink into worms. They speak of improvisation and extravagance, but they work. "The wash still is key to Pulteney's character," says Stuart Harvey, master blender at owner Inver House. "You get massive reflux and

Wick harbor—and Old Pulteney—were both built to satisfy the demands of the town's herring fleet.

capture those top-end esters, but you also get leather. Pulteney has less spice and more fragrance than Balblair, but it's got more oil." Idiosyncratic. What else would you expect from such a location?

OLD PULTENEY TASTING NOTES

NEW MAKE
Nose: Heavy. Struck-match with an almost creamy oiliness. Linseed oil. Hint of salinity/spice. Citrus peel/orange crates.
Palate: Thick and oily with juicy, soft fruit. Touch of vanilla.
Finish: Fruity.

12YO 44%
Nose: Fruit is now bulging out. Persimmon and peach. Slightly salty and oily. Melon.
Palate: Unctuous feel. A thick bubble of oil. Juicy but slightly green fruit.
Finish: Fragrant.
Conclusion: Thick and tongue-coating.

Flavor Camp: Fruity & Spicy
Where Next? Scapa 16yo

17YO 46%
Nose: Lightly bready (bread and butter) with quince and toasty wood. More cask-driven.
Palate: Physically broader than 12yo. Touch more cream.
Finish: Juicy and long.
Conclusion: The cask has made more drive and cut down on the oiliness.

Flavor Camp: Fruity & Spicy
Where Next? Glenlossie 18yo, Craigellachie 14yo

30YO 44%
Nose: Amber. Big, resinous. Racing stable: saddle soap, hoof oil, sweet nuts. Cedar. Yeasty hint. Clean.
Palate: Marzipan. Again, the lift of citrus fruit, but now the oil has come back forcefully.
Finish: Thick.
Conclusion: A typically Pulteney weird complexity.

Flavor Camp: Fruity & Spicy
Where Next? Balmenach 1993, Glen Moray 30yo

40YO 44%
Nose: Amber. Hugely perfumed. Preserved lemon, cinnamon, that saddle-soap note again; light smoke and dried flowers. A late blossoming. Oddfellows.
Palate: Rosemary. Intense and then typical Pulteney oiliness coats the tongue. The smoke adds a new dimension.
Finish: Fragrant and long.
Conclusion: Concentrated and reduced.

Flavor Camp: Fruity & Spicy
Where Next? Longmorn 1977

WESTERN HIGHLANDS

Welcome to Scotland's smallest whisky "region," which, although it stretches the length of the long, indented, western coastline, currently boasts only two representatives. The reasons they have survived is not only down to their towns' good transport links, but because of their individual personalities and, maybe, a shared belief in an older way of making whisky.

Seil Island lies close to Oban, the gateway to the Western Isles.

Oban

OBAN • WWW.DISCOVERING-DISTILLERIES.COM/OBAN • OPEN TO VISITORS • FEB–DEC • SEE WEB FOR DETAILS

Oban's distillery is jammed between a cliff and the harborside buildings, giving it the air of being a slightly furtive operation, as if the town were trying to put on a different face to show the world. Respectability is an important element in Calvinist Scotland, and drink is, for some, decidedly not respectable. Not that this would have bothered John and Hugh Stevenson, who took advantage of a scheme in the late eighteenth century when the Duke of Argyll offered 99-year leases at nominal *tack* (rent) for anyone who would build a house. The Stevensons ended up effectively building a town and a brewery, which, by 1794, had become a licensed distillery. As far as the Stevensons were concerned, whisky was decidedly respectable. They, their son, and grandson ran the distillery until 1869.

Other whisky ventures have tried and failed on this coastline, the result of problems over transportation. Oban, however, was perfectly positioned. It remains a major hub: railway station, ferry port, the end (or the beginning) of the road between Glasgow and the Western Isles.

It's another of those distilleries which, today, works against type. Its two small, onion-shaped stills are linked to worm tubs, leading you to conclude, logically, that this should be a heavy and possibly sulfury new make. Far from it.

Instead, Oban has an intense fruitiness with a jag of citrus fruit—the result of air-resting the stills between distillations to allow the copper to revive itself and get ready to grab the sulfury compounds as they try to sneak across the lyne arms. Warmer worms also help prolong the conversation between the vapor and the copper, revealing the fruit behind and adding a spicy tingle to the new make which could be interpreted as saltiness.

Fermentation kicking off in one of Oban's washbacks.

OBAN TASTING NOTES

NEW MAKE

Nose: Fruity. Touch of rooty smoke to start. Baked peach and high citrus fruit/orange crate. Perfumed and complex. Has depth.
Palate: Creamy and gentle. Then the orange peel arrives and spreads across the tongue.
Finish: Smoke.

8YO REFILL WOOD, CASK SAMPLE

Nose: Earthy, perfumed, green banana/green orange. Weighty and slightly saline.
Palate: Sweet and dense. Masses of citrus-fruit tones. Concentrated. Numb.
Finish: Tickle of smoke.
Conclusion: The impression is of freshness and weight. This is one that might need time but it can cope with an active cask.

Flavor Camp: Fruity & Spicy

14YO 43%

Nose: Clean and crisp. Light vanilla, some milk chocolate, and lots of sweet spice. Fragrant with just a touch of smoke. Dried peels. Firm oak.
Palate: Soft sweet start with a zesty character running all the way through. Very clean, with orange notes, mint, and syrup.
Finish: Very spicy and tingling.
Conclusion: Clean and balanced and now open.

Flavor Camp: Fruity & Spicy
Where Next? Arran 10yo, BenRiach 12yo

Ben Nevis

FORT WILLIAM • WWW.BENNEVISDISTILLERY.COM • OPEN ALL YEAR • MON–FRI; EASTER–SEPT, SAT ALSO; JULY–AUG, SUN ALSO

If we return to our loose theory that "old" stills tend to produce a heavier style of spirit, then Ben Nevis would be a prime example of this in action. It also seems only appropriate that a distillery close to the buttresses of Britain's highest mountain makes a powerful dram – something light and ethereal would simply seem wrong in these surroundings.

Founded (legally) in 1825, Ben Nevis (the distillery that is) has had an intriguing career. At one point it had a Coffey still installed and was the only whisky in Scotland to marry the grain and malt components for its blend in cask before maturation.

In 1989, when it was bought by Japanese distiller Nikka, many believed that a new phase of modern-style whisky-making would be ushered in. If anything, the opposite has been the case. Old-school beliefs help to produce this "old-style" whisky, which is rich, fruity, and chewy, with an intriguing leathery note that deepens with age.

It is appropriate, too, that long-serving manager Colin Ross is a proud traditionalist. "Having being brought up on the traditional distilling practices, I've tried rigorously to maintain these within

our distillery," he explains. "Distilling has evolved over these past 185-plus years as a traditional way of life. All these changes that are being rushed through are destroying not only the industry but, in my mind, the quality of the drams emanating from each distillery."

This adherence to time-honored values means, in Ben Nevis's case, a reversion to wooden washbacks and "traditional" yeasting. Indeed, Ben Nevis is probably the only single-malt distillery in Scotland that continues to use brewer's yeast at the insistence of its manager—and its Japanese owner. This is specifically for flavor creation.

"It could well be that these two factors might have contributed to the character," says Ross. "My first manager always told me that fermentation was the most important of all, but there are so many other contributing factors: having the right conditions for distillation, keeping the copper clean inside the spirit stills to allow the vapors to come into close contact."

Physically remote it may be in whisky terms, but this distillery stands at the heart of traditional whisky-making.

BEN NEVIS TASTING NOTES

NEW MAKE

Nose: Rich and oily, with a little meaty sulfur note. Fruity behind.

Palate: Thick and sweet. Heavy mid-palate. Very chewy and clean. Rich. Less meat on the palate and more red licorice and red fruit.

Finish: Thick.

10YO 46%

Nose: Full gold. A mix of coconut, even some soft suede. Has the fatness of the new make. Thick, almost syrupy fruit-paste quality. The oak adds a nutty background.

Palate: Coconut again: coconut cream this time. The feel remains thick and sweet, with toffee notes.

Finish: Long, lightly nutty.

Conclusion: A bold whisky that is welcoming the attentions of pretty active casks.

Flavor Camp: Fruity & Spicy
Where Next? Balvenie Signature

15YO CASK SAMPLE

Nose: Pale gold. Lifted, clean, and lightly fragrant, as if a new delicacy has emerged. Still, the leather is the dominant character. Heavy and sweet. Light peat smoke.

Palate: Thick and chewy, but now an added chestnut-honey flavor. Quite creamy with water, and an added praline touch.

Finish: Supple and long.

Conclusion: Remains a substantial malt that simply continues to take whatever the cask throws at it.

Flavor Camp: Fruity & Spicy

25YO 56%

Nose: Dark amber. Rich with runny toffee; light dried fruit. The thread to follow here is leather: from soft suede to this old armchair.

Palate: Hugely concentrated. Bitter toffee, dark chocolate, black cherry. Akin to a very old bourbon.

Finish: Dry coconut. Sweet and long.

Conclusion: The thick, sweet power allows this to mature well.

Flavor Camp: Rich & Round
Where Next? GlenDronach 1989, Glenfarclas 30yo

LOWLANDS

Drumchapel, Bellshill, Broxburn, Airdrie, Menstrie, Alloa. While it may sound
more like a list of soccer teams in the Irn-Bru Scottish Third Division, this is a
list of the hidden power bases of Scotch whisky. If we glance at the map of the
Lowlands and dismiss it as a whisky desert dotted with a few single-malt oases,
we overlook the fact that this is where the bulk of Scotland's whisky is
produced, matured, and blended.

The mind-set of the Lowland distiller has always been different from
that of his Highland counterpart. By the eighteenth century, the gin craze
in London had created a healthy export market for distilling families
such as the Haigs and Steins, whose spirits were shipped south,
rectified, and poured down the gullets of the denizens of Spitalfields
and Southwark. It was the gin craze that stimulated so much of the
bungling legislation which gave birth to the Highland smuggler.

The Lowland distillers were equally affected. Export to England
was the way to make money, but export licenses were hard to obtain,
and their stills were charged on capacity (peaking at an astounding
£54/$80 per gallon). The only solution was to distill more rapidly.
As the Scottish Excise Board reported in 1797, a 253-gallon (958-liter)
still in Canonmills distillery "worked at the rate of 47 charges and
discharges in the space of 12 hours … which, even at the rate of £54
per gallon (capacity) … reduces the duty on the gallon of spirit far
below anything we had the honor formerly to represent."

They may have stayed in business, but what was the spirit like?
Burnt and brimming with fusel oils. It might have been acceptable
after rectification into gin, but for local Lowland drinkers? Even if the
quality of the illicit Highland malt was not to today's standard, it was
significantly better than this.

When legal single malt arrived post-1823, Lowland distillers once
again began to up production, but this time with a new design of still
that gave both volume and quality. In 1827, Robert Stein of Kilbagie
invented a "continuous" still. Then, in 1834, Aeneas Coffey's patent
still was installed at Grange in Alloa (*see* p.197). The Lowlands
became the capital of grain production.

But what of the Lowland malts? Traditionally they have been light,
but each distillery has approached lightness in a different way. High
demand equals larger stills; the arrival of Irish distilling expertise
equals triple distillation; there's no need to use peat. Maybe, simply,
Lowland sensibilities demanded light.

The arrival of blending in 1853 was a pragmatic and symbolic
linking of the dual approaches to whisky-making. It was this which
established the power bases and Scotch's worldwide rise. Because
of it, Glasgow is as much a whisky capital as Dufftown, a place of
dockside warehouses, cellars, elegant dining rooms, and dark-wooded
blending labs, white coats, and flat caps, the clatter of bottling lines,
the amber working-class fuel.

Whisky is more than just hills and stills. It can also be urban.

Border lands—looking across Wigtown Bay to Ben John and Cairnharrow from Carrick Point.

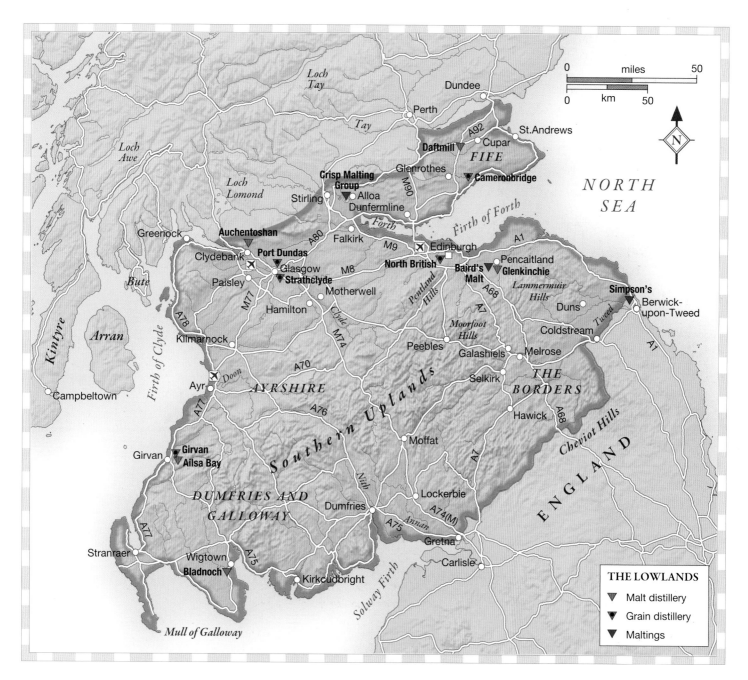

Placid and gentle—just like Wigtown's sole single malt.

Bladnoch & Ailsa Bay

WIGTOWN • WWW.BLADNOCH.CO.UK • OPEN ALL YEAR • SEPT–JUN, MON–FRI; JULY–AUG, MON–SUN / AILSA BAY • GIRVAN

A mile out of Wigtown on the banks of the meandering river from which it takes its name, Bladnoch is a big, rambling site whose considerable warehouse complex heads off up into the fields to the back of the distillery. A walk around the site leaves you with the distinct impression that every building you have entered has been accessed through the back door—there may not even be a front door.

Bladnoch is less of a purpose-built distillery and more of a random collection of dark-stoned, slate-roofed buildings, one of which happens to house whisky-making equipment. The others house a shop, a café, offices, a bar that doubles as a village hall, an old kiln that can also double as a venue, and a campsite. Bladnoch is less of a distillery and more of a community, which is what you expect from a place that has been the focal point of the village since 1817.

This feeling that every room contains a surprise starts in the mashhouse (entered through the side door), where slightly cloudy worts go through to one of the half-dozen Oregon pine washbacks, where they're allowed to ferment in a leisurely fashion for what owner Raymond Armstrong calls "four hours short of three days." The stillhouse is more of a still room. There are none of the usual bars, ladders, and guards around the stills, which poke through the floor. Stillman John Herries controls things from a rickety table, next to which is a wooden box with switches and valves. Bladnoch, it strikes you, is improvised whisky-making.

The fact that it's working at all is a surprise. It was closed from 1938 until 1956, and ran from then until 1992 (latterly as part of Bell's) before closing again in 1993. Armstrong, a Belfast-based chartered surveyor, bought it the next year, intending to convert the site into holiday homes, but then he fell in love with the place. The garrulous Ulsterman had to go back to Diageo to ask if he could restart production.

Eventually the company relented, allowing him to make 26,417 gallons (100,000 liters) a year. Spirit started flowing again in 2000,

AILSA BAY: THE NEWCOMER WITH A MISSION

An hour's drive north from Bladnoch on the Clyde coast is William Grant's Girvan grain distillery, home to one of Scotland's newest malt plants, Ailsa Bay. This wasn't, however, built as a new "Lowland" distillery but, as Grant's master blender Brian Kinsman explains, "as something flexible to take all the things we liked in our Dufftown site and replicate them."

Modeled on Balvenie, Ailsa Bay exists in order for the malt brand to grow. "The stills are Balvenie-shaped for the simple reason that it's growing as a single malt but is also a major component in blends, so there is pressure on supply." Kinsman hasn't stopped there. Four styles—estery, malty, light, and heavy peat—are produced on the site.

the interim being taken up with legal issues and the need to re-engineer the plant. "When [Bell's] left, they took a chainsaw to the electrics to ensure it would never run again. Everything bar the stills and the washbacks was either removed or destroyed," Armstrong says, looking at the new make running into the spirit safe and smiling.

The fragrant character is back as well. "They were churning it out before they closed it down," recalls Herries. "Everything was just

Scotland's most southerly distillery comes complete with café, village hall, and campsite.

Resting the stills between distillation helps preserve Bladnoch's fragrant character.

forced through. Now we're more relaxed again." That would explain the Blair Athol-like character that you pick up on the 17yo and 18yo and also why the new make and Armstrong-era 8yo all seem to resemble nectar-heavy flowers.

"The trouble with the whisky business is that a lot of enthusiasts don't appreciate the subtleties and elegance of Lowland malts," says this born-again whisky evangelist. "We just have to convince them."

BLADNOCH TASTING NOTES

NEW MAKE
Nose: Fresh and gentle, with clean floral notes and light citrus fruit.
Palate: Clean and zesty with good acidity, blossom, and a little touch of honey.
Finish: Clean and short.

8YO 46%
Nose: Light gold. Bulrushes, cut flowers, and sweet apple with a light hint of beeswax. Lemon puffs. With water a slow lift of clover honeycomb.
Palate: Clean and slightly buttery. Soft center, with fragrant flowers and that honeyed note. Becomes lightly spiced on the finish.
Finish: Light and clean.
Conclusion: Fresh as a spring day.

Flavor camp: Fragrant & Floral
Where Next? Linkwood 12yo, Glencadam 10yo, Speyside 15yo

17YO 55%
Nose: Light gold. Broader and more nutty, with that sweet undertone still in evidence, although this is more mash-like than honeyed. Freshly baked bread and apricot jam. Hot buttered toast.
Palate: Slightly perfumed quality, then settles into honey-nut cornflakes.
Finish: Spicy and a little soapy.
Conclusion: Typical of the last days of the *ancien regime*.

Flavor camp: Fragrant & Floral
Where Next? Glenturret 10yo, Strathmill 12yo

AILSA BAY TASTING NOTES

No mature spirit has been released. Nor do the new makes have names. There are six examples of the different spirit types being made.

1.
Nose: Light and estery. Sesame. Pineapple with a little brassy note. Dry.
Palate: Very pure; that estery pineapple, pear, bubblegum note along wth melon.
Finish: Soft and gentle.

2.
Nose: Clean, light, crisp with light cereal undertones.
Palate: Whistle-clean. Very pure, with green-grassiness. Has mid-palate fatness.
Finish: Crisp.

3.
Nose: Nutty with a hint of cooked-vegetable sulfur. Pot ale. Heavier.
Palate: Fatter on palate. Ripe and heavy. Lentils.
Finish: Broad and ripe.

4.
Nose: Cereal and acetone. Green almond. Less roasted than the previous.
Palate: Pure. Big, nutty, with fruit in the background. Light nuttiness/nutshell. Dry and clean.
Finish: A sudden sweetness. Will develop in an interesting fashion.

5.
Nose: Fragrant peat smoke. Rooty, with cigar and light ham. Burning wood, pear, and new tennis shoes.
Palate: Dry smoke hits immediately. Solid but with a sweet core. A big hitter.
Finish: Smoke now lifts and floats gently away.

6.
Nose: Garden bonfire with a hint of oils. Heavy and dry.
Palate: Powerful and sightly earthy. Clean but more of a foggy effect.
Finish: Long.

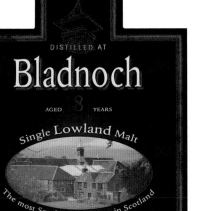

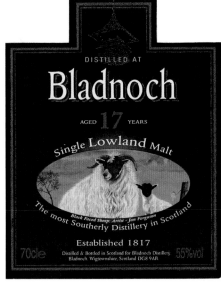

Auchentoshan & Daftmill

AUCHENTOSHAN • CLYDEBANK • WWW.AUCHENTOSHAN.COM • OPEN ALL YEAR / DAFTMILL • CUPAR • WWW.DAFTMILL.COM

Although the fourth of the handful of Lowlanders may be less than romantically situated (between the Clyde River and the main road from Glasgow to Loch Lomond), it offers another way of producing a light style: triple distillation. In the nineteenth century, this was a fairly common method of production, especially in the Lowland belt, perhaps as a result of Irish immigration, or even as an attempt to copy what, at that time, was a more successful whisky style—economics at work again. Today, however, Auchentoshan (aka "Auchie") is the only Scottish distillery that does it exclusively.

Here, triple distillation is used to build up strength and lighten character, ending up with a fresh, highly focused new make. The charge for the third (spirit) still is made up of high-strength "heads" from the intermediate. When this is distilled, the spirit cut is taken between 82–80 percent abv/164–160 proof (*see* pp.14–15).

"It's on spirit for maybe 15 minutes," says Iain McCallum, blender at owner Morrison Bowmore. "Obviously that's giving us a light character, but I don't want neutrality. Auchentoshan should have sweetness, a malty note, citric fruit, and, as it matures, a hazelnut character." Auchie's inherent delicacy of character means that McCallum cannot be too heavy-handed with oak.

DAFTMILL: SMALL BUT WITH STRONG IDEAS

Ailsa Bay is not the sole new Lowland distillery. In 2003, Fife farmer Francis Cuthbert's tiny custom-made Daftmill distillery began to produce. Unlike many new ventures, he has decided to hold on to the whisky until he deems it ready for release. Judging by the clean, rich new make and the cask samples so far, it is destined to become a cult.

"It's such a light spirit that it could easily be swamped. I believe strongly in having the character of the spirit coming through the heart of the brand," says McCallum. "And with Auchie, you have to take it easy with the oak." Light but with guts. It's another facet of the too easily dismissed Lowland style.

AUCHENTOSHAN TASTING NOTES

NEW MAKE
Nose: Very light and intense. Pink rhubarb, sweet cardboard, banana peel, leafy.
Palate: Tight and hot. Slight cookie tone, intense lemon lift.
Finish: Quick. Apple.

CLASSIC NAS 40%
Nose: Light gold. Sweet oak. Slightly dusty with a light floral note; touches of coconut from the oak.
Palate: Sweet and nutty with plenty of vanilla which takes things into a chocolate realm. The high-toned notes of new make are still in evidence.
Finish: Fresh.
Conclusion: Deftly handled oak allows character to show.

Flavor Camp: **Malty & Dry**
Where Next? Tamnavulin 12yo, Glen Spey 12yo

12YO 40%
Nose: Again, oak leads the way. Touches of hot cross bun, paprika-covered roasted almond. Citric lift.
Palate: Soft and clean, the cereal note now drifts towards spice. Still that leafy quality.
Finish: Crisp and clean.
Conclusion: Identifiably Auchie.

Flavor Camp: **Malty & Dry**
Where Next? Macduff 1984

21YO 43%
Nose: Slghtly funky maturity. Concentrated dark fruit, then come dry spices: coriander, roast chestnut, but still that intense dustiness and freshness.
Palate: Rich and liquorous, with a lavender-like flavor on the palate.
Finish: Perfumed.
Conclusion: Even at 21 years, a light spirit holds its own.

Flavor Camp: **Fruity & Spicy**
Where Next? The Glenlivet 18yo, Benromach 25yo

DAFTMILL TASTING NOTES

NEW MAKE
Nose: Sweet. Medium to full. Fat fruits and a little oily. Turkish delight.
Palate: Intense top notes play above pear and a thick, creamy texture. Clean.
Finish: Sweet and fresh, but with real substance.

EX-BOURBON CASK SAMPLE
Nose: Straw, herbal, scented grass, lily, and lemon. Becomes intensely minty with a hint of coconut.
Palate: Sweet and slightly floral. Oak is balancing and giving grip. In process of assembling itself. Soft feel.
Finish: Long and smooth.
Conclusion: Although still a work in progress, this is showing great potential.

Flavor Camp: **Fruity & Spicy**

EX-SHERRY CASK SAMPLE
Nose: Dark mahogany. Light fruitcake, walnut loaf, some resin. Big cask effect. Still young.
Palate: Assertive oak. Walnut oil. Very sweet still, especially with water. A very active cask has pulled this along quickly.
Finish: Nutty.
Conclusion: Precocious—could either be bottled soon or give weight and structure to a vatting.

Flavor Camp: **Rich & Round**

Glenkinchie

PENCAITLAND • WWW.DISCOVERING-DISTILLERIES.COM/GLENKINCHIE • OPEN ALL YEAR • DEC–MAR, MON–FRI; APR–NOV

The Lowlands are nothing if not spread out in whisky terms. To find the next distillery you have to travel east to the edge of the Borders and a similarly bucolic setting. Glenkinchie lies within arable farmland, meaning that there would have been little problem with raw materials when it was founded in 1825 on land that had belonged to the deQuincey family (hence "Kinchie").

Rebuilt in the 1890s, today Glenkinchie presents an air of solid bourgeois respectability. It's tall, brick-built, solid, and speaks of a feeling of prosperity and sureness of intent. This place was built to make whisky—a lot of whisky, and its owners were going to make a lot of money out of it.

It's little surprise, then, that when you enter the stillhouse you look down on a pair of enormous pots: the wash still, with a capacity of 8,454 gallons (32,000 liters), is the largest in Scotch whisky. It is somewhat reminiscent of the style and size distillers in Ireland were building at roughly the same time as Glenkinchie was rebuilt. As demand rose, the stills got larger, and as the stills got larger, the style of whisky changed from heavy to light. The fact that the Lowlands make gentle whiskies has nothing to do with the environment, it is down to market forces.

However, gentle is not the descriptor you'd come up with if you were to nose the new make. Cabbage soup might be closer to the mark. The clue to this also lies in the stillhouse. Those fat country squires of stills have lyne arms that go through the wall into worm tubs. Like Dalwhinnie, Speyburn, and anCnoc, this is a light, mature spirit that starts sulfury, and like those other distilleries, it's what lies beneath that is important.

An uphill struggle. Lowland whiskies are sadly overlooked by many.

The cabbagey notes fly off quicker than at Dalwhinnie, leaving a whisky that is clean and delicate, with a background grassiness but also that distinctive, worm-derived palate weight. A recent shift of the standard bottling from 10yo, where there was the occasional hint of vestigial sulfurousness, to 12yo has proved to be a sound move: those extra couple of years have helped to build weight and to reveal its full, mature character.

GLENKINCHIE TASTING NOTES

NEW MAKE

Nose: Struck-match and light cabbage water. Fragrant behind. Quite agricultural aromas.
Palate: Big sulfur hit, then dry grass, cooked vegetable. What's hiding underneath?
Finish: Sulfur.

8YO REFILL WOOD, CASK SAMPLE

Nose: Damp hay, then clover, washed linen. The sulfur is already almost gone. With water, jellied fruit: guava.
Palate: Intense sweetness. Pure and clean with a light, dry floral edge, then comes the residual sulfur.
Finish: Gentle, with a hint of struck-match.
Conclusion: A butterfly emerging.

Flavor Camp: Fragrant & Floral

12YO 43%

Nose: Clean, meadow-like. Lightly floral, apple, orange.
Palate: Sweet with a little nut, but generally a good, silky feel. Direct and clean with a little vanilla.
Finish: Lifted. Lemon cake and some flowers.
Conclusion: Attractive, with substance. Butterfly takes wing.

Flavor camp: Fragrant & Floral

Where next? The Glenlivet 12yo, Speyburn 10yo

1992, MANAGER'S CHOICE SINGLE CASK, 58.2%

Nose: Early summer aromas of thyme, lemon balm, green melon, Muscat grapes, night-scented stocks.
Palate: Gentle, with those flowers once more, along with some creaminess and fresh fig.
Finish: Lightly bitter. Lemon.
Conclusion: A light and perfumed example.

Flavor Camp: Fragrant & Floral

Where Next? Bladnoch 8yo

DISTILLER'S EDITION 43%

Nose: Gold. Fatter than 12yo, with riper, semi-dried fruits. Baked apple. Some dry oak. More substantial. Slightly more liquorous. Yellow cake, white raisins in the background. No sulfur.
Palate: Less overtly sweet to start, and wider on the tongue. Some barley sugar, dried apricot, heavier florals. Fleshy, slightly more tropical in character.
Finish: Light, sweet spice and citrus-fruit oils.
Conclusion: Here, the finish has added a new element while not killing the distillery character.

Flavor Camp: Fruity & Spicy

Where Next? Balblair 1990

ISLAY

Flat calm off the south coast of Islay. The boat's wake is barely managing to flop the bronze seaweed lazily against the chain of islets which protects this channel from the sea. Seals gaze at us, big-eyed. White sand runs under the keel. Black letters scroll slowly across a white wall opposite: journey's end. You can fly to Islay, but to appreciate the island fully you must sail there. After all, the sea as much as the land has dictated Islay's wider *terroir*. Islands behave differently than the mainland.

All of Islay's distilleries are on the coast. This allowed raw materials in … and whisky out.

Sit on the top of Opera House rocks on its west coast at sunset and look out. The sea is rolling in under a blue and turquoise sky, the wind riffling through the *machair* (plain), the world is suffused with a soft light. Everything glows as if lit from within. The next landfall is Canada. You are on the edge of the world.

Islay has been inhabited for 10,000 years, but its "modern" era starts on the coast, in places such as the tiny chapel of St. Ciaran (Kilchiaran). The monks from Ireland sought out this northern and western desert for their retreats.

It would be ideal if someone like St. Ciaran had brought distillation with him from Ireland, but it's unlikely. The art only passed into Western thought in the eleventh century. However, Islay could lay claim to being the spiritual home of distillation in Scotland, thanks to the arrival of the MacBeatha family (aka Beaton), who knew the secret of distillation. In 1300, they became the hereditary physicians of the Lords of the Isles (the MacDonalds), landing as part of Aine O'Cathain's wedding party on her marriage to Angus MacDonald. This island, therefore, is the fulcrum around which distillation, and in time, whisky, revolved. Islay isn't insular. It is part of the wider world.

By the fifteenth century whisky was being made, although it was far from the spirit of today. It would have been made from a range of cereals, sweetened with honey and flavored with herbs, but it would have been smoky. You cannot escape peat on Islay. It is the DNA of its malts. Here, the geographical *terroir* doesn't just speak, it roars.

Islay's malts start life on the peat moss. Their aromas are the product of thousands of years of maceration, compression, decay, and transformation. Islay peat is different from mainland peat; maybe that's where the seaweedy, medicinal, kipper-like aromas originate.

I asked Mike Nicolson, a former manager of Lagavulin, what being an incomer on the island was like. "There's a tighter relationship between the managers and the community here. You begin to think further out when you make decisions. You know you're part of a community which has been there for a very, very long time indeed, and that takes you into that continuum thing, where you're reminded that life is short and that you're following on from those who went before, who made an exceptional spirit in that place, for generations."

Loch Indaal. The shores of this shallow loch are the perfect place to sit with a sunset dram (or two) and contemplate the magic of Islay's location.

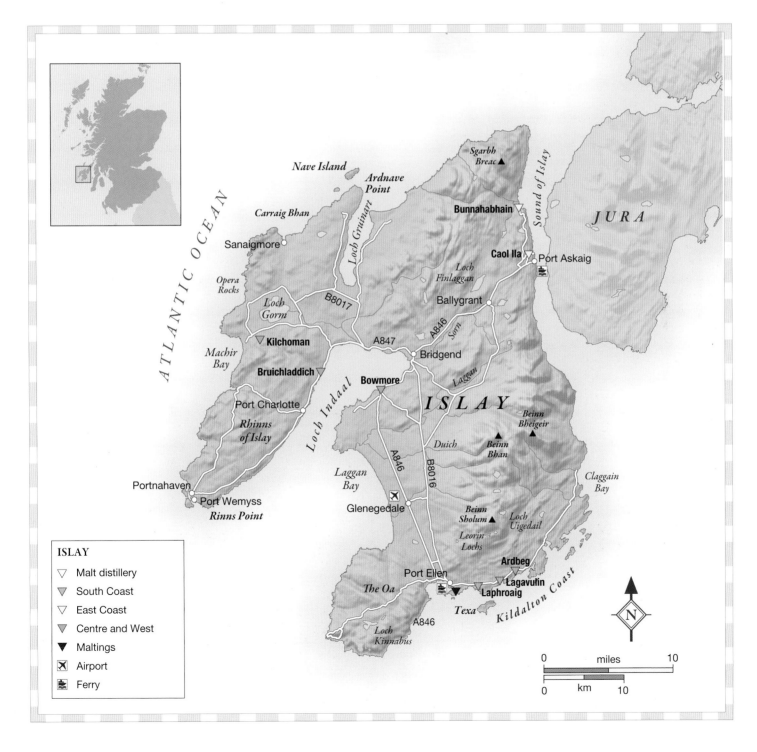

ISLAY

▽	Malt distillery
▽	South Coast
▽	East Coast
▽	Centre and West
▼	Maltings
✕	Airport
⛴	Ferry

JURA

Sgarbh Breac ▲

Sound of Islay

Nave Island

Ardnave Point

Bunnahabhain ▽

Carraig Bhan

Caol Ila ▽

Port Askaig

ATLANTIC OCEAN

Sanaigmore

Loch Gruinart

Loch Finlaggan

Opera Rocks

B8017

Ballygrant

Loch Gorm

A846

Sorn

Kilchoman ▽

A847

Bridgend

Machir Bay

Bruichladdich ▽

Laggan

Port Charlotte

Bowmore ▼

ISLAY

Beinn Bheigeir ▲

Rhinns of Islay

Duich

Beinn Bhan ▲

Loch Indaal

A846

B8016

Claggain Bay

Laggan Bay

A846

Portnahaven

Beinn Sholum ▲

Loch Uigedail

Port Wemyss

Glenegedale ✕

Leorin Lochs

Rinns Point

Ardbeg ▽

Port Ellen ⛴

Lagavulin ▼

The Oa

▼ Laphroaig

Kildalton Coast

Texa

A846

Loch Kinnabus

N

0	miles	10

| 0 | km | 10 |

Maintaining tradition. Bowmore is one of a small band of distilleries still to malt some of its own barley.

SOUTH COAST

Islay's south coast is a place of offshore reefs, tiny, seal-haunted bays, and ancient Celtic Christian sites. It is also home to the Kildalton Trio, three legendary distilleries that make the biggest, peatiest whiskies of all. Don't be fooled by first impressions, though: beneath their smoky exteriors beat hearts filled with sweetness.

Islay doesn't just attract flocks of whisky-lovers; it is also a renowned bird-watching center.

Ardbeg

PORT ELLEN • WWW.ARDBEG.COM • OPEN ALL YEAR • SEPT–MAY, MON–FRI; JUN–AUG, MON–SUN

Soot. That's what comes at you. A chimney being swept, but there's a citric edge; is it grapefruit? Then there's dulse, the local seaweed, on the rocks; a burst of violet, then banana; wild garlic in the spring woods. Ardbeg new make is a balancing act between the smoky and the sweet, between soot and fruit. The smell is with you all the way through the distillery; it's built into the bricks. But what of that sweet element? Go to the stillhouse.

There's a pipe linking the lyne arm of the spirit still to its belly, diverting any liquid that has condensed back into the still. This reflux not only helps build complexity but will help to lighten the spirit by giving the vapor more contact with copper. Result? That sweetness.

Ardbeg's recent history mirrors perfectly the vicissitudes of the whisky industry. This is a long-term business; stocks are laid down by a mix of experience and optimistic market projections. In the late 1970s it was blind optimism. Sales fell but stocks continued to be laid down. By 1982, the whisky loch resulted in a mass culling of distilleries. Ardbeg was one.

By the 1990s the place was forgotten, ghostly. When you turn the heat off in a distillery you're left with a coldness that seeps into your soul. The echo of cold metal makes you realize that distilleries have a spirit of their own.

The barrrel-roofed warehouses of Ardbeg face the sea. It is interesting to consider what effect that might have on the character of the whisky.

PEAT AND SMOKINESS

That Ardbeg is heavily peated is true, but simplistic. Ardbeg, Lagavulin, Laphroaig, and Caol Ila all happen to be peated to more or less the same level, yet the nature of the smokiness in each is substantially different. Why? It's down to distillation, mostly. The shape and size of the still, the speed at which it is run and, vitally, the cut points (see pp.14–15). Phenols don't just appear at the end of the spirit run; they drift across all the way through. Their concentration and composition change as well, meaning that those captured early in the run are substantially different from those that appear at the end. Cut points are set in order to retain—or reject—specific phenols.

Yet by the late 1990s malt's fortunes were rising, and Glenmorangie bought the site and stock for £7.1m ($10.5m) in 1997. A further few million have since been spent getting it up and running.

There have been a few tweaks. "We're running longer ferments," says Dr. Bill Lumsden, Glenmorangie's distilleries director and whisky creator. "Short ferments give you pungency from the smoke, but with long ferments you get creaminess and slightly more acidity. The stills are the same, the peating is the same, but the spirit run has been tweaked a little."

Islay peat—and lots of it: a key ingredient in the creation of Ardbeg's individual character.

on these inconsistencies. Whisky-makers may hate vintage variations, but whisky-nuts love them. Trying to keep both happy has involved a balancing act: a core range supplemented by a selection of "wonderful oddities," as Lumsden calls them. Examples include the recent heavily peated Supernova.

A wood policy has been put in place with more first-fill American oak in the system. "The main change was that the quality of wood is now higher," says Lumsden. "Now we can flesh out the rawness."

It has been a long haul between purchase and the release of the first Glenmorangie-owned Ardbeg, a process charted by releases that marked the incremental progress of the spirit: "Very Young," "Still Young," "Almost There."

"My objective was to re-create the original house style," says Lumsden. "The 'Young' range was tongue-in-cheek, but it showed what we were doing. Old Ardbeg was sooty and tarry, but the quality was also inconsistent; every year was different. We needed consistency." The problem was that the cult of Ardbeg was built

Holes in the stock profile have also meant a need for creative blending, which in turn has liberated Ardbeg from age statements.

"Uigeadail was to give an idea of the old style; Corryvreckan to show Ardbeg in French oak; Airigh nam Beist was my homage to the old 17yo," Lumsden explains.

There's a swagger to Ardbeg these days as if the distillery itself had reclaimed its destiny.

"It's difficult to talk empirically about how much a distillery dictates what it is going to make," says Lumsden, "but I'd reckon it's 30 percent us and the rest is the character of the place, the history. We've had to work sympathetically around what was there. Distilleries are somehow alive."

ARDBEG TASTING NOTES

NEW MAKE

Nose: Sweet-and-sooty touch of dulse and rock pools. Lightly oily then peat smoke, unripe banana, garlic, violet root, tomato leaf. With water, creosote and Chinese cough medicine, solvent.

Palate: Big, sooty, and intense, slightly peppery. Sweet-centered. Mossy peat, grapefruit.

Finish: Oatcake.

10YO 46%

Nose: Pale gold. Lots of American oak, custard apples, vanilla. Lightly medicinal, then grapefruit. The seaweed has changed to wet kelp. With water, Band-Aids and antiseptic cream.

Palate: Sweet and concentrated, moving into pepper, then the build of smoke. Sweet pear in middle.

Finish: Smoked toffee.

Conclusion: The pungency of new make has gone as the wood now starts to integrate.

Flavor Camp: Smoky & Peaty
Where Next? Caol Ila Cask Strength

AIRIGH NAM BEIST 1990 46%

Nose: Extends the seaweed notes, but also now brings in some fresh coconut. The peat has become more turfy, along with marram grass. Then comes a big, thick, oily note, tar, and lime.

Palate: High salinity, then black licorice, creosote, charcoal. Lime leaf/oil. Scented, heavy, and ripe. The smoke shifts to the back.

Finish: Oily. Tar and creosote.

Conclusion: A powerful yet somehow elegant expression.

Flavor Camp: Smoky & Peaty
Where Next? Lagavulin 16yo, Longrow 14yo

LORD OF THE ISLES 25YO 46%

Nose: Concentrated mix of decaying fruit and storm beach: dried seaweed, timbers. The smoke and creosote have been reduced to balsam and bog myrtle. Gentle oiliness as it slows.

Palate: Old with touches of fish box, mint, and bay leaf. Smooth but still sweet underneath. Tarry rope and pipe smoke.

Finish: Smokehouse. Long.

Conclusion: The smoke hasn't gone; it has just been absorbed.

Flavor Camp: Smoky & Peaty
Where Next? Laphroaig 25yo

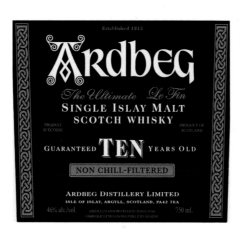

Lagavulin

PORT ELLEN • WWW.DISCOVERING-DISTILLERIES.COM/LAGAVULIN • OPEN ALL YEAR • SEE WEB FOR DAYS & DETAILS

The Kildalton coast is indented by small rocky bays, its rocks fracturing the thin earth—a place of hideouts and hermetic practices. From here, you can see the other points of the cradle of distillation: Kintyre slumping opposite, the blue hills of Antrim on the horizon. Guarding Lagavulin Bay are the ruins of Dunyvaig Castle, the final destination of Aine O'Cathain's wedding flotilla in 1300 (*see* p.152).

If Ardbeg sprawls across its bay, then Lagavulin seems compressed by its location, the buildings forced upwards, the present dominating the past, the sheer white-painted walls looking down on the black stumps of the ruined castle, the silent bell on the hill. The lords' days are over, it seems to say. Now is the time for whisky.

The scene wouldn't have been nearly as grand when the two legal distilleries that once stood here were established at Lagavulin Farm in 1816 and 1817. The bay was regarded as the center of production on the island, with up to ten small-scale illicit operations working here before the Islay *gaugers* (tax officers) and landlords clamped down on the practice. By 1835, there was a single plant, and it had grown into Islay's largest distillery by the end of the century.

Water rushes in from hill lochs down the *lade* (channel) into the mash house as you enter what looks like the original late Victorian office complex, but which in fact are the original malt barns given

PORT ELLEN MALT WHISKY: GONE BUT NOT FORGOTTEN

Lagavulin's owner, Diageo, also owns Caol Ila and the Port Ellen Maltings, which supplies peated malt for some of the island's plants. Until 1983 it also had a third distillery whose shell now sits in the shadow of the maltings. Port Ellen was built in 1830 and had been exported as a single malt in the nineteenth century, but the combination of the expansion at Caol Ila in the early 1970s and the slump at the end of that decade sealed its fate. It is now a cult malt whose austere, pier-head aromas have become revered.

a sympathetic makeover. Breathe in: there's smoke once again. One previous manager, fresh from the mainland, hit the fire alarm when he first arrived here—but the smoke seems different to Ardbeg's. All of Lagavulin's malt is peated at the same place: the Port Ellen maltings, and it is also in the "high smoke" bracket.

The trail of smoke leads you through the prickling CO_2-laden tun room, past the hot, cereal smells of the mash tun into a short, covered

Lagavulin's bay was originally the site of one of the castles occupied by the Lords of the Isles.

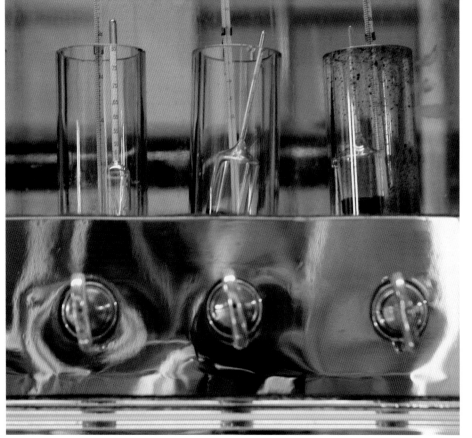

A very slow second distillation is one of the secrets of Lagavulin's complexity.

bonfire, but with an intense sweet core. Clearly, then, it's the stills that make the difference here. The wash stills are huge, but with acutely angled lyne arms that swoop into condensers (this is the only one of Diageo's old "Classic Six," without worms). Heaviness being built in? The spirit stills are significantly smaller, fat-based and plain, looking like stylized elephant's feet. In these, the heat is turned down, allowing maximum reflux, polishing, removing; retaining smokiness but taking away sulfur.

It's a surgical dissection of heaviness, a slow revelation of the sweet core that must be at the heart of any smoky spirit if it is to be a balanced, mature whisky.

They are aged, for single malt, in refill casks that are overseen by Iain MacArthur, crofter, warehouseman, wit. Here, pulling samples from a selection of casks, he shows how the fieriness of youth is slowly tempered by oak, introducing a new complexity. Lagavulin is about peeling away layers as it pulls you onto the pier, looking out past the castle, thinking of Aine and her bevvy of boats, out into the cradle.

passageway. The smoke seems to billow out, but halfway round the aroma changes: smoky still, but now with an overwhelming sweetness, a strange exotic pungency. Pour some of the new make on your hands and inhale. If Ardbeg is sooty, then Lagavulin is more like a beach

LAGAVULIN TASTING NOTES

NEW MAKE

Nose: Sooty smoke. Bonfire-like. Dense and foggy. Kiln-like. Gentian, fish boxes, seaweed. Sulfur hint.
Palate: Big, complex, with lifted aromatics; almost floral but held in check by earthy/seashore smoke.
Finish: Long and peaty.

8YO REFILL WOOD, CASK SAMPLE

Nose: Complex. Drying crab creels, seaweed. Wet peat bank, little hint of rubbery immaturity, pipe smoke. Kilns. Sweet and smoky. Heavy and lifted.
Palate: Sooty. Smothered fire. Ripe fruit. Heather and blueberry, seaweed. Vibrant, deep.
Finish: Explosive. Peat. Spice, oatcakes, and seashells.
Conclusion: Ready to go.

> **Flavor Camp: Smoky & Peaty**

12YO 57.9%

Nose: Straw. Intense smoke. Carbolic soap, lightly smoked haddock, but also sweet. Bog myrtle. Wasabi on fresh herring. Ozone. Light sootiness.
Palate: Dry, with intense smoke to start; smoked cheese rolled in oatmeal. Tight yet effervescent. Hugely fragrant. Uncompromising but open. Water allows its sweet center to show, and also youth.
Finish: Firm, smoked, dry.
Conclusion: Intense, but the key here is the growing complexity in both smokiness and sweetness.

> **Flavor Camp: Smoky & Peaty**
> **Where Next?** Ardbeg 10yo

16YO 43%

Nose: Big, robust, and complex. Seriously smoky, pipe tobacco, kiln, beach bonfire, smokehouse, all allied to ripe fruitiness. Touch of creosote and lapsang souchong tea.
Palate: Lightly oily and defiantly smoky. Fruit comes first, with a medicinal touch alongside bog myrtle while smoke builds steadily towards the finish. Elegant.
Finish: Long and complex mix. Seaweed and smoke.
Conclusion: Opens quickly. Its effusive character starts to concentrate into an essence of shoreline peatiness.

> **Flavor Camp: Smoky & Peaty**
> **Where Next?** Longrow 14yo, Ardbeg Airigh nam Beist 1990

MANAGER'S CHOICE, 54.7%

Nose: Deep amber. A powerful range of aromas here: squid ink, dried seaweed, rosemary thrown on a beach BBQ, creosote, tobacco, dried fruit. Fruity, tarry, and smoky.
Palate: Full-bodied and concentrated. It starts with dried fruit with background smoke, but this begins to build and scent everything (it's the tobacco again). Mulberry, earthiness, burning pine, and brine hints.
Finish: Dry smoke, but sufficient dried fruit to sweeten.
Conclusion: Massive but sophisticated.

> **Flavor Camp: Smoky & Peaty**
> **Where Next?** Ardbeg Lord of the Isles

DISTILLER'S EDITION 43%

Nose: Mahogany. Woodier than the 16yo and slightly vinous. The black fruit is now dried and there's generally less definition on the nose, as if all the almost paradoxical complexities have been tidied up. Almost discreet, it does open with time and water.
Palate: The smoke seems to have been shunted forward (if only because the finish is so much sweeter). A good mix of rich spirit, dried fruit, and a touch of cinnamon toast.
Finish: Thick and only lightly smoked. Generous and sweet.
Conclusion: Lagavulin with added sweetness.

> **Flavor Camp: Smoky & Peaty**
> **Where Next?** Talisker 10yo

Laphroaig

PORT ELLEN • WWW.LAPHROAIG.COM • OPEN ALL YEAR • SEE WEB FOR DAYS & DETAILS

The final member of the Kildalton Trio lies little more than a couple of miles from Lagavulin. It, too, is smoky, yet once again the character of that smoke is fundamentally different from that of its neighbors. Laphroaig is heavy and rooty, like walking down a freshly tarred seaside road on a hot day. At one time, it was a style that was envied by its neighbor. Sir Peter Mackie, who owned Lagavulin, had lost the agency for Laphroaig in 1907. He built a replica, called Malt Mill, at Lagavulin using the same water, same stills, and even (after financial inducement) the same distiller. The whisky was different. "It's something that scientists try to explain, but can't," says Laphroaig manager John Campbell. "Character is about location. Maybe that's why distilleries are all across Scotland, rather than in one super-distillery. It could be down to altitude, it could be proximity to the sea, it could be humidity; I don't know, but it exists."

It does also lie within the creative process at the distillery. Laphroaig still operates its own floor maltings which provide up to 20 percent of its requirements. For Campbell, the maltings aren't there as a sop for tourists; they certainly don't offer any savings in fixed costs, but they do provide a different character. "We get a different smokiness here than we get from Port Ellen [malt]," he says. "We kiln differently, we peat and then dry at low temperatures. This gives us higher levels of cresol [a key phenol] and it's this that gives you that tarry note in the spirit. It wouldn't be there without the floor maltings."

The stillhouse is, inevitably, different. There's seven stills for starters, while on the spirit side there are two different sizes, with one twice the size of the other three. "We are effectively making two different spirits which we then marry before casking," says Campbell.

Ardbeg and Lagavulin both strive for an element of reflux to get sweeter estery notes. Laphroaig, on the other hand, steers the other way. Here, Campbell wants to hold on to that heavy, tarry

weight that means having the longest foreshot run in the industry (45 minutes) so that those sweet esters at the start of the run are recycled rather than collected (see pp.14–15). "We cut at 60 percent, which isn't as low as some, but because we get less of the estery notes there is a larger percentage of smokiness, so the spirit seems heavier."

The sweetness that does exist within Laphroaig is found from its virtually exclusive use of American oak barrels—all of which come from Maker's Mark. "For consistency," says Campbell. It's this vanilla character that smooths away the more rugged edge of the new make and adds a subtle sweet drive to the mature spirit. A good example of this process is the Quarter Cask release, in which young Laphroaig is given a short period of extra maturation in new tiny, "quarter" casks made from American oak. The vanilla and the smoke are here at their peak.

For Campbell, though, Laphroaig is more than just technology; it's people. "I'd say that we were the result of the people who have worked

Low tide at the seaweed-strewn strand at the third of the mighty Kildalton malts, Laphroaig.

Laphroaig believes that its signature flavors come partly from its own floor maltings.

here. People have influenced the style and the attitude to making whisky, none more so than Ian Hunter [who owned it from 1924–54]. It was he who created the recipe that we have now. In the 1920s we were mucking around, and it really wasn't until 1940, after Prohibition, that he began to source ex-bourbon casks and mature the whisky on site."

So, it comes back to location again. "A traditional warehouse gives more body to the whisky, maybe because you get more oxidation

in a damp dunnage than the rack. We have both on site, and I know that there is a difference."

Maybe he should have told Sir Peter Mackie.

LAPHROAIG TASTING NOTES

NEW MAKE

Nose: Heavy, tarry smoke. Oilier than its neighbors. A light, medicinal note (iodine, hospital) along with a crisp maltiness and gentian root. Has complexity.
Palate: Hot embers followed by the rich spread of smoke. Both dark and clean. Hot roads on a summer day by the sea.
Finish: Dry, clean, smoky, Crisp.

10YO 40%

Nose: Rich gold. Smoke is beng both restrained by and manipulated by sweet oak. Wood oils, pine woods. Seashore, wintergreen. Nutty background and, with water, iodine.
Palate: Smooth, soft start with plenty of vanilla accents then a slow uptake of smoke, but the oak is balanced. Becomes tarry at the finish.
Finish: Long, lightly peppery smoke.
Conclusion: The key here is the balance between the dry (smoke) and the sweet (oak).

Flavor Camp: Smoky & Peaty
Where Next? Ardbeg 10yo

18YO 48%

Nose: Rich gold. Restrained and gentle. The smoke, having been given more time with the oak is now mossy and has picked up a spicier edge alongside that creamy oak. Light iodine and that rootiness of new make.
Palate: Nutty start. Walnuts, and whisky-soaked raisins. A little citric note rising above the slightly shy smoke.
Finish: Smoked salted cashew.
Conclusion: A toned-down example.

Flavor Camp: Smoky & Peaty
Where Next? Caol Ila 18yo

25YO 51%

Nose: The smoke has returned! Soy sauce, fish boxes, dried tar, heavy tobacco, burning lobster creels. Rich. Funky.
Palate: After the huge impact of the nose, this seems almost gentle. Age has thickened it. It has become coherent with full integration (and therefore complexity) of distillery character and oak plus new exotic flavors.
Finish: Still tarry.
Conclusion: Smoke doesn't disappear, it simply becomes more concentrated and absorbed into the overall flavor.

Flavor Camp: Smoky & Peaty
Where Next? Ardbeg Lord of the Isles

BY APPOINTMENT TO HRH THE PRINCE OF WALES,
DISTILLER AND SUPPLIER OF SINGLE MALT SCOTCH WHISKY,
D. JOHNSTON & CO., (LAPHROAIG) ISLE OF ISLAY

LAPHROAIG®

ISLAY SINGLE MALT SCOTCH WHISKY

10 Years Old

LAPHROAIG DISTILLERY
ESTABLISHED 1815

ARE YOU A FRIEND
See Inside
for Details
OF LAPHROAIG?

Distilled on the remote island of Islay off the West coast of Scotland, Laphroaig is the most richly flavoured of all Scotch whiskies

70 cl e DISTILLED AND BOTTLED IN SCOTLAND BY D. JOHNSTON & CO., LAPHROAIG DISTILLERY, ISLE OF ISLAY   40% vol

BY APPOINTMENT TO HRH THE PRINCE OF WALES,
DISTILLER AND SUPPLIER OF SINGLE MALT SCOTCH WHISKY,
D.JOHNSTON & CO., (LAPHROAIG) ISLE OF ISLAY.

LAPHROAIG®

ISLAY SINGLE MALT SCOTCH WHISKY

ESTABLISHED
1815

AGED **25** YEARS

CASK STRENGTH
2009 EDITION

MATURED IN A COMBINATION OF THE FINEST OLOROSO
SHERRY AND AMERICAN OAK CASKS AND BOTTLED IN 2009
THE MOST RICHLY FLAVOURED OF ALL SCOTCH WHISKIES.

Distilled and Bottled in Scotland by D. Johnston & Co.,
Laphroaig Distillery. Isle of Islay

70cl e   1LAPH25F05   51% vol.

EAST COAST

Islay's east coasters enjoy views across the fast-running tidal race of the Sound of Islay to the raised beaches of Jura and north to the shores of Colonsay and Mull. In some ways, their remoteness is surprising, because this pair of distilleries are the island's largest producers—and in some ways Islay's least known.

Gazing over to the raised beaches of Jura; Islay's east-coast distilleries have a spectacular outlook.

Bunnahabhain

PORT ASKAIG • WWW.BUNNAHABHAIN.COM • OPEN TO VISITORS • APR–SEPT, MON–FRI

Islay's northeast coast was deserted in the late nineteenth century when the Islay Distillery Company started work on not just a new distillery but an entire village in what is now known as Bunnahabhain. A road, a pier, houses, a village hall, as well as a substantial distillery, Bunnahabhain is a fine example of the optimism that surrounded Scotch whisky in the 1880s and the paternalistic attitudes of the new distilling companies.

The Islay Distillery Company's (IDC) endeavors certainly met with the approval of Alfred Barnard when he visited in 1886. "This portion of the island was bare and uninhabited," wrote whisky's first chronicler, "but the prosecution of the distilling industry has transformed it into a lifelike and civilized colony"—which was probably meant to be less patronizing than it now reads.

Bunnahabhain was built to provide spirit for blends. Six years after its founding it merged with Glenrothes to form Highland Distilleries, a move that undoubtedly saved this high-capacity site on a remote island when the downturns of the early 1900s and 1930s came along.

Though launched as a single malt in the late 1980s, Bunna' has never received the backing it needed (and deserved). Its huge stills produced a clean, slightly ginger-accented new make that was ignored by the peat freaks who flooded into Islay from the 1990s.

That situation is being addressed by new owner Burn Stewart, which took over in 2003. Heavily peated malt is now being used every year, a style which its previous owner denied was ever produced. "Rubbish!" says Burn Stewart's master blender, Ian MacMillan. "Bunnahabhain was peaty until the early 1960s, and only changed because they didn't need smoky [whisky] for their blends. I want to re-create what it would have been like in the 1880s and

Looking across to the cloud-shrouded "Paps of Jura" hills, it is not hard to believe that Bunnahabhain is Islay's most remote distillery.

show that it could be what people think of as an 'Islay' whisky." Islay permeates the gentle unpeated style as well.

"There's a difference in maturation cycles on the island," says MacMillan. "There will be a coastal influence. The Bunna' matured in Bishopbriggs is a different beast to the same whisky matured on Islay."

BUNNAHABHAIN TASTING NOTES

NEW MAKE

Nose: Sweet and full, with a slight oiliness and a little yeasty note and a hint of sulfur. In time, an aroma akin to tomato sauce (spiciness) and when diluted, lots of malt.

Palate: Violet-like rootiness and sweet mid-palate weight before drying considerably.

Finish: Gingery spice.

10YO CASK SAMPLE

Nose: Pale straw. Clean and crisp. Light, slightly fluffy, and crisp, with juicy citrus fruit behind. Still quite firm, suggesting it might need time to open. Chestnut flour, shortbread.

Palate: Medium-bodied. Sweet, with the same solid center seen in new make. Again, a cereal note, then apricot jam. It is picking up wood, but remains tense.

Finish: Nutty and that violet note again.

Conclusion: All the components are there, but it's still coming together.

Flavor Camp: Malty & Dry

16YO CASK SAMPLE

Nose: Mahogany. Camp coffee/chicory, bitter chocolate, aniseed, crystallized ginger stems, and would you credit it, tomato paste.

Palate: Dried cherry, licorice. Chewy; the tannins from the sherry cask are forced back as the spirit's weight stirs and pushes them to the fringes of the mouth. Only now is there fruitiness.

Finish: Light malt and fruitcake.

Conclusion: On this evidence, Bunnahabhain just needs time to rouse itself from its slumbers.

Flavor Camp: Rich & Round

34YO CASK SAMPLE

Nose: Elegant. A seamless flow of oxidized and sweet aromas, mixing peach, fig, and ripe plum alongside polished floors, gun oil, and leather. In time a hint of old paper.

Palate: Restrained start. Dried cherry, fruitcake, ginger in syrup, nutmeg, pepper.

Finish: Fresh spiciness.

Conclusion: As if to underline that this is a distillery that benefits from time …

Flavor Camp: Rich & Round

Caol Ila

PORT ASKAIG • WWW.DISCOVERING-DISTILLERIES.COM/CAOLILA • OPEN TO VISITORS • MID–FEB–DEC, MON–FRI, APR–OCT, SAT ALSO

Although it sits little more than a stone's throw from Port Askaig, which is one of Islay's two ferry terminals, until you set sail you wouldn't know Caol Ila existed. It was built in 1846 by Hector Henderson, who, smarting after two other distilling projects had foundered, saw whisky-making possibilities in a cliff-backed bay next to one of the fastest tidal races in Scotland.

Islay was, as now, popular as a single malt. It grew in importance as the century progressed and blenders realized that a little touch of smoke in their blend added complexity and a touch of mysteriousness. Blends are Caol Ila's lifeblood. It's the largest distillery in terms of capacity on the island, but in many ways it is also the least known: the quiet man of an island on which some robust personalities vie constantly with each other for attention. Its manager, Billy Stitchell, is a perfect personification of this calm.

Its importance in blending resulted in the old distillery being demolished in 1974, when today's new, larger, plant was constructed. Here, the SMD stillhouse design, with its car dealership window, works to its greatest effect. Caol Ila has the finest panorama of any stillhouse in Scotland, looking across the Sound of Islay to hills known as the Paps of Jura, the view framed by its huge stills.

Caol Ila's malt sneaks up on you. There's smoke, but it is understated. The creosote and seaweed of the Kildalton coast has been replaced by smoky bacon, seashells, and a grassy lift. It's less "peaty," yet the malted barley is exactly the same as that which goes to Lagavulin. Everything in Caol Ila is run differently: mashing regime, fermentation, and, most importantly, the size of those stills and the cut points. Knowing the phenolic parts per million (ppm) of malt

The huge Caol Ila is somehow wedged into a tiny coastal gorge.

(i.e. peatiness) might win a Trivial Pursuit quiz but it means nothing, since peatiness is lost during the whisky-making process.

You may even find Caol Ila with zero ppm because, since the 1980s, it has run for part of the year unpeated, and with a different distillation regime. Occasional releases show a malt with a fresh, green-melon character.

The quiet ones always surprise.

CAOL ILA TASTING NOTES

NEW MAKE

Nose: Fragrant and smoky. Juniper and wet grass. Cod liver oil and wet kilt. Lightly malty with a seashore freshness.
Palate: Dry smoke, then an explosion of oil and pine. Hot.
Finish: Grassy and smoky.

8YO REFILL WOOD, CASK SAMPLE

Nose: That grassiness continues. The oiliness is now bacon fat, the juniper continues. Fat and smoky: a mix of sweet, oily, and dry.
Palate: Oily and chewy. Saltier than the new make. Pear and ozone. Salty skin and fresh fruit.
Finish: Intense smoke.
Conclusion: All the components are there, with smoke to the fore.

Flavor Camp: Smoky & Peaty

12YO 43%

Nose: Balanced mix of ozone freshness, smoked ham, and a little touch of seaweed. Very clean and lightly smoky with some sweetness behind. Angelica and seashore-fresh.
Palate: Oily and tongue-coating. Pears and juniper. Dries towards the finish, although the smoke is a constant thread adding fragrance and a drying, balancing element.
Finish: Gently smoked.
Conclusion: Again, it's all about balance here.

Flavor Camp: Smoky & Peaty
Where Next? Kornog (Brittany, France), Highland Park 12yo, Springbank 10yo

18YO 43%

Nose: Intense. Briny/seashore, smoked fish, smoked ham. Sweet woods.
Palate: Soft, quite rich, and less oily as well. The smoke has receded a little as the wood has combined with the fruit.
Finish: Lightly smoky and herbal.
Conclusion: A more active cask has calmed down the peatiness.

Flavor Camp: Smoky & Peaty
Where Next? Laphroaig 18yo

CENTER & WEST

A trio of distilleries are found in this final Islay cluster. Two sit on the shores of Loch Indaal, while the third is Scotland's most westerly, and one of its newest sites. Welcome to the Rhinns, with its round church, some of Scotland's most ancient rocks, restless innovation, and the place where Scotland's first distillers may have settled.

A picture of tranquility; sunset on Loch Indaal. Now turn the page...

Bowmore

BOWMORE • WWW.BOWMORE.COM • OPEN ALL YEAR • MON–SAT; JULY–AUG, SUN ALSO

Bowmore's distillery walls form part of the sea defenses for this neat, white-painted village on the shores of Loch Indaal, which itself only dates back to 1768, a time when the agricultural improvements that significantly changed the Scottish landscape were building in momentum. In 1726, "Great" Daniel Campbell of Shawfield purchased Islay using the £9,000 ($13,320) he received as compensation for his house being burned down during the Malt Tax riots in Glasgow. His improvements were carried on by his grandson, Daniel the Younger, who built Bowmore. The island was run like a business. There was flax for weaving into linen, a fishing fleet, and the introduction of two-row barley on the newly enlarged farms, which, with its better yields and easier malt-ability, gave a chance to distill on a more commercial scale.

It means that, instead of being an isolated facility built because of access to the sea (or because its obscure location was perfect for moonshining), Bowmore's distillery sits in the heart of this small community. The waste heat warms the swimming pool (a former warehouse), the smoke from its kilns scents the air. It is rooted in its location.

The smoke issuing from the pagoda roof is evidence that Bowmore, like Laphroaig, has retained its own malting floors. "We're meeting 40 percent of our own needs," says Iain McCallum, blender at owner Morrison Bowmore Distillers (MBD). "As an industry, we always talk of heritage and tradition, but we actually do things traditionally; it's why people come to see us." There's a pragmatic reason as well, since floor maltings can allow the distillery to run if the barley supplies are held up from the mainland because of weather.

Bowmore's peaty note is different again. While not the most heavily peated of the island's malts, it is the most overtly smoky, with the clearest peat reek. Just as sulfury new-make sites on the mainland are hiding something, peaty new makes conceal background characters that only reveal themselves in maturation.

In Bowmore's case it is tropical fruit that is there in the new make but it can be obscured by peat when young, sat on by first-fill sherry casks. In refill casks, however, and with age it suddenly and startlingly blossoms, imparting an exotic Caribbean edge to a whisky from a small, chilly Hebridean island. It's a characteristic Bowmore-lovers have always revered.

"Some of the 1970s coming through now are as good as the legendary 1960s," says McCallum. "We have fantastic whiskies; we've just not been good at telling people what we are good at. As a firm, we were blend, we were bulk, but now we're single malt, which allows us to focus on the portfolio, slim it down, and release some spectaculars."

Storms on Loch Indaal frequently batter the Bowmore warehouses, which help act as the town's flood defenses.

Bowmore still malts a significant percentage of its own barley. Any that isn't dried over peat, however, will start to sprout!

It takes time to change a whisky firm's fortunes but there is plenty of evidence that MBD's improved wood policy is now bearing fruit (if you pardon the pun) with casks from its Loch Indaal-backed warehouses.

"Effectively, all our single malt is matured at Bowmore," says McCallum. "We're right next to the water and the microclimate will be different. There's always a saltiness to Bowmore. Now, I'm a chemist and I know there's not actually salt in there, but I can discern that character in the whisky. Maybe there's some magic in those damp, low-roofed vaults."

BOWMORE TASTING NOTES

NEW MAKE

Nose: Hugely sweet, with fragrant peat smoke, broom/pea pod, and a touch of wet grass, barley, and vanilla. With water, and concentrated jellied fruit in the back.

Palate: Dense, damp peat smoke blanketing the tongue. A nutty undertone. Sweetness with water. Hazelnut.

Finish: Fragrant smoke.

LEGEND NAS, 40%

Nose: Light gold. The smoke drifts upwards while crisp oak adds a fresh, dry note to the fragrant smoke.

Palate: Clean, sweet, and appealing. Some spicy paprika, banana. Lightly salty, preserved lemon.

Finish: Seashore.

Conclusion: Oak adds a crisp element.

Flavor Camp: Smoky & Peaty
Where Next? Laphroaig Quarter Cask

12YO 40%

Nose: Rich gold. Again, toasty oak, some date. Thicker, with a charred wood melding with the peat reek. Touches of mango chews. Ripe and fleshy. Orange zest.

Palate: Deeper, with more fruitiness. Sweet herbs, toffee, lightly salty. The smoke shifts towards the back.

Finish: A build-up of smoke, along with light chocolate malt.

Conclusion: Balanced and showing a steady integration.

Flavor Camp: Smoky & Peaty
Where Next? Caol Ila 12yo

15YO DARKEST 43%

Nose: Amber. Deep with significant sherry notes, moving into chocolate-covered cherry, molasses, orange zest, beach bonfire.

Palate: Concentrated, with a hint of lavender. PX-like sherry, bitter/salted chocolate and coffee. The oiliness of the new make now comes back, thanks to the sherry casks.

Finish: Thick and long. Now the smoke is released, but the tropical fruit has gone.

Conclusion: Rich and powerful, with balanced smoke.

Flavor Camp: Smoky & Peaty
Where Next? Laphroaig 18yo

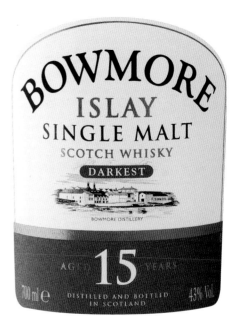

Bruichladdich & Kilchoman

BRUICHLADDICH • WWW. BRUICHLADDICH.COM • OPEN ALL YEAR • MON–SAT; SEE WEB FOR TIMES
KILCHOMAN • BRUICHLADDICH • WWW.KILCHOMANDISTILLERY.COM • OPEN ALL YEAR, NOV–MAR, MON–FRI; APR–OCT, MON–SAT

May 29, 2001. The Rhinns of Islay. The sun is splitting the sky. Iron gates swing open and it seems like everyone on the island piles into a freshly painted distillery courtyard. After seven years of silence, Bruichladdich was open for business once more, but the symbolism reached further. After some tough, lean years stretching back to the collapse of the 1980s, with the re-emergence of Islay's last mothballed distillery, the island itself was truly back.

Built in 1881 by the sons of the owner of the Yoker distillery in Glasgow, Bruichladdich was modern in its time. Now it has some of the oldest equipment in the industry: the mill is a thing of mad-inventor genius: the mash tun is an open-topped rake system; there are wooden washbacks and its slender-necked quartet of stills sit in a wooden-floored stillhouse producing a honeyed, sweet, lemon-drop-like spirit.

Bruichladdich hasn't been slow in making a name for itself. Taking a leaf out of Springbank's book, it started bottling on site, raised the strength to 46 percent, did away with chill-filtering and stopped caramel adjustments. But after the elation of the opening day, the hard work had to start—and that meant master distiller Jim McEwan (who left Bowmore to join the new team) taking a long, hard look at what was in the warehouses. It wasn't a pretty sight.

"We had a seven-year hole in stock and what was there was in fourth-, fifth-, seventh-fill hoggies," he says. "I've had to manage that gap in production and change every single cask in this distillery. Every single one! Our whole principle is to fill first-rate wood. We've now got warehouses full of every type of cask you can imagine."

And therein lies one of the criticisms leveled at Bruichladdich: that it has released too many expressions, too many finishes. "We need the money!" laughs McEwan. "For example, we had casks from First Growth Bordeaux *châteaux*, so the choice was one single whisky or six, one from each First Growth. What would you do?

"I really don't see why people are bothered about us; we're 0.09 percent of the industry. It's like America being worried that it's going to be invaded by the Isle of Man!"

The multiplicity of expressions has been matched by multiple distillates. "We're doing Laddie unpeated, Lochindaal medium-peated, Port Charlotte heavy-peated, Octomore

The open-topped mash tun at Bruichladdich is one of the few in the industry that is still operational.

KILCHOMAN: SITED NEAR WHERE IT ALL BEGAN

Islay's newest distillery is located on its west coast, near where the MacBeathas (Beatons) settled. Operational since 2005, at the time of writing it had just bottled its first official whisky—earlier than expected. "What has surprised us is how quick-maturing the spirit is," says owner Anthony Wills. "We had planned to wait until it was five, but it jumped the gun." Good planning or fortuitous? "We knew what style we hoped for, and we've been fortunate that we never needed to tweak. It's been consistent from the start." Two expressions, a medium-peated from its own maltings and an "Ardbeg spec" from Port Ellen maltings, are made, though all the barley is grown on site—something that sets Kilchoman apart. Given that the first release sold out instantly, is expansion on the cards? "No!' says Wills. "We'll produce 26,417 gallons (100,000 liters) a year. It's quite enough."

super-heavy-peated; then there's organic, Islay barley, bere barley, triple-distilled, quadruple-distilled … and I've just installed a Lomond still. You don't need 22 distilleries."

There's an irrepressible and infectious enthusiasm to McEwan as he expounds his vision of the future, but it is rooted in a belief in people, quality—and Islay. "This distillery is a community of 46 people," he

Ribboned out along the shore next to the beach, Bruichladdich's buildings are now home to a huge number of whisky-making experiments.

says, "and we're trying to do our best by them. I still get that buzz every day. It's just been great to take this old lady back and watch her get more beautiful by the day."

BRUICHLADDICH TASTING NOTES

NEW MAKE ORGANIC

Nose: Full, fat, and very sweet with lemon drops, vanilla, light esters, a touch of carnation, and deep cereal in the background.
Palate: Thick and sweet, with hints of butterscotch, then come the sticky sugars with a fresh citric lift.
Finish: Creamy nuttiness.

2002 FRESH BOURBON, 65.5%

Nose: Light gold. Big, toasty, oak notes. Coconut, praline, custard, and butterscotch. The generous sweet character of new make has been retained.
Palate: More vegetal, with grassy notes and light floral touches. Has the thickness of the new make with an added scented (rosemary) note.
Finish: Orange and cumin.
Conclusion: Has freshness and energy.

> Flavor Camp: **Fruity & Spicy**
> **Where Next?** Glen Moray 12yo, Macallan 10yo Fine Oak

16YO OLD BOURBON 46%

Nose: Sweet. Vanilla. Light-brown sugar and a little lime. Lifted and fresh. Toasted oak.
Palate: Soft and clinging. Peach then vanilla bean. With water, tangerine, orange oil.
Finish: Clean and sweet.
Conclusion: American oak enhancing the sweetness of the distillery character.

> Flavor Camp: **Fruity & Spicy**
> **Where Next?** Aberfeldy 12, Glenmorangie Original, Miyagikyo 15yo, Oban 14yo

OCTOMORE 5YO 63.5%

Nose: Roasted malt. Burning sappy wood, green bean, light oil. Burning moors and cowsheds.
Palate: Similar to PC's grassiness but significantly oilier. Peppery Italian olive oil. With water, burning boats.
Finish: Paprika. Oil. Cookies.
Conclusion: Still young but coming together.

> Flavor Camp: **Smoky & Peaty**
> **Where Next?** Chichibu New Born (heavy peat)

PORT CHARLOTTE PC8 60.5%

Nose: Gold. A roasted peatiness. Wood smoke, burning leaves with dry grass. Scented. Young.
Palate: Intense heathery character. A fog of smoke over the palate.
Finish: Hot embers.
Conclusion: Clean and developing interestingly.

> Flavor Camp: **Smoky & Peaty**
> **Where Next?** Longrow CV, Connemara

KILCHOMAN TASTING NOTES

INAUGURAL RELEASE 3YO 46%

Nose: Has the pleasant putty/linseed-like nose typical of young peaty whiskies. Very clean, with light smoked fish (hot smoked salmon, perhaps), even some scallop shell and a soft, dried-fruit note: fig.
Palate: This is a sweet, smoky spirit with a definite seashore air. Good feel in the center of the tongue where a burst of sweetness enhanced by the sherry casks anchors it as the smoke begins to ignite.
Finish: Light citrus fruit: preserved lemon.
Conclusion: One to watch.

> Flavor camp: **Smoky & Peaty**
> **Where Next:** ever upwards!

ISLANDS

We are entranced by islands. The notion of being cut off somehow excites us, while getting there involves not only a physical transportation but a psychological one as well. We leave the familiar for "that land over there," and making that journey off Scotland's coasts involves traveling on some of the best sailing grounds in the world. This is a place of bright-jade seas, pink granites, ancient, gritty, zebra-striped gneiss and lava flows; of raised beaches, winds, and sheltered bays; a thrilling, living landscape, home to orca, minke, dolphin, gannet, and sea eagle.

Its aromas are those of wet rope and salt spray, of heather and bog myrtle, of guano, seaweed, and sump oil, of drying crab shells, bracken, and fish boxes. Its secrets also lie below the ground, in the rock and what lies upon that rock: heather, or the windblown sand which has rooted the fertile *machair* (beach grass) and how both have been compressed into fragrant peat. In Orkney's case, peat that's different from that of Islay.

Whisky would have been made on every one of these islands at some stage and in some form, whether that be farmers making it for their community or in a commercial fashion. Tiree, the westernmost Inner Hebridean island, had two licensed distilleries and was a whisky exporter in the eighteenth century. Mull and Arran, too, were noted whisky islands, and the Outer Hebrides was also whisky territory.

Now? Distilleries are scattered around the Hebrides, the exception rather than the rule. Yet the spaces are as interesting as those which have survived. The Highland Clearances put paid to most farm distilling—157 moonshiners were arrested on Tiree alone, and many were then evicted—as well as creating the larger sites such as Talisker and Tobermory. Others tried and failed; many more simply didn't continue as the changed market demands of the nineteenth century made this an expensive place to distill on a commercial scale. It still is.

In our state of entrancement we overlook the realities of living on an island: communication, raw materials, higher fixed costs, the lack of things we take for granted on the mainland. "If I want to buy a new pair of trousers I have to drive to Inverness," a former manager of Talisker once told me. Newcomers who come here with their get-rich-quick schemes soon realize that getting rich isn't going to happen. Neither is quick. Island life works to a longer time frame—but time suits whisky. Island life may be wonderful, but it is hard.

Is there any surprise that the whiskies made out here on the fringed western coast, while generous in their natures, have something of this uncompromising landscape about them? You have to meet them on their own terms. That is why they have been so successful. Island whiskies, with their scents that seem to drift in from the landscape, by and large haven't been steered by the requirements of the market; they are as they are. Take them or leave them.

Rugged and individualistic, the landscape of the Scottish islands is reflected in the uncompromising nature of its whiskies.

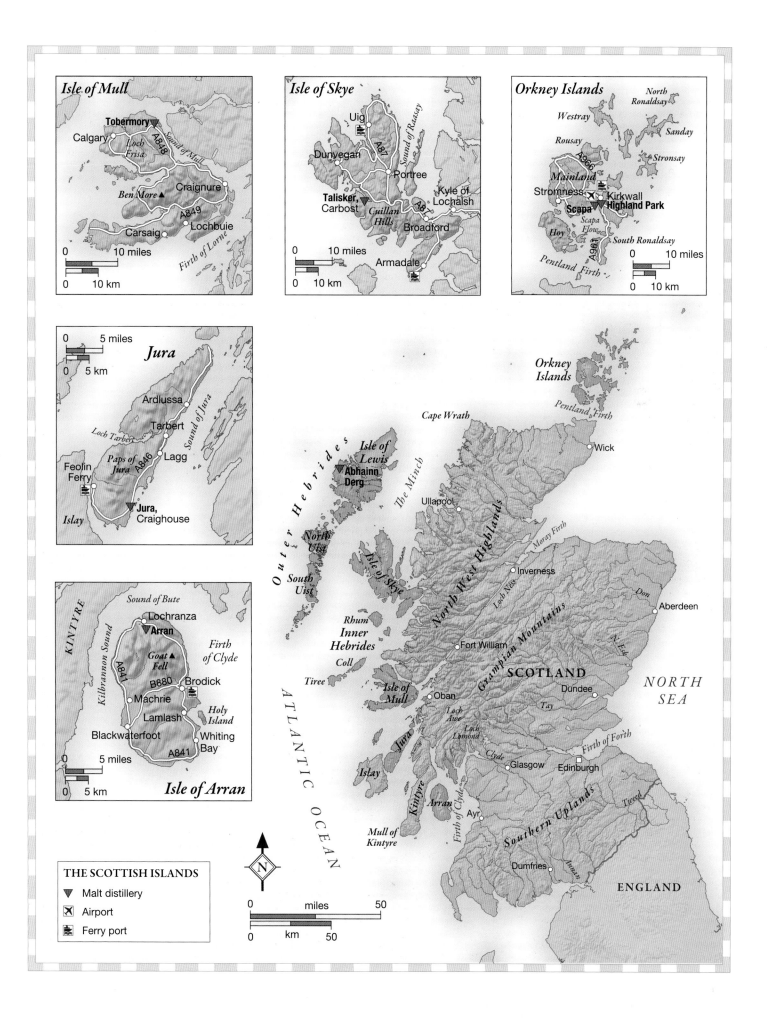

Isle of Mull

Calgary
Tobermory
Loch Frisa
A848
Sound of Mull
Ben More ▲
Craignure
A849
Carsaig
Lochbuie
Firth of Lorne

0 — 10 miles
0 — 10 km

Isle of Skye

Uig
A87
Sound of Raasay
Dunvegan
Portree
Kyle of Lochalsh
Talisker, Carbost
A87
Cuillan Hills
Broadford
Armadale

0 — 10 miles
0 — 10 km

Orkney Islands

North Ronaldsay
Westray
Sanday
Rousay
Stronsay
A966
Mainland
Stromness
Kirkwall
Scapa
Highland Park
Hoy
Scapa Flow
South Ronaldsay
A961
Pentland Firth

0 — 10 miles
0 — 10 km

Jura

0 — 5 miles
0 — 5 km
Ardlussa
Sound of Jura
Tarbert
Loch Tarbert
Paps of Jura
A846
Lagg
Feolin Ferry
Jura, Craighouse
Islay

Isle of Arran

Sound of Bute
KINTYRE
Lochranza
Arran
Kilbrannon Sound
Goat Fell ▲
Firth of Clyde
A841
B880
Brodick
Machrie
Holy Island
Lamlash
Blackwaterfoot
Whiting Bay
A841

0 — 5 miles
0 — 5 km

SCOTLAND

Orkney Islands
Pentland Firth
Cape Wrath
Wick
Outer Hebrides
Isle of Lewis
Abhainn Derg
The Minch
Ullapool
North Uist
South Uist
Moray Firth
Loch Ness
Inverness
North West Highlands
Rhum
Inner Hebrides
Coll
Tiree
Isle of Skye
Fort William
Grampian Mountains
Don
Aberdeen
N. Esk
Isle of Mull
Oban
Loch Awe
Loch Lomond
Tay
Dundee
NORTH SEA
Jura
Islay
Clyde
Glasgow
Edinburgh
Firth of Forth
Kintyre
Arran
Firth of Clyde
Ayr
Southern Uplands
Tweed
Mull of Kintyre
ATLANTIC OCEAN
Dumfries
Annan
ENGLAND

THE SCOTTISH ISLANDS

▼ Malt distillery
☒ Airport
⛴ Ferry port

N

0 — miles — 50
0 — km — 50

Loch Scavaig and the back door to the Cuillins. Behind these mighty peaks is Talisker.

Arran

LOCHRANZA • WWW.ARRANWHISKY.COM • OPEN ALL YEAR • DAYS VARY IN WINTER; MID-MAR–OCT, MON–SUN

Arran is hard enough to define as an island, let alone as a whisky. Split by the Highland Boundary Fault, it's a geologist's paradise: granite intrusions, Dalradian metamorphic rocks, sedimentary layers, glaciated valleys, raised beaches. Its northerly half is craggy and mountainous, the south is all undulating pasture. Highland or Lowland? Maybe simply Scotland distilled. In whisky terms, it's more complex. The distillery is sitated in Lochranza in the north, therefore legally it's Highland, but it's on an island, so surely it's an island dram? Maybe definitions mean nothing. It is the small-scale specificity of the site that matters. And it's the attitude of the people at the distillery that helps create its individuality.

Arran has always been both bewildering and revelatory. It was at Lochranza that the father of geology, James Hutton, discovered one of his "unconformities," where younger rocks sit horizontally on top of deeply eroded older ones that have been raised to the vertical, revealing the immense time over which geological processes take place.

The distillery was built in 1995—a very belated return to whisky-making for an island once famed for its moonshining. That just leads to another question. Why, after almost 160 years, was Arran's new distillery built in the north rather than in the south, where, history shows, most distilling activity took place?

"They looked at a dozen sites," the original manager (and distilling legend) Gordon Mitchell says. They settled for Lochranza because of the water. "Loch na Davie gives us volume, a good pH to help with fermentation—and there's nae dead sheep in it, either!"

Like most new distilleries, it is a one-room layout, which also features, somewhat incongruously though appealingly, a large pot plant. Originally grist was brought in, but now a mill has been installed. "I want control over the whole process," says current manager James MacTaggart, a native Ileach with over three decades

CREATING A SUSTAINABLE BUSINESS

Building your own distillery is a dream for many whisky-lovers. The commercial reality is somewhat different. Getting started and making spirit is perhaps the easiest bit. In Scotland, you must then wait for three years before you can call it whisky, and while people might buy your three-year-old out of curiosity, the reality is that the market only takes you seriously when your whisky has ten years behind it. All the time you are laying out money on making more spirit and buying wood to age it in. That necessitates one very understanding bank manager. Income can be generated from the distillery's visitors' center, but ultimately you only survive through having a good spirit.

of whisky-making experience at Bowmore under his belt. Not surprisingly, there's some peaty make being produced every year.

Arran kicks up an intense spray of citrus fruit from day one, providing a lifted counterpoint to the bedrock of crisp cereal. "It's hard to say exactly where it comes from," shrugs MacTaggart, "but I just run these wee stills very slow and give it lots of time for reflux. I'd guess that's where that light citrus comes from."

Built in 1995, Arran's distillery brought whisky-making back to the island after a gap of 160 years.

Cleverly designed on one floor, Arran is the perfect place to learn about the intricacies of distilling.

The light character was a commercial decision. Arran was built just before the boom in young, peaty whiskies and there was a commercial necessity to make a relatively quick-maturing spirit. It's sometimes been described as "easy," but that is rather disparaging. Arran, now at its 15th birthday, is still growing. It's shown in recent years that it can deal with the attentions of sherry as part of the wood mix, and, for this writer at least, the scaling back of the number of finishes has been a positive move, allowing the true Arran character to reveal itself. Arran has done that most difficult thing: it has survived.

Unconformity might just be a neat enough descriptor for this distillery. Neither classic Highland, Lowland or, indeed, what one would assume Island should be. But this is only right and proper because, as we have seen, Arran itself hardly conforms to any neat definition. Arran (the island and the whisky) is Arran.

ARRAN TASTING NOTES

NEW MAKE
Nose: Lifted and very citric: fresh orange juice, unripe pineapple undercut with a bran/oaty note. Green.
Palate: Tingling effect. Clean and masses of citrus fruit. Very focused and sweet. Cereal.
Finish: Clean and intense.

5YO, SCOTTISH MALT WHISKY SOCIETY
BOTTLING NUMBER 121.25, 61.6%
Nose: Dark ruby. Huge sherried nose with lots of walnut oil, some tomato paste, even a little blood. Dried fruits and tight tannin. The citric tone has gone into Olde English marmalade. In time, wet leather and a little rubber.
Palate: Sweet and savory. Quite hot, with some phenolic notes. Firm and tight. The cask has taken charge.
Finish: Firm.
Conclusion: An instructive whisky: this is what an over-active cask can do to a light spirit. A good drink, but is it Arran?

Flavor Camp: Rich & Round
Where Next? Glenfiddich 18yo

10YO 46%
Nose: Starts with a cereal note, then come dried orange pith and lemon with soft banana. A little touch of vanilla from oak.
Palate: Light and sweet. Hard candy, then mixed peel, and then fragrant flour (the cereal and citrus fruit are reversed on the palate). Medium-weight.
Finish: Dried banana.
Conclusion: The mid-palate sweetness is the key here. Clear distillery character development.

Flavor Camp: Fruity & Spicy
Where Next? Hazelburn 12yo, Oban 14yo

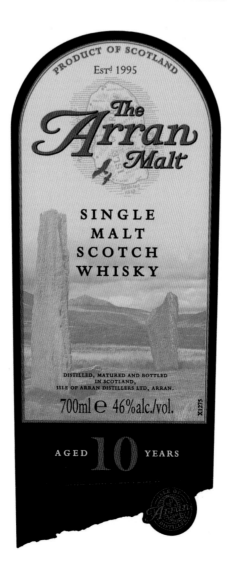

1996 SINGLE CASK CASK SAMPLE
Nose: The crisp malt continues at first, but the peel has now turned into marmalade held alongside light sherried notes. The maltiness then returns, but is now mixed with nutty oxidized wine. Plump dates and a lift of sulfur.
Palate: Chewy, and the stewed peel comes through, leaving the cereal in a supporting role. Ripe and long.
Finish: Juicy with tangerine.
Conclusion: Arran develops a little like Balvenie: with a slow shedding of the barley husk revealing the sweet spot in the middle.

Flavor Camp: Rich & Round (just)

Jura

That there is a distillery on Jura is no mean achievement. This is hardly one of the most populous islands of the Hebrides, and transport (everything must go via Islay) is hardly conducive to keeping control of fixed costs. When the distillery in Craighouse (called variously Caol nan Eilean, Craighouse, Small Isles, Lagg, and Jura) closed in 1910, it seemed likely that the locals would have to import their drams from neighboring Islay.

In 1962, however, two landowners, Robin Fletcher (George Orwell's landlord during his time on the island) and Tony Riley-Smith (uncle of the publisher of *Whisky Magazine*), worried at the decline in population, hired William Delmé-Evans to build a new plant.

There's one thing which Jura has plenty of and that's peat, but until recently none was used in its whisky production. Whereas records show that Small Isles made heavily peated whisky, Fletcher and Riley-Smith's main client was Scottish & Newcastle, which wanted light and unpeated for their blends. So, like most of the distilleries from the 1960s, that was the style it made, with huge stills installed to assist the process.

It's what lies above the island's peat that gives Jura one of its defining aromatic characteristics: fern, green in its humid summer woods, drying over time into bracken, all backed with a cereal rigidity. Jura is a tough one. "It has to settle before you put it into sherry," says Richard Paterson, master blender at owner Whyte & Mackay. "It's almost saying I'm happy in a suit, not a mink coat. Put me in sherry too early and I'll head off in another direction."

This slow process of coaxing takes the best part of 16 years to start and hits its peak at 21 (or older). The old "no peat" rule has gone, with heavily peated single-cask bottlings showing a fog of

Jura, the singular island: one road, one village, one whisky.

pine alongside that bracken, while the turfy Superstition offers a different—and in some ways more complex—character. Embracing its environment rather than working against it may be the best for Jura in the long run.

JURA TASTING NOTES

NEW MAKE

Nose: Dusty, dry green bracken. Light, grassy note.
Palate: Intense and light, with a touch of perfume in the mid-palate, then flour. Very tight.
Finish: Sweet as this is, it's a hard nut to crack.

9YO CASK SAMPLE

Nose: Gold. The flour/dust has now taken shape as green malt with a back note of hazelnut. Citrus fruit now coming through (lemon) and that green-fern character remains along with a little nougat. Still crisp.
Palate: Very dry and firm. Flaked almond, unripe fruit, malt.
Finish: Begins to open at the very end, offering a nodule of sweetness.
Conclusion: Simple and a clear extension of the new-make character. Still that firm undertow.

Flavor Camp: Malty & Dry

16YO 40% ABV

Nose: Amber. Rich, extractive wood notes: vanilla, sweet dried fruit, prune, chestnut, and blackberry jelly. Slight lactic touch. A dry character behind.
Palate: More rounded and soft compared with the 9yo. Silky feel and gentle. Ripe fruit cut with dry grasses (the evolution of that green bracken).
Finish: Mix of sweet sherry and firm spirit.
Conclusion: The active cask mix has helped to coax the underlying sweetness out.

Flavor Camp: Rich & Round
Where Next? Balvenie 17yo Madeira Wood, The Singleton of Dufftown 12yo

21YO CASK SAMPLE

Nose: Mahogany. Mature, with allspice, ginger, raisin, dried peel. Then come molasses, a tweedy note (maybe the dryness finally disappearing). The beginnings of concentration.
Palate: Huge sherried influence: palo cortado. Sweet/savory character. Fruitcake and walnut. Mellow and long.
Finish: Ripe, sweet fruit.
Conclusion: The intriguing spiciness is late to emerge in Jura's evolution.

Flavor Camp: Rich & Round

Tobermory

TOBERMORY • WWW.TOBERMORYMALT.COM • OPEN ALL YEAR • MON–FRI

Anyone who has sailed on Scotland's west coast appreciates that you have to balance being on one of the most spectacular cruising grounds in the world with having lots of challenging weather being flung at you. Tobermory, the capital of the Isle of Mull, is one of the main havens for spume-lashed yachties, weary after another day of battling with the elements. As you stagger up from the anchorage, heading for the Mishnish Hotel, the first building that greets you seems in a similar state to yourself: wave-blown and blasted. Tobermory distilllery, it must be said, is hardly one of Scotland's most beautiful.

In some ways its story parallels the islands themselves. Starting life in the late eighteenth century as a brewery, it passed through a succession of owners (who treated it like many absentee landlords treat their Hebridean tenants), while the wood policy prior to 1993 came straight from the "If it's from a tree, we'll use it" era. Now in the care of Burn Stewart, it is another plant being brought back round by general distilleries manager Ian MacMillan. (*see* p.110, Deanston).

He has succeeded, and, while the oily, vegetable-like new make is somewhat odd, there's an interesting mossy character that develops, along with a red fruitiness. There is certainly something odd about the stills, which have an S-shaped bend at the top of the lyne arm. "The kink is the key here," MacMillan says. "It gives lots of reflux, which helps with that underlying lightness."

This lightness of character also lurks underneath Ledaig (pronounced *Lea-Chick*), this distillery's heavily peated version, whose new make is full of mustard, limpets, and smoke, like a puffer's funnel. The release of 30yo+ versions of both, however, shows how refined this pair can become.

The gable end of the Tobermory distillery is a welcome sight for many a weary mariner.

In other words, both drams are highly individual and, like Jura, need time. "They do take a while to get going, but that's just the style," says MacMillan. "Who said whisky should just take five minutes?"

TOBERMORY TASTING NOTES

NEW MAKE

Nose: Oily, vegetable, with some candy notes. When this clears, there's moss and brass, artichoke and bran.
Palate: Oily. Fat and solid to start, but bone-dry on the finish.
Finish: Hard and short.

9YO CASK SAMPLE

Nose: Very fruity (lime cordial), strawberry chews. Then wet cookies, fenugreek, oily, then a sherried note.
Palate: Linseed oil. Rather than the fruit, now a wholegrain character emerges, becoming sweeter as it moves. With water, there's some balsa wood.
Finish: Crisp.
Conclusion: The sweet and dry characters seen on the new make are still tussling.

Flavor Camp: **Fragrant & Floral**

15YO 46.3%

Nose: Deep amber. Big, sherried impact: white raisins on top of the green notes seen in the new make. Some minty chocolate and a mature jamminess developing.
Palate: Spicy, some cherry (as well as sherry) showing the red fruit developing in an interesting manner. Hazelnut.
Finish: Dry, with a lick of molasses.
Conclusion: The cask has rounded things out, but the feeling remains that this has a way to go.

Flavor Camp: **Rich & Round**
Where Next? Isle of Jura 16yo

32YO 49.5%

Nose: Deep amber. Mature, elderberry, raisin, slightly smoky, autumn woods, leaf mulch, that moss once more.
Palate: Firm grip with assertive, heavy sherry notes. Cedar and a gentle soft creaminess.
Finish: Lingering.
Conclusion: Finally it emerges.

Flavor Camp: **Rich & Round**
Where Next? Tamdhu 18yo, Springbank 18yo

Talisker & Abhainn Dearg

TALISKER • CARBOST • WWW.DISCOVERING-DISTILLERIES.COM/TALISKER • OPEN ALL YEAR • MON–FRI
ABHAINN DEARG • CARNISH, ISLE OF LEWIS • WWW.ABHAINNDEARG.CO.UK

Situated at the head of Loch Harport in the village of Carbost, Talisker is one of the most spectacularly situated distilleries in Scotland. This is a place of mountain and shore. Behind the distillery rise the Cuillin Hills, their shattered and fractured ridge acting as a barrier to the south. Stand on the shore and inhale, deeply: seaweed and brine. Then do the same with the new make: smoke, oysters, lobster shell. Talisker distills itself. But surely this is romantic nonsense, brought about by the extreme location, this island where you confront the insignificance of mortality?

Hugh MacAskill, "Big Hugh," didn't build a distillery here for any metaphysical reasons. The nephew of a Mull landowner, whose Mornish estate he would inherit, MacAskill took control of Talisker in 1825 and applied the brutal economics of "improvement" upon his tenants—or those who still remained after the previous landlord, Lauchlan MacLean, had finished.

Talisker, like Clynelish (*see* p.138), is a Clearance distillery. The people had an option: stay in Carbost and work at the distillery or clear off to the colonies. Skye's desolate beauty isn't just the effect of its geology, but the result of nineteenth-century capitalist economics. "Skye isn't empty," writes British author Robert MacFarlane. "It is emptied."

The whisky, too, doesn't initially appear to be about abstract connections. Talisker is about reflux, purifiers, and peat. It's about "process"… and yet that procession of flavors on the tongue still

ABHAINN DEARG: LEWIS GETS ITS OWN DISTILLERY

If you think Loch Harport is remote, think again. Scotland's newest distillery (at the time of writing) is located on the west coast of Lewis. Here, at Red River, Marko Tayburn has built a tiny and (hopefully) self-sufficient distillery in the grounds of an abandonded salmon fishery, complete with a still that looks like a cross between a witch's hat and a crashed rocket. The new make is fragrant, yet with a distinct oily nature.

leads you back to the littoral. Skye's thin soils mean there are 21 springs feeding into the distillery; the barley is peated (and these days comes from Glen Ord), the ferments are long and in wood. All this gives a wash that goes into two of the more intriguingly shaped stills in the industry.

Caught between the shore and the Cuillins, Talisker is one of the most spectacularly situated distilleries in Scotland.

Talisker's secrets start here in these tall pots, whose lyne arm has a dramatic U-bend in it. Vapors will reflux here and can be led back into the still through a purifier pipe. The lyne arm rears back up to its original height, goes through the wall and coils around in a cold worm tub. These are pretty remarkable flavor-making machines. The low wines then go to two of three plain spirit stills (maybe a hangover from when Talisker was triple-distilled) and yield that complex new make.

Checking the *cratur* (whisky). Talisker's peppery, smoky style is in constant interplay with the subtle caresses of oak from its time spent in cask.

There's smoke, obviously, but also sulfur in here: that's the combination of worms plus exhausted copper, but also an oily sweetness from all of that reflux in the big wash still with its purifier. It's that sulfur note that eventually recedes to the back of the palate to give Talisker its giveaway peppery note.

So, is Talisker a factory making whisky or are these white-painted buildings a manifestation of the place itself? "Of course you can capture the place in the whisky," says Diageo's master distiller and blender, Douglas Murray. "You can't condense the spirit without capturing some of the essence of the location. There's something about this site which makes Talisker Talisker. We'll never know how it happens—and we don't want to." Site-specific *terroir*.

All of these island whiskies have survived because they are both pragmatic—whisky-making is one of the few businesses that work here—and also because their flavors (driven predominantly by peat) are uncompromising, as is the landscape. In this way the whisky reflects both where it is from and the people who make it. This is cultural *terroir* as well.

TALISKER TASTING NOTES

NEW MAKE

Nose: Light smoke to start. Very sweet, with sulfur in the background. Oyster brine, lobster shell. Perfumed smoke at the end.

Palate: Dry, smoky, and sulfury. Light tar. New leather. Soft fruit. Salty.

Finish: Long, smoky, and peppery with sulfur underneath.

8YO REFILL WOOD, CASK SAMPLE

Nose: Scented. Heathery/earthy peatiness. White peppercorn, developing a medicinal edge. Still has the briny/oyster-like notes of new make. Iodine and dried mint. With water, bog myrtle and larch.

Palate: Big white peppercorn hit. Marine. Solid, thick texture with some oil. Complex.

Finish: Dry, then sweet, then dry and peppery again.

Conclusion: Already hitting its mature character.

Flavor Camp: Smoky & Peaty

10YO 45.8%

Nose: Gold. Smoky fires. Heather, licorice root, and bilberry. A mix of earthy smoke (bonfires), pork rind, and a light seaweed touch. Sweetness runs underneath. Balanced. Light complexity.

Palate: Immediate. A rich, complex mix of pepper flakes, then a really sweet, soft fruitiness, all linked by a sooty/mossy smokiness. Hint of sulfur. A mix of sea and shore, the sweet, the fiery, the smoky.

Finish: Peppery and dry.

Conclusion: Balance struck between seemingly contradictory elements.

Flavor Camp: Smoky & Peaty
Where Next? Caol Ila 12yo, Springbank 10yo

1994 MANAGER'S CHOICE SINGLE CASK 58.7%

Nose: Full gold. Very briny. All sea-washed pebbles and wet dulse, before the hickory/heather, root-like smoke emerges on top. There's a hint of violet root, pears poached in red wine, and a broom-like pea-pod lift.

Palate: Balanced and peaty with a salty surge. Akin to eating apple-wood-smoked cheese beside the sea in a gale. Water makes it considerably more gentle, allowing that very sweet, white fruitiness to reveal itself alongside that smoked rock salt.

Finish: Long with a characteristic long pepper-scented quality.

Conclusion: Takes no prisoners.

Flavor Camp: Smoky & Peaty
Where Next?: Manager's Choice Yoichi 12yo

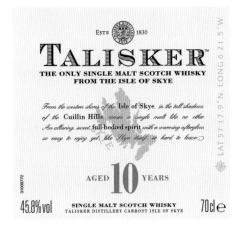

18YO 45.8%

Nose: Gold. Complex, burning heather, sweet tobacco, old warehouse, spent bonfire. Underneath is almond paste/nougat/butter cookies and a lightly herbal note. Plenty of smoke. Rich and complex.

Palate: A slow start, then pepper, a light, smoked-fish note, but the key is the sweet fruit syrup which gives a balancing element. Builds in stages to an explosive finish.

Finish: Red peppercorn.

Conclusion: Retains Talisker's identifiable attack but with a growing sweet center.

Flavor Camp: Smoky & Peaty
Where Next? Bowmore 15yo, Highland Park 18yo

25YO 57.8%

Nose: Gold. Rooty (heather/orris), earthy peatiness. Then come oilskins, magic markers, damp coal shed in winter, then fruit: freshly baked apple cake, banana, quince ... oh and seaweed. Ever-changing. Then comes salt spray.

Palate: Softness of apple cake in custard to start with, then it reaches the middle of the tongue and changes dramatically, with a drier, crisper character emerging. Builds in power (and heat) as the pepperiness begins to come forward. This flares, then returns to its unctuous starting point.

Finish: Starts gently then pounces. Pepper, peppermint.

Conclusion: Has been aged in a refill cask, which allows distillery character to develop with only little nudges from oak.

Flavor Camp: Smoky & Peaty
Where Next? Highland Park 40yo

ORKNEY ISLANDS

Orkney stands apart from the rest of Scotland. Here is a place of standing stones, neolithic burial chambers, and ancient roundhouse forts, a place where the relentless sea beats at the cliffs and Viking sagas still seem contemporary. All seem to coexist in this enchanted collection of islands, whose two distilleries take different approaches to expressing their location.

Temporal simultaneity: Orkney's ancient past is palpably alive.

Highland Park & Scapa

HIGHLAND PARK • KIRKWALL • WWW.HIGHLANDPARK.CO.UK • OPEN TO VISITORS • SEPT–APR, MON–FRI; MAY–AUG, MON–SUN
SCAPA • KIRKWALL • WWW.SCAPAMALT.COM

The propellers cut the cloud, revealing an undulating coastline which, from this height, looks more like a gentle waltz between land and sea than the drunken stagger of the Scottish west coast. Orkney is unlike the rest of Scotland, in landscape, in culture, in people—and in whisky. This archipelago of low green disks remains an outpost of Norse culture, while not being Scandinavian; in Scotland, yet not Scottish. Again, here we have islands whose inbuilt insularity and self-sufficiency have created their own solutions, and the islands' two distilleries, Highland Park and Scapa, represent two different creative approaches to whisky-making: one naturalistic, the other technological.

Highland Park, as the name suggests, sits on top of the hill above Kirkwall, its layered, dark stonework making it look as if it sprang directly from the rock. Passing under its ornate gateway ("Estd. 1798") is like entering a strange other dimension, with flagged winding alleys leading between buildings that seem to have grown organically as the distillery's needs increased.

It floor malts 20 percent of its own barley requirements on site, one day on peat, and one day on coke, creating a medium/heavy character. This is then blended with unpeated malt from the mainland. Dried yeast is used in a long ferment regime, distillation is slow. The result is a new make which mingles fragrant smoke and a citric uplift. "HP" is sweet from the word go, and this dance between smoke, sweetness, orange, and rich fruit continues throughout all its expressions. Sometimes peat has the upper hand, at others the sweetness eases itself forward, while age steadily draws both elements into a dense, honeyed compact. Balance is the key.

HP's DNA lies at the front and back ends of its creation. As part of the Edrington Group, its wood is under the eye of master of wood George Espie, and since 2004 no bourbon casks have been filled (nor,

SCAPA: A VARIATION IN STYLE

Overlooking Scapa Flow and about a mile as the crow flies from Highland Park, Scapa's whisky couldn't be more different. Unpeated and juicily fruity, the key to its character lies in the stillhouse where a Lomond still stands. Though its baffle plates have been removed, its broad neck and the use of a purifier give huge amount of copper conversation. Now renovated by new owner Chivas Brothers, this pretty distillery and its hugely drinkable make is finally becoming better known.

incidentally, does any caramel tinting take place). This is a whisky from ex-sherry casks made from four-year, air-dried seasoned European and American oak. "That wood policy gives consistency of character," says brand ambassador Gerry Tosh. "That's the biggest challenge when you have seven expressions ranging from 12yo to 50yo, with no finishing."

The steep paved alleyways of the Highland Park distillery give it the air of being a self-contained medieval town.

If Espie and whisky-maker Max MacFarlane have their hands on controlling unwanted surprises at the end, then the beginning is down to Orkney.

Walk on to Hobbister Moor, where Highland Park extracts 350 tons of peat a year, and you'll notice a change in the land's aroma: a pine-like, herbal fragrance that's replicated in the whisky. To get a true understanding of why HP is different, travel from there to the cliffs of Yesnaby, where that aerial illusion of a gentle coastal dance is blasted away. Here, on top of these wave-pounded, multicolored strata, the winds reach over 100 mph (160 km/hr) 80 days a year.

"It's Orcadian peat which makes Highland Park different," says Tosh, "and this is where it starts. The salt spray means there's never been trees on Orkney, leaving only heather, and because of that the peat is different, and because of that the aroma when it's burned is different … and that makes Highland Park."

A distillery character rooted in its place of birth.

HIGHLAND PARK TASTING NOTES

NEW MAKE

Nose: Smoke and citrus fruit. Very lifted and sweet. Fresh, kumquat peel, and light, juicy fruit.
Palate: Light nut. Big spread of sweet citrus fruit, then comes fragrant smoke.
Finish: Continues to sweeten with a touch of pear on the finish.

12YO 40%

Nose: Light gold. The fruit has come through, softening the peat. Still that big citric hit, moist fruitcake, berry fruit, and that olive oil. With water, there's baked fruit and gentle smoke.
Palate: Soft and gentle, with hints of white raisins and peat creeping in slowly from the mid-palate. Everything is concentrated in the center of the tongue.
Finish: Sweet smoke.
Conclusion: Already open and picking up complexity.

Flavor Camp: **Smoky & Peaty**
Where Next? Springbank 10yo

18YO 43%

Nose: Full gold. Ripe and fatter than the 12yo with fleshier fruit rather than the peels of the 12yo. Pound cake, sweet cherry, and more spice. Fudge, light honey. Smoke is dying in the fireplace.
Palate: This more dense progression continues. Dried peach, honey, polished oak, walnut. Juicy with a little marmalade.
Finish: Integrated smoke.
Conclusion: A clear family resemblance, and picking up weight from the oak.

Flavor Camp: **Rich & Round**
Where Next? Balvenie 17yo Madeira Wood, Springbank 15yo, Yamazaki 18yo

25YO 48.1%

Nose: Amber. Luscious with masses of sweet dried fruit. More heathery smoke/heather honey than the 18yo. There's also the start of whisky *rancio* notes of furniture polish and moist earth.
Palate: Molasses and concentrated fruit sugars. Allspice, nutmeg. Remains sweet.
Finish: Dried orange peel and fragrant smoke. Darjeeling tea.
Conclusion: Beginning to enter its third age, but the distillery character is there.

Flavor Camp: **Rich & Round**
Where Next? Springbank 18yo, Jura 21yo, Ben Nevis 25yo, Hakushu 25yo

40YO 43%

Nose: Mature. Light *rancio* touches. Highly exotic. Suede and a sexual, sweaty muskiness. There's smoke on the back and then a return of the fudge-like sweetness. Grows with water and keeps on giving for hours, moving into perfumed smoke and light, orris-like rootiness.
Palate: Dry start, then becomes oily and tongue-coating. The leather comes back alongside notes of bitter almond, raisin, and dried peel. In time, the smoke emerges and eventually takes the upper hand.
Finish: Crisp, then sweetens.
Conclusion: Mature and evolved but clearly Highland Park.

Flavor Camp: **Smoky & Peaty**
Where Next? Laphroaig 25yo, Talisker 25yo

SCAPA TASTING NOTES

NEW MAKE

Nose: Estery with banana, green pea, quince, plums. Some damp earth behind and a touch of wax.
Palate: Sweet and lighty oily. Fruit chews.
Finish: Clean. Short.

16YO 40%

Nose: Gold. Lots of American oak overlay. Banana and fruit chews. Light and aromatic with a hint of fresh thyme.
Palate: Light oiliness still. Quite a fat feel, yet somehow airy. Light, toasty notes from the oak. The fruit anchors it to the center of the tongue.
Finish: Unctuous and ripe.
Conclusion: Bouncy and eager to please.

Flavor Camp: **Fruity & Spicy**
Where Next? Old Pulteney 12yo, Clynelish 14yo

1979 47.9%

Nose: Gold. More integrated character with light cacao, mashed banana /black banana. The quince returns. Full and vibrant.
Palate: Complex and rich. British bourbon biscuit, guava. Toasted oak. Sweet.
Finish: Gentle spiciness. Fruit.
Conclusion: Still has masses of distillery character, but calmer than the puppy-like 16yo. Needs time to become serious.

Flavor Camp: **Fruity & Spicy**
Where Next? Craigellachie 14yo

CAMPBELTOWN

Campbeltown Loch, I wish ye were whisky went the old Scottish music-hall song. Well, at one point the singer's dream was reality. This small town at the foot of the Kintyre peninsula has been home to at least 34 distilleries. Fifteen of those disappeared during the depression of the 1850s, but by the end of the nineteenth century, Campbeltown malt was a desirable commodity, its smoky, oily character an integral part of blends. Campbeltown was a boom town.

A deep and sheltered harbor enabled Campbeltown to become a major fishing port and whisky-producer with quick access to the Lowland markets.

The villas on the east side of its bay are evidence of the wealth that existed here. It was whisky-making paradise: there was a deep natural harbor, a local coal seam, 20 maltings in the vicinity working from a mix of local barley and grain from nearby Ireland and southwest Scotland. Distilleries were crammed into its streets, up alleyways. Yet by the end of the 1920s only one, Riechlachan, was operational, and even that fell silent in 1934, when today's survivors, Springbank and Glen Scotia, reopened.

The question of why the other 17 distilleries failed has never been fully answered. Various theories have been put forward: overproduction leading to a drop in quality (though we can dispense with the myth that the whisky was filled into herring barrels); an inability to get rid of effluent (an issue in the nineteenth century when "The free-ranging pigs of Dalintober relished pot ale and were frequently seen indulging that taste at the Pottle Hole"), the working out of the Machrihanish coal seam. All had a part to play, but there isn't a single answer to its decline. It was simply the most exposed region in a perfect storm.

By the 1920s, blenders had fixed on their most popular styles, thereby restricting the requirements of Campbeltown's predominantly smoky/oily character. They were also dealing with the consequences of a fall in consumption during World War I, and a decline in production that had left stock levels even lower than this level of demand. In addition, UK duty had risen significantly in 1918 and 1920, but distillers weren't allowed to pass this on to the consumer, making it more expensive to replenish stocks.

At one point the produce of 34 distilleries would have been shipped out of these waters. Today, there are just three left.

Export was equally difficult, thanks to Prohibition in the US and the Great Depression. Caught between rising costs and falling sales, whisky-making became uneconomical, especially for small, independent distillers.

We tend to forget that the entire industry was affected. Fifty distilleries across Scotland were closed in the 1920s and only two pot-still sites were operational in the whole country in 1933. When the crisis passed, the industry had been rationalized by the Distillers Company Ltd (an echo of the 1850s, a precursor of the 1980s' cull). It was "leaner," maybe even "fitter." What is clear is that the (primarily) small distilleries of Campbeltown simply didn't fit into this new whisky world. This notion that Scotch whisky has lived a charmed life is false.

And yet, there is a happy ending. Today, Campbeltown has been reinstated as a whisky region in its own right and is home to three distilleries making five different whiskies. One of these producers acts as a template for the new wave of small, independent distillers; another has been brought back from the grave. The loch may not be filling with whisky, but Campbeltown is back.

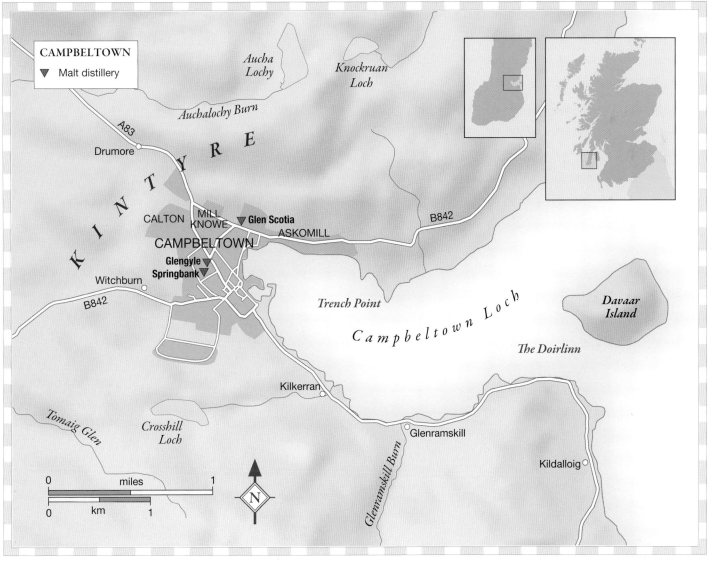

Springbank

Hidden up a narrow street behind a church, the Springbank distillery buildings have been owned by the same family since 1828, the longest such example in Scotch whisky. Self-sufficiency is the byword here. All the distillery's requirements are malted, distilled, matured, and bottled on-site: the only such Scottish distillery to have everything under one roof. This total self-reliance is relatively new, however. Like any distilleries reliant on contracts for fillings, it found itself exposed during the 1980s' crash and responded by going back to fundamentals. The message was clear: Springbank's destiny should lie in its own hands—not by being in hock to the majors.

It's this balance between a retention of old ways while having an eye to the future that intrigues the most. Take what happens inside the boatskin larch fermenters. "We always try to replicate conditions which existed as far back as records allow us to check," says production director Frank McHardy. That means low-gravity worts (around 1,046°), extra-long (100 hour) ferments, and a low-strength wash (between 4.5–5 percent—the industry standard is 8–9 percent. "That lengthy fermentation in larch promotes loads of fruitiness, the lower OG helps create esters."

The distillery's three stills—a direct-fired wash still and two low-wines stills, one of which runs into a worm tub—produce three distinct new makes. Springbank itself is 2.5 times distilled: the wash still giving low wines, the low-wines still yieldng "feints," and the final mix in the second low-wines still, which is a mix of 20 percent low wines and 80 percent feints (*see* pp.14–15). The new make is big, one of the most complex in Scotch, capable of prolonged aging and giving a sense that all of Scotland's styles are here, compressed into one package.

"It's a method of production which has gone on for as long as we have records," says McHardy. "One thing we're pretty sure of is that Springbank Distillery was the only one in Campbeltown to carry out this process." It could be the reason for its survival.

Of the other two styles, the fragrant, appley, unpeated, triple-distilled Hazelburn looks to the Lowlands, or maybe to northern Ireland, where McHardy spent 13 years as manager of Bushmills. Meanwhile, heavily peated Longrow is "normal," i.e. double-distilled, but maybe closer to the original "Campbeltown" template. Bold when young, it lacks any of the rubbery immaturity that can mar young, peaty whiskies and can also grow in complexity (*see* p.192).

Springbank remains an upholder of traditional whisky-making customs, yet it is also the template for many new distilleries.

From barley to bottle. Springbank is the only distillery to malt, distill, mature, and bottle on the same site.

museum of whisky-making. Its calculated belief in the old ways, but also in multiple streams, a tight wood policy, and self-sufficiency has made it a template for other newer (and often noisier) distillers. It's not just the past, it's a future.

All three are defiantly non-linear. This is a distillery in which flavors jump through hoops, run against the norm, are nudged, boosted, and refined. Don't, however, patronize Springbank by thinking it is some

Ultimately, it's Springbank's ability to stay ahead of the times that has allowed it to survive over the years.

SPRINGBANK TASTING NOTES

NEW MAKE

Nose: Huge, luscious, and complex. Baked, soft fruit, some vanilla, touch of Brylcreem, and very light cereal. Sweet, rich, and heavy. With water, smoke and a little yeast.

Palate: Heavy, oily. Very full-bodied, with rich smoke and a litle briny tingle. Heavy, earthy, and ripe.

Finish: Earthy and full.

10YO 46%

Nose: Light gold. Light, additive oak-shaving notes. Smoke, ripe fruits, extra-virgin olive oil, and fragrant wood. Rich and charred. Toasty, with a light, citric lift.

Palate: Sweet start, and then the black olive comes through before briny smoke builds. Still tense.

Finish: Smoke. Long.

Conclusion: A slow, gentle development from the new make. Like a young white burgundy or Riesling, it's hugely drinkable but with so much more to come.

Flavor Camp: Smoky & Peaty

Where Next? Ardmore Traditional Cask, Caol Ila 12yo, Talisker 10yo

15YO 46%

Nose: Light gold. Aniseed, ashy smoke, charcoal, and that earthy note on new make returning. Some marzipan, olive tapenade, then comes the ripe, soft fruit mixing with hazelnut. With water, old bookshops/old paper.

Palate: Sweet start. The feel is still similar to the oily/chewy new make but now there is added semi-dried fruit. Rich.

Finish: Light smoke and a touch of brine.

Conclusion: Now it has opened fully and the wood is fully integrated.

Flavor Camp: Rich & Round

Where Next? Benromach 1981, Glendronach 15yo, Highland Park 18yo

18YO 46%

Nose: Full gold. Baked fruit and integrated wood. Smoke and coconut, dried fruit and caraway. Still that black-olive character running through. Heavy and perfumed.

Palate: More overt smoke but balanced by an intense spearmint and eucalyptus tone that shifts into cough syrup/cherry. Remains earthy and rooty. Needs water for the sweet fruit to come through, and also that briny note.

Finish: Mossy.

Conclusion: Distillery character all through, just building in complexity.

Flavor Camp: Rich & Round

Where Next? Highland Park 25yo

HAZELBURN TASTING NOTES

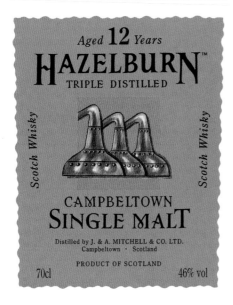

NEW MAKE

Nose: Clean and spicy. High-toned and limey with a little touch of starch behind. Intense and pure. Green apple.
Palate: Light and rapier-like intensity but good, soft feel.
Finish: Green plum.

HAZELBURN 12YO 46%

Nose: Full gold. Sherried notes: amontillado-like nuttiness mixed with molasses, prune, and white raisin. Real lifted sweetness behind.
Palate: Soft. The wood has thickened the feel but the penetrating intensity cuts through the oak, adding a zesty intensity to the top. Becomes more citric as it moves: orange and sweet dried fruit.
Finish: Clean.
Conclusion: Full, balanced integration of distillery and oak.

Flavor Camp: **Fruity & Spicy**
Where Next? Arran 12yo

HAZELBURN CV 46%

Nose: Pale gold. Very fresh and citric with lots of jasmine tea. Light oak and apple cake. Orange blossom. Lifted. Oil paint: artist's studio.
Palate: Very soft with quite firm oak before the lilies and jasmine take control. Green tea and white chocolate.
Finish: Lightly oily.
Conclusion: A fresh and direct expression that shows Hazelburn's floral aspects.

Flavor Camp: **Fragrant & Floral**
Where Next? Bladnoch 8yo, anCnoc 12yo

LONGROW TASTING NOTES

NEW MAKE

Nose: Very sweet. Cassis. Earthy smoke. Wet slate.
Palate: Intense and sweet start before a huge purple cloud of smoke. Touch of tomato-sauce spiciness.
Finish: Bone-dry, smoke, and a hint of tingling salt.

14YO 46%

Nose: Rounded. The smoke is obvious but not dominant since more wood coming through; think moorland and chimneys, lilac and bracken. Bonfire and wet slate character suggest there's more.
Palate: Big and lightly malty. Dry wood smoke, then that ripe black fruit seen on the new make makes its move, mixing with some sweet date.
Finish: The smoke surges through and is sustained.
Conclusion: Now on a roll.

Flavor Camp: **Smoky & Peaty**
Where Next? Yoichi 15yo, Ardbeg Airigh nam Beist 1990

LONGROW CV 46%

Nose: Light gold. Smoky. Rooty, sooty. Some orris and violet with touches of lanolin but a vibrant energy that stops it from becoming too heavy. With water, a waxiness.
Palate: Pepper, then wintergreen/balsam and a slight grassiness as smoke rumbles below. With water, there's lemon and an unctuous and waxy feel.
Finish: Throat-coating. Smoky.
Conclusion: A big but fresh whisky.

Flavor Camp: **Smoky & Peaty**
Where Next? Ardbeg 10yo, Yoichi 10yo

KILKERRAN TASTING NOTES

NEW MAKE

Nose: Clean. Wet hay. Bakery and light sulfur. Yeasty and a slippery weight.
Palate: Similar weight to its neighbor but fatter. Starts fruity, then drier and malty.
Finish: Perfumed.

3YO CASK SAMPLE

Nose: Rich gold. Precocious. Lots of additive coconutty notes. Sweet, damp hay/raffia and patisserie.
Palate: Ripe and sweet, with mango balanced by oak and that cereal grip. Mouthfilling.
Finish: Long and sweet.
Conclusion: Been given a big leg up by an active cask, but moving speedily.

Flavor Camp: **Fruity & Spicy**

2004 WORK IN PROGRESS NO 2, 46%

Nose: Pale. Quite light and shy. Dusty hay loft/wheat chaff. Some oak shavings. With water, there's a huge, aromatic lift into angelica and dried oregano.
Palate: Very sweet, then a sudden citric shift. Has focus and attack, with perfumed note seen in new make. Palate has that distillery fatness anchoring things.
Finish: Scented.
Conclusion: Complex. Developing in an interesting way.

Flavor Camp: **Fruity & Spicy**
Where Next? Arran 10yo

Glengyle & Glen Scotia

CAMPBELTOWN • WWW.KILKERRAN.COM • CONTACT DISTILLERY FOR VISIT

The decline of Campbeltown's whisky is written upon its architecture. Tantalising glimpses of old sites remain – a cracked and faded sign, the shape of the windows on a block of flats, the incongruous sight of a supermarket with a pagoda roof. It's a fascinating but sobering experience which exposes the fragility of the whisky industry. Yet dwelling on its past is to do the town's distillers a disservice. Campbeltown is not a place for whisky archaeologists, but whisky lovers.

In 2000 Hedley Wright, whose family has owned Springbank since its founding in 1828, bought a shell of a distillery next door. This had been Glengyle, closed for 80 years.

The derelict building was refitted into a neat single-level design and its pair of stills were salvaged from Frank McHardy's first distillery, Ben Wyvis, which operated briefly in the Invergordon grain distillery. "These were subjected to some changes when installed here," McHardy explains. "We got the coppersmith to reshape the ogee and also sweeten the angle of the pot's shoulders. The lyne arm was also angled upwards to give the still some reflux qualities." The early releases show a lightly peated, medium-bodied character.

The whisky is called Kilkerran as the brand name, Glengyle is owned by Campbeltown's third distillery: Glen Scotia. When Alfred Barnard arrived in Campbeltown he wrote that this plant, then just called Scotia, "seems to have hidden itself away out of sight, as if the art of making whisky ... was bound to be kept a dark secret".

Not a lot has changed. Glen Scotia remains one of Scotland's more elusive distilleries, famed for its alleged haunting by former owner Duncan MacCallum. Now owned by Loch Lomond Distillers it's been in full production since 1999, "and never with the aid of people from Springbank," says director Gavin Durnin at Loch Lomond, scotching one persistent rumour. At the time of writing, a peated 12yo is on the market.

Back from the dead. Glengyle was reopened in 1999 after 80 years of silence.

GLEN SCOTIA TASTING NOTES

12YO 40%

Nose: Coal, wet plaster, bandages, and smoke with a fresh cereal undertow.
Palate: Smoky. Heavy and rounded, with a tongue-clinging quality. Dense. Nuttier with water.
Finish: Lingering smoke and very light oak.
Conclusion: This could be the old Campbeltown style.

Flavour Camp: Smoky & Peaty

Where Next? Ledaig (peated Tobermory)

The nose knows.
Edrington's master
blender, Gordon
Motion, at work.

**Opposite: Although
the personnel** may
have changed, the
process of blending
remains the same.

SCOTCH BLENDS

Scotch single malt may link the spirit with the land, but the majority of these distilleries would not exist were it not for blended Scotch, which accounts for over 90 percent of the Scotch whisky sold throughout the world. When the world talks of "Scotch," it is talking blends. And blends have their own story to tell.

Blends are less about place, but more about occasion, and flavor lies at the heart of it. Scotch whisky has faced numerous crises throughout its history. Each time it has reinvented itself by looking at flavor.

In the 1830s, whisky distilling was seen as a get-rich-quick scheme, but within two decades the industry was over capacity. Rum was Scotland's preferred spirit, while Irish whiskey was outselling Scotch in Scotland. "Chiefly on account of its uniformity of style," as William Ross, managing director of key player Distillers Company Ltd (DCL), noted. He was addressing the Royal Commission on Whisky and Potable Spirits, which was set up in 1908 and formalized the legal definition of Scotch whisky.

A legal change in 1853 had allowed whisky of different ages from the same distillery to be blended "in bond" (i.e. prior to tax being paid), which allowed the mixing of different ages and enabled more experimentation in a bid to achieve flavor consistency. Within a year, Usher's Old Vatted Glenlivet (initially a vatted malt) appeared. The blending houses we know today developed in 1860, in tandem with the first issuing of "grocers' licenses," a move that enabled a wider range of retailers (especially grocers) to sell direct to the public.

It was the grocers who took advantage of this opportunity; people like John Walker and his son, Alexander, the Chivas brothers, and wine merchants like John Dewar, Matthew Gloag, Charles Mackinlay, George Ballantine, and William Teacher.

Understanding the principles of bringing together different flavors and textures to create a uniform and consistent whole was familiar to them. The significant shift wasn't just in the liquid, where light patent-still grain calmed the rambunctious temperaments of the single malt, but in the merchants putting their names on the bottle as a personal guarantee of quality. From this point on, blends were the future of Scotch, and the blender become the arbiter of style.

By the end of the nineteenth century, new malt distilleries were being built specifically to tap into the blended market, or at the behest of blenders themselves. This happened particularly in Speyside, as the blenders tried to give their blends a gentler character. Why? The market.

The genius of blenders such as the Walker and Dewar families and James Buchanan was that they went to the English market, saw what the middle class wanted to drink, and fitted a blend around those requirements. The same process happened around the world. Blends were being made to suit a serving style (whisky and soda) and an occasion (pre-dinner, pre-theater). Scotch became a signifier of success.

This process has continued through the lightening years of Prohibition and postwar times to today's market, moving from the cut-glass tumblers of London to the beach bars of Brazil, the nightclubs of Shanghai or the *shebeens* of Soweto. Blends by their nature are fluid: they shift in accordance with changing tastes. They live in the real world.

Grain Whisky

Grain whisky is conceivably the most misunderstood of all whisky's styles. For the majority of drinkers, column-still whisky equals neutral alcohol. Grain whisky? Nothing more than Scottish vodka whose existence in a blend is simply to dilute and bulk up the malts, right? No. None of that is true. Grain has character of its own and performs a vital function within a blend.

By law, grain must have flavor. The Scotch Whisky Act of 1988 states that it must be distilled "at an alcoholic strength by volume of less than 94.8 percent, so that the distillate has an aroma and taste derived from the raw materials used in and the method of its production." In other words, although grain can be high in strength, the regulations say it must have flavor and character.

Its production is different (*see* p.16). The chosen cereal (these days wheat, in the past corn) is cooked in order to hydrolize the starch. "It's like boiling tatties," says Billy Mitchell at Cameronbridge Distillery in Fife. "The hot water changes them [the grains] from hard to soft." Malted barley is then added for its natural enzymes, which convert starch into sugar. The resulting worts are drained, fermented, and then distilled in a column still.

At the start of the nineteenth century, distillers around the world were trying to make production more efficient. A still where you could put fermented wash in one end and get alcohol out the other was a vision pursued by engineers such as Blumenthal, St Marc, and Robert Stein, who installed two at Kirkliston, Edinburgh, and Wandsworth, London, in 1827.

Then, in 1831, Irishman Aeneas Coffey, who was familar with all these designs, patented an improved variation. His design is still in use today. It comprises two linked columns (the analyzer and the

Through a glass darkly. Diageo's master blender, Maureen Robinson, using tinted *copitas* so as not to be distracted by the color of the whisky.

Opposite: Column stills come in all shapes and sizes, but the principle remains the same: to produce a consistent, light-bodied spirit.

Opposite right: Steel-clad, but the insides of column stills are usually made of copper.

rectifier), each of which is divided horizontally by perforated plates. Wash travels in a pipe from the top to the bottom of the rectifier and then is sprayed out at the top of the analyzer. As it descends, it meets live steam that vaporizes the alcohol, which is piped back to the foot of the rectifier and released.

As it rises, the vapor begins to cool and the heavier elements begin to reflux out. In this way, plate by plate, the increasingly light-flavored vapor rises until it is diverted into a condenser. Because the columns are huge, only the highest and lightest-flavored alcohols can reach this collection point. Today, more complex setups (such as the multiple-column vacuum still at William Grant's Girvan site) are also

used, on the principle that the more columns there are, the lighter and cleaner the spirit will be. Coffey still spirit tends to be slightly richer and oilier in texture. This means that every Scottish grain distillery produces a different new-make character: intense and citric from Girvan, oily from Cameronbridge's Coffey's, clean from North British, and so on.

Most distillers will age the new-make grain in first-fill ex-bourbon casks. This both adds a vanilla/coconut character and also helps to "season" the cask for long-term maturation of malt. Mature grain is luscious and gentle, with a silky, tongue-coating quality, and it is this that the blender particularly wants.

The Art of Blending

CHIVAS BROTHERS • WWW.CHIVAS.COM • SEE ALSO WWW.MALTWHISKYDISTILLERIES.COM
DEWARS • ABERFELDY • WWW.DEWARSWOW.COM • OPEN ALL YEAR • MON–SAT
JOHNNIE WALKER • WWW.JOHNNIEWALKER.COM • WWW.DISCOVERING-DISTILLERIES.COM/CARDHU
GRANT'S • DUFFTOWN • WWW.GRANTSWHISKY.COM • WWW.WILLIAMGRANT.COM

In principle, the creation of a blend is a simple one. You take some grain whiskies and some malt whiskies and mix them together to give an acceptable final flavor. We can all do this as a one-off and make maybe one bottle that we find satisfying. What if you are making millions of bottles every year? Each time you make your blend it must be the same. Again, in principle that doesn't sound too difficult. As long as you have a recipe, you can ask the computer to pick the casks you need and away you go. Can't be too difficult, can it?

There's a problem, however. Every cask is different. Your original recipe may include whiskies from distilleries that no longer exist, or from firms which you have fallen out with. Blending isn't about following a recipe; it is about making a consistent product with a constantly changing range of components. It cannot be done by a computer, only a person.

The blender must have an intimate knowledge of his palette of flavors. He must know not just what whisky A tastes like, but what it tastes like when put with whisky B, C, and D. He also needs to build in as many options for himself as possible.

We have a tendency to look at the malt component within the blend as being made up of the single malts we know as bottled brands. Nothing could be further from the truth. In principle, today, you can draw from 96 single-malt distilleries, each with its own distillery character. They are then aged in three sizes of cask, each of which will give you a different flavor. These casks are made from two different species of oak, each of which will give you a different flavor. The casks can be filled once, refilled, and then recharred. Each one of these will give a different flavor.

You can also draw from any of these casks once their contents is more than three years old, and carry on drawing up to whatever age you want. Each year will give you a different flavor. You need to know all the options and permutations. It's a bit more complex than just taking some Distillery X 12yo plus some of its buddies and bunging them together. Now, tell me, do you still think you can be a blender?

Then there's the issue of grain, which, as we have seen, cannot be considered as just a filler. It has a character of its own. Grain adds texture to a blend—that tongue-coating quality—as well as pulling flavors out from the malts. It enhances the malts, warps them, and melds them. Grain is the ameliorator.

It is normal to want answers to questions like how many malts are in this blend? What are they? And how old are they? The answers are: the right number for the flavor to be delivered; the right ones for the flavor to work; and the right ages for the flavor to work. The numbers don't matter, the recipe doesn't matter. The flavor does.

Putting together a blend is one thing. Blends succeeded because the blenders gave the consumers what they wanted. Yet consumers' tastes change.

Writing about blends in 1930, Aeneas MacDonald noted:

> *Blending made it possible to make a whisky which would suit a different climate and different classes of patrons. The great export trade in whisky is almost entirely due to the elasticity which blending brought to the industry. Even today the aesthetics of whisky have a very definite geographical aspect. London likes a milder, less pronounced whisky than Lancashire, [which prefers one] less pungent than Edinburgh, which is surpassed by Glasgow where they revel in the denser and fuller-bodied joys of the Campbeltown malts.*

Blends succeeded because blenders understood MacDonald's "elasticity." At his time of writing, a major change was taking place in the USA. During Prohibition, America went light. Seeing this trend, London wine merchant Berry Bros. & Rudd hired a blender, Charles H. Julian, to make a light whisky: Cutty Sark. It was a speakeasy hit. In 1933, Cutty's former US agent went to another St. James's Street wine merchant, Justerini & Brooks, and asked for the same style of blend. They hired a certain Charles H. Julian, who came up with J&B. This lightening process continued postwar. Lighter blends such as Johnnie Walker Red Label began to be promoted, and in 1954, Seagram relaunched Chivas Regal 12yo reformulated by … Charles H. Julian.

Julian demonstrated the thinking behind every new blend: When is this going to be drunk? How is it going to be drunk? And now I know this, what whiskies can I use to deliver a blend that suits the occasion? The blender's first question when creating a blend isn't what whiskies are to be used, but when is the blend going to be consumed? It also must remain true to the house style and play variations on that theme. Walker is about big flavor with smoke; Chivas is more delicate and fragrant, Dewar's is sweet and honeyed, Grant's is about richness, Famous Grouse is medium-bodied but underpinned with sherried notes.

Looking at blends in this way moves you away from worrying about age statements to concentrate instead on the flavor and the occasion. Is Johnnie Walker Blue "better" than Red? Dewar's Signature better than White Label? In certain circumstances, yes, but the reverse is often just as true. Blends are about the right flavor at the right time.

SCOTCH BLENDS TASTING NOTES

CHIVAS REGAL 12YO 40%

Nose: Straw. Fragrant and floral: apple blossom, freesia. Nutty, with a lick of cream.
Palate: Light, with green fruit and grassy, perfumed notes.
Finish: Lightly spiced. Short.
Conclusion: Light and delicate.

Flavor Camp: **Fragrant & Floral**
Where Next? Cutty Sark

CHIVAS REGAL 18YO 40%

Nose: Sweet and medium-weight. Baked fruit, nuts, and fresh citrus fruit. With water, sweet maltiness.
Palate: Gentle, fruity. Very sweet. Butterscotch, a touch of pine nut/chestnut and mocha. Shows maturity.
Finish: Vanilla toffee.
Conclusion: Much difference between this and the 12yo.

Flavor Camp: **Fruity & Spicy**
Where Next? Dewar's 12yo

DEWAR'S WHITE LABEL NAS, 40%

Nose: Soft, with fresh vanilla. Smooth grain and some honey and a light grassiness. Sweet and clean.
Palate: Gentle and ultra-creamy. Cocoa butter. Silky feel with a little lemon zest, peach; a wheaty note.
Finish: Lightly spicy with firm, young grain giving grip.
Conclusion: The sweetest and softest of the major players.

Flavor Camp: **Fruity & Spicy**
Where Next? Ballantine's Finest

DEWAR'S 12YO 40%

Nose: Gold. Crisper, with more coconut and cookie-like oak. The chocolate is there, but now crackly and praline-like. With time, orange zest and fruitcake. Still some green melon and airy grain.
Palate: More sherry influence. Similar silky feel to White Label but deeper. Dark honey. Ripened fruit.
Finish: Spicy again.
Conclusion: More complex; balanced. Firm and rounded.

Flavor Camp: **Fruity & Spicy**
Where Next? Famous Grouse 12yo

DEWAR'S SIGNATURE NAS, 43%

Nose: Sweet, with lots of ripe red fruit and a heavy floral character. Little stewed apricot, sealing wax, raisins, sweet spice, and crystallized fruit.
Palate: Fragrant and blossom-like. Lily alongside dry hay and that soft fruit typical of the house style, alongside dried apple and bitter chocolate. Thicker feel. Slow to open.
Finish: Classic Dewar's sweet spiciness.
Conclusion: Like Walker Blue, this is a super-premium blend of rarer whiskies which is wholly in the luscious, fruity Dewar's style.

Flavor Camp: **Fruity & Spicy**
Where Next? Royal Salute 21yo

GRANT'S FAMILY RESERVE NAS, 40%

Nose: Gold. Medium-weight and clean. Crisp malt with touches of spice. Overripe banana and a touch of white raisin. Ripe apple and smoke with water.
Palate: Soft and generous, with tangerine. Quite intense in the middle of the tongue before becoming richer and more fruit-driven on the back. Coconut.
Finish: Spicy and dry.
Conclusion: Balanced, and one of the richest NAS brands.

Flavor Camp: **Fruity & Spicy**
Where Next? Famous Grouse

GRANT'S 25YO 40%

Nose: Amber. Mature, with classic whisky *rancio* notes: baked fruit, rum-soaked white raisins, cedar, plum, and toffee. With water, the caramelized *crème brûlée* notes of old grain.
Palate: Quite perfumed: lavender and sage. Lightly smoky. Some fig, black olive. Ripe and long.
Finish: Full, with that perfumed note continuing.
Conclusion: Another blend that can stand its ground against single malt.

Flavor Camp: **Rich & Round**
Where Next? Johnnie Walker Blue Label

JOHNNIE WALKER RED LABEL NAS, 40%

Nose: Reddish(!) in color. Vibrant with ginger root. Hint of malt and ozone-like freshness. Zestiness. Lightly heathery smoke, then a touch of gorse and lemongrass. Very clean.
Palate: Vivacious with a silky mid-palate. Tongue-coating.
Finish: Spicy, with that ginger note coming through.
Conclusion: An open, outdoors style of whisky.

Flavor Camp: **Fragrant & Perfumed**
Where Next? Grant's Family Reserve

JOHNNIE WALKER BLACK LABEL 12YO, 40%

Nose: Amber. Ripe black fruit (damson, mulberry) with a little prune and raisin. Sandalwood and a jammy richness to it with the signature heathery smoke hanging in the background. Complex.
Palate: Ripe and rich. Silky once more. Dark honey (almost molasses), raisin. Mouthfilling.
Finish: Long, with fragrant smoke.
Conclusion: The freshness of Red has been replaced by chewy, mellow notes.

Flavor Camp: **Rich & Round**
Where Next? Grant's 12yo

JOHNNIE WALKER BLUE LABEL NAS, 43%

Nose: Amber. Mature. Field mushrooms. Preserved-lemon-scented, dried flowers, iris. An old country house with many rooms: floor polish, hint of leather, raisin, plum skin, and cedar. Complex. Needs time.
Palate: Rich and seamless. Rose petal, fig, molasses, dunnage warehouse. Dried fruit, but also a fresh lift. Supple and highly complex.
Finish: Very smoky.
Conclusion: It has Walker's immediacy of character, palate weight, and smoked complexity.

Flavor Camp: **Rich & Round**
Where Next? Grant's 25yo; Whyte & Mackay 40yo

IRELAND

Aine scanned the gray sea. There, a smudge on the horizon, was the coastline of Islay, her future husband's island. Two great families, the O'Cathains and the Macdonalds, would be linked; the two ancient *dalriadas* (kingdoms) joined. An important marriage, so much so that among her retinue was Padraig MacBeathad, her physician, as his father had been to hers. In this way, conceivably, the knowledge of distillation slipped across the North Channel to Scotland. Padraig's family, who changed their name to Beaton, translated ancient texts on distillation into Gaelic. The first Irish distillers? The first Scottish ones? We don't know …

Previous page: Whiskey-making has been part of rural Ireland for centuries.

Until the nineteenth century, most of Ireland's whiskey was made by small farmers.

Irish whiskey's early history is sketchy. There's evidence that whiskey was widely drunk by the sixteenth century, and in 1608 licenses which gave their owners (i.e. the King's cronies) exclusive rights to distill. Among them was Sir Thomas Phillipps, who was allowed to distill, "within the countrey [sic] of Colrane otherwise called O'Cahanes countrey … in Co. Antrim." Aine's ghost stirs.

Irish whiskey's history parallels that of Scotch: a struggle between small-scale distillation of *poitín* (or poteen: illegal "moonshine") and larger licensed "Parliamentary" whiskey. The major change took place after the liberalization of the industry in 1823. Immediately, Irish distillers began to think BIG. In Dublin, distillers such as John Jameson began to produce huge volumes of whiskey from massive pot stills—and put their names on the bottle as a seal of quality. Crucially, these new Irish whiskeys were consistent in quality. They became the gold standard for whisky distillation, but the nineteenth century was their high point.

Jameson's Bow Street distillery in Dublin is still there, but it's a heritage center. Irish whiskey has been through the cruelest run of luck, bad management, and government interference ever to beset an industry. By the end of the nineteenth century, the Scottish Distillers Company Ltd (DCL) began a slash-and-burn operation in Ireland, buying grain plants in north and south and closing them down in order to protect its Scottish base. By 1930, managing director William Ross noted: "Ireland is an irrelevance." Independence put paid

to the sales in the British Empire, a refusal to do business with bootleggers closed off Prohibition-era America, and Irish Prime Minister Éamon de Valera then capped whiskey exports and hiked domestic taxes. By 1966, the Republic's last three distillers merged operations, and, in 1975, centralized production at a new distillery at Midleton. In 1986, Irish Distillers Ltd (IDL) bought Bushmills, the sole distillery in the north.

But then, slowly, incredibly, things begin to change. In 1988, whiskey started trickling from an ugly industrial unit in the Cooley peninsula; IDL's production team's world-leading work on wood management changed their whiskeys immeasurably, and then, in 2005, IDL's parent, Pernod Ricard, sold Bushmills to its biggest rival, Diageo. Suddenly, there was an Irish category once more. Just as we went to press, William Grant & Sons announced plans to build a new distillery to produce Tullamore Dew.

Look hard and you realize there's no single thing that can be defined as "Irish whiskey." There are three distillers in Ireland making whiskey in three very different ways. This is diverse.

Ireland exists on stories and memories of old silent stills, piles of stones, half-forgotten tastes; a place of soft melancholy and the quiet smile which accompanies it. But Irish whiskey is not dead. It lives again: in pubs, in songs, in folk memory, and in distilleries. An irrelevance? Not anymore.

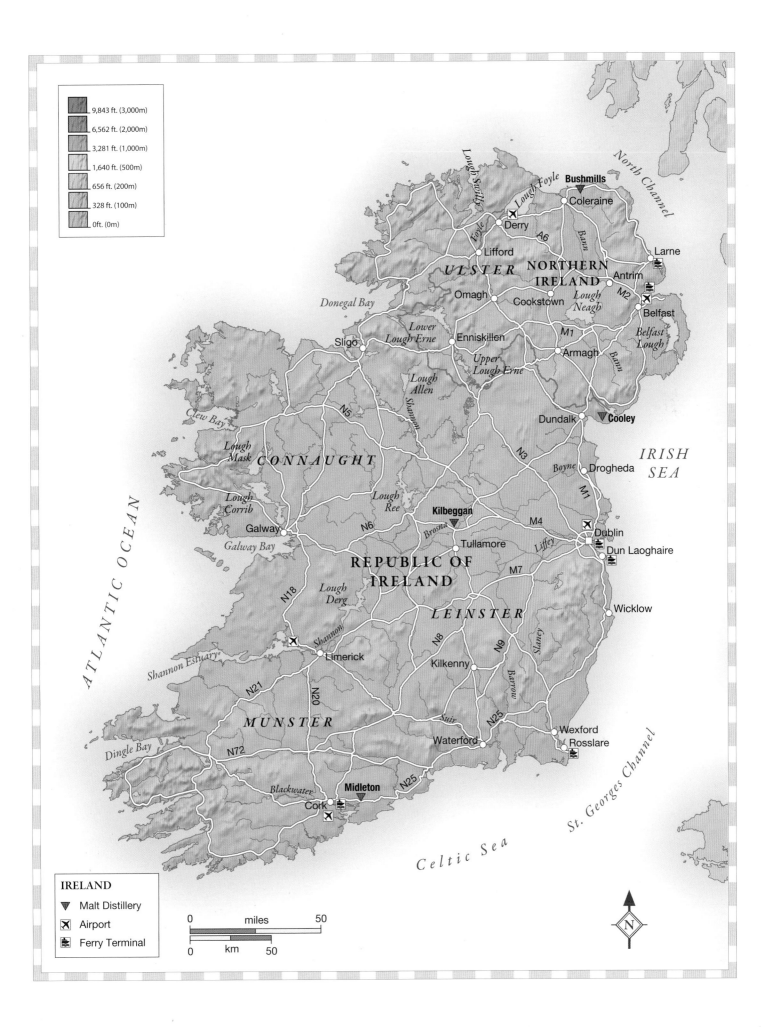

9,843 ft. (3,000m)
6,562 ft. (2,000m)
3,281 ft. (1,000m)
1,640 ft. (500m)
656 ft. (200m)
328 ft. (100m)
0 ft. (0m)

Lough Swilly

Lough Foyle

Bushmills

North Channel

Coleraine

Derry

A6

Lifford

Larne

Bann

U L S T E R

NORTHERN
IRELAND

Antrim

M2

Omagh

Cookstown

Lough
Neagh

Belfast

Donegal Bay

Foyle

Lower
Lough Erne

Enniskillen

M1

Belfast
Lough

Sligo

Upper
Lough Erne

Armagh

Bann

Lough
Allen

Shannon

Dundalk

Cooley

Clew Bay

N5

Lough
Mask

C O N N A U G H T

Boyne

Drogheda

IRISH
SEA

Lough
Corrib

Lough
Ree

Lough
Allen

M1

Galway

N6

Brosna

Kilbeggan

Galway Bay

REPUBLIC OF
IRELAND

Tullamore

M4

Liffey

Dublin

Dun Laoghaire

Lough
Derg

N18

L E I N S T E R

Wicklow

Shannon

Shannon Estuary

Limerick

N8

M7

N9

Slaney

Kilkenny

Barrow

N21

N20

M U N S T E R

Suir

N25

Dingle Bay

N72

Waterford

Wexford

Rosslare

Blackwater

Midleton

N25

Cork

St. Georges Channel

Celtic Sea

ATLANTIC OCEAN

IRELAND

▼ Malt Distillery
✈ Airport
⛴ Ferry Terminal

miles
0   50

km
0   50

N

The art of distilling spread from Ireland's rocky coastline to Scotland.

Bushmills

BUSHMILLS • WWW.BUSHMILLS.COM • OPEN ALL YEAR • MON–SUN, EXCEPT HOLIDAYS

The North Channel has long been a busy waterway between Ireland and Scotland. There are years of shared tales, songs, and poetry, of politics and science, a great tidal flow of humanity and ideas. Whiskey is an integral part of this. Specifically, Bushmills is part of this, although this being Ireland, to get to the facts you first need to clear away the brush of half-truths.

For example, the distillery wasn't founded in 1608. The license to distill in the district was granted then, but Bushmills' distillery first appeared in 1784, complete with two small pot stills. By 1853 it had been "improved" and had just had electric light installed, although two weeks after the power was switched on, the distillery was destroyed by fire. Whether the two are connected isn't clear.

When whiskey chronicler Alfred Barnard visited in the 1880s, he reported enthusiastically that the now enlarged distillery was "alive to all modern inventions." It wasn't making triple-distilled whiskey though. That only started in the 1930s, after Jimmy Morrison was employed as manager to improve the make. His solution was to try "a triple type of pot still [distillation] not in use anywhere else" (*see* p.17). Oh, and it was peated until the 1970s.

Today, it makes a light, grassy triple-distilled malt as well as its own blends: the rich, fruity Black Bush and the fresh, gingery Original. It is both immediate and easy-sipping, but at the same time complex—more or less what you would expect from such a shape-shifting place.

Bushmills' heart is the spirit that comes out of its nine stills, scattered in seemingly random fashion in the stillhouse, whose slender necks have squeezed the vapor into an intimate conversation with the copper, increasing reflux.

Light is the desired flavor here, achieved by cutting the spirit from the intermediate stills into three. The heads are run into the low-wines receiver, then a middle cut is taken which goes into the strong-feints receiver. The remainder, the weak feints, ends up in the low-wines receiver (*see* p.17).

The two stills being used for the spirit run are then each charged with 1,849 gallons (7,000 liters) of strong feints. Only a tiny cut (from 86 percent down to 83 percent) is collected as spirit. The distillation continues, however, with the rest of the distillate being collect as strong feints. Of course, the weak feints and the excess from the spirit still keep being redistilled, cut, redistilled, and topped up. It makes Mortlach and Dalmore seem simple.

"We say it's triple distillation," says manager Colum Egan, "but we're probably distilling some of this six or seven times. The fact that we have four, maybe even six cut points through the process also gives us a better opportunity to add strength or take out flavors we don't want."

Today, the new make is matured in a high percentage of first-fill casks. "This whiskey is light, complex, but there's less fusel oils," says Egan. "If you have a delicate spirit you daren't put it into poor casks."

Everything about the distillery and its evolving whiskeys speaks of a place that has always been self-aware. It has taken what may appear

Whiskey on the rocks. The basalt columns of the Giants Causeway are close to Bushmills distillery.

to be the unconventional route, the awkward path, but that decision, whether conscious or intuitive, has been the very reason why it has survived. It never quite made "Irish whiskey"; it made Bushmills. The very thing that sets Bushmills apart—its flavor and the way in which that flavor is made—speaks of its heritage, its cultural *terroir*. This is a part of the world where whiskey-making is in the blood.

A large, rambling site, Bushmills has been through a range of different incarnations in its long and varied history.

Antrim's quiet lanes, its serrated coastline, have produced people who are born distillers, who revel in their questioning mentality and a belief in an unconventional individuality.

BUSHMILLS TASTING NOTES

ORIGINAL BLEND, 40%

Nose: Light gold. Very fresh, with a delicate herbal twinge. Hot clay and scented grasses.
Palate: Sweet, with a little dustiness. Sweet centered with a little orange-blossom honey, becoming grassy to the back.
Finish: Crisp and gingery.
Conclusion: Made for mixing—and that's a compliment.

Flavor Camp: **Fragrant & Floral**
Where Next? Johnnie Walker Red Label

BLACK BUSH BLEND, 40%

Nose: Full gold. Clean oak. Spice and honeydew melon, with a little date, black grape juice, then coconut and cedar. With water, it's plum clafoutis and stewed rhubarb.
Palate: Juicy, fruity, and ripe. Fruitcake. Deep. Pools in the center.
Finish: Creamy and long.
Conclusion: Serve with one rock of ice.

Flavor Camp: **Rich & Round**
Where Next? Johnnie Walker Black Label

10YO 40%

Nose: Gold. Green-grassy moving into light hay, malt bin, then fresh plaster, balsa wood. Clover.
Palate: Crisp, but with vanilla sweetness from ex-bourbon casks. Lightly fragrant.
Finish: Dry grasses and dusty spices.
Conclusion: Slightly fuller than in the past.

Flavor Camp: **Fragrant & Floral**
Where Next? Cardhu 12yo, Strathisla 12yo

16YO 40%

Nose: Deep amber. Big, sweet-sherry character, lots of concentrated black fruit, prune but also sweet oak. Has retained the juiciness of character. Raisins, teacakes.
Palate: Ripe and vinous. Mulberry jam, currant. Just a little touch of tannin; then black cherry before toffee.
Finish: Grapes again.
Conclusion: Maturation in three oak types, yet not grippy.

Flavor Camp: **Rich & Round**
Where Next? Balvenie Madeira Cask

21YO MADEIRA CASK FINISH, 40%

Nose: Big and generous. Shifting into coffee cake with butter icing. Water makes it reminiscent of a sherry *bodega*. Then come mint, citrus zest, and fresh tanned leather. Grist-like sweetness.
Palate: Sweet and gripping, with dark dried fruit, molasses, red licorice.
Finish: Firm, nutty, and clean.
Conclusion: Double-cask treatment has added weight.

Flavor Camp: **Rich & Round**
Where Next? Dalmore 15yo

Cooley & Kilbeggan

COOLEY • DUNDALK • WWW.COOLEYWHISKEY.COM / KILBEGGAN • TULLAMORE • WWW.KILBEGGANWHISKEY.COM • OPEN ALL YEAR

If the Bushmills' story takes a while to untangle, it is nothing on Ireland's newest whiskey distiller, Cooley. Its saga touches on legend, agriculture, cars running on potatoes, the breaking of a monopoly, and the country's newest yet oldest distillery. Ireland, you soon realize, doesn't do linear.

The Cooley peninsula in Co. Louth is one of the settings of *The Táin*, the medieval Irish epic in which a king and queen battle over the ownership of a magical bull, which is a pretty neat analogy for the fight for the soul of Irish whiskey, at which Cooley has been in the center since its birth.

Now 20 years into its life, Cooley has been characterized as the odd one out, defined (by its rivals) as much by what it didn't do as for what it did. To purists, Cooley was simply making Scotch in Ireland. After all, hadn't Irish whiskey always been triple-distilled and unpeated? "Says who?" asks Cooley's production director, Noel Sweeney. "That idea is a misnomer. Read Alfred Barnard. There was triple-distilled, double-distilled, all malt, mixed malt—and peat was used. Irish Distillers Ltd (IDL) needed to differentiate itself from Scotch, but that didn't ever mean that all Irish whiskey had to be made that way. No, I thought it was arrogant to claim we weren't making 'proper' Irish whiskey."

The view across Dundalk Bay may be bucolic, but the distillery is a utilitarian, green-painted collection of concrete boxes, which started life as one of five Irish government-owned plants that originally produced car fuel from potatoes—although by the end of the 1970s it was making spirit for Bailey's.

In 1989 it was sold to John Teeling, who had decided to take on the IDL monopoly. The fact that Cooley is still here suggests

he succeeded, but it has been a struggle. At one point, with mounting debts he was going to accept IDL's offer to buy the business and close it down. Only a massive order from Heaven Hill saved it from becoming another of the abandoned distillery sites that can be found littered across Ireland.

Why, though, take a production position diametrically opposed to the IDL model? To create clear green water? Economics? Perversity? "I reckon a bit of each," says Sweeney. "We were lacking in expertise as far as triple distillation went and IDL wouldn't talk to us. We also had a Scottish distiller [Gordon Mitchell of Arran], so we went that way."

The Cooley pot-still method involves charging the spirit still with the equivalent of 1.5 fills from the wash still. This, plus a slow distillation regime and upward-angled lyne arms (with cooling pipes inside), encourages reflux. The result is a very sweet, honeyed distillate. An identical regime is used for Connemara (bar the use of heavily peated barley), which gives that brand a sweet center balancing the pugnacious, turfy smoke. Cooley's buttered-popcorn-accented grain is corn-based and run through a Barbet column setup, adding a clinging texture to blends such as Kilbeggan.

With financial security and a growing reputation, Cooley finally seems grounded, and in 2008 it turned its attention to the remarkable eighteenth-century water-powered Kilbeggan distillery some 65 miles to the southwest. Old Kilbeggan is a white-painted, thick-walled museum of distilling, whose murky, rambling, low-beamed

The good old days. Kilbeggan was a famous brand before the great collapse of the twentieth century.

interior houses artifacts from the early days of the country's whiskey-making heritage: a working steam engine, millstones, a mash tun that's more of a vast, side-draining, shallow pond, and worms which were sunk in the mill-race, the stream leaving the watermill. Outside are three verdigris-streaked, fat-bellied stills. Like bankrupted squires they bear witness to Irish whiskey's past—but now there's life in the

After years of silence, Kilbeggan is now producing whiskey once more: evidence of the new optimism in the Irish industry.

old place. Sweeney has started distilling once more, in a tiny ball of a copper pot. "People think this is all well planned," laughs Sweeney. "Mostly it happens by accident!"

COOLEY & KILBEGGAN TASTING NOTES

NEW MAKE GRAIN

Nose: Sweet and lightly grassy, with touches of lime and popcorn. Very clean.
Palate: Fat, juicy, and mouthwatering. Fat-corn notes. Chewy and ripe.
Finish: Hot and zesty.

NEW MAKE MALT

Nose: Honey. Very sweet, with some raspberry leaf. Scented. Very pure. With water, a little sealing wax.
Palate: Very light, with the honeyed note dominating. Full feel, then a delicate floral lift on the back.
Finish: Buttery. Clean.

NEW MAKE PEATED MALT

Nose: Less smoky than you'd expect. Lightly farmyardy notes. With water, sweetness and a wisp of turf.
Palate: Big, sweet peatiness. Damp fires with a lightly sulfury youthfulness, but underneath is that honey/waxy note of the unpeated new make. Balanced.
Finish: Hugely medicinal. Antiseptic and hospitals.

CONNEMARA 12YO 40%

Nose: Scented, with cut grass, bamboo leaves, dried apple, and a little peat. Like the new make, the peat seems shy.
Palate: But not on the palate where it now mingles among almond, fennel seed, and banana.
Finish: Smoked paprika. Turfy smoke.
Conclusion: Balanced.

> **Flavor Camp: Smoky & Peaty**
> **Where Next?** Ardmore Traditional Cask, Bruichladdich, Port Charlotte PC8

TYRCONNELL 10YO MADEIRA 46%

Nose: Firm and slightly nutty, with a scented quality. Burnt sugars, frangipane, damson. Sweet oak.
Palate: Soft and gentle, with a steadily paced flow through sweet tropical fruit (mango/guava), lightly honeyed, then some stewed red plum.
Finish: Chocolate and fruit.
Conclusion: The inherent sweetness of the malt spirit is not overwhelmed by the cask.

> **Flavor Camp: Rich & Round**
> **Where Next?** Bushmills 16yo

KILBEGGAN 15YO BLEND, 40%

Nose: Solid and thick, with lots of juicy grain, hot sawdust, red cherry, cinnamon, and that almond note once more, this time sugar-coated.
Palate: Sweet. Greek yoghurt. Banana and coconut with some runny toffee. Just enough grip to stop it becoming flabby. Lightly grassy with water.
Finish: Juicy and sweet.
Conclusion: Balanced and lightly spiced.

> **Flavor Camp: Fruity & Spicy**
> **Where Next?** Nikka Super

Connemara
Aged 12 *Years*
PEATED SINGLE MALT IRISH WHISKEY

Irish Distillers

MIDLETON • WWW.JAMESONWHISKEY.COM/HERITAGE/VISITOR-CENTRES/MIDLETON_EXPERIENCE_TOUR_INFO.ASPX • OPEN ALL YEAR

The sheer scale of Old Midleton distillery always comes as a shock. There is nothing in this land of pastel-colored shops and wild, fuschia-laden lanes to warn you that around the corner is a collection of enormous buildings which look more like barracks than a distillery. That is, until you discover that it was once barracks, then a woolen mill, before in 1825 the Murphy family, having made a fortune in tea, decided to try their hands at the newly liberalized trade of whiskey-distilling. They immediately installed a pot still of 37,829 gallons (143,200 liters).

Its size was in direct proportion to both the ambition and, for most of the nineteenth century, the success of Irish distillers. Ireland had the world's first recognizably commercialized whisky industry, and at its heart lay traditional Irish pot-still whiskey, whose birth came as a direct result of the vaulting ambition of the major Irish distillers. Seeing the tax on malted barley eating into their profits, in the 1850s they began to use a mix of unmalted and malted barley to save money (see p.17). Flavor may have been a secondary consideration, but it changed the whiskey. In fact, it made the whiskey.

Traditional Irish pot still has a mouth-coating oily texture, mixed with apple and spice. There are none of the cereal notes you get in Scottish malt; this is juicy, spicy, and yielding, but with a firmness when young. Look at the fragrant standard Jameson and then work through the range, seeing how the pot-still element increases, adding weight and succulence and spice; then go to the combination of American oak and heavy pot still in the unctuousness of Powers, before culminating in the 100 percent pot still of Redbreast 15yo, a whiskey you could cut with a knife.

These days, the ratio of unmalted to malted barley tends to be 60:40, but different ratios are used. There's no one way of making whiskey at Midleton (to be precise at New Midleton, which sits behind the old distillery). Irish Distillers Ltd's (IDL) amalgamation means that this site produces all the whiskeys for all of the firm's blends, and some contract bottlings like Tullamore Dew and Green Spot.

One wall houses the three column stills, the other has four pot stills: two wash, one feints, and one spirit. All are the same size, but the filling charge will vary depending on the style of whiskey being made (that vapor/copper conversation thing at work again). One light, two medium, and one heavy 100 percent pot-still style is made, but after gentle quizzing, master distiller Barry Crockett admits there might be more styles—and indeed, variations—since the distillate streams can be diverted from pot to column, or vice versa.

The final secret lies in the warehousing. IDL is a pioneer in bespoke casks (initiating the strategy before Scottish distillers) and currently lays down 4,000 new sherry casks a year, as well as US oak and bespoke casks previously holding port and Madeira. "We had a

"New" Midleton is one of the world's most remarkable distilleries. Created out of a spirit of adversity, it kept the Irish whiskey flag flying.

Masters of wood. IDL pioneered many approaches in wood management now accepted as the norm in the world of whiskey.

serious look at wood in 1979 and then had a fundamental review," says master of wood Brendan Monks. "Basically, we said to the bosses that if we were to be a serious player we needed investment in wood."

Historical and economic factors forced IDL to shift production to a single site. Once there, however, it has been the skills of distillers, blenders, and wood masters that have ensured that this one distillery can make whiskeys as different as Paddy, Powers, Jameson, and the mighty Redbreast by remaining true to tradition, even in an ultra-modern distillery and at a time when they could have retrenched and made just one whiskey. If Old Midleton shows the demise of the old Ireland, New Midleton shows its renaissance.

IRISH DISTILLERS TASTING NOTES

JAMESON ORIGINAL BLEND, 40%

Nose: Full gold. Highly scented. Herbs, hot earth, amber, scented wood, and caramelized apple sugars. Mead-like. Fresh and zesty.

Palate: Soft with lots of vanilla. Succulent mid-palate then start to dry, becoming slightly finer. The spices begin to creep in.

Finish: Cumin. Balsa wood. Clean.

Conclusion: Balanced and aromatic.

> **Flavor Camp: Fragrant & Floral**
> **Where Next?** Grant's Family Reserve, Hibiki 12yo

JAMESON 12YO BLEND, 40%

Nose: Less perfumed than the "standard" with more honey, some white raisins, toffee, and butterscotch. Cooked apple. Dried herbs and hot sawdust.

Palate: Juicier and fuller than standard, with more coconut, vanilla, and a hint of dried-fruit concentration. Succulent. Little hint of camphor.

Finish: Allspice.

Conclusion: More pot still adding weight and feel.

> **Flavor Camp: Fruity & Spicy**
> **Where Next?** Dewar's 12yo

JAMESON 18YO BLEND, 40%

Nose: Full gold. Little closed to start but then heavier pot still begins to develop. The most polished and oiliest (linseed oil) of the trio. Some resin but also that lifted note now gone into dried herbs.

Palate: Chewy and full with more sherried notes. Raisins. With water, sweet gingerbread.

Finish: Again it's spicy, this time mace along with chestnut honey.

Conclusion: Clear family resemblance but a weightier proposition.

> **Flavor Camp: Rich & Round**
> **Where Next?** Chivas Regal 18yo

POWERS 12YO BLEND, 46%

Nose: Big, succulent, blossom-like. More peachy. More freshly fruited and generally fatter than Jameson.

Palate: Massive shot of banana milkshake sweetened with peach nectar and honey. Thick texture before a cashew/pistachio note. Mouth-filling.

Finish: Ripe, then coriander and turmeric.

Conclusion: Unctuous.

> **Flavor Camp: Fruity & Spicy**
> **Where Next?** Glen Elgin 12yo

REDBREAST 12YO 40%

Nose: Amber. Resinous, oily with cloves, supple leather. Pure peach/baked banana quality, sweet spice.

Palate: Generous and mouthfilling. Thick. Soft orchard/pulpy fruits, quince paste, plus spiciness: mace.

Finish: Oils and blackberry. Tobacco.

Conclusion: A complex mouthful.

> **Flavor Camp: Rich & Round**
> **Where Next?** Macallan 12yo

REDBREAST 15YO 100% POT STILL, 46%

Nose: Huge. Autumn fruit (red and black). Toffee and light leather, sandalwood. Polished oak. Rich.

Palate: Fat and rounded. Chamois leather then masses of spice. Layered effect of cumin, ginger, mixing with new leather, dried fruit, baked apple. Complex.

Finish: Long, ripe, throat-clinging.

Conclusion: Like Jameson on steroids. Classic pot still.

> **Flavor Camp: Rich & Round**
> **Where Next?** Old Pulteney 17yo

JAPAN

On a visit to Karuizawa distillery I saw a poster of a fierce-looking man with pebble-thick glasses and jutting goatee. It turned out to be the haiku poet Santoka. It was the perfect synchronicity. Santoka famously liked a drink, and what is haiku if not a distillation of words into the essence of experience? Or, in Santoka's words, tapping "the deep breath of life." Whisky is a haiku. Its creation is concerned with the concentration of flavor, but behind its technical aspects it is a manifestation of a wider culture.

Previous page: Somehow familiar yet so very different, the Japanese landscape is reflected in its whiskies.

Although it is impossible for any *gaijin* (non-Japanese) to understand Japanese culture fully, some appreciation of the Japanese sensibility does make the creative processes behind its whiskies a little more understandable. Japan's whisky history has taken on the gloss of a folktale. It began with the arrival of western spirits in the late nineteenth century, the case of Old Parr brought back in 1872 by the Iwakura trade mission; then there was the subsequent creation of imitation foreign spirits in Japanese laboratories; the founding of Kotobukiya by the young Shinjiro Torii in 1899; the sending of young science student Masataka Taketsuru to Glasgow to study chemistry in 1918. Add to that Taketsuru's seduction by Scotland, his marriage to Rita Cowan, his apprenticeships at Hazelburn and Longmorn; his subsequent hiring by Torii-san, by then casting around for a Japanese distiller for Japan's first dedicated whisky distillery at Yamazaki in 1923; how they worked together and then split, and you end up with Torii founding Suntory and Taketsuru founding Nikka, which remain the two pillars of whisky-making in Japan.

There is an assumption that, because the Japanese have adhered to the Scottish template of whisky-making, their whisky is a copy. Nothing could be further from the truth. From the outset, the aim was to create a Japanese style, which is precisely what's happened. It's also widely believed that these are technological whiskies, made in labs, disconnected from the land. Again, fundamentally wrong.

Yes, Japanese whisky-makers turned to science to answer their questions. What else were they to do: wait for 200 years to build up a residue of folk wisdom? This was an industry starting from scratch, it had to be rigorous in its approach. But while Japanese whisky may have been driven initially by practical considerations grounded in science, it has evolved in the manner it has because Japan the country then came into play: its climate, its economics, its food, its culture, its psychology—a need for release after a day's work.

Japanese whisky isn't necessarily lighter, but it possesses a clarity of aroma that singles it out. Its absence of a cereal background note also differentiates it from Scotch, as does the use of the intensely aromatic Japanese oak. If Scottish single malt is a rushing mountain burn (stream), all the flavors jostling for position, Japanese malt is a limpid pool where all is revealed.

There's a Japanese term, *wabi-sabi*. This is the aesthetic philosophy that prizes transient beauty, an aesthetic which is focused on the understated; simple, and impermanent. It holds that imperfections are beautiful. Whisky can never be "perfect" in chemical terms; that's neutrality. The flavors within whisky are "imperfections"; finding the balance between technical brilliance and the curve balls thrown by nature (climate, wood, copper) is what whisky-making is about. As Taketsuru said, "Whisky-making is an act of cooperative creation between the blessings of nature and the wisdom of man." *Wabi-sabi*.

Cool, calm, collected, yet also enigmatic. The world is now unraveling the secrets of Japanese whisky.

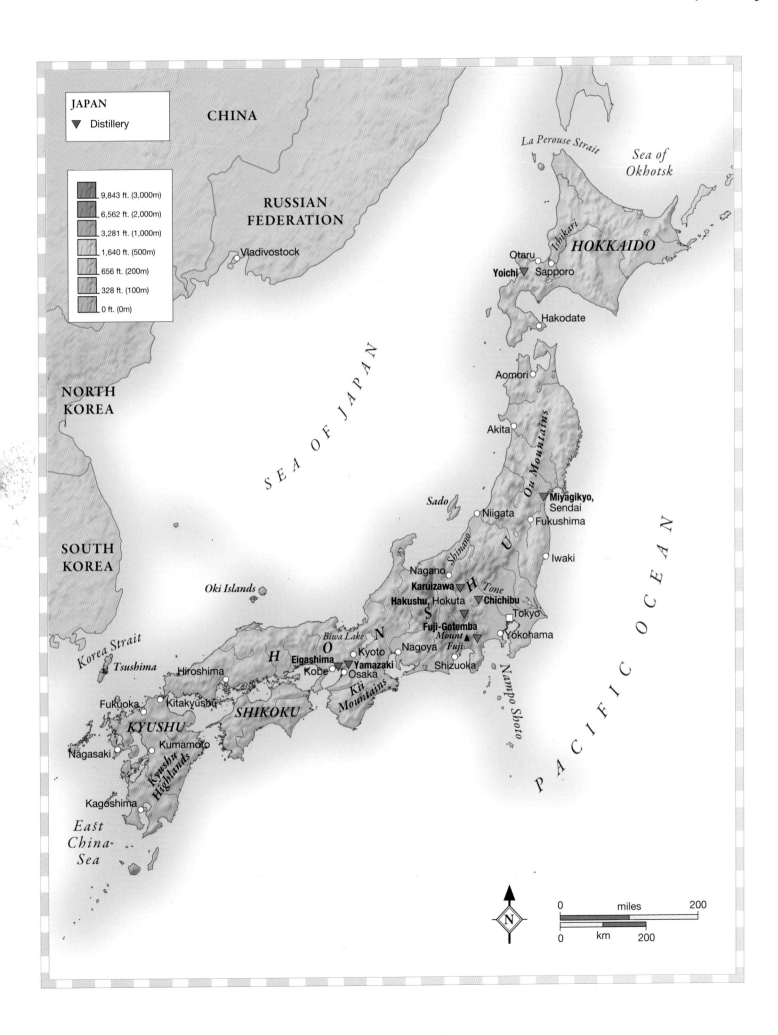

CHINA

RUSSIAN
FEDERATION

NORTH
KOREA

SOUTH
KOREA

Vladivostock

La Perouse Strait

*Sea of
Okhotsk*

HOKKAIDO

Otaru

Ishikari

Yoichi ▼ Sapporo

Hakodate

Aomori

Akita

On Mountains

Miyagikyo,
Sendai ▼

Sado

Niigata

Fukushima

Shinano

Iwaki

U

SEA OF JAPAN

Nagano

Karuizawa ▼

H

Tone

Hakushu, Hokuta

Chichibu ▼

S

Tokyo

Oki Islands

N

Yokohama

Fuji-Gotemba ▼

*Mount
Fuji* ▲ ▼

O

Biwa Lake

Kyoto

Nagoya

H

Eigashima ▼

Shizuoka

Kobe

Yamazaki ▼

Osaka

*Kii
Mountains*

Tsushima

Hiroshima

Korea Strait

SHIKOKU

Fukuoka

Kitakyushu

Nampo Shoto

KYUSHU

Kumamoto

Nagasaki

*Kyushu
Highlands*

PACIFIC OCEAN

Kagoshima

*East
China
Sea*

N

Mount Fuji's slopes provide water for one of Japan's distilleries—Fuji Gotemba.

Yamazaki

OSAKA • WWW.THEYAMAZAKI.JP/EN/DISTILLERY/MUSEUM.HTML • OPEN ALL YEAR • CHECK HOLIDAYS • SEE WEB FOR DETAILS

It starts here, next to the old road that linked Kyoto with the port of Osaka, across the railway where today bullet trains hurtle; a place of stifling summer humidity and winter chill. This is Yamazaki. Torii-san chose to build here in 1923 for a number of reasons. It made shrewd commercial sense to be situated between two important markets with good transport links, plus it was the meeting place of three rivers, meaning a plentiful supply of water. There's a deeper resonance, however. This was where Sen Rikyu, the sixteenth-century creator of what we know as the tea ceremony, built his first tea house—because, some believe, of the water quality. This is more than just a convenient bit of flat land beside the railway tracks.

Yet this rootedness doesn't mean that it is hog-tied by the past. Japanese distillers have an almost alarming willingness to scrap the old and start afresh. Yamazaki has been rebuilt three times, most recently in 2005. In this last renovation, the stillhouse was totally refitted, the stills replaced by smaller models, direct fire brought back in (naked flames at the base), and the styles changed. Note the plural. When you try to understand Japanese whisky, it is wise to put Scotland to the back of your mind. The creation of styles is another example of Japan's fusing of the pragmatic and the creative.

Scotland has 96 malt distilleries, allowing its blenders to draw from a huge variety of whisky styles which they exchange with each other. In Japan, the Big Two (Suntory and Nikka) have four malt plants between them—and they don't exchange. If they want a variety of whiskies for their blends then they have to make them in-house.

Yamazaki has two mash tuns, mashing low and heavily peated barley, producing startlingly clear wort (hence the lack of cereal notes in the spirit) that's fermented with a mix of two yeasts in either wooden (considered better for longer flavor-generating lactic fermentation) or steel washbacks. It's the stillhouse that takes the first-time visitor by surprise: six pairs of stills, all different shapes and sizes. All the wash stills are direct-fired and one has a worm tub. Aging is in five different types of cask: sherry (American and European oak), ex-bourbon, new, and Japanese oak.

This allows a different approach to single malt. In Scotland, each distillery will tend to produce one style, meaning that the difference between an 18-year-old and a 15-year-old is, in simple terms, three years plus any tunes you play with wood. At Yamazaki, the constituent parts of each age expression are diferent: Yamazaki 18yo isn't just six

Located across the tracks from the ancient road between Kyoto and Osaka, Yamazaki was Japan's first purpose-built whisky distillery.

Going for a spin. *A new maturation technique—or the result of the large scale of the distillery?*

Multiple styles of *whisky are made at Yamazaki.*

years older than the 12yo; it's made up of different whisky types, all of which are married for six months prior to bottling.

What is fascinating, however, is that, for all its diversity, there is a unifying character to Yamazaki, a moment when the whisky dips and holds in the center of the tongue, when the fruit comes through. It can cope with boldness of sherry and the incense-scented *mizunara* (Japanese oak), whose intense, acidic character acts as a counterpoint to the richness of the spirit. Thus it embodies the arc of Japanese

whisky's life: from its early days when Shinjiro Torii and his successors were searching for lightness to suit the needs of the Japanese consumer, to the new, malt-centric consumer who wants more character.

For all of its technological innovations (and there are many more hidden from sight), Yamazaki remains a place of tranquility, a place where this Japanese fusing of opposing elements (which in the West may seem diametrically opposed)—the modern with the ancient, intuition and science—appears perfectly natural.

YAMAZAKI TASTING NOTES

NEW MAKE MEDIUM STYLE

Nose: Gentle, sweet, fruity with heavy florals (lily), apple, strawberry.
Palate: Rounded, with the "Yamazaki dip" mid-palate (*see main text*). Fruity, with a spicy edge. Vibrant.
Finish: Smooth and long.

NEW MAKE HEAVY STYLE

Nose: Deep and rich, with very light vegetable notes. Rich fruits.
Palate: Chewy and full, with a big vanilla hit. Clinging and ripe. Thick, with hints of smoke.
Finish: A little closed.

NEW MAKE HEAVY PEATED STYLE

Nose: Clean. Iris and artichoke. Smoke is solid and fragrant.
Palate: Sweet and thick (the dominating character). Smoke confined mostly to the back palate. Beach bonfire.
Finish: Spiced.

10YO 40%

Nose: Light gold. Fresh, with more of the spicy aspects on show. Toasty oak. Estery.
Palate: Clean and zesty, light citrus fruit, hint of *tatami* (Japanese reed mats). Green fruit.
Finish: Soft, then crisps up.
Conclusion: Delicate and clean. Suited to *soda-wari* style (on the rocks with soda). Spring-like.

Flavor camp: **Fragrant & Floral**
Where Next? Linkwood 12yo, Strathmill 12yo

12YO 43%

Nose: Gold. The fruit begining to show. Ripe melon. Pineapple, grapefruit, and also some of the floral notes. Again, the hint of *tatami* and a little dried fruit.
Palate: Sweet fruit. Has a succulent feel; syrupy, mid-apricot, and a hint of vanilla.
Finish: Lightly smoked with the dried fruit continuing.
Conclusion: Medium-bodied but packed with character. Summery.

Flavor camp: **Fruity & Spicy**
Where Next? Longmorn 16yo, Royal Lochnagar 12yo

18YO 43%

Nose: Light amber. Autumn fruit. Ripened apples, semi-dried peach, raisin. Light leaf mulch. Little more smoke. Florals now deepened. More perfumed.
Palate: Woods. Fuller sherry notes, walnut, and damson. Lightly mossy. Still clings to the center of the tongue. Complex.
Finish: Sweet oak. Rich.
Conclusion: A further and deeper journey into the woods. Autumnal.

Flavor camp: **Rich & Round**
Where Next? Highland Park 18yo, Glengoyne 17yo

THE
YAMAZAKI
SINGLE MALT
WHISKY
AGED **12** YEARS
The oldest distillery in Japan
YAMAZAKI DISTILLERY
PRODUCED BY SUNTORY
PRODUCT OF JAPAN
ウイスキー
山崎
"YAMAZAKI"

Hakushu

HOKUTO CITY • WWW.SUNTORY.COM/BUSINESS/LIQUOR/WHISKY.HTML / WWW.SUNTORY.CO.JP/FACTORY/HAKUSHU/GUIDE

There's a cool breeze blowing through the pines that stretch far up the granite slopes of Mount Kaikomagatake in the southern Japanese Alps. Dotted among the trees are warehouses and distillery buildings, although it is hard to comprehend the size of Suntory's Hakushu distillery until you climb to the air bridge: the glass corridor linking the two tower tops in its museum. This is a vast site—part national park, part distillery complex—which still holds upwards of 450,000 casks. An indication of the scale of Japanese distillers' ambition in the 1970s when a booming economy, and a seemingly insatiable thirst for (blended) whisky, led to the building of what, for a period of time, was the world's largest malt distillery.

It was water that led Suntory here. Soft mountain spring water (which the firm now bottles) in sufficient quantities to match the company's grand vision. Unfortunately, however, it wasn't to be. Japan's whisky boom ended in the early 1990s, when the Asian financial crisis started the deflation through which the country continues to walk, zombie-like.

A clear manifestation of the effects of this decline in whisky's fortunes lies behind a pair of vast iron doors in the West Distillery. Head blender Shinji Fukuyo pushes them open and we enter a chill mausoleum. Dwarfed by massive copper pots, he speaks of how this distillery was making 7,925,161 gallons (30 million liters) of spirit a year from two stillhouses: East and West.

Now, production has shifted to the East site and has been reduced by a third. Just as at Yamazaki, the vagaries of the market have resulted in Hakushu changing itself, with the biggest refit taking place in 1983. Before its closure, Fukuyo had experimented in the West site. One of the stills has a flat top. "Oh yes, I did that," he says blithely. "I wanted to make a different style, so I thought I'd see what would happen." It's very typical of the dramatic changes Japanese distillers do, seemingly without a second thought.

If anything, Hakushu is even more radical than Yamazaki. Here, four types of barley, from unpeated to heavy peated, are used, and the clear wort is given a long fermentation in wooden fermenters using a mix of distillers and brewer's yeast. "Wooden fermenters and the brewer's yeast help to encourage lactic bacteria," says Fukuyo. "It's this which helps to produce esters and a creaminess to the spirit." Or to be accurate, spirits.

There are six pairs of direct-fired, golden-sheened stills in a mind-boggling variety of shapes and sizes: tall, fat, thin, minuscule; lyne

An obsessive control of wood is key to Japanese whisky's quality. **Left:** a cask is being recharred. **Right:** a sample is about to be drawn.

Idyllic location. Hakushu is situated in a nature reserve in the Japanese Alps.

arms go up, down, can be detached and diverted into worm tubs or condensers. The permutations are baffling, but again, as with Yamazaki, there seems to be a coherence to the variations in spirit type.

Hakushu, even in its heaviest and peatiest expression, has a focus and directness that sets it apart from Yamazaki's depth. In its youth it seems directly to encapsulate its location, a single malt that's filled with a green, leafy character: wet bamboo, fresh moss after rain, and, yes, that creaminess—which is partly from the

preference for American oak casks here and conceivably from this longer fermentation regime. The peat is there but almost like an afterthought.

The Hakushu style could also conceivably come from the ambient temperature. "Here the temperature range goes from 39°–72°F (4°–22°C)," says Fukuyo. "At Yamazaki it's between 50°–81°F (10°–27°C) and with greater humidity in summer." The pine-fresh 10yo gives no indication that Hakushu has the capability of extended aging. The 25yo is heavier—peatier, too— but always with this pebble-fresh directness and a touch of cool mint that ripples through, like the wind in the pines.

HAKUSHU TASTING NOTES

NEW MAKE LIGHTLY PEATED
Nose: Very clean. Cucumber, fruit chew. Touch of grassiness, white pear, plantain. Smoke, very subtle.
Palate: Sweet and intense. Green melon. High acidity. Fresh. The smoke drifts in the background …
Finish: … then comes through on the finish.

NEW MAKE HEAVY PEAT
Nose: Robust and firm, with a touch of nuttiness. Less "foggy" than Scottish peatiness. More clarity and lightly scented. Wet grass and lemon.
Palate: Zesty and citric, with building smoke.
Finish: Recedes gently.

12YO 43.5%
Nose: Straw. Cool and green and lightly perfumed. Grassy and lightly floral, touch of pine and sage. Green banana.
Palate: Smooth and silky with a little mintiness and green apple. Bamboo and wet moss. Lime and chamomile.
Finish: The merest touch of smoke.
Conclusion: Fresh and seemingly delicate but has substance. Focused.

> **Flavor Camp: Fragrant & Floral**
> **Where Next?** Teaninich 10yo, anCnoc 16yo

18YO 43.5%
Nose: Gold. Cookie-like, with ginger and almond/marzipan. Lightly waxy, plums, and sweet hay. Marzipan, green grass, green apple. Currant leaf.
Palate: Medium-bodied and clean (again, good acidity). Mango, ripe honeydew melon. Grassy still. Delicate wood smoke and toasty oak.
Finish: Clean and lightly smoky.
Conclusion: Poised. Still modest, with a little more smoke.

> **Flavor Camp: Fragrant & Floral**
> **Where Next?** Miltonduff 18yo

25YO 43%
Nose: Amber. Intense with lots of dred fruit and waxed furniture. Lightly caramelized fruits. Baked apple, white raisins, ferns/moss, and mushrooms. Dried mint and smoke.
Palate: Big, ripe, and generous, with the broadest spread of the range. Vinous and silky with light tannin. Praline.
Finish: Smoke drifts through the wood.
Conclusion: Bold, but still has the fresh acidity that typifies the distillery.

> **Flavor Camp: Rich & Round**
> **Where Next?** Highland Park 25yo, Glencadam 1978

THE CASK OF HAKUSHU HEAVY PEAT, 61%
Nose: Golden. Intense and appetizing with an ozone-like freshness. Carnation, scallion with smoke building in the background, released fully by water. Retains aromatics. Fleshy fruits and moist peat.
Palate: Equally intense—partly the alcohol, partly the distillery. Spreads across the tongue. Melon and huge smoke.
Finish: Green and long.
Conclusion: Balanced and typically idiosyncratic.

> **Flavor Camp: Smoky & Peaty**
> **Where Next?** Ardmore 25yo

Miyagikyo

SENDAI • WWW.NIKKA.COM/ENG/DISTILLERIES/MIYAGIKYO.HTML • OPEN ALL YEAR

The first of Nikka's two malt distilleries lies in the northeast of Honshu, around 45 minutes west of the city of Sendai. This is a place of twisting roads and gnarled, maple-covered hills, one of those secret parts of Japan that the stranger rarely visits. Hot water gushes from the earth, discreet old *onsen* (hot springs) are dotted around in the mountain valleys.

Once again, water looms large in the story of the distillery's founding. By the late 1960s, Masataka Taketsuru, the legendary co-founder of Japanese whisky who had created Nikka in the 1930s, wanted another distillery site. If his first search had led him directly to the cold north (*see* Yoichi, p.226), this time the whole of Japan was considered as having potential. Company legend has it that it took him three years of traveling to find this spot in the Miyagi Valley (*Miyagikyo*) where the Nikkawa and Hirose rivers meet. He walked onto the rounded gray pebbles of the riverbank, drank the water, and pronounced it good. In 1969 the Sendai distillery was in production.

Taketsuru's concern about water quality is not unusual among distillers. Although water may not have a direct impact on flavor, distilleries need it in plentiful quanitites, at the right temperature (cold), and the mineral content could have an effect on fermentation. When Taketsuru started his apprenticeship at Longmorn distillery in 1919 (*see* p.91), two of his 13 initial questions to his manager concerned water. After discovering the distillery's water source, he asked, "Have you ever analyzed the water?" The answer was in the negative. He then asked if there was any distillery in Scotland where a microscope was used. The answer was, "I don't think so." One can guarantee that once he tasted Miyagikyo's water, he also had it analyzed. Things are not left to chance these days.

Miyagikyo has subsequently been expanded twice and makes spirit in a malt and a grain plant. The malt side conforms to the Japanese multiple-stream approach to whisky-making, although the Nikka technique is different to Suntory's.

Mostly unpeated barley is used, but medium and, occasionally, heavy peat is also processed into either clear (mostly) or cloudy wort. The fermentation takes place with a combination of various different yeast types. The stills are all the same shape: large capacity with fat bottoms, a boil bulb, and fat necks—similar, in fact, to Longmorn's.

In a landscape of blunted hills, forests, and hot springs, the Miyagi Valley was chosen for the quality of its water.

When tasting Miyagikyo, Taketsuru's intentions become clear. At Yoichi, he created a heavy, smoky, richly textured single malt. Here, lightness of touch was the key. If Yoichi is a winter whisky, all smoke and leather armchairs, Miyagikyo is filled with the fruits of late summer. Here's the balance in the portfolio, the new element for the blends. The grain plant adds the final element and is further evidence of the way in which Japanese distillers, while always investigating new techniques, have retained those elements of the past that work.

As well as a modern column still, it houses a pair of Glasgow-built Coffey stills, which produce three different types of grain spirit: corn only, a corn/malted barley mix, and an all-malt distillate. The last, which is bottled in small quantities as "Coffey Malt," has been (rightly) hailed for its quality—and also as a typical example of Japanese innovation. In fact, "Coffey Malt" was widely made across Scotland at the time when Taketsuru was studying. Maybe it was simply another technique he stored away, waiting for the right moment … and the right location; maybe a place where crimson autumn leaves dance in the eddies of the river and children's shrieks of pleasure rise in the crisp air.

Four distinct seasons have their own influence on the way Miyagikyo evolves in the cask.

MIYAGIKYO TASTING NOTES

15YO 45%
Nose: Full gold. Soft and sweet. Lots of runny toffee, milk chocolate, and ripe persimmon.
Palate: The gentle and lifted character seen in the 10yo is now given a little more peachy depth and spin with a touch of sherried elements. Light raisin, touch of pine again.
Finish: Long and fruity.
Conclusion: Sweet and easy-drinking.

Flavor camp: Fruity & Spicy
Where Next? Longmorn 10yo

1990 18YO SINGLE CASK, 61%
Nose: Oolong tea, preserved lemons; light and clean. Hard caramel, then come strawberries, oak lactone, a little hint of oiliness. With water, it's chocolate cookies, fragrant oak.
Palate: Immediate and direct. Quite fat, jammy, and tongue-coating. Builds steadily to the back palate. Stewed apples and currants. Opens into thyme, citrus fruit. Slightly acidic
Finish: Lightly oaky.
Conclusion: Has a lovely pooling effect on the palate.

Flavor Camp: Fruity & Spicy
Where Next? Balblair 1990, Mannochmore 18yo

NIKKA SINGLE CASK COFFEY MALT 45%
Nose: Suntan lotion, latté. Macadamia nuts. Sweet, with ripe, tropical fruit. In time, fragrant wood and shoe leather. Water brings out a lightly floral touch alongside caramelized fruit sugars. Balanced, with some complexity.
Palate: Almost creamy to start, then flambéed banana and white chocolate.
Finish: Long and unctuous.
Conclusion: Highly individual.

Flavor Camp: Fruity & Spicy
Where Next? Crown Royal

Karuizawa & Fuji-Gotemba

KARUIZAWA • NAGANO • WWW.KIRIN.CO.JP/BRANDS/SW/KARUIZAWA/INDEX.HTML • VISITOR CENTER & WHISKY MUSEUM
FUJI-GOTEMBA • MT FUJI • WWW.KIRIN.CO.JP/BRANDS/SW/GOTEMBA/INDEX.HTML • OPEN ALL YEAR • ENGLISH TOURS ON REQUEST

It is somewhat surprising to the foreign visitor to Japan that two of its malt distilleries are built next to active volcanoes, but where there is lava, there are also *onsen* (hot springs) in which you can relax while keeping an eye on any imminent eruption. It was these hot springs which in turn prompted the building of the small town of Karuizawa, whose wide streets lined with half-timbered buildings give it the air of an English market town crossed with a settlement in the American midwest. The rich volcanic soils laid down by the permanently smoking Mount Asama also attracted wine producers in the early 1950s, one of which, Daikoku-budoshu, turned its winery into a distillery.

Karuizawa (currently mothballed) is a more straightforward distillery than the big operations run by the major players. There is one style: Golden Promise barley, mostly heavily peated, small stills, ex-sherry casks. It's like a throwback to a mostly forgotten Scotland. Yet in taste Karuizawa could only be Japanese. There is a depth and intensity of focus to its malts—resinous, sooty, scented with cardamom, thick with beeswax, spotted with blood—that only Japan can produce.

This feral edge could be the barley; it might be the yeast. It's certainly helped by the minuscule stills and by the smaller-than-normal sherry casks, cut down so that they'd fit onto the old wine racks. There is a

FUJI-GOTEMBA: THE LIGHTER TOUCH COMES TO THE FORE

Fuji-Gotemba's situation is even more surprising. Spectacularly situated next to Mount Fuji, it has a Japan Defence Force firing range in its backyard. Stylistically, it couldn't be more different from Karuizawa. This is a light, almost fragile malt, aged in American oak and made to partner Japanese cuisine. Created in 1973 as a joint venture between Kirin and Seagram, it is composed of a malt and grain site (the latter makes the fuller whisky) and is much like a mini-Gimli (*see* p.276)—even with that distillery's kettle and column setup.

reassuring solidity to these malts, and an enigmatic quality. Run this regime in Scotland and the result would be very different.

FUJI-GOTEMBA TASTING NOTES

FUJI SANROKU 18YO 40%
Nose: High-toned and estery. Quite restrained. Polished wood, peach pit, violet. With water, there are white flowers, grapefruit.
Palate: Sweet, fragrant, and honeyed. Very light grip with a little lemon and hot sawdust.
Finish: Gentle. Lychee.
Conclusion: Very clean and precise.

Flavor Camp: **Fragrant & Floral**
Where Next? Royal Brackla 15yo, Glen Grant Cellar 1992

18YO SINGLE GRAIN 40%
Nose: Gold. Very sweet and intense, with a buttery, fat character. Lots of honey and sesame and coconut cream.
Palate: Thick, soft, and sweet. The fat-corn quality comes through, along with baked banana.
Finish: Long and syrupy.
Conclusion: Gentle, mellow and sweet. Very amenable.

Flavor camp: **Fragrant & Floral**
Where Next? Glentauchers 1991, Glenturret 10yo

Specially coopered sherry casks sit outside the Karuizawa warehouses.

KARUIZAWA TASTING NOTES

1985 CASK #7017, 60.8%
Nose: Pigeon blood. Deep and slightly feral, turned earth with molasses, geranium, cassis, and cedar before prunes come through, along with stewed Assam tea. With water there's damp coal bunker, varnish, raisin, and sulfur.
Palate: Big, quite tarry smokiness with a slight rubbery note. Gripping and masses of eucalyptus reminiscent of an ancient expectorant. Again, the sulfur becomes a little too obtrusive with water.
Finish: Sooty and long.
Conclusion: Classic Karuizawa. Uncompromising.

Flavor Camp: **Rich & Round**
Where Next? Glenfarclas 40yo, Benrinnes 23yo

1995 NOH SERIES CASK #5004, 63%
Nose: Resinous. Varnish, balsam/tiger balm, geranium, shoe polish, prune, heavily oiled woods. Barberries and rosewood casket. Water makes it evergreen, with coal smoke and leather.
Palate: Light astringency when neat, wood oils, teetering into bitterness. With water, there's eucalyptus. Strange things are going on; it could be a smoky Armagnac. Fragrance stops it becoming too grippy.
Finish: Tight and exotic.
Conclusion: Do you drink this or rub it on your chest?

Flavor Camp: **Rich & Round**
Where Next? Benrinnes 23yo, Macallan 25yo, Ben Nevis 25yo

Chichibu & Eigashima

CHICHIBU • BY APPOINTMENT ONLY / EIGASHIMA • KOBE • WWW.EI-SAKE.JP

The ethics of sustainability as envisioned by the Lifestyles of Health and Sustainability movement is not a topic you normally find yourself discussing on a distillery visit. Things are different at Chichibu—but then again, owner Ichiro Akuto is not your average distiller. His family has been making alcohol (sake, then *shochu*) in quiet Chichibu since 1625. In the 1980s they started distilling whisky in the industrial town of Hanyu, trucking water in from Chichibu for mashing. Timing couldn't have been worse. The whisky market collapsed; by 2000, Akuto-san was left with the ruins of a distillery and 400 casks of old stock (now being released through his Card Series). In 2007, he went back home to Chichibu, bought a plot of land—two razorback ridges outside town—and within a year had a tiny distillery operational.

So is this Hanyu Mark II? He shakes his head. "No. Chichibu's environment affects the character. I never wanted to replicate Hanyu here because we couldn't have made Hanyu here." The new distillery, staffed by a team of enthusiastic youngsters and under the tutelage of the former distiller at Karuizawa, is tiny; the space, no more than a large room, is winery-clean and gleaming with new, miniaturized equipment.

A mix of imported and local barley (predominantly unpeated: "Heavy peat obscures the subtle differences we are trying [to obtain]") is used, although Akuto intends both to peat with local fuel and malt on-site in the future. The self-draining mash tun (no lauter rakes here: just a wooden paddle) yields wort that goes to small Japanese-oak washbacks, while the stills, from Forsyth's of Rothes, are equally small.

Currently he is making three distillates (including heavy peat) by adjusting the temperature of the condensers: cold for heavy and hot for light. Chichibu's size allows him to focus intently on each part of the process. "Every day's ferment is a little different," he explains. "Ask me

EIGASHIMA: IS THIS WHERE IT ALL BEGAN?

Eigashima (aka White Oak) is an enigma. This distillery on the Akashi Strait near Kobe could be Japan's first whisky distillery (it had a license in 1919), but has specialized in sake and *shochu*, and like Hanyu got into whisky too late. These days, production of its light, fragrant Akash single malt is squeezed into two months of the year, but there are tentative moves to expand production.

what it's like in 15 years!" The make is aged in a wide mix of casks, everything from red oak and the normal whisky selection to local *mizunara*. What comes next excites him most—a vision of total sustainablity: on-site cooperage, local barley, malting, local peat. Maybe it's what 385 years of perspective give you. And what has surprised him most? "The interrelated cycle: forestry, farming, and distilling you need to make good whisky. Community. I used to think the cask was everything; now I know how important distillation is, but in reality it is a totality."

CHICHIBU TASTING NOTES

2008 NEWBORN CASK #447, DOUBLE-MATURED, 61.3%

Nose: Rich gold. High nose burn. Light, malty note alongside dried grapefruit peel, desiccated coconut, fresh-baked muffins, and a whiff of pineapple. Very toasty/creamy with water, moving into butterscotch, fudge, and hazelnut.

Palate: Very sweet. Light spirit and quite estery, with more florals on show. Freesia, then some cream. With water, tight and slightly jangly. Hard candy. Clean and balanced.

Finish: Slightly green.

Conclusion: Remarkably advanced for such a youngster. A prodigy.

Flavor Camp: Fragrant & Floral

Where Next? Allt-a-Bhainne

Hanyu was Ichiro Akuto's prevous distillery. It is now demolished, but he is releasing the last remaining whisky as single-cask bottlings.

HANYU MIZUNARA CASK #370, 57.3%

Nose: Amber. Soft and gentle with pine-like notes, spruce, and citric funkiness. Hint of marmalade and distant resinous notes.

Palate: Gentle and restrained, almost shy, before an ambush of lemon acidity. The wood has now shifted to cedar/yew. Smooths with water, where all those extremes are calmed down. Good weight.

Finish: With water, it is long, sweet, and satisfying.

Conclusion: The intensity of *mizunara* oak adds another layer to Hanyu's rigid character.

Flavor Camp: Fruity & Spicy

Where Next? Balmenach 1993, Macduff 1984

Yoichi

YOICHI • WWW.NIKKA.COM/ENG/DISTILLERIES/YOICHI.HTML • OPEN ALL YEAR • CHECK HOLIDAYS • TOURS IN JAPANESE

Although spread out across central and northern Honshu, all of Japan's malt distilleries are easily accessible from Tokyo. There's good reason for that: ease of transport and access to the main markets. All of them, that is, except one. Where is Yoichi? Your eyes finally head north to Hokkaido; you trace the line to the ferry crossing between Aomori and Hakodate, past Sapporo, then 30 miles west to the coast. This is the northlands, this is opposite Vladivostock. Why, when everyone concentrated on Honshu, would the co-founder of Japanese whisky head here?

Masataka Taketsuru always had a vision of making whisky in Hokkaido. It was his perfect location. While in Hazelburn, worrying (again) about water quality in Japan, he wrote: "Even in Scotland there is occasionally a shortage of good water; therefore it is totally unreasonable to build a pot-still factory at Sumiyoshi [Osaka] where we cannot have water without digging a well.

"If we consider the geography of Japan, a place would be needed that would constantly supply good-quality water, where barley can be obtained, with a good supply of fuel (coal or wood), with a railway link and with water navigation."

All signs, he felt, pointed to Hokkaido, but his boss, the pragmatic Shinjiro Torii, thought it was nowhere near the markets, so Yamazaki it was. No one knows the true story behind the foundering of the relationship between the two men; maybe it is simply coincidence that Taketsuru was moved to manage a brewery in Yokohama the same year as his whisky, "Shirofuda," was launched—and flopped. It was too heavy, too smoky, not "Japanese" enough.

At the end of his contract in 1934, and with finance from backers in Osaka, Taketsuru and his Scottish wife, Rita, headed north, finally, to Hokkaido, ostensibly to make apple juice. In reality, he was going to

Scotland or Japan? Yoichi was Masataka Taketsuru's homage to his spiritual home, but also one of the sites of the creation of a uniquely Japanese type of whisky.

Coal-fired stills remain a vital component in Yoichi's heavy, oily character.

satisfy his vision, which he made reality in the small fishing port of Yoichi, encircled by mountains, next to the great, gray, chill Sea of Japan.

And the whisky that appeared in 1940? Big. Smoky. Not, in Torii's terms, "Japanese." Today, Yoichi's tall, red-roofed kiln is no longer puffing out clouds of smoke from Japanese peat, cut on the Ishikari plains. Like all Japanese distilleries, the malt comes from Scotland. Inevitably, a number of styles (Nikka remains politely opaque about how many) are made: there are different peating levels (unpeated to heavy), different yeast strains, fermentation times, and cut points.

The clear point of difference is the coal fire sitting under the quartet of hefty wash stills. It's an art, running coal: the stillman always anticipating what is about to happen, getting ready to damp down,

to boost heat, and to maintain control of a living flame. Yet the result is a density given to the final spirit. The worm tubs help, as might a maturation temperature profile running from 39°F (-4°C) in winter to 72°F (22°C) in summer.

Yoichi is big. It is oily, smoky, yet fragrant. It has depth, but also the clarity of character that allows the complexities to be seen clearly. Its weight isn't the same as Karuizawa's four-square solidity; this has salty touches. At times there are glints of Ardbeg, but then a touch of black olive. And the smoke: it takes you not to Islay, but Kintyre. You look round to see a small fishing port, miles from the nearest main town and a cussedly different style of whisky-making. It could be Campbeltown, where Taketsuru worked, where he could have stayed to work. Yoichi is not a copy by any means. It can only be Japanese, but there's a psychic link.

Taketsuru remains an enigma. Pragmatist or romantic? Probably both. Was his move to Hokkaido only for practical reasons, or was there also a wish for a physical distancing from the past, a need for the sea air, the space to breathe?

YOICHI TASTING NOTES

10YO 45%

Nose: Light gold. Clean and fresh. Vibrant smoke. Sooty and slightly salty. Needs water to bring out its real depth and oily base.

Palate: That oiliness allows the flavors to cling to the tongue. Light, oaky, crisp apple notes behind the big smoke.

Finish: Once again, an acidic edge.

Conclusion: Balanced and young: have it with soda water.

Flavor Camp: Smoky & Peaty
Where Next? Ardbeg Renaissance

12YO 45%

Nose: Full gold. Immediate briny-accented smoke with a touch of marzipan behind. Weightier than the 10yo, with a heavy floral note, some baked peach, apple, and the start of a cacao tone.

Palate: Oily, with that baked-apple character coming through. Sweet and cake-like, a little butter, then cashews and smoke.

Finish: Smokiness develops.

Conclusion: A balance between the pull of the shore and that of the orchard.

Flavor Camp: Smoky & Peaty
Where Next? Springbank 10yo

15YO 45%

Nose: Deep gold. Less overtly smoky and more of the deep, rich oiliness that typifies the distillery's makes. Cigar, cedar, and walnut cake. Hint of black olive behind.

Palate: Has all of the distillery's density of character. Again, the tongue-coating oiliness clamps the flavors to the tongue. Sherried notes: eugenol (clove essential oil) and the cacao note seen in the 12yo now moved to a full, bitter chocolate.

Finish: Slighty salty.

Conclusion: Robust but elegant.

Flavor Camp: Smoky & Peaty
Where Next? Longrow 14yo, Caol Ila 18yo

20YO 45%

Nose: Amber. Intense and maritime. Drying fishing nets, wet seaweed, boat oil, lobster shell. Sandalwood and intense, dense fruitiness. Tapenade and soy sauce. Becomes spicier with water: fenugreek, curry leaves.

Palate: Deep and resinous. The smoke now starts to build through the thick, black oiliness. Light leather that's cut with a surprisingly fresh top note.

Finish: Linseed oil and a touch of spice before the smoke returns.

Conclusion: Powerful and contradictory.

Flavor Camp: Smoky & Peaty
Where Next? Ardbeg Lord of the Isles 25yo

1986 22YO HEAVY PEATED, 59%

Nose: Gold. Orange zest, incense, and peat smoke. Fleshy fruit, black olive with assertive smoke, buddleia, hard toffee, and roasting sweet spice. The balsamic note suggests age.

Palate: Big smoke and a solid mix of fruitcake and tarred twine. Substantial and complex, though needing a touch of water to show it's got a gentle and fruity side.

Finish: A smooth build-up of all the complexities on the palate.

Conclusion: Boldness remains in force.

Flavor Camp: Smoky & Peaty
Where Next? Talisker 25yo

Just one sample of the multiplicity of styles produced at Yoichi.

Japanese Blends

NIKKA • WWW.NIKKA.COM/ENG/PRODUCTS/WHISKY_BRANDY/NIKKABLENDED/INDEX.HTML • SEE YOICHI & MIYAGIKYO
HIBIKI • WWW.SUNTORY.COM/BUSINESS/LIQUOR/WHISKY.HTML

Japanese whisky, like Scotch, was built on blends. It was the complex needs of the blended market that triggered the innovations in distilling at the single-malt distilleries which so define Japanese whisky. Even today, with a boom in malt whisky among a new generation, blends make up the bulk of sales; blends lie behind the need for so many expressions from single distilleries. Yet, while the mechanics of blending are the same as in Scotland, Japan itself, its climate and its culture, has dictated what the style of those blends should be. Blends reflect society.

Japan's first blend, "Shirofuda" (White Label), released in 1929, was heavy and smoky. It wasn't a success. Shinjiro Torii went back to the drawing board and went light. His next release, Kakubin, remains one of Japan's top-selling whiskies. A lesson had been learned, one that would be fully exploited in the postwar period when the Japanese economy began to heat up.

Suddenly there were bars full of hardworking men needing to relax and let off steam. What would they drink? In Japan, beer has much the same status as in Germany: a foodstuff. "Breakfast beer" is served without any eyebrows being raised in business hotels. Whisky? Not neat certainly. In humid Japan you needed something light and refreshing. The answer? Whisky *mizuwari*: blended whisky, ice, heavily diluted with water. It might be politically incorrect to suggest this today, but the *mizuwari* served meant that you could drink a lot. A LOT.

Blended Japanese whisky was enormous. In the 1980s, Suntory Old was selling 12.4 million cases in its home market. That's almost as much as all Johnnie Walker variants sell globally today. "You can't compare it with today," says Suntory head blender Seiichi Koshimizu. "Our big sellers at that time were [Suntory] Red, White [aka Old], Kakubin, Gold, Reserve, and Royal. It was a pyramid with a unified 'Suntory' style. In society there was also a pyramid and if you were promoted, you would try a higher-level whisky. As you moved up through that hierarchy, you changed your whisky."

Who said blending was easy? An array of bottles—and flavor possibilities for the Japanese blender to play with.

Has that changed? "The idea of hierarchy has gone," Seiichi Koshimizu says. "Now you drink a 'higher' whisky because you want to try it! So, even as beginners, younger drinkers are trying premium and malt whiskies." It's a generational and social shift reflected in whisky.

Interestingly, it is currently moving in two ways. A young generation (including a higher-than-average percentage of women) that turned its back on their fathers' drink and drank *shochu* is now coming to whisky, either with the single-malt style or through—guess what?—heavily diluted whisky highballs.

New, top-end blends are now being developed. Suntory's premium Hibiki range (launched in 1989) has a new member: a 12yo variant which contains whiskies filtered through bamboo charcoal and a malt that's been aged in plum liqueur casks. Nikka's From The Barrel is offering malt drinkers an entry into a world they had rejected, while the firm's Blender's Bar offers a snapshot of the possibilities afforded by blending, but featuring wildly different flavored whiskies made from different ratios of the same components.

Blending may seem coldly analytical, but it is creative. "We are artisans," says Shinji Fukuyo, another of Suntory's senior blending team. "We all strive to become artisans, but you cannnot lightly call yourself one. Artists aim to create something new; they are creators. We artisans are responsible for creation but also for sustaining the quality in our products. We have a promise to keep."

Every whisky will be tasted, assessed, and noted.

JAPANESE BLENDS TASTING NOTES

NIKKA, FROM THE BARREL 51:4%

Nose: A wood in springtime: bark, moss, and green leaves and a light floral underpinning along with rosemary oil. New car. Water makes it more dense. Coffee cake.
Palate: Modest and soft, with melon, peach, sweet persimmon. Dries towards the back, where that mossy note reappears.
Finish: Tight oak.
Conclusion: Intense and balanced. A blend for malt-lovers.

> Flavor camp: **Fruity & Spicy**
> **Where Next?** Johnnie Walker Green Label

NIKKA SUPER 43%

Nose: Copper. Fleshy and crisp, light dried fruit, caramel, and hints of smoke. Raspberry with a light, rooty, floral note.
Palate: Clean and lean with some slick grain helping the flow. Light citrus fruit. More sweet than the nose.
Finish: Medium length. Clean.
Conclusion: A sound and mixable blend.

> Flavor Camp: **Fragrant & Floral**
> **Where Next?** Chivas Regal 12yo, Grant's Family Reserve

HIBIKI 12YO 43%

Nose: Spice (dusty, nutmeg). An intense, green mango/Victoria plum note. Pineapple and lemon.
Palate: Gentle, sweet. Vanilla ice cream, peach. Spicy.
Finish: Long pepper, menthol, then coriander seed.
Conclusion: Highly innovative blending.

> Flavor Camp: **Fruity & Spicy**
> **Where Next?** Jameson

HIBIKI 17YO 43%

Nose: Soft and gentle fruit with touches of lemon balm and orange leaf, then come cacao, apricot jam, banana, and hazelnuts.
Palate: Gentle grain giving a lush toffee character. Dried-fruit notes sit underneath. Black cherry and raisin cake. Long and ripe.
Finish: Smooth and honeyed.
Conclusion: A layered effect justifies the Japanese approach to whisky-making.

> Flavor Camp: **Fruity & Spicy**
> **Where Next?** Chivas 18yo

17 Years Old
HIBIKI
SUNTORY WHISKY
A harmonious blend of handcrafted select specially aged whiskies

THE USA

Distillers use what grows around them. A new country holds no fears for them; they just adapt to the change in circumstances, take a new base ingredient and improvise upon it. In Mexico settlers learned to turn agave into tequila; in the Caribbean they did the same with cane and made rum. In the early days of the settling of the United States, it was apple and fruit which were transformed into brandies. It wasn't until the mid-eighteenth century that whiskey began to be made in any quantities, by *émigré* farmers from Germany, Holland, Ireland, and Scotland who settled in Maryland, Pennsylvania, West Virginia, and the Carolinas and planted rye, the basis for America's first indigenous whiskey style.

Corn-based spirit had to wait until 1776, when "corn patch and cabin" rights were granted to new settlers in the virgin territory of Kentucky County. They took that "Indian corn" and distilled it. It made economic sense. A bushel of corn sold for 50 cents, whereas the five gallons of whiskey you could make from that bushel could net you $2. They used what grew around them.

By the 1860s, the industrial revolution had created a commercial whiskey industry. Distilleries grew in size, railroads allowed national distribution, and, importantly, the quality had improved, thanks to scientific advances spearheaded by James Crow at the Old Oscar Pepper distillery in Kentucky (*see* p.236, pp.240–1).

It's interesting to speculate what today's whisky world might look like had America not fallen under the fell influence of the Temperance movement. It is quite likely that it would have become the dominant player, not Scotch. We'll never know.

What we do know is that by 1915, 20 states were dry, including Kentucky. Whiskey production stopped in 1917 in order to produce industrial alcohol for the war effort and three years later, on January 17, 1920, the Great Drought started.

Although social historians point out that more spirits were drunk in the 13 years of Prohibition than ever before, this was little consolation to American whiskey-makers, who watched a new generation drinking Scotch and Canadian whisky. By the time Prohibition was repealed in 1933, not only was there little stock, but the American palate had also changed. Maybe drinkers could have been persuaded back to rye and bourbon were it not for World War II closing the industry down again. When it restarted postwar, it had been effectively closed for almost three decades. American whiskey was a stranger in its own country.

Its renaissance has been a long and patient one. In many ways, distillers had to wait for tastes to change; their attempts to go light simply diluted the essence of the American whiskey style. It was only when big flavor began to swing back into fashion, triggered by Californian wine as well as single malt, that there were signs that a new generation of American drinkers were ready to rediscover their own spirit.

Now rye is back, and the bourbon industry is in a flurry of creativity. In addition, on the back of the craft-brewing revolution— something that was driven by consumers giving up on the bland and wanting flavor—there's a craft-distilling revolution underway, with new pioneers heading out to points as yet unknown. Their messages from the new frontiers make fascinating reading. American whiskey is alive and well.

Kentucky's limestone bench is good not just for bourbon-making, but for horse-breeding as well.

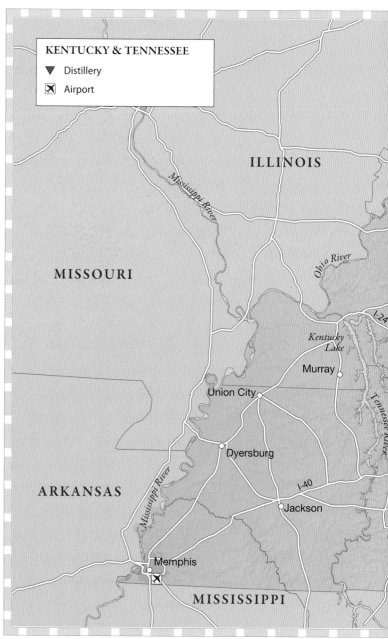

KENTUCKY & TENNESSEE
▼ Distillery
☒ Airport

ILLINOIS

MISSOURI

Mississippi River

Ohio River

I-24

Kentucky Lake

Murray

Union City

Tennessee River

Dyersburg

I-40

ARKANSAS

Mississippi River

Jackson

Memphis

MISSISSIPPI

Previous page: **Looking towards the** Rocky Mountains from Sweet Grass County, Montana.

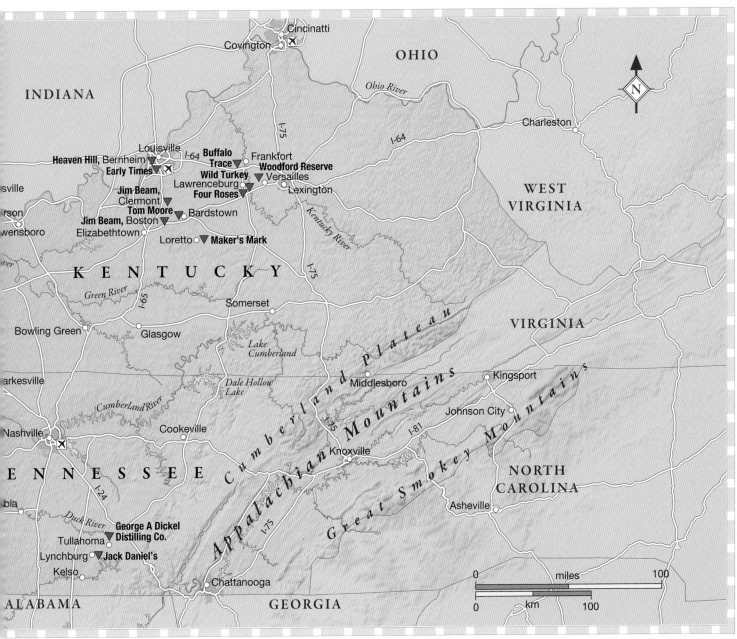

Columbia River, Crown Point State Park, Oregon, looking across to Washington state.

KENTUCKY

We start in New York in the late 1980s. It's late. You're in a bar. "Make it a Manhattan. Rocks." The barkeep gives you a funny look. You look around. Everywhere there are uptown yuppies sipping vodka martinis. It's the era of the skeletal cocktail, the triumph of packaging over content, the high point of the anti-flavor movement which had slowly been gaining momentum since the 1950s. You look at your drink.

It pulses red: a drink of danger. A *noir* cocktail. Even in those days, when small-batch bourbons were appearing on the market, it was a hard sell. What a long way from the days when bourbon and rye were America's spirit. You sip the drink. Where did it all go so wrong?

It started optimistically enough. The free land given to eighteenth-century settlers on the understanding that they planted corn had given Kentucky a head start in whiskey production. Farmstead stills became small distilleries. By the start of the nineteenth century, whiskey barrels were being shipped down the Ohio to the Mississippi to New Orleans.

It was rough stuff, aged for as long as it took to get to market. It took a Scot, James Crow, to change things. From 1825 until his death 31 years later, he brought scientific rigor to whiskey-making: sour-mashing, saccharometers, pH testing. Crow created consistency.

With better spirit and a changing market, aging and new charred barrels became the norm. No one knows who started this, although it could well have come from the Americas' first spirit: rum. Rum distillers knew about the transformative effect wood had on a rough spirit and had been using charred barrels since the seventeenth century.

With each development, the flavors of bourbon began to become fixed—even in law. Today, "Straight Bourbon" is a whiskey distilled no higher than 160° (80% alcohol by volume, or abv; equal to 160 proof) made from a fermented mash of not less than 51 percent corn, which is put in barrel at not more than 125° (62.5% abv), and aged in new charred oak containers for a period of two years or more.

There's a certain flexibility: there's no restriction on cask size, nor does it say that American oak must be used, while the 51 percent allows plenty of variation in mash bills, the precise corn/grain proportions. Bourbon is a series of improvisations on these themes: upping and lowering the corn-to-rye ratio to bring out spice or corn fatness, substituting rye for wheat to smooth things out, utilizing different yeast types to produce specific aromas. Finally, there's Kentucky itself.

Bourbon was born in Kentucky and has survived in Kentucky because of Kentucky. Its hard limestone water requires sour-mashing which in turn gives flavor. The wild yeasts in its air have helped generate distilleries' own strains; its soils give the corn and rye, and its climate impacts hugely on the final flavor of the bourbon. Finally, there's a cultural *terroir* in the shape of whiskey-making dynasties: the Beams, the Samuels, the Russells; bourbon legends like Elmer T. Lee.

New York 2010. It's late. You're in a bar. "Make it a Manhattan. Rocks." The barkeep smiles. Asks you if you'd like bourbon or rye and what brand. Look around. Everywhere people are drinking bourbon.

Bourbon Street, New Orleans: destination for the Mississippi-shipped whiskeys from Kentucky.

Maker's Mark

LORETTO • WWW.MAKERSMARK.COM • OPEN ALL YEAR • MON–SAT; MAR–DEC, SUN ALSO

In 1844, the *Nelson Record*, living up to its name, recorded that Taylor William Samuels' distillery in Deatsville, Kentucky, was "well-constructed and equipped with all the modern improvements known in the distillery business." Taylor William, it would seem, was following in a family tradition. The Samuels family, Scots-Irish in origin, had apparently been turning their corn into whisk(e)y since 1780. Nothing's changed. They still are.

The Maker's Mark story is one of heritage and perseverence, shot through with the cussedness that permeates all of the distillers in this part of the world—but with an important twist. The tales which swirl around bourbon are drawn from family histories, half-truths, and suppositions all stitched together like an old-time patchwork quilt. It may annoy historians, but it makes great marketing. One *leitmotif* is that after Prohibition, the distiller picked himself up, dusted off the old recipe, and got down to business once more. It's very American, it's laudable, and it's often true.

When Bill Samuels Sr. decided to revive the family tradition in 1953 at Star Hill Farm, he deviated from this. He picked himself up, looked around, and said, "We're going to do it differently this time."

In other words, not just start a distillery from scratch, but start everything from basics. To Bill Sr., the bourbons on the market were hard, harsh, low-priced, and, most importantly, being outsold by Scotch. If bourbon were to have a future, he mused, it would have to up its quality and change its flavor.

Here in the woodsy hollow next to Hardin Creek, in a distillery that had been producing since 1805, he planned his single style of whisky (Bill Sr. stuck to the Scottish spelling). No rye in the mash bill, but wheat. Maker's, contrary to popular belief, is not the sole wheated bourbon on the market. Bill Sr. consulted with the greatest advocate of the wheated style, Pappy van Winkle, and came up with a mash bill of 70 percent corn, 16 percent wheat, and 14 percent malted barley.

Charred barrels are an essential element in the creation of the Maker's Mark character.

"He did a lot of different things," says Maker's brand ambassador Jane Conner. "Things were bad, so he just did the opposite." These "different things" are seen today at the distillery: a roller mill to stop the grains scorching, slow cooking in open cookers ("to get the essence of corn"), the use of its own house jug yeast. Distillation to 130 proof (65% abv) in a copper beer column and pot-still doubler. This gives a pleasantly focused "white dog" (the American term for new make).

"Maturation is key," says Conner. "Our oak is air-dried for 12 months and given a lighter char for flavor reasons. We don't want the sickly sweetness of other bourbons. What he wanted was a smoother bourbon. 'Easy-drinking' is a bad thing to say these days, apparently, but I don't see why. Surely it's nice to create something that's drinkable?"

Maturing its whisky in black-painted rick warehouses dotted around the property, Maker's still rotates its barrels: taking the slow-maturing casks from the cooler bottom floor and replacing them with the ones that have been baking on the top floor. Conner says that this is for consistency, but if only one bourbon is being made, wouldn't a cross section be easier? "A cross section might work if you just had one warehouse, but we have 19 and every one is different. Rotating makes sense because maturation is just crazy in Kentucky."

Maker's has stuck with its gentle, yet bright style since 1953. "There's been a lot of pressure for us to do another line," says Conner, "but there's nothing worse than paying $60 for a bottle and being disappointed. While we wanted to do it, we had to find a way to enhance what we already had." That enhancement was about to be released at the time of writing: a Maker's that's been given a period of maturation in casks fitted with inner staves, effectively increasing the interaction with oak. "It's in your face," says Conner. "It's Maker's on steroids."

Black and red. The slightly ominous-looking company livery of Maker's Mark couldn't be in greater contrast to this most open-hearted of bourbons.

MAKER'S MARK TASTING NOTES

WHITE DOG 90°/45%
Nose: Sweet, gentle, and pure with good corn oiliness. Touch of heavy florals, apple, and lint.
Palate: Fleshy and ripe, with red summer fruits. Fragrant with a gentle texture. Very bright and dynamic.
Finish: Focused, with a little fennel.

MAKER'S MARK
Nose: Soft, with buttery oak. Creamy feel. Maraschino cherry, sandalwood, and upfront apple. Fruit is now fully ripe. With water, more blossom-like. Balanced wood.
Palate: Smooth, sweet, and gentle. Quite chewy. Some laurel, syrup, coconut.
Finish: Soft.
Conclusion: Rather than rye acting as the gripping agent, here the oak is allowed to exert a gentle squeeze on the soft spirit.

Flavor Camp: Sweet Wheat
Where Next? W. L. Weller, Crown Royal

Early Times & Woodford Reserve

EARLY TIMES • LOUISVILLE • WWW.EARLYTIMES.COM
WOODFORD RESERVE • VERSAILLES • WWW.WOODFORDRESERVE.COM • OPEN ALL YEAR • TUES–SAT

Louisville is a fascinating amalgam of the grand and the blue collar: a state capital with impressive brick buildings festooned with wrought ironwork, a museum to a baseball bat, and hotels with hidden passageways for bootleggers to escape through. It's also the birthplace of Muhammad Ali and a quiet revolution in American music. But in areas such as Shively are the shells of warehouses and old plants, once home to mighty whiskey producers.

Both of Louisville's two operational distilleries are situated around here: Heaven Hill's Bernheim and Brown-Forman's Early Times. Operational since 1940, Early Times produces Early Times and Old Forester from two distinct recipes. "They are two very different whiskeys," says master distiller Chris Morris. "Early Times is relaxed. Old Forester is focused."

That "old-fashioned, country style" found in Early Times starts with a mash bill that is 79% corn, 11% rye, and 10% barley malt (*see* p.18). "We use the IA yeast strain, in use since the 1920s," says Morris. "This gives a low congener profile which helps create that mild character. We also sour it to 20 percent [i.e. 20 percent of the mash is backset, whereby the acidic ("sour") spent lees from the bottom of the beer column is added to the fermenter]. Old Forester's mash bill has a higher rye-to-malt ratio, 18% to 72%, which helps to up the spiciness. It, too, has its own yeast and is soured only to 12 percent."

Sour-mashing can be a confusing issue, with many bourbon drinkers claiming to prefer "sour-mashed" brands over others simply because the term is on the label. In reality, all straight whiskeys are sour-mashed. Kentucky and Tennessee sit on a limestone bench, meaning that the water is mineral-rich but also hard and alkaline. Adding backset helps to acidify the mash, stop potential infection, and ease the fermentation.

The percentage of sour used has a significant impact on flavor, as Morris explains. "The more sour you use, the less sugar the yeast has to work with, so a 20 percent sour and a three-day ferment [as with Early Times] gives a lower congener level, while Old Forester's 12 percent sour and five-day ferment gives more flavor and a fresher beer because there's more material for the yeast to work with. Old Forester's beer smells like rose petals; Early Times' is nachos." Both are taken off the thumper at 140° (70%) and diluted to 125° (62.5%), then barreled.

While Early Times is happy to stick to its image as a down-home, easy-sipping bourbon (or, when aged in refill barrels, Kentucky whiskey), Old Forester has been moving into the area of special release with its Birthday Barrel selection of older bourbons (on average ten to 14 years) taken from a single day's production. "It allows us to look for unusual profiles," says Morris. "Once, for example, a squirrel got itself in a junction box and blew the power— killed himself as well—and left us with a three-day ferment, which gave us different congeners."

The squirrel might have felt more at home at Brown-Forman's other distillery, Woodford Reserve, which lies in the heart of horse-breeding territory next to Glenn's Creek in Woodford Co. Here, in the 1830s,

Oscar Pepper hired the father of modern bourbon, James Crow. Today, these pale limestone buildings contain a unique bourbon distillery that uses pot stills, like miniaturized versions of Glemorangie's, to triple-distill.

"This distillery honors Pepper and Crow," says Morris, "but it isn't a re-creation of nineteenth-century whiskey." Instead, Woodford Reserve

Barrels fitting snugly behind the thick limestone walls of the Woodford Reserve distillery.

is more of a continuation of Crow's analytical exploration of what was possible. Made to the same mash bill as Old Forester but with only 6 percent souring and a different yeast, it has a week-long fermentation. Although the white dog comes off the third still at 158° (79%), the "less-efficient" pots build in more flavor than a spirit of the same strength out of a column. Barreled at 110° (54.5%) in air-dried oak, the Distiller's Select always has bourbon from the Shively distillery blended in.

Crow's "why not?" ethos extends to the Master's Collection limited release program. "We have five sources of flavor in bourbon," Morris says. "Grain, water, ferment, distillation, and maturation. Distillation and water are constants, so any innovation involves looking at the possibilities in the other three." So far, the releases have included a four-grain mash bill, finishing in ex-Sonoma-Cutrer Chardonnay barrels, a sweet ("unsoured") mash—"We figured we should find out why we do sour"—and there are plans around wood types and coopering. Crow's legacy lives on.

Originally the Old Oscar Pepper Distillery, Woodford Reserve was where James Crow brought scientific rigor to the art of bourbon distilling.

EARLY TIMES & WOODFORD RESERVE TASTING NOTES

EARLY TIMES 80°/40%
Nose: Gold. Perfumed and honey-like, with lots of spun sugar and sweet popcorn. Coconut and a lick of honey.
Palate: Medium-weight and soft. The corn shows well, mixing with vanilla fudge, with a deeper tobacco note behind showing an unexpected seriousness.
Finish: Gentle and long.
Conclusion: Sweet and easy-drinking.

Flavor Camp: Soft Corn

Where Next? George Dickel Old No.12, Jim Beam Black Label, Hedgehog (France)

WOODFORD RESERVE DISTILLER'S SELECT
86.4°/43.2%

Nose: Dark amber. Waxy, honeyed notes. Lemon thyme and intense citrus fruit. Stewed apple, nutmeg, and lemon cake. The oak adds a syrupy character. With water, there's charred wood, corn shucks, and wood oils.
Palate: Clean and light to start. Precise and almost angular. Zesty and tight. The thyme comes back along with the citrus peels. Rye eases in subtly.
Finish: Mix of citrus fruit and sweet spice.
Conclusion: Balanced and very clean.

Flavor Camp: Spicy Rye

Where Next? Tom Moore, Maker's Mark

LABROT & GRAHAM

WOODFORD RESERVE

DISTILLER'S SELECT

Wild Turkey

LAWRENCEBURG • WWW.WILDTURKEYBOURBON.COM • OPEN ALL YEAR • MON–SAT

Iron-clad and black-painted, sitting on the edge of a cliff above the Kentucky River, Wild Turkey's location is a physical metaphor of the past state of the bourbon industry. The fact that it has survived is down to the efforts of one man: Jimmy Russell, who has been distiller here for 55 years. In fact, it could be argued that the values of old-time bourbon have only survived because of the distillers of Jimmy's generation, who resisted change if it meant compromising on character and quality.

Jimmy and Wild Turkey have achieved a form of symbiosis: Wild Turkey is a big bourbon whose thick, rich physicality makes drinkers take their time. It represents a slower, less hectic age. He has an old-style distiller's polite contempt for scientists and expresses benign amusement when fielding questions about Turkey's DNA. I just do it the way I've always done it, he seems to say, the way I was taught and the way I've taught Eddie. (Eddie is Jimmy's son. He's in his 30th year at Wild Turkey.)

The Wild Turkey rationale is all about building in flavor, about anchoring this bourbon in the mouth. "We're in the low-70s when it comes to corn and therefore close to 30 percent in small grains," says Jimmy. "Some of the other fellows are in the high-70s, some are mid-70s. A couple even use wheat. We're the lowest. We're traditional, with more body, more flavor, and more character."

That character starts with open-topped cookers and fermenting with a single yeast strain. "How old is the strain? Well, I've been here for 55 years and it was here when I arrived," says Jimmy. "It, too, has an effect on flavor. It's there to help promote that heavier flavor."

Collected off the still at 124–126° (62–63% abv) the white dog is barrelled at 110° (55%). "My feeling is that the higher percentage of alcohol, then the less flavor you'll have. Because we go into the barrel at a low proof and then bottle at 101° (50.5%), we're not losing much in terms of flavor, and that helps in making that older style."

The huge warehouses at Wild Turkey, each with their own microclimate, play their part in making this one of the biggest-boned of bourbons, seen arrayed **below**.

It might even be a style recognizable to the Ripy brothers, who moved here in 1905 from their family distillery in Tyrone, Pennsylvania, which had been making bourbon since 1869. In the 1940s, the Ripy Distillery was bought by Austin Nichols and renamed Wild Turkey after its bourbon became the favored drink at the directors' annual wild turkey shoot. It ended up as part of Pernod Ricard, which never seemed to grasp its potential, and in 2009 was bought by Campari. Maybe the hands-off approach worked out for the best. Jimmy has kept on making his style of bourbon and now the market has gone full circle.

"I think the consumer is coming back to what they wanted years ago," he says. "It's not just the older generation drinking Wild Turkey, but new drinkers looking for a bourbon with flavor and body that they can sip and have a good time with. It's going back to pre-Prohibition times. Everything comes around." Even straight rye, a style which only a few distillers (including Turkey) persevered with, is back.

Was he tempted to change when bourbon went light? "We couldn't have competed in that market, so I s'pose it was part economics on the part of the bosses and partly my philosophy. We wanted to stay true to what bourbon was all about, which is not watered down."

Now under its new ownership, capacity is being doubled. Bourbon has looked over the abyss and stepped back into a world of flavor. Jimmy Russell has been vindicated.

The sweetness of American oak mingles with the rich corn and rye and some magic to make Wild Turkey.

WILD TURKEY TASTING NOTES

101 101°/50.5%

Nose: Amber. Heavy and richly flavored. Walnut leaves, maple syrup/chestnut honey, and rock candy that's cut with a lemon lift and then dusty rye. With water, cream toffee.
Palate: Immediately deep and mouth-filling. Tongue-clinging, sweet, and heavy, then a solid mentholated kick as the rye starts to come through. Freshening as it moves.
Finish: Spicy with a little clove.
Conclusion: A massive flavor package.

Flavor Camp: Rich & Oaky
Where Next? Old Forester Birthday Bourbon 13yo

RUSSELL'S RESERVE BOURBON 10YO
90°/45%

Nose: Huge and sweet with vanilla, chocolate, caramel, baked peach, fruit syrups, then the chestnut honey seen on the 101 with Greek pine honey. Thick, almost waxy feel. With water, more rye. Nutmeg.
Palate: As nose with added Turkish delight and plenty of oak giving support to the liquorous thickness of the weight. Almond. Sweet.
Finish: Rye lift but balanced by the sheer weight. Cinnamon. Tobacco.
Conclusion: Complex and layered.

Flavor Camp: Rich & Oaky
Where Next? Booker's

RARE BREED 108.2°/54.1%

Nose: Deep amber/coppery glints. Less thick than Russell's Reserve and also a cleaner sweetness. Orange and allspice with a previously unseen leathery note. Fragrant and, for Turkey, subtle.
Palate: Overtly spicy. Varnish, that tobacco-leaf quality then spiky rye.
Finish: Long, mixing sweet toffee and jags of spice.
Conclusion: A small-batch blend of bourbons between six and 12 years old and bottled undiluted.

Flavor Camp: Rich & Oaky
Where Next? Pappy van Winkle Family Reserve 20yo

RUSSELL'S RESERVE RYE, 6YO 90°/45%AV

Nose: Light gold. Intense rye to start with but very honeyed behind. Less dusty than some ryes but still bold, with green fennel seed, spruce, and garden twine. With water there's camphor, sourdough, and sweet oak.
Palate: Slow, honeyed start. Hard candy, then a dry-rye character begins to change the sweetness to a clean acidity.
Finish: Fizzy spice.
Conclusion: Quite a gentle rye.

Flavor Camp: Spicy Rye
Where Next? Millstone 5yo rye (Holland)

Heaven Hill

LOUISVILLE • WWW.HEAVEN-HILL.COM • HERITAGE CENTER: BARDSTOWN • OPEN ALL YEAR • TUES–SAT; MAR–DEC, SUN ALSO

There are warehouses as far as you can see. Massive metal-clad tenements of whiskey spilling across the rolling Kentucky landscape, looking a little like a housing project that's been dumped here by some stray tornado. The extent of the warehousing is testament to the volume of different whiskeys produced here by the various Heaven Hill distillers. This, after all, is the American distiller with the largest roster of brands on the market.

There's a feeling of permanence about this scene. This is bourbon's heartland. Two of the Heaven Hill brands are named after legendary pioneers of distillation in this corn-rich land: Evan Williams and Elijah Craig. Yet the Heaven Hill story is a relatively recent one, starting from the distilling wasteland that was left by Prohibition. Only a tiny fraction of the hundreds of distillers who plied their trade before the Volstead Act came into force in the 1920s took up whiskey-making after the repeal. Some of these restarted operations.

There were also, however, some newcomers who sensed an opportunity. The Shapira brothers were in the latter camp. Storekeepers by trade, they bought a plot of land outside Bardstown in the 1930s and started distilling in 1935. They called their distillery Heaven Hill: not, as many imagine, out of some romantic allusion, but after the original owner, William Heavenhill. When the operation got going properly after the war, they hired a master distiller—and in Kentucky, who better to get than a Beam? In this case Earl Beam, Jim's nephew.

THE BOURBON / SCOTCH DIVIDE

One way in which the bourbon industry differs from Scotch is in its intense personal crafting of whiskey styles. Due to Prohibition, American whiskey had to start afresh. The styles that emerged from its distilleries were very much the creations of the distiller. Parker learned from his father; he didn't follow an approach handed down for over a century as is the case in Scotland. There is a direct physical and emotional attachment. Sometimes it isn't location but the personality of the people.

Earl's son, Parker, and grandson, Craig, now rule the whiskey-making roost here while the Shapira family still owns the business.

Today, the Heaven Hill Bardstown site contains the company HQ, a prize-winning visitors' center, and that warehousing, but there's no distillery. There's a reason for that. There used to be one, at the bottom of the hill. Then, in 1995, a lightning strike on a warehouse

Not a Bardstown housing project: just part of Heaven Hill's huge warehousing complex.

Full of color and life, the bourbon is now ready for the next phase—a bottle—and your glass.

sent a river of flaming liquor straight into the distillery and it exploded.

Today, all the Heaven Hill brands are produced at what used to be United Distillers & Vintners' [now Diageo's] Bernheim distillery in Louisville, which the drinks giant closed in 1999. Switching site is no easy task, and as Parker says with typical understatement, "There were some kinks in here which we had to iron out before we could get the Heaven Hill character right."

Bernheim was fully computerized, but Parker and Craig were used to a sleeves-rolled-up approach. "Whiskey is a hands-on business," Parker says. "You need to make it personal. That's the way in which we've always worked and I guess I just don't know any other way." He likes his whiskeys with age on them; even the Heaven Hill flagship, Evan Williams, is seven years old: a fair age for a bourbon.

Indeed, the father-and-son team craft whiskeys from across the American tradition songbook. There are corn- and rye-based bourbons in Evan Williams and Elijah Craig; corn and wheat with Old Fitzgerald;

straight rye in Rittenhouse and Pikesville; and the most recent innovation is the straight-wheat Bernheim Wheat.

I see Parker and Craig's quiet personalities writ large in Parker's releases, and across this calm, understated yet innovative portfolio.

HEAVEN HILL TASTING NOTES

BERNHEIM ORIGINAL WHEAT 90°/45%
Nose: Gentle, with butter and fresh baking, red fruit, and allspice. Clean and defined.
Palate: Tingle of fresh-planed oak. Reminiscent of melted rock candy with a hint of toffee and a menthol note. Very fine.
Finish: A stunning glass, gentle yet exotic.
Conclusion: Gentle and dangerously drinkable. A new world of opportunity opens up.

Flavor Camp: **Sweet Wheat**
Where Next? Crown Royal

OLD FITZGERALD 12YO 90°/45%
Nose: Complex earth tones with licorice, cigar smoke, leather, walnut cake.
Palate: A deep, brooding bourbon, with butterscotch and vanilla underpinnings showing a lovely interplay between honey and chocolate. Wood has a presence, but nuttily so.
Finish: Oak, but lovely balance.
Conclusion: Deep and powerful. Demands a cigar.

Flavor Camp: **Rich & Oaky**
Where Next? W. L. Weller, Pappy van Winkle

EVAN WILLIAMS SINGLE BARREL VINTAGE 1999 86°/43%
Nose: Immediate and expressive. A scented, exotic lift of Peychaud bitters, dandelion, maraschino juice, rock candy. In time, a mix of redwood, yew sap, and assertive rye. Great vibrancy. Balance.
Palate: Light and clean, then cotton candy, spearmint, and a blast of spiciness to the finish, making it increasingly mouth-tingling.
Finish: Clean and crisp. Cherry tobacco.
Conclusion: Each vintage plays a subtle variation on this very precise sweet/spicy interplay.

Flavor Camp: **Soft Corn**
Where Next? Four Roses Single Barrel, Blanton's

RITTENHOUSE RYE 80°/40%
Nose: A teasing mix of sweet and sour. Camphor, turpentine, varnish, rich oak. Hugely spicy. With water, nuts, shaved wood, flamed orange peel.
Palate: Intensely spicy, a firm grip, and mouth-tightening tannins overtake surprising sweetness. Scented lemon, dried rose petal.
Finish: Long, wonderfully bitter. Rye!
Conclusion: A great start for newcomers to the rye world.

Flavor Camp: **Spicy Rye**
Where Next? Wild Turkey, Sazerac

ELIJAH CRAIG 12YO 94°/47%
Nose: Sweet and dense. Apricot jam, stewed fruit, charred oak. Custard, cedar, and a little tobacco leaf.
Palate: Rounded. A very sweet start, licorice, before spiced apple takes over on the finish.
Finish: Sweet. Candy. Oak.
Conclusion: Sweet and rich. An approachable old-style bourbon.

Flavor Camp: **Rich & Oaky**
Where Next? Old Forester, Eagle Rare

On the hunt for another magic barrel ...

Buffalo Trace

FRANKFORT • WWW.BUFFALOTRACE.COM • OPEN ALL YEAR • MON–SAT

First there came the buffalo, finding a fording point on a bend in the Kentucky River on their annual migration. Then came the Lee brothers, who set up a trading post, "Leestown," in 1775. Today, there's a massive distillery that seems to have acquired more names than most along the way: OFC, Stagg, Schenley, Ancient Age, Leestown—and now Buffalo Trace.

This is a university of straight whiskey distillation. Even the red-brick buildings add to that air. The polar opposite to Maker's Mark with its single recipe, here the aim is to be as diverse as possible: there's wheated bourbon (W. L. Weller); ryes (Sazerac, Handy); corn/rye bourbon: Buffalo Trace; and single barrels (Blanton's, Eagle Rare). The Pappy van Winkle range is also made here.

In addition, there's an annual Antique Collection of limited releases and the occasional experimental bourbons. It's as if Buffao Trace is trying single-handedly to restore the number of bourbon brands to its pre-Prohibition levels.

Given his multitasking responsibilities, master distiller Harlen Wheatley seems remarkably laid-back. "We have five big recipes," he says, "but we only run one at a time. So we'll be on wheated for six to eight weeks, then rye/bourbon, and then one of the three different rye recipes. We like to have a bit of everything."

While the specifics are a secret, there's no addition of backset at the cooking stage, which takes place under pressure (*see* pp.18–19). "It is a better way to get all the sugars," Wheatley explains, "and results in a more consistent ferment." Only one yeast strain is used, but the fermenters are different sizes, creating different environments. The distillation for each brand is, however, totally different, with varying degrees of reflux and distillation strength.

Distillation is only half of the story. The complex range of differently flavored white dogs (new makes) is matched by a complex range of maturation conditions. It's easy to think that when a barrel is placed in a warehouse that it matures in a even fashion. Each barrel is, however, different, and the microclimate within each warehouse is different. Warehousing, especially in the extreme conditions in Kentucky, is therefore a vital component in flavor creation.

If you're making a variety of products and specializing in one-offs, then building in complexity of warehousing and maturation conditions is vital. "We have 75 different floors in total," explains Wheatley. "These are split across three sites. We have brick-built, stone-built, heated, and rick [wooden beams surrounded by a brick shell or iron]. Because each floor and each warehouse is different, the location of barrels is important for each brand, and since we go from 3yo to 23yo we have to figure it all out." In other words, it's not just mash bill and distillation, but the physical placement of the barrel which makes the difference.

Buffalo Trace's mastery of a wide range of styles has made it the red-brick "University of Bourbon."

"We have to anticipate," he continues. "Weller, for example, we know will be a 7yo, so we're not going to put that on the top floor, or the bottom floor either, because that would be too slow. Pappy 23yo we have to watch very carefully—that's probably a second or third floor—while Blanton's has its own warehouse which produces a very specific effect." He laughs. "We understand it. We've been doing it a while."

He's right there. Wheatley is only the sixth master distiller here since the Civil War. Master distiller emeritus Elmer T. Lee, who still oversees Blanton's, was trained by Colonel Blanton, who joined in 1897. Diversity is a result of this human matrix of knowledge.

The final seal of approval at the distillery for the bottles of Buffalo Trace.

BUFFALO TRACE TASTING NOTES

WHITE DOG, MASH NO. 1

Nose: Sweet and fat. Cornmeal/polenta. Hot with lily, nutty roasted corn/barley. Hint, with water, of a vegetal *rhum agricole* note.
Palate: Lifted. Big violet hit, then a spreading, chewy corn.
Finish: Long and smooth. No harshness.

BUFFALO TRACE 90°/45%

Nose: Amber. Mix of cocoa butter/coconut and a scented violet/herbal note. Touch of apricot and spice. Clean oak. Spiced honey, butterscotch, and tangerine.
Palate: Spicy start with sweet citrus fruit, then vanilla and eucalyptus, then Peychaud bitters. Fat and generous. Medium-bodied. In time, lots of freshly grated nutmeg.
Finish: Light grip and rye spices.
Conclusion: Mature and rich. Balanced.

Flavor Camp: Soft Corn
Where Next? Blanton's Single Barrel, Gentleman Jack

EAGLE RARE 10YO SINGLE BARREL 90°/45%

Nose: Amber. Deeper than Buffalo Trace, this has more dark chocolate and dried orange peel along with that scented note that is one of the distillery's signatures. Molasses and lively spices, some cherry cough medicine, star anise. Mellow oak. With water, polished wooden floors.
Palate: Soft and very thick. Quite a different feel to BT, with more tannin and crisper oak. Vetiver.
Finish: Dry, then an acidic hit.
Conclusion: Altogether a bigger prospect.

Flavor Camp: Rich & Oaky
Where Next? Wild Turkey, Ridgemont Reserve

W. L. WELLER 12YO 90°/45%

Nose: Clean and light. Grated nutmeg, vellum, roasting coffee bean. Honeycomb and rose petal with a little hint of heavy florals.
Palate: A clean and very honeyed palate, with crisp spice from the oak that softens into melted chocolate.
Finish: Sandalwood.
Conclusion: A wheated bourbon showing the characteristic gentle mellowness of that grain.

Flavor Camp: Sweet Wheat
Where Next? Maker's Mark, Crown Royal

BLANTON'S SINGLE BARREL

NO. 8/H WAREHOUSE, 93°/46.5%

Nose: Amber. More cooked fruit and caramel. Lots of vanilla bean, corn, and peach cobbler. Sweet, clean, and lightly spicy.
Palate: Starchy start, then a floral lift—almost the jasmine/lily of the white dog. Wood begins to tighten but this is toffee-like. Almost smoky, charred.
Finish: Turmeric and dry oak.
Conclusion: Rounded compared with the Eagle's talons.

Flavor Camp: Soft Corn
Where Next? Evan Williams SB

PAPPY VAN WINKLE FAMILY RESERVE 20YO

90.1°/45.2%

Nose: Rich amber. Ripe and oaked. Sweet fruit jams and heavy maple syrup. A little spice. With water, has the funky/fungal qualities of wood-aged spirits.
Palate: Oak and dry leather. Cigar, then mothballs before drifting to dried mint, dried cherry, and licorice.
Finish: Gentle bite and oak.
Conclusion: Old and wooded.

Flavor Camp: Rich & Oaky
Where Next? Wild Turkey Rare Breed

SAZERAC RYE & SAZERAC 18YO BOTH 90°/45%

Nose: The younger has a nose of dust, violet, and proving sourdough bread with orange bitters and a red-cherry jag. The 18yo is also scented, but the attack has lessened and moved to an integrated leathery/varnish note. Cherries are now black.
Palate: Flinty and intense. Lots of camphor. Classically zesty. The 18yo shows more oak and baked rye bread. Oily rather than flinty, but scented still.
Finish: Allspice and ginger. The 18yo retains the ginger, adds anise and a throat-thickening sweetness.
Conclusion: Like peatiness in Scotland, the rye character isn't lost but absorbed into the spirit.

Flavor Camp: Spicy Rye
Where Next? Young: Eddu (France), Russell's Reserve Rye 6yo; **Old:** Four Roses 120th Anniversary, Four Roses Mariage Collection 2009, Rittenhouse

Jim Beam

CLERMONT • WWW.JIMBEAM.COM • OPEN ALL YEAR • MON–SUN

Scottish distillers are rightly proud of their whisky-making tradition, yet to the best of my knowledge there's no dynasty in Scotland like the Beams. The family history claims Jacob Beam (originally Boehm) started distilling in 1795 in Washington County. In 1854, his grandson, David M. Beam, moved the operation near to the railroad in Clear Springs, where his sons, Jim and Park, then learned their trade. So far, so normal. It's what happened after Prohibition that is remarkable.

Aged 70 in 1933, Jim applied for a license to distill and built a new distillery in Clermont, with Park and his sons making the whiskey. Jim handed over to his son, Jeremiah, then his grandson, Booker Noe, took up the reins. Now Booker Noe's son, Fred, is there. When you consider that Parker and Craig Beam at Heaven Hill are Park's grandsons, too, and that it was a Beam who started Early Times, you begin to wonder whether the state should be renamed.

It's only when you understand that lineage that you can begin to understand why an old man started up the family business again, at the age of 70. What else was James Beauregard Beam to do? Bourbon ran in his veins.

Did he change things? Yes and no. The sweet, hopped yeast cooked up in the family home was a re-creation of the original, but distillation was able to take advantage of twentieth-century developments. I well remember Booker Noe guffawing as I spluttered through a fusel-heavy glass of (another firm's) pre-Prohibition bourbon. "I like true bourbon," he rumbled, "but you know, some things just needed changing."

Beam's post-Prohibition story is very much a balance between the commercial necessities faced by a big brand in an ever-changing

market and this adherence of Booker to his belief in Big Bourbon. It's a creative tension that gave the world its biggest-selling bourbon brand, but also saw, in 1988, the launch of the uncompromising "straight from the barrel" brand, Booker's, and then, four years later, the Small Batch Collection.

The downside of being a major brand is that aficionados can be dismissive of the whole range, yet there is as much creativity at Beam's two distilleries in Clermont and Boston as at any other plant. Not that there's any great emphasis placed on secret mash bills as being the main driver for flavor. "The yeast is obviously important," says brand ambassador Ernie Lubbers. "And yes, we do have more than one recipe, but the first questions you should ask about any bourbon is what is the proof off the still, what's the barreling strength, and where are the barrels stored? Look at Scotch. It's just barley, yet you get hundreds of different flavors. It's not just the recipe!"

The Beam range uses the flavoring potential of strength and location to its fullest. White and Black Label come off at 135° (67.5% abv), are barreled at 125° (62.5%), and the barrels are scattered around the warehouses: top, bottom, sides, and middle. Old Grandad is a high-rye recipe but is otherwise the same as White and Black. The rye is lower strength: 127° (63.5%) and it's barreled at 125° (62.5%).

Things have certainly changed in Clermont since the Beams first started distilling.

JIM BEAM TASTING NOTES

WHITE LABEL 80°/40%

Nose: Fresh and zesty. Has a youthful energy. Light rye lemon spiciness, then ginger and tea. Scented and vibrant.

Palate: After such a sassy nose, the palate starts very silkily with real menthol. Cool mint cigarettes. Butter toffee. Crisp.

Finish: Sweet.

Conclusion: Balanced and vibrant.

> Flavor Camp: **Soft Corn**
>
> **Where Next?** Jack Daniel's

BLACK LABEL 8YO 80°/40%

Nose: Soft with a little molasses, spiced orange, and a similar fresh spiciness to the White Label. Cacao and cigar ash.

Palate: The oaky notes continue: cedar and char balanced by the punchy spirit. More overtly spicy than the White Label.

Finish: Molasses.

Conclusion: Oak and energy.

> Flavor Camp: **Soft Corn**
>
> **Where Next?** Jack Daniel's Single Barrel, Buffalo Trace, Gentleman Jack

KNOB CREEK 9YO 100°/50%

Nose: Amber. Rich and sweet. Pure fruit. Caramelized fruit sugars, agave syrup. Light coconut and apricot. Cigar leaf.

Palate: Big, sweet, and luscious. Full-bodied, with lots of cinnamon, blackberry, and spun sugar.

Finish: Oak and butter.

Conclusion: Rich, but has that Beam energy.

> Flavor Camp: **Rich & Oaky**
>
> **Where Next?** Wild Turkey Rare Breed

BOOKER'S 126.8°

Nose: Huge and soft. Baked fruits with blackstrap molasses. Tropical fruit and black banana. Deep and powerful.

Palate: Sweet and almost liqueur-like. The spirit coping with the attack of the oak. Blackberry jam and burnt sugar. Orange-blossom honey.

Finish: Wood and heat.

Conclusion: A huge, no-holds-barred experience.

> Flavor Camp: **Rich & Oaky**
>
> **Where Next?** Russell's Reserve 10yo

There's even greater variation with the small batches. Knob Creek is distilled to 130° (65%) and barreled at 125° (62.5%). "It's a 9yo product so we're not going to have any [barrels that] touch the sides or the top floors of the warehouses," explains Lubbers. Basil Hayden is high in rye but distilled and barreled at 120° (60%) and aged in the center of the warehouses as is Knob Creek. Baker's is distilled and barreled at 125° (62.5%) but is aged for seven years on the top floor; "That's why it's so intense." And Booker is distilled and barreled at 125° (62.5%) and aged in the fifth and sixth floors.

"You know," says Lubbers. "Booker would go up there all the time, just stand there and see what was happening."

Dreaming, working things out. The human touch.

Four Roses

LAWRENCEBURG • WWW.FOURROSES.US • OPEN ALL YEAR • MON–SAT

If Buffalo Trace is a red-brick university, then the yellow-painted Four Roses is less the Spanish Mission its architecture suggests and more of a specialized postgraduate college with master distiller Jim Rutledge as its professor. He revels in complexity, seeing the creative possibilities in the Four Roses five yeast strains and two mash bills. This breadth of choice came about thanks to the distillery's former owner, Seagram, which used to have five plants in Kentucky, each with its own yeast specification.

Though Seagram sold off its assets, all the yeasts ended up at Four Roses, now owned by Japanese brewer/distiller Kirin. Today, Jim Rutledge oversees the production of ten different spirits. There are two high rye content mash bills: OE, 75% corn, 20% rye, 5% barley; and OB (60:35:5). Each are then fermented with five different yeasts, producing that kennel of white dogs.

The yeast strains create very specific flavors. F, for example, lends a vegetal almost *rhum agricole* note to the OE and a herbal lift to OB; K gives violet and spices on OE and intensifies the focus on rye on OB; O is fat and mashy on OE and heavy with ripe fruit on OB; Q is broad and jasmine-like on OE and has an intense rose perfume on OB; while the V strain gives an estery banana note on OE and carnations and steeliness to OB. All Four Roses, all different.

This wealth of riches allows Rutledge to have a different blend for each of his brands, meaning that the age and blend for Yellow Label is different from that of the single barrel (in 2009, an 11yo OE/Q), which is different from that of Mariage (in 2009, a blend of 19yo and 12yo OB/K with 12yo OE/O). What is intriguing is that the high rye percentage doesn't deliver the eye-blinking bite seen in many other bourbons but a freshness and vibrancy. Four Roses, however, does not have just a PhD in yeast; it has one in blending as well.

This should be enough Four Roses to keep someone happy.

FOUR ROSES TASTING NOTES

120TH ANNIVERSARY 12YO 110.8°/55.4%
Nose: Upfront and rich. Classic aromatic notes of cinnamon balls, dust, rose oil, powdered lemon.
Palate: Perfumed start, all roses and talc. Quite dry but central sweetness. Slightly acidic on the finish.
Finish: Pacharan (sloe liqueur).
Conclusion: Well-balanced

Flavor Camp: **Spicy & Rye**
Where Next? Ridgemont Reserve

BARREL STRENGTH 15YO SINGLE BARREL 104.2°/52.1%
Nose: Cotton-candy sweetness, green plum, eucalyptus, oak.
Palate: Perfumed, silky, and sweet, with fizzing spices. Succulent flow balanced by spice and caramel apple.
Finish: Tight and spicy.
Conclusion: Balanced and fine-boned.

Flavor Camp: **Spicy & Rye**
Where Next? Sazerac 18yo

MARIAGE COLLECTION, 2009
Nose: Dark amber. Balanced sweet spiciness. Powdered rose petal. Lime marmalade, light vanilla toffee, and mint chocolate. Typically lifted and precise. Not oaky.
Palate: Camphor-like and tightly focused. Palate is more orange peel and that light floral lift, and then just sufficient butteriness to soften the grip of the rye. Again, no oak. Quite penetrating
Finish: Very zesty and dry.
Conclusion: Almost austere in its delivery. Iconoclastic to the last.

Flavor Camp: **Spicy & Rye**
Where Next?: Evan Williams Single Barrel

SINGLE BARREL, 2009 116°/58%
Nose: Fruit market (apple crates), oak, and a little sandy note. Becomes more fragrant/heavy floral in time with some added black cherry. Perfumed. Cigar wrapper and rhubarb.
Palate: Highly scented. Good maturity. Ripe, red fruit and a decent spread of flavors over the tongue. Water brings out a fine-grained spiciness.
Finish: Crisp oak.
Conclusion: That range of options at Jim Rutledge's fingertips shows its worth in this complex mixture.

Flavor Camp: **Spicy & Rye**
Where Next? Woodford Reserve

Tom Moore

BARDSTOWN • WWW.SAZERAC.COM • OPEN TO VISITORS • CHECK WEB FOR DETAILS

You'd think that being hidden from sight in a ravine would bother most distillers, but it strikes you that it suits the guys at Tom Moore pretty well. If other distilleries are good at getting their distillers working on ever more innovative new expressions, then the guys down in the hollow outside Bardstown just kept their heads down and got on with making damned good bourbon, which they then sold at a (very) fair price. If no one visited them, that was fine. Not that they were (or are) in any way unfriendly; they just didn't see the necessity of having to play the marketing game. In this respect, it's like the Kentuckian equivalent of one of the multiplicity of Speyside distilleries that sit in the background.

Since Tom Moore's former parent company at one point owned both Loch Lomond and Glen Scotia distilleries, there is what you may call a history. Until recently it was the Barton distillery. Even that name had a solid, unpretentious air about it. It was close to the 1876 site of "Mattingly & Moore" before Tom Moore set up here in 1899. Its post-Prohibition life started in 1944, when it was bought by Oscar Getz's Barton Brands (the same Getz who gave his name to the marvellous bourbon museum in Bardstown).

The 1940s red-brick distillery uses a number of mash bills (details are secret), its own yeast, and a copper-headed beer column where the reflux is played and prolonged before the doubler does its work. The first sign that Barton (sorry, Tom Moore) was breaking out of its self-imposed reticence was the Ridgemont Reserve 1792 launch and the news that it was offering tours. Now part of media-savvy Sazerac (owner of Buffalo Trace), maybe there's a change on the horizon.

High-grade corn is the basis of Tom Moore's range of bourbons.

TOM MOORE TASTING NOTES

WHITE DOG FOR RIDGEMONT

Nose: Sweet, fat, and clean with a tight back note. Corn oil and a light dustiness.
Palate: Intensely spicy from the word go. Big impact, then a slow softening (almost works in reverse to normal). Intense.
Finish: Tight. Will need time in wood.

TOM MOORE 4YO 80°/40%

Nose: Fresh, young, and oak-driven. Oak posts. Lumberyard. In time, geranium leaf and cedar and fresh-turned earth.
Palate: Aromatic, all rosewood and subtle sweetness. Light, wth popcorn tones.
Finish: Toffee.
Conclusion: Young and energetic. Made to mix.

Flavor Camp: **Spicy Rye**
Where Next? Jim Beam White, Woodford Reserve

VERY OLD BARTON 6YO 86°/43%

Nose: Tea-like. Polished oak, rubbing spices. Vibrant, fresh, and dry: very much in the house style.
Palate: A sweet and soft entry to the palate. Nutmeg in butter, rose, grapefruit, and coffee.
Finish: Cigar box.
Conclusion: Crisp and clean.

Flavor Camp: **Spicy Rye**
Where Next? Evan Williams Black Label, Beam Black Label, Sazerac Rye

RIDGEMONT RESERVE 1792 8YO 93.7°/46.8%

Nose: Has that deep, slightly oily note of the white dog but now polished by oak into a fine sheen.
Palate: Ripe, with some fresh citrus fruit, a little touch of vanilla. The tea note seen in the young. Weightier.
Finish: Cigar (now out of the box).
Conclusion: This is a bourbon with which to convince Scotch drinkers.

Flavor Camp: **Rich & Oaky**
Where Next? Eagle Rare

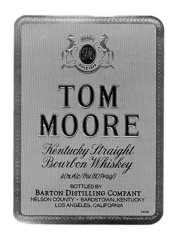

TENNESSEE

In some ways, the story of Tennessean whiskey parallels that of Kentucky's: boom, Prohibition, and slow recovery. The difference is that while in Kentucky most of the major distillers came back after Prohibition in the 1930s, Tennessee had been dry since 1910 and had operated a smaller-scale industry even in those days. The result was that only one distillery started up immediately after repeal: Jack Daniel's. It would be 25 years before the state's second (legal) distillery, George Dickel, opened.

The word "legal" is used deliberately. Tennessee is a microcosm of America's ambivalent relationship with alcohol. Its hills and hollows continue to hide numerous moonshining stills, many of them close to fundamentalist churches preaching against the evils of drink. Its music (and this state is rich in its musical heritage) both celebrates and castigates whiskey-drinking. For as many songs as there are about the joys of drinking 'shine, there are more that use drink (usually whiskey) as a symbol of dissolution and despair, the refuge of the self-pitying, broken-hearted fool. George Jones, no stranger to booze, sums it up in "Just One More": "Put the bottle on the table and it stays right there/'till I'm not able to see your face in every place I go/One drink, just one more/and then another."

This dichotomy is seen clearly in Lynchburg, conceivably the most famous small town in the world, home to the world's bestselling American whiskey—just don't expect to be able to wander into a bar in the town and order one. Lynchburg's dry. You won't even get a taste when you tour the distillery.

In other words, they do things a little differently in Tennessee and this extends to their whiskeys: the rye percentage in the mash bill is very low, for example (*see* pp.18–19). Conforming to the same legal framework as straight bourbon, to become Tennessee whiskey the white dog (new make) must be put through the Lincoln County Process: filtration through a bed of sugar-maple charcoal before being barreled. The result is a softer and slightly sootier spirit.

Is this wholly a Tennessean invention? There's evidence that filtration was being used in Kentucky as far back as 1815, but it appears to have been dropped soon after. As Jeff Arnett at Jack Daniel's points out, it's expensive.

The fact that it is known as the Lincoln County Process also points to it being not only a Tennessee specialty, but one fixed in a specific location: Cave Springs, where the Jack Daniel's distillery is now situated. Before the distilling prodigy arrived, one Alfred Eaton was using Cave Springs' limestone water to make his whiskey—and using the charcoal-filtering method from 1825 onwards. If Eaton didn't invent it, then he certainly exploited it to the full.

Quite where it came from, no one has been able to say. Vodka was being charcoal-filtered by that time, but unless there was a Russian *émigré* distiller in the area, it's unlikely that the technique could have been directly passed on. It remains a mystery, just another one of Tennessee's many secrets.

Charcoal filtration (here, at Jack Daniel's) is the key difference between Tennessee whiskey and bourbon.

Opposite: Jack Daniel's has always prided itself on its old-time charm.

Money up in flames: Every year, Jack Daniel's spends over $1 million on charcoal—here, being made.

Jack Daniel's

LYNCHBURG • WWW.JACKDANIELS.COM • OPEN ALL YEAR • MON–SUN

Iconic is a word too freely bandied around in the world of drink, but occasionally its use is appropriate. Jack Daniel's is one of those times. Clutched by numerous rock stars, the square bottle with the black and white label has become a signifier both for hedonistic rebelliousness and down-home, small-town values. Brand-building 101 starts with Jack Daniel's.

Its founding has all the hallmarks of a folktale. Born round about 1846, the young Tenesseean Jack Daniel fell out with his wicked stepmother and ran away from home to live with an "uncle." By age 14 he was helping out a storekeeper and lay preacher called Dan Call, who was running a still in Louse Creek. When Dan was away in the Civil War, Jack learned the art of whiskey-making from Nearest Green, an old slave, and when Jack moved from Louse Creek (maybe he already had an eye for marketing) in 1865, Green's sons, George and Eli, went with him.

Jack moved to take up the lease of the old Eaton distillery in Cave Springs on the outskirts of Lynchburg, where, it is generally agreed, the Lincoln County mellowing process originated (Lynchburg was in Lincoln County at the time).

"Our uniqueness starts with that water," says Jack Daniel's master distiller Jeff Arnett. "It is 56°F (13°C) all year and it provides minerals and nutrients that become part of the distillery character. If we had different water, the character would change." That water from the echoing cool cave is added to a low-rye (8 percent) mash bill to reduce any pepperiness in the final spirit, and the soured mash is fermented with the aid of the distillery's own yeast. Distillation is via a copper still, and the doubler yields a 140° white dog, which then undergoes the process that makes Jack a Tennessee whiskey: charcoal mellowing through 10 feet (3m) of sugar-maple charcoal.

Hidden in the woods: just one of Jack Daniel's many warehouses.

Why, though, were Tennessee whiskeys mellowed in the first place? "I reckon that there were things in those old days that Jack couldn't control, and mellowing got rid of them" says Arnett. "It evened things out, and he could use fast-growing local sugar maple. He did a lot of things for purely practical reasons.

"If you taste the white dog coming off the still it's astringent. After mellowing, there's a different mouthfeel: it's clean and light," he adds. "Technically speaking we don't have the same issues as Jack faced, but without mellowing our character changes."

Why, then, if it's so beneficial, wasn't the technique more widespread? "It's expensive! We have 72 vats and each has to have its charcoal changed every six months. That's $1million a year."

The more you investigate Jack Daniel's, the greater the realization that it is all about wood, be that charcoal or barrels. "We make our own barrels," says Arnett. "We have our own wood buyer, our own drying process, our own toasting process. It all creates complex characters to give that toasty, upfront sweetness which tells you it's Jack."

The long-running campaign, which has never exploited the more notorious party-animal side to Jack, has you believing that this is some small-scale operation from Sleepy Hollow. Nothing could be further from the truth. The operation is vast—and all for one make, albeit with three expressions. Is Arnett not tempted to push the boundaries a little more? After all, look what his Brown-Forman colleague, Chris Morris, is doing.

"I can't rule anything out," he says. "Old No.7 has taken the focus, but as a master distiller you look at different ideas. A rye? We could. Finishing? Maybe. We're open to possibilities. We're ready to play." Wouldn't it be good if, when this happens, Nearest Green was given some credit?

Copper, here in the beer still, helps to lighten the white dog.

JACK DANIEL'S TASTING NOTES

BLACK LABEL, OLD NO.7 80°/40%

Nose: Golden amber. Sooty, with caramelized sugars and felt, then an iris note. Eucalyptus wood on a barbecue. Sweet.

Palate: Light, sweet, and clean, with vanilla and marmalade cake, but young and firm underneath.

Finish: A touch of spice and a touch of balancing bitterness.

Conclusion: Easy, sweet, and mixable.

Flavor Camp: Soft Corn
Where Next?: Jim Beam White Label

GENTLEMAN JACK 80°/40%

Nose: Less sooty and oaky than standard Jack with more creamy vanilla. Bonfire in the woods. More custard and ripe banana.

Palate: Very smooth and soft. Chewy and fleshy fruit with the rigidity of the standard underneath.

Finish: Spiced.

Conclusion: Softer and more gentle.

Flavor Camp: Soft Corn
Where Next? Jim Beam Black Label

SINGLE BARREL 90°/45%

Nose: Dark amber. More banana. Bigger and more estery. Wood. Pine-like. With water, a charred note.

Palate: Has the energy of the standard and the sweetness of Gentleman with an added spicy attack. Balanced.

Finish: Clean and lightly spiced.

Conclusion: Takes the best points of the two styles.

Flavor Camp: Soft Corn
Where Next? Jim Beam Black Label

George Dickel

CASCADE HOLLOW, BETWEEN NASHVILLE & CHATTANOOGA • WWW.DICKEL.COM • OPEN ALL YEAR • TUES–SAT

Tennessee's final distillery takes us back to the quilt of tales and the myths that have been bundled around brands. American whiskey's tempestuous history, with brands changing hands many times, distilleries disappearing then reappearing on another site and with a new name, not to mention the devastation wreaked by Prohibition, has meant that company archives have been shredded. In addition, what was normal behavior in Tennessee in the nineteenth century might not seem too respectable in the twenty-first. The blanket is pulled over the truth.

Such is the case with George Dickel, whose actual and somewhat convoluted history is actually much more interesting than the official, sanitized version. In this, George and his wife, Augusta, are trotting along in their horse-drawn buggy to Cascade Hollow, where they taste the water and decide to build a distillery. Fact is, George Dickel never owned the Cascade distillery; nor did he ever make whisk(e)y, which the company that bears his name spells in the Scottish manner.

Dickel was a German immigrant who arrived in Nashville in 1853, where he set up a store selling boots before branching out into grocery goods, including whisky wholesaling. A profitable business ensued. By 1881 he was joined by his brother-in-law, Victor Shwab, who was also the owner of the Climax Saloon in Nashville—a fairly appropriate name for a den of iniquity in the town's "Men's Quarter." Shwab got the position through his brother-in-law's superintendent, Meier Salzkotter, who had been a bootlegger during the Civil War. The former bootmaker and bootlegger and their gambling-den magnate were about to become whisky barons.

In 1888, Victor Shwab bought a two-third share in the Cascade distillery (estd 1877) and George Dickel was granted exclusive rights to bottle and distribute the whisky. A decade later, Shwab owned the distillery outright. It was the Shwabs and Dickel's widow who switched production, complete with charcoal mellowing, of Cascade

The Cascade distillery has changed somewhat since the days when Victor Shwab owned it.

Sugar-maple rick ready to be fired into charcoal...

... **through which the** white dog from this still will be filtered.

whisky to the Stitzel distillery in Louisville, Kentucky, in 1911, the year after Tennessee went dry. The firm was sold in 1937 by George Shwab to Schenley Industries, which, in 1958, sent Ralph Dupps to Tennessee to start up production of George Dickel in a new distillery close to the original Cascade plant. Now that's a story—and my thanks go to Chuck Cowdery for his help in its telling. There's nothing wrong with George Dickel being a successful wholesaler. After all, it's true to say that some of the greatest names in bourbon were just that.

Today, the George Dickel Cascade distillery is situated on a narrow, tree-shaded valley on the highland rim of the Cumberland plateau, close to Normandy Lake. The grains and corn are pressure-cooked and fermented for three to four days with the aid of Dickel's own yeast. Because this is a Tennessee whisk(e)y, it is charcoal-mellowed prior to barreling, but here the technique is different to the one at Jack Daniel's 18 miles to the southwest.

At Dickel, the white dog is chill-filtered prior to mellowing, which removes fatty acids. The vats are then flooded with the white dog (rather than the drip-feed of Jack Daniel's). Woolen blankets are also placed in the top and at the base of the vat: at the top to allow an even distribution of the white dog and at the bottom to stop any charcoal being pulled through. Ten days later, it's barreled and then left to age in single-storey, hilltop warehouses. It's this combination of extra filtration, charcoal buffing, and new oak that gives Dickel its distinctive smoothness.

At the time of writing, there's a shortage of Dickel whisky, the result of the distillery being closed between 1999 and 2003, and its owner Diageo's haphazard handling of the brand has left it remaining in a strange limbo where legend takes the place of fact. Hopefully by the time you read this, the situation will have changed. Shwab and Dickel deserve it to.

GEORGE DICKEL TASTING NOTES

OLD NO.12

Nose: Amber. Very sweet and slightly waxy. Apple pie and lemon. Light clove and yellow corn syrup.
Palate: Very smooth and lightly herbal notes: back to thyme and dried oregano, then ginger, lime blossom, and honey.
Finish: Clean and soft with baked apple and a final cinnamon twist.
Conclusion: Gentle and smooth but has real personality.

Flavor Camp: Soft Corn
Where Next? Early Times, Hudson Baby Bourbon

REST OF THE USA

There is, writes rock critic Greil Marcus in *Invisible Republic*, his book on Dylan's *Basement Tapes*, something in the music that taps into an "old, weird America," a country whose boundaries were first charted by *Harry Smith's Anthology of American Folk Music*. It is the sound of a country creating and then losing itself, the sound of the liminal, songs from the woods and under the floorboards. This musical (re)creation of America inevitably includes whiskey: in blues, in country tunes, stomps, and ballads, a boon and a curse, a constant, raucous presence.

Bob Dylan himself turned to it in *Self Portrait,* when he inhabits Frank Beddoe's "Copper Kettle". "Get you a copper kettle/Get you a copper coil/Fill it with new-made corn mash/And never more you'll toil./You'll just lay there by the juniper/While the moon is bright/Watch them jugs a-filling in the pale moonlight."

There's a truth to his account. It starts lazily as the moonshine trickles, then he throws in tips on what wood to use before, seemingly under the influence, comes a louder, cracked defiance, a song being sung by a moonshining family who "ain't paid no whiskey tax since 1792." Across America today and for the past decade, musicians, food producers, writers, poets, philosophers, drink from this well, whiskey is part of it once more.

"We reckon that there are 264 distilleries in the US at the moment," says Bill Owens, who heads craft-distillers organization the American Distilling Institute (ADI). "Most of them are very small. In seven years from now, some might be doing 10,000 cases, maybe more, but most will be less than 2,000." Small they may be when compared to the output of the major commercial distillers, but it is a significant shift in mindset that will have positive ramifications for the whole American spirits industry.

But who are these people who have suddenly decided to make their own spirits? "They come from a lot of different walks of life," says Owens. "Maybe they've started in beer, but that's an area where you can get a lot of know-it-alls and so they have moved to spirits, where there's a different degree of sophistication and curiosity."

Owens himself started as a brewer and is perhaps best-known in craft-brewing circles as the man who revived pumpkin ale, a type of beer that harks back to George Washington's time. Owens' Buffalo Bill's Pumpkin Ale started a mini trend: the style is now being made in 40 or 50 small breweries across the US. In many ways, the growth of craft distilling mirrors that of the burgeoning American craft-brewing movement. Today it is almost impossible at any one point to say accurately how many craft breweries there are in the US—and it is getting to be much the same with distilleries.

As Owens points out, many of the new breed of craft distillers are brewers who have either added a distillery onto their beer business, or quit beer in favor of ardent spirits. Equally, however, many have come from wine or farming, or they may simply be spirits- (often Scotch) lovers who want to try their hand at making their own.

The range of spirits being made reflects the eclectic nature of the distillers themselves: apple brandy, fruit *eaux-de-vie*, gin, rum, vodka, and whiskey, the latter covering rye and corn, but mostly single malt. "It's a different template to just making whiskey," says Owens. "Who

THE UNITED STATES
▼ Craft distillery

wants to wait two years or so to drink your spirit?" Are they just, as in the title of one of Owens' textbooks, modern moonshiners? "Not the old sense," he says. "Anyone who wants to produce anything illegal will be growing marijuana, not making 'shine. Neither do I meet anyone coming into this to become rich. The bar in terms of knowledge and financing is high. They're entrepreneurs, not just guys who've built a distillery in their garage."

In other words, these craft distillers are legitimate, questing individuals who are interested in quality and character. Some of the whiskey distillers will also be producing fruit brandies or vodka, which allows capital to come into the business immediately rather than only after their whiskey is mature. Others on the whiskey side

have got round the time issue by maturing in small casks to accelerate the maturation process, or even by using wood chips.

It is this area of innovation—by necessity, or simply because they can—that intrigues most on the whiskey side. With bourbon covered by the majors, it makes sound business sense to make American single-malt whiskey. "I don't see anyone wanting to make bourbon," observes Owens. "A lot will use peat, or smoke the barley in some way. Some are using inner staves, and the big bourbon guys are looking at what they are doing."

They have also now been given official legitimacy, with the industry body, the Distilled Spirits Council of the United States (DISCUS), creating an affiliate program for the craft distillers. They are inside the tent.

Craft distillers

CLEAR CREEK • PORTLAND • WWW.CLEARCREEKDISTILLERY.COM • OPEN ALL YEAR • MON–SAT • SEE WEB FOR TOUR DETAILS
ST GEORGE SPIRITS • WWW.STGEORGESPIRITS.COM • OPEN TO VISITORS • WED–SUN • SEE WEB FOR DETAILS
STRANAHAN'S • COLORADO • WWW.STRANAHANS.COM • OPEN TO VISITORS • SEE WEB FOR DAYS & DETAILS
TUTHILLTOWN • GARDINER • WWW.TUTHILLTOWN.COM • TASTING ROOM, THURS–SAT • TOURS, SAT & SUN; RESERVATIONS ESSENTIAL
WWW.ANCHORBREWING.COM/ABOUT_US/ANCHORDISTILLING.HTM • WWW.CHARBAY.COM • WWW.COPPERFOX.BIZ

Craft distillers also hark back to the origins of spirits in America: to George Washington's Mount Vernon estate, the peach brandies of Georgia, and the small-scale farm distilleries which grew into today's bourbon industry. The wheel turns. "For me, it's part of a green revolution," says Bill Owens, head of the American Distilling Institute: "the revival of small-town bakers, brewers, and now distillers. They've gone back to basics." In doing so, they've opened a new chapter in the tale of American whiskey.

Fritz Maytag, the godfather of American micro-brewing, believes in authenticity. His gin, Junipero, is 100 percent juniper spirit instead of a mix of botanicals, and since rye was the first American whiskey style, his Old Potrero is made of 100 percent rye (*see* p.232). Made since 1994 at Maytag's Anchor Steam distillery in San Francisco, his single malt is an "eighteenth-century" style (i.e. aged for just one year), while the oily, spicy Straight Rye is his homage to the nineteenth-century whiskeys and spends three years in barrel. The folks at Templeton in Iowa have taken a similar approach: their rye whiskey is a direct re-creation of an old Prohibition-era recipe.

Those original distillers which Maytag is paying tribute to followed the adage that you distill what grows around you, a maxim taken up in

1982 by Jorg Rupf at Alameda's St. George Spirits distillery in California. St. George started as an *eaux-de-vie*/brandy site using Holstein stills. Now, distiller Lance Winters has turned his attention to whiskey.

"Fourteen years ago, I started work here with the express goal of making a single-malt whiskey," he says. "I thoroughly enjoyed Scottish malts, had a fair appreciation for rye, even liked a few bourbons, but Jorg prompted me to be original. The approach that we chose was that of an *eaux-de-vie* distiller, one in which the new spirit is smooth, complex, and layered.

"I drew upon my brewing experience to formulate a mash that would give soft, sweet notes of roasted hazelnut, cacao, and light smoke. We chose barley smoked over alder and beech because it layered in nicely and also because anything we did with peat ended up smelling

CRAFT DISTILLERS TASTING NOTES

CLEAR CREEK, MCCARTHY'S OREGON
SINGLE MALT BATCH W09/01, 42.5%

Nose: Grass and smoke to start. Bonfire in the woods, touch of hickory and birch smoke. Gentle and sweet behind. Seems young and fresh. Very lifted.

Palate: Smoke again hits immediately, but the lift of the aromatics is what separates this from a Scotch. Lapsang souchong tea.

Finish: Smoked cashews.

Conclusion: Iconoclastic.

> **Flavor Camp: Smoky & Peaty**
>
> **Where Next?** Chichibu Newborn, Kilchoman

ST. GEORGE CALIFORNIAN SINGLE
MALT 43%

Nose: Lifted and intensely fruity. Pure mango and apricot. Effusive, sweet, and clean with a little touch of smoke undernneath.

Palate: The ripe, fleshy, intense aromatics now backed with drier, more cereal-driven texture that then softens into the center to American cream soda.

Finish: Firm yet juicy.

Conclusion: An eye-opening single malt showing the possibilities that exist.

> **Flavor Camp: Fruity & Spicy**
>
> **Where Next?** Glenmorangie, Imperial

STRANAHAN'S COLORADO STRAIGHT MALT
WHISKEY BATCH 52, 47%

Nose: Crisp and dry initially, with roasted notes. Quite understated, then orange, rich malt, cinnamon, and a scented dusty note. Again, very lifted. With water, geranium, toffee, and roasted coffee.

Palate: Charred oak giving a lightly sooty note. Fruity with a toffee edge and plenty of sweet spiciness. Moves into cassis/*mures* but always cut with firm oak..

Finish: Zesty.

Conclusion: Balanced and clean. Another new and welcome definition of whiskey.

> **Flavor Camp: Fruity & Spicy**
>
> **Where Next?** Arran

and tasting like a whiskey made by someone else." The intense, lifted aromas of the St. George whiskey shows that he has succeeded.

Steve McCarthy at Portland's Clear Creek distillery in Oregon also comes from a fruit spirit background but while his distillation techniques were honed through visits to *eaux-de-vie* specialists in Europe, his whiskey is made from peated Scottish malt. The result (*see* above) is a remarkable fusion between the two.

Like Winters and McCarthy, Marko Karakasevic at family-owned Charbay in the Napa Valley has blended two approaches to his whiskey-making. "Since I was a kid, I always wanted to make whiskey," he says. "Even though I grew up distilling brandy and making wine and liqueurs, whiskey had a mystique to it. When I looked at it, though, I wondered why, if it is distilled from beer,

that whiskey-makers produce a "distiller's beer" that nobody bottles, nobody drinks, nobody likes?" The result is that Charbay's 6yo whiskey is double-distilled Pilsner beer—"Hops and all."

There was something of the spirit of the old-time moonshiner in Jess Graber when he started making whiskey in Boulder, Colorado, in 1972, using a small still given to him by a friend, "Larry, The Missouri River Rat." After inquiring about going legit in 1990, but then putting it off for six years after receiving the short version of the Code of Federal Regulations, his breakthrough came after a party at George Stranahan's ranch when he distilled the remnants of a couple of half-full kegs of Flying Dog beer. "The spirit was immediately cleaner, smoother," he recalls. "The light bulb went on. If great brandy is made from wine, not grape skins, then why not use the same principle and make a whiskey out of a purified mash?"

His Stranahan's distillery was finally established in 2002, with production starting two years later. Graber has stuck to his original recipe—although the wash now comes from his own Heavenly Daze brewery. The barley is 90 percent Colorado-grown, fermented with brewer's yeast, and given a long, temperature-controlled ferment before being double-distilled in Vendome pots and aged in top-quality, new Independent Stave barrels with an alligator char (the heaviest kind) that adds a sweet, spiced toffee note to his Colorado Straight Malt Whiskey.

"To my knowledge, no one in America, let alone in Colorado, had made a 'Straight Malt Whiskey' before," Graber says. "We were therefore not bound by the conventions that every other distillery was encouraged to follow."

Functional rather than romantic—but with plenty of room for expansion—the St. George distillery in California.

The beer theme is picked up on the east coast at Nantucket Island's Triple Eight distillery, whose Notch (i.e. Not-Scotch) is a distillation of Cisco Brewery's Whale's Tail Pale Ale.

In the orchards of Sperryville, Virginia, two miles from the boundary of the Shenandoah National Park, is Rick Wasmund's Copper Fox distillery. Apples feature strongly in Wasmund's approach. Not only was the distillery a former apple juice plant, but he kilns his malted barley over a mix of apple, cherry, and oak woods. The same mix of woods is chipped and added to the barrels, upping the wood extractives and resulting in Wasmund releasing his whiskey when it is just months old. "I made my first still in my high-school chemistry class," he says. "I loved good whiskey, but

I figured that there were things other than peat that could be used in the barley-malting process. I was cooking frequently with apple wood and cherry wood, so I reckoned that we would be true to the process and our location and see where the flavor path led us. We did not want to make another Scotch or another bourbon."

The thread that links all of these distillers is one of innovation. "It made sense to make use of our flexibility and innovations as a business strategy, but it turned into a lifestyle strategy," Wasmund admits. "Why should we exist if we just made something 'as good as' some other whisky which was already being made?"

It's a similar philosophy to that of Ralph Erenzo, who moved into Gardiner, upstate New York, in 2001 to establish a rock-climbing center. Forced to change plans after objections from neighbors, he read that New York state had just lowered the annual permit for distilling from $60,000 to $1,250 for two years and capped production at 35,000 gallons (132,489 liters) per annum. Two years later, Tuthilltown Spirits was making New York state's first legal whiskey since Prohibition. There are now eight whiskeys and two vodkas.

"We want to capture the flavor of the thing we are making our spirits from," says Erenzo. "Whiskey should taste like the grain from which it is made. We use no peat and focus on individual grains for specific whiskeys. Our Corn Whiskey tastes and smells corny. Our Rye Whiskey is grainy and spicy and full of character. American whiskeys are also about the wood. Storage in new charred oak results in deeper color, more caramel and vanilla aromas and flavors, and more spice.

"We knew we couldn't do it the same way as others. We are both by nature and by necessity innovative."

The same theme is repeated in many more distilleries across the US. As Jess Graber says: "The genie is out of the bottle, and the innovators, with a gleam in their eye, will find a way to give us all something new to taste and talk about."

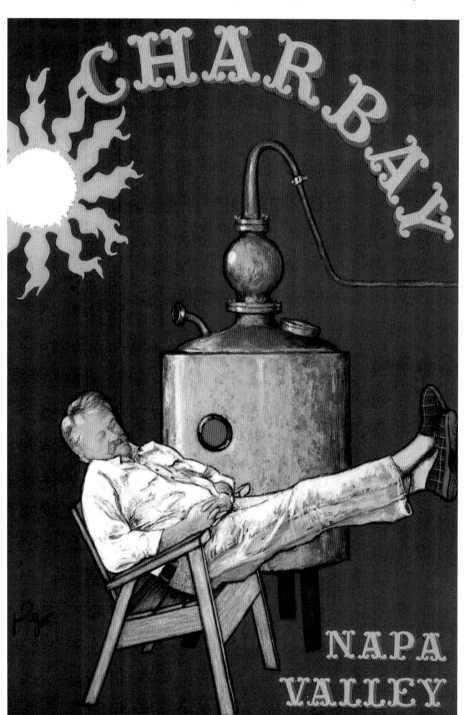

Don't be fooled by the image; distillers need to stay awake!

Opposite: Production of craft whiskeys is speeding up across the US.

TUTHILLTOWN SPIRITS TASTING NOTES

HUDSON BABY BOURBON 46%

Nose: Strangely, less spicy than the malt. Broader, creamier, and sweeter. More ginger and cinnamon and a little pine.

Palate: Fragrant: the same rose note seen in the corn. Gentle and quite thick.

Finish: Long and smooth.

Conclusion: Made from 100 percent NY corn and aged in new small oak. Kentucky, watch out.

Flavor Camp: Soft Corn

Where Next? Early Times

HUDSON NEW YORK CORN 46%

Nose: Clear: corn whiskey does not need to be aged. Sweet, with popcorn and the wild floral notes that come off corn. Heavy rose/lily and then berry fruit.

Palate: Mashy but has bite and energy. The corn gives this fatness to the palate which is cut with green corn leaf.

Finish: Nutty/powdery.

Conclusion: Fresh and characterful.

Flavor Camp: Soft Corn

Where Next? Heaven Hill Mellow Corn

HUDSON SINGLE MALT 46%

Nose: Intensely spicy, allspice, cassia bark, clove. Very aromatic and sweet with a touch of wholewheat bread behind. Light citrus fruit behind it all.

Palate: Lightly bready, with a little yeast, then cherry wood. Slow and sweet with an oatmeal-like note underneath.

Finish: Clean and nutty.

Conclusion: Made from 100 percent malted barley and aged in new (small) oak.

Flavor Camp: Malty & Dry

Where Next? Glen Spey 12yo

CANADA

Despite the scale of Irish and Scottish immigration, their influence on Canadian whisky-making remains more legend than fact. Yes, they distilled, but a strong seafaring tradition and ready access to Caribbean molasses led these settlers in Canada's Atlantic provinces to distill rum.

However, in 1821, Thomas Molson, a Montreal brewer, fired up his father's copper pot still, turning Canada into a commercial whisky-making nation. A decade later he moved west, opening his second distillery in Kingston. Popular history credits United Empire Loyalists as the pioneer whisky-makers: American settlers, who, loyal to Britain, moved to Canada following American Independence. Their tiny, farm-based operations never became commercially viable.

Up until the 1880s, during the formative years of Canadian whisky-making, English and Western European influences did prevail. Culturally, Molson, Gooderham, Worts, Corby, and Seagram were English; Wiser, Dutch; Hespeler, German; and Randall and Walker, were New Englanders. All but Molson began as millers, distilling excess grain. More recently, Rieder, a Swiss distiller, built Kittling Ridge in 1972, while Canadian Mist, founded by Barton Brands in 1967, and Valleyfield, set up by Schenley Industries in 1945; both are successors to Jewish-American bourbon distillers.

There were two main dynamics behind the emergence of the Canadian whisky style. In pioneer central Canada, it was delineated by water, following the flow of the St. Lawrence River and the lakes that feed it, while further west in the Prairies it was the climate and the ease with which grain grew in that part of the country.

In the provinces of Quebec and Ontario, from Montreal to Windsor, distillers stayed close to the St. Lawrence shorelines. Early settlers in this region found the short summers and rocky soils ill-suited to most grains, so Dutch and German settlers began planting rye, which could endure the bitter cold. Through their efforts, rye became a staple Canadian whisky grain.

The westward expansion continued in 1837, when Gooderham and Worts began distilling in York (now Toronto). Corby set up shop near Belleville in 1855, and Wiser in Prescott in 1857. That same year, near Berlin (now Waterloo) William Hespeler and George Randall launched what became Seagram. Hiram Walker opened in Windsor the following year. Although these brands and methods survive, only Hiram Walker's distillery remains operational.

Canada's second whisky region, the Prairies, is defined by its abundant grain. George Reifel built the first Prairie distillery, Alberta Distillers, in Calgary in 1948. Seagram's Gimli distillery followed in Manitoba in 1968. Gilby established Black Velvet in Lethbridge in 1973, and in High River, Highwood Distillers opened for business in 1974.

Consolidations in the 1980s resulted in the closure of more than half of Canada's distilleries, leaving just four on the Prairies and four in Central Canada. In 1990, Glenora, Canada's only malt-whisky distillery, began production on the east coast.

Canada's whisky style derives from its production methods. A mash of cooked grains—corn, barley, wheat, and rye—is fermented for three to five days, then distilled, unfiltered, in column stills. The resulting distillate is then diluted with water and redistilled. A third distillation in a rectifier concentrates the alcohol and the desirable congeners. It gives

a distillate of about 94 percent alcohol which is aged to produce base whisky. Although referred to as "neutral," it's really quite flavorful.

A second whisky, known as "flavoring," is made from a rye-rich mash. The distillate may be put in barrels after a single pass through

Previous page: **The raw ingredients:** wheat fields in Manitoba.

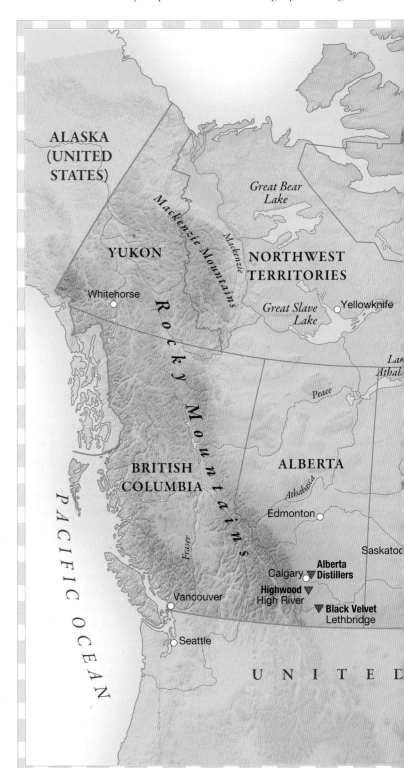

the beer still, or a second run in one of several unusual stills such as the "kettle and column" combination at Gimli. Canadian distillers take several cuts, separating various streams of flavoring distillate for reblending in carefully controlled proportions.

Base and flavoring whiskies are aged between three and 25 years in charred white oak barrels before blending to produce light, though flavorful whiskies. Although referred to as blends, many Canadian whiskies might better be described as single distillery whiskies.

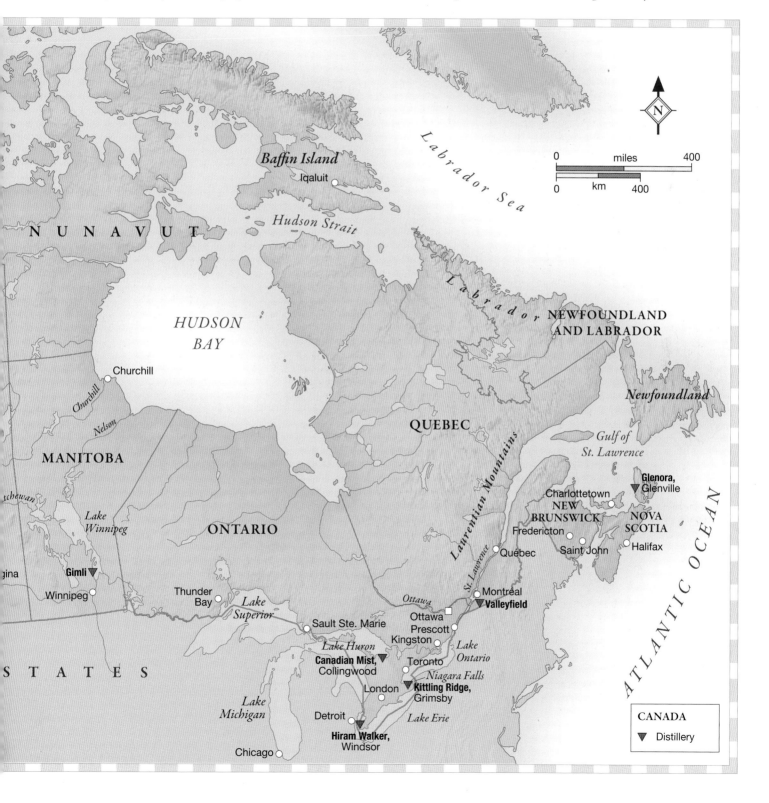

CANADA
▼ Distillery

Imposing neighbors: Ogilvie Mountains, Territorial Park, Yukon.

Eastern Canada

CANADIAN MIST • COLLINGWOOD • WWW.CANADIANMIST.COM

HIRAM WALKER • HERITAGE CENTER, WINDSOR • WWW.CANADIANCLUBWHISKY.COM

KITTLING RIDGE • ONTARIO • WWW.KITTLINGRIDGE.COM • OPEN TO VISITORS • JUNE–SEPT

GLENORA • GLENVILLE • WWW.GLENORADISTILLERY.COM • OPEN ALL YEAR / VALLEYFIELD • QUEBEC

The massive grain elevators at Collingwood on Lake Huron remind visitors that when the Canadian Mist distillery was built there in 1967, boats still carried western grain to market. Some grain remained in Collingwood to be made into one of Canada's bestselling whiskies, Canadian Mist.

Canadian Mist operates around the clock as its master distiller Harold Ferguson explains, "Making great whisky is like making great rock 'n' roll: you have to crank up the volume." A five-day ferment using proprietary yeast brings out the fruitiness of Mist's rye flavoring whisky, while a three-day fermentation yields cereal-rich spirit for the base whisky. Six shiny, stainless-steel columns—the upper trays packed with sacrificial copper—and a copper doubler produce clean flavorful spirits. They spend three years in ex-bourbon casks from Brown-Forman Cooperage before being blended on-site.

Downstream from Collingwood in Windsor, an iconic Canadian Club sign faced Detroit for decades from atop Canada's largest and oldest distillery, Hiram Walker, built in 1858 and rebuilt nearly a century later in 1955. Walker himself introduced Canadian Club to the world in 1882, but the sign came down after Pernod Ricard bought the distillery in 2005. It's called Wiser's now, as was Wiser's previous home in Corbyville, and the original distillery in Prescott, Ontario. As a result of the fallout after the takeover, Canadian Club (now a part of Jim Beam) is a tenant in the very distillery it built.

A standard column distillation produces base whisky, while two rye flavorings and a barley-malt distillate are made in a copper beer still and a 3,170-gallon (12,000-liter) copper pot. Uniquely in Canada, these base and flavoring spirits are blended together prior to aging for Canadian Club, with each of the four main expressions having a different recipe. All the CC barrels are also decharred and recharred prior to filling and aging for a minimum of six years. The spirits are aged separately for Wiser's, Gibson's, and other brands produced at Walker. Hiram Walker is the only Canadian distillery to make whisky using malted rye.

Further downstream again, at the foot of the Niagara Escarpment, near a creek that is 40 miles from Niagara Falls, Kittling Ridge distillery sits sandwiched between a forest and a multilane highway. From the little Lake Ontario town of Grimsby, Forty Creek whiskies is making quite a name for itself in Canada and in the US.

John Hall, a winemaker, bought this former *eaux-de-vie* distillery in 1992, crafting whiskies the same way that he creates wine: using brewer's and wine yeasts to ferment the different grains (malted barley, rye, and corn) for between five and seven days. These are then given a single distillation in a small 132-gallon (500-liter) still before aging in barrels selected to suit the individual personalities of the grains.

Sweet corn spirit goes into heavily charred barrels, the nutty barley spirit into medium char, and rye into gently toasted oak to showcase its zesty, spicy character. Hall is also experimenting with aging in local

Kittling Ridge distillery has adopted the modern approach of standing its barrels upright on pallets for filling, maturation, and emptying.

Canadian oak. As with wine, these whisky "varietals" are blended when mature: six to ten years for Forty Creek.

Valleyfield is Quebec's last remaining whisky distillery. It sits in the heart of Salaberry-de-Valleyfield, a typical *Québeçois* town built around a silver-roofed, double-steepled Roman Catholic church. Situated on an island in the St. Lawrence River, the town is just upstream from the site of Thomas Molson's original Montreal distillery.

Valleyfield is best known for its OFC brand and Golden Wedding, a failing American bourbon reformulated and rehabilitated as a fine Canadian mixing whisky. Production shifted to Black Velvet distillery over in Alberta shortly before Diageo bought Valleyfield in 2008.

Down the St. Lawrence on the Atlantic coast sits Glenora, a tiny malt whisky distillery made famous by its David-and-Goliath fight with the Scotch Whisky Association over its Glen Breton single malt. In 1990, when Glenora was built in the Gaelic-speaking town of Glenville on Cape Breton Island, Nova Scotia, a whisky with a Scottish heritage finally flowed from commercial Canadian stills.

It's an unpeated Scottish-style malt whisky distilled in a pair of copper pots before aging for ten years. A recent innovation sees the whisky finished in Nova Scotia Icewine casks. Glen Breton is still developing its flavor profile, and for now is most popular with expatriate Cape Bretoners across Canada.

CANADIAN MIST TASTING NOTES

CANADIAN MIST 40%

Nose: Full gold. Grassy, with cranberries, oranges, green fruit, sweet baking spices, toffee, corn, cereal, and mash. Nutty, with a unique hint of cola.

Palate: Very sweet, with cleansing citric zest. Not complex. Hot pepper and baking spices. Then comes sweet fruit, vanilla, and perfume. Creamy mouthfeel with a hint of milk chocolate.

Finish: Fades quickly on hot pepper, mash, and citric zest.

Conclusion: Well-made, tasty cocktail; unique cola twist.

Flavor Camp: Malty & Dry
Where Next? Centennial 10yo, Rosebank 10yo

GLENORA TASTING NOTES

GLEN BRETON 10YO, ICE 40%

Nose: White-wine color. Mash, hints of fruit, slight bitter smell, wet clay, exotic fruit, slightly butyric.

Palate: Sweet, mashy with pleasing peppery warmth. Slightly woody and bitter. Slight astringency.

Finish: Medium on pepper, and vague sweetness.

Conclusion: Getting there, but has yet to hit its stride.

Flavor Camp: Malty & Dry
Where Next? Sullivan's Cove, Allt-a-Bhainne

KITTLING RIDGE TASTING NOTES

FORTY CREEK PREMIUM BARREL SELECT 40%

Nose: Full gold. Sweet, creamy corn with notes of dusty rye. Dried fruit, vanilla, and cream sherry. Pickles and slightly floral notes.

Palate: Toffee, ripe fruit, peppery spices, hint of ginger, some earthy rye, sweet sherry, and refreshing notes of grapefruit peel. Luscious and weighty.

Finish: Medium and fading on spice and cleansing zest. Sour fruit, licorice, and prune juice.

Conclusion: A solid Canadian sipper, but feel free to mix.

Flavor Camp: Fruity & Spicy
Where Next? Crown Royal Limited Edition, Canadian Club Black Label 8yo

VALLEYFIELD TASTING NOTES

VO GOLD

Nose: Full gold. Rich butterscotch toffee, Christmas baking spices, hint of mint.

Palate: Creamy toffee, developing hot pepper and spicy rye. Weighty.

Finish: Long. Sweet and hot, with refreshing zest, ginger and other baking spices.

Conclusion: A robust version of VO to mix or sip.

Flavor Camp: Fragrant & Floral
Where Next? Alberta Premium, Gibson's Finest 12yo

HIRAM WALKER'S TASTING NOTES

CANADIAN CLUB RESERVE 10YO 40%

Nose: Orange-amber. Plenty to amuse the nose: hard sharp rye, tobacco, dry grain, fresh wood, pencil shavings, fresh-tilled soil, rye bread, concentrated fruit juice, and a hint of rubber. Floral and vaguely citric.

Palate: Toffee, hottest pepper, incense, cloves, cinnamon, cedar, almond skins. Meaty, with a hint of tomato sauce, and lots of citric bitterness. Nice weight.

Finish: Longish. Hot, pepper, peppermint, and ginger, caramel, prunes, earth, and underlying citric zest. Slightly sweet with the vaguest tobacco.

Conclusion: With its hard-rye edginess, the best of the popular CC line.

Flavor Camp: Spicy Rye
Where Next? Century Reserve 15yo

GIBSON'S FINEST 12YO

Nose: Fuller gold. Wood with rye spices, cedar notes, then back to fresh lumber.

Palate: Toffee and wood with a slight tannic pull, then cloves and cinnamon beautifully balanced by underlying bitterness. Hot white pepper.

Finish: Long. Fading on hot pepper, with some sweetness.

Conclusion: A solid favorite right across Canada, and for good reason.

Flavor Camp: Rich & Oaky
Where Next? VO Gold, Wiser's Small Batch

WISER'S 18YO 40%

Nose: Orange-gold. Fresh-sawn wood, spicy rye, sourdough bread, dry grain, cigar box, and glue stick.

Palate: Complex, richly flavored. Burnt sugar, lumberyard, white pepper, perfumed, dusty rye, dark fruits, baking spices, some pulling oak tannins.

Finish: Long and peppery, fruity sweetness giving way to oak tannins and palate-cleansing bitter lemon.

Conclusion: A cedar box filled with sweet and spicy delicacies.

Flavor Camp: Rich & Oaky
Where Next? Gibson's Finest 18yo, Alberta Premium 25yo

Western Canada

ALBERTA DISTILLERS • CALGARY / BLACK VELVET DISTILLERS • LETHBRIDGE • WWW.BLACKVELVETWHISKY.COM
HIGHWOOD, HIGH RIVER • WWW.HIGHWOOD-DISTILLERS.COM / GIMLI • MANITOBA • WWW.CROWNROYAL.COM

The Manitoba/Ontario border is more than a geographical marker. It serves almost as a psychological point of division within Canada. To the east, where the landscape is defined by the lakes and rivers of the Canadian Shield, the mind is on business, while to the west, an agrarian population occupies the Prairies: a wide expanse of flat, fertile grassland that runs all the way to the Rockies.

In addition to prodigious yields of wheat, the Prairies are also a primary source of rye and barley. No wonder four Canadian whisky distilleries prosper here. Gimli, Manitoba, on the shores of Lake Winnipeg, is a commercial fishing center with a seasonal fishing fleet. In the frigid winters, 18-wheelers are known to take shortcuts across the lake's frozen surface.

Originally settlers from Iceland, this community is also responsible for all six versions of Crown Royal, Canada's bestselling whisky. In 2008, the campaigning Hillary Clinton knocked back Crown Royal to grunts of blue-collar delight. It's so ubiquitous and so rich in Canadian-made "bourbon," she can be forgiven for thinking it was a US distillation.

Master blender Jim Boyko can draw from five different whisky streams: a bourbon mash bill ("But it's not bourbon"); a corn/rye/barley malt; a high-percentage rye/barley malt; a rye from Canada's last remaining Coffey still; and a corn spirit that's been distilled in Gimli's distinctive kettle-and-column combination (also seen at Fuji-Gotemba in Japan, *see* p.224). "This is a method that gives a spirit which lends itself marvellously to mouthfeel," says Boyko. "This is a whisky that you can roll around the mouth." With 26 different types of barrel pressed into service, Boyko has a hugely varied base from which to draw.

Nine hundred and thirty miles of prairie highway to the west lies Calgary, a city that seems to have grown up around its distillery, founded some 60 years ago. A huge maltings next door could be mistaken as part of the distillery, but it is not. At Alberta Distillers, malted rye or barley never make their way into any of the whiskies. Unmalted rye is difficult to distill because it is sticky and blocks the flow, forming unprocessable "rye balls": little beads of flour, wet on the outside and powdery on the inside. Still, from the start, Alberta Distillers has focused on making whisky from 100 percent local rye grain because of its availability. The distillery also processes corn and wheat. Although it only claims 100 percent rye for Alberta

A grain truck with two hoppers delivers corn to the Black Velvet distillery in Lethbridge, Alberta.

Premium, many of its other brands (and a lot of its bulk whiskies) are also made up from 100 percent rye spirits.

South of Calgary in the farming community of High River, Highwood Distillers, Canada's smallest whisky distillery, is half-hidden behind a farm implement dealership on the western edge of town. Highwood is the only Canadian distillery using 100 percent wheat to produce the closest thing to a genuinely neutral-base whisky spirit in Canadian distilling. Highwood's Glen Hopkins admits, though, that it could never pass for vodka. The wheat is pressure-cooked whole, releasing its starches after exploding like popcorn. The fermented mash passes through a beer still, then is rectified in an unusual pot still with a tall column above it.

In 2005, Highwood acquired the brands and maturing stocks from Potter's, a whisky-broker, and maintained Potter's corn-based profiles, as Potter's did, with spirit purchased elsewhere. White Owl, Highwood's clear rye whisky, harks back to earlier days, when the Quebec market demanded a clear, but fully aged rye whisky. How does a little distillery make such interesting whiskies? "It's Western Canada," Hopkins explains. "They're used to cowboys. They know their whisky."

Further south, not far from a rattlesnake-infested desert called The Alberta Badlands, the town of Lethbridge is home to the Black Velvet Distilling Company, founded in 1973. Continuous jet cookers at Black Velvet process eight railcar-loads of corn each week. At 94–96 percent alcohol, the base spirit retains a sweet, grainy, pepperiness. In a unique "blending at birth" process, corn and rye high wines and some partially matured rye flavoring whisky are added to the base spirit, before it matures in oak barrels. Annually, 100 railcars of Black Velvet, its flagship mixing whisky, are shipped to the US for bottling, while Black Velvet whiskies destined for Canada and the rest of the world see glass in Lethbridge itself.

To maintain consistent high quality, a "Quality Panel" tastes each Canadian whisky at least five or six times at different stages of maturation.

ALBERTA DISTILLERS TASTING NOTES

ALBERTA SPRINGS 10YO 40%

Nose: Fire orange. Wood, dry grain, baking spices, cedar, with a hint of hot mustard.
Palate: Rich and creamy. Quickly gets hot. Refreshing bitter lemon restrains the toffee, while fresh-sawn wood and the unmalted rye balance the pepper.
Finish: Hot peppermint with hints of wood and citric zest.
Conclusion: Alberta Premium 25yo gets the attention, but this is what the folks at the distillery drink.

Flavor Camp: **Spicy Rye**
Where Next? Kittling Ridge, Canadian Mountain Rock

BLACK VELVET TASTING NOTES

DANFIELD RESERVE 21YO 40%

Nose: Mahogany. Linseed, Christmas baking spices.
Palate: Toffee, caramel, lots of fresh-cut cedar, old barn boards. Nice citric hint. Classic rye baking spices.
Finish: Long. Sweet, woody, cinnamon, ginger, pepper.
Conclusion: At Black Velvet they really know how to use the citric notes to advantage.

Flavor Camp: **Richly Oaked**
Where Next? Wiser's 18yo, Banff 32yo

HIGHWOOD TASTING NOTES

CENTURY RESERVE 21YO 40%

Nose: Straw. Cow barn, hints of oak, sawdust, peppermint, lime peel, dry grain, and corn.
Palate: Toffee, hot pepper, cedar, oak tannins, and sweet lemon. Ever-changing with no dominant notes.
Finish: Medium fade; peppery with hints of wood.
Conclusion: A weighty if understated 100 percent corn whisky.

Flavor Camp: **Rich & Oaky**
Where Next? Gibson's Finest 18yo

CENTENNIAL 10YO 40%

Nose: Light amber. Unusual. Cloves with hints of flint, dry grain, very ripe black fruit, and cooked green vegetables.
Palate: Weighty. Toffee, pepper, sawdust, and some baking spices, then sweet lemonade with a subtle bite.
Finish: Long but subdued. Fading out on toffee, sweet spices, and pepper.
Conclusion: The softness of wheat whisky but with a bite.

Flavor Camp: **Sweet Wheat**
Where Next? Maker's Mark, Bruichladdich 16yo Bourbon, Littlemill

GIMLI DISTILLERY TASTING NOTES

CROWN ROYAL LIMITED EDITION 40%

Nose: Amber. Slowly opens to nutmeg, cinnamon, hints of apple juice, toffee, and vague vanilla. Austere.
Palate: Complex mix of barley sugar, rye spices, hot pepper, and grapefruit zest. Good weight. Creamy fruit. Spicy, with a flash of peppermint.
Finish: Medium-creamy fade on pepper and wood with a citric finale.
Conclusion: Top-of-the-line for Crown Royal.

Flavor Camp: **Spicy Rye**
Where Next? Crown Royal Black Label

REST OF THE WORLD

One look at the whisky-making map of the world shows that what used to be a style of spirit dominated by very few players has become a global phenomenon. While it is true that the new whisky distillers do not have the capacity to threaten the hegemony of the Old Countries, their approach and attitude point to a subtle shift in the way whisky is perceived. After tasting a range of these new whiskies, you realize that they challenge fundamentally your belief in what "whisky" is.

Previous page: whisky is now being made across Europe, from the Pyrenees to the Danube, Andalusia to Scandinavia.

It is interesting to compare the approaches of these distillers to those of their equivalents in nineteenth-century Scotland and Ireland. Like them, this new breed of whisky distiller is faced with the important philosophical questions of what do I make, what should it taste like—and how can I sell it?

This was the issue faced by Fred van Zuidam when, after years of making *genever* (a traditional Dutch style of gin) for a major company, he set up his own business. "We are one of the last specialist distilleries," he says, "but maybe we're not a dying breed. Maybe instead we are at the start of the next cycle." The fact that his son, Patrick, has added single malt and rye to the firm's portfolio of aged *genever* and *corenwijn* ("corn wine") is symptomatic of how this new specialist distiller thinks.

These distillers have usually started life as Scotch-lovers who decided to branch out on their own. The creation myths of many of these distilleries are variations on the same theme: "We were on a climbing/fishing/shooting/skiing trip, and over a bottle of single-malt Scotch we started talking about making our own whisky." What is perhaps surprising to the newcomer to these products is how their creators have then consciously and deliberately *not* copied Scotch, the spirit from which they took their inspiration.

When asked the style question, the response is immediate. "I wanted to make Tasmanian/Swedish/Danish/Dutch/Breton/ Corsican whisky." There are two motivating factors for this. Firstly, it would be suicidal commercially to try to replicate the dominant whisky style. Second, there is a deeper belief on the part of the most successful exponents of this new world of whisky that they are actively tuned into their location.

If they are in Sweden, for example, they'll use juniper twigs to help perfume the malted barley or turn to Swedish oak. If in Tasmania they'll use the local (and aromatically very different) peat. If in Brittany, why not use the indigenous grain, or in Corsica, what about aging in local wine barrels? They have freed their thinking and thus opened up new flavor possibilities. They don't have to stick to the same yeasts as used in Scotch; they can use a thick mash, a temperature-controlled fermentation, they can age in small barrels. Whisky distillers in wine-producing countries with access to "wine-quality" wood are in a significantly better position than Scotch distillers. Neither do they have to stick to the Scotch-type pot still. They may design their own, or go to still-makers like Vendome, Holstein, or Faraday, all of which will produce different aromatics. They are, these distillers, by necessity and inclination, innovative.

The spectacular scenery of the Brecon Beacons shelters Penderyn, Wales's only whisky distillery.

This is both exciting and occasionally disconcerting for the drinker. These whiskies should not be compared with single-malt Scotch, but judged in their own right. The issues of quality of spirit, complexity, and balance apply, but it is wrong to approach these thinking that they will be the same as single-malt Scotch. They are different. That's the point.

It is too early to say whether a Nordic or Australian or French style is emerging. I suspect it won't. While there might be shared characteristics, it will be the individuality of the distillery that will turn out to be the most important factor. Not all will succeed, but those who do will be those who ally commercial savvy with an obsessive concern for quality and individuality.

These are the ground-breakers within the whisky world. They are creating their own traditions.

Theirs is a world of opportunity.

EUROPE

▼ Distillery
▽ Mothballed distillery
▽ Planned distillery

N

0   miles   400

0   km   400

Lofoten Islands
Lofotr

Buran
Rein

Ådalen

NORWAY   SWEDEN

Norwegian Sea

*Faeroe
Islands*

Mackmyra

Oslo
Egge   Gammelstilla

Vänern

Agder
Brenneri

Stockholm

Vättern

*Shetland
Islands*

*North
Sea*

Gotland

see inset

DENMARK   Wannborga

Öland

Copenhagen   Hven

Baltic Sea

Dublin
IRELAND   UNITED
KINGDOM

RUSS. FE

Hamburg

Elbe

Vistula

Penderyn   St George's
London

see inset

NETH.
Amsterdam

Berlin

Wars.

*ATLANTIC
OCEAN*

Claeyssens

Brussels

Rhine

Sonnenschein

POLAN

Menez-Bré
Warenghem
Menhirs   Northmaen
Glann ar Mor
Holl
Jacques
Fissilier   Paris

BELGIUM   Höhler
Luxembourg   Frankfurt

GERMANY

Mößlein   Stock   Prague   Teset

*Bay of
Biscay*

Guillon
Lehmann
Pays d'Othe
Grallet-Dupic
FRANCE   Meyer
Monsieur   Whisky Castle
Balthazar   Hedgehog
Les Vignettes

Hepp &
Bertrand
Elsasser
Hohenheim
Sloupitsi
Lanten-
hammer
Bern   LIECH.
Telser
SWITZ.   Brennerei-
Zentrum
Bauernhof   Reisetbauer
Blaue Maus   Slyrs

CZECH
REPUBLIC

Roggenhof

SLOVAK

Vienna   Bratislav
Rabenbrau

AUSTRIA   Ortner   Budapest
Ljubljana   HUNGARY

Loire

Garonne

Rhône

Ebro

ALPS

SLOV.

Danube

Bordeaux

Toulouse

SAN
MARINO

Zagreb
CROATIA   SER

Destilerias
Y Crianzas
Del Whisky   ANDORRA

ITALY

MONACO

BOS.
& HERZ.
Sarajevo

PORTUGAL   Segovia

Douro

Madrid
SPAIN

Lisbon

MONTENEGRO
Podgorica

Corsica
Mavela

KOSOVO
Tirana

Guadalquivir

Rome

Granada
Liber

Balearic Islands

Barcelona

ALBAN

Sardinia

Mediterranean Sea

Sicily

MALTA

Map 1 (Denmark inset):

North Sea

Skaggerak

SWEDEN

Åalborg

Viborg   Randers   Kattegat

DENMARK

Århus

Stauning

Faery Lochan   Horsens

Gourmetbryggeriet

Ørbæk   Roskilde   Copenhagen

Esbjerg   Odense   Sjælland   Braunstein

Fyn

Bornholm

Vingården Lille Gadegård

GERMANY   Baltic Sea

Map 2 (Netherlands/Belgium inset):

North Sea

Groningen

Leeuwarden

Den Helder   Us Heit

NETHERLANDS

Amsterdam

The Hague   Vallei, Leusden

Utrecht

Kampen   Rhine   GERMANY

Bruinisse   Rotterdam

Eindhoven

Zuidam, Baarle-Nassau

Antwerp

Gent   Het Anker, Mechelen

Brussels   Rademacher, Raeren

Lille   Owl,   Liège

Grace-Hollogne

FRANCE   BELGIUM

LUXEMBOURG

Main map:

NLAND

ck   Teerenpeli

Helsinki   Lake Onega

Tallinn   Lake Ladoga

STONIA

Riga   RUSSIAN FEDERATION

LATVIA

UANIA   Moscow

ius

Minsk

BELARUS

Kiev

Dnieper

UKRAINE

MOLDOVA

Chisinau

MANIA

Bucharest

Danube   Black Sea

BULGARIA

Sofia

a

oje   Istanbul

EDONIA

Ankara   Tekel

TURKEY

ECE

hens

Nicosia

Crete   CYPRUS

England

EAST HARLING, NORFOLK • WWW.ENGLISHWHISKY.CO.UK • OPEN ALL YEAR • MON–SUN

When Norfolk farmer Andrew Nelstrop opened the St. George's distillery in November 2006, he was reviving a lost English tradition. While never achieving the scale of whisky distilling in Scotland or Ireland, English whisky did exist in the nineteenth century, with large distilleries operating in London, Liverpool, and Bristol (the last two were probably originally rum distilleries that had made spirits to barter for slaves).

When they all closed, English whisky disappeared. The malting barley grown on the fields of East Anglia headed north to Scotland. "My father claims he's been talking about making whisky for years for that very reason," says Nelstrop. "The issue came up every year in the 1990s, but the time wasn't right. It was hard enough to find Scottish malt whisky in those days. Making an English whisky was never going to work economically."

In September 2005, however, he felt that the market had changed enough. "Originally it was to be a microbrewery in a shed, but the smallest still we were permitted was 476 gallons (1,800 liters), so it became a more serious enterprise." Planning consent was granted in October, construction started in March, and spirit ran from the stills in November. Having his own land and building firm helped, but St. George's opened without any windows or doors in place because Nelstrop had heard rumors (unfounded) that a distillery was being built in the Lake District. With stills and engineering from Forsyth's of Rothes and former Laphroaig and Edradour distiller Iain Henderson at the helm, St. George's soon found its own style. "The stills decide the overall character," says Nelstrop. "You might want to make a certain style,

but it dictates the only cut that works." Being released in "Chapters" through new make to official whisky has allowed connoisseurs to see the evolution of this light and quite delicate style, whose character suggests it will hit its peak in its mid-teens.

"We want to make a good and drinkable whisky," says Nelstrop. "Iain persuaded us to make peated as well; now it's 50 percent of the production." Availability is limited because he is holding back 60 percent of each year's production.

Could this be the start of an English whisky movement? "We'd be delighted if others started up," he says, "but it's a lot of money. It's OK for farmers who've been trading for 600 years, but it is a big commitment."

English whisky is once again emerging from the mists of the past.

THE ENGLISH WHISKY COMPANY TASTING NOTES

CHAPTER 3 EX-BOURBON CASK, 18 MONTHS OLD, 46%

Nose: Light, with a touch of green grass and a hint of cooked vegetable (sulfur). Some very light cereal touches when dilute.

Palate: The start of some wood coming into the conversation. Sawdust and very light vanilla. Still tight.

Finish: Light spices.

Conclusion: This will develop interestingly. Clean spirit.

Flavor Camp: Fragrant & Floral
Where Next? On its way towards Speyburn

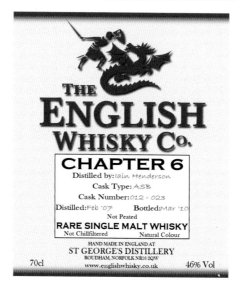

CHAPTER 6 EX-BOURBON CASK, 3YO (THEREFORE OFFICIALLY WHISKY), 46%

Nose: Pale straw. The fresh grain note seems to have come forward and any of the light sulfur has disappeared, showing a little citrus fruit and just a hint of soft oak.

Palate: More of a green/crab-apple bite. Again, some floury notes. Lightly scented.

Finish: That hint of grassiness seen on the 3rd Chapter's nose has now reversed and appears here.

Conclusion: An important marker. Will keep growing.

Flavor Camp: Fragrant & Floral
Where Next? Bladnoch

Wales

PENDERYN • WWW.WELSH-WHISKY.CO.UK • OPEN ALL YEAR • MON–SUN

Finding your style is always an interesting philosophical adventure for a new distiller. What are your reference points? Do you follow what has gone before, or do you reject your neighbors' approaches and strike out on your own? It's hard enough to find your voice when there are these markers; what happens when you really are all alone? That was the issue faced by the Welsh Whisky Company (WWC), when, a decade ago, it built its Penderyn distillery in the Brecon Beacons National Park. The fact that there was no other Welsh whisky to compare itself against was, one would imagine, both a daunting challenge but also a liberation. Welsh whisky was what Penderyn said it was.

Why, for example, did they have to mill, mash, and ferment on site when there was Brains brewery close by? "The wash is made to our specification and arrives here at 8% abv," says distiller Gillian Macdonald. "Brains uses its own strain of yeast—you know what brewers are like about yeasts: they're obsessed with them—and it gives a really fruity punch. It sets us apart."

This freedom of technique extends to the still. Rather than following the normal route and install pot stills, the firm turned to engineer Dr. David Faraday's design, which is a pot linked to a rectifying column allowing spirit to be made in a single pass. "Actually, it's two rectifying columns," says Macdonald. "If it had been just the single column, then the building would have been too high and we would have broken the strict building regulations!"

The pot is filled with 660 gallons (2,500 liters) and heat is then applied. The vapor rises up the neck and into the first column, which is itself divided by six plates. It then travels to the second column and rises once more. This column has 18 plates and the spirit is collected on the seventh one.

"Any distillate that refluxes out on the plates flows back down the column," Macdonald explains. "This is carried back to the first [column] and from there back to the pot. We say it's a single distillation, but it could be redistilled millions of times." The end result is 53 gallons of spirit (200 liters) at between 92 percent and 86 percent. Its focused, mossy-green, floral character is then aged in a selection of barrels chosen by WWC's consultant Dr. Jim Swan, the great guru of maturation.

The standard Penderyn (none of the whiskies carry an age statement) is aged in ex-Buffalo Trace first-fill barrels and then spends six months in ex-Madeira casks. The sherry wood is 70% ex-bourbon and 30% ex-sherry, while the latest addition is a peated expression. Welsh peat?

"It was an accident!" says Macdonald. "When we started, we had no refill barrels, so we got some from Scotland and although we specified no ex-peaty ones, half a dozen slipped through. Initially we thought it was a problem, but when we bottled them as a one-off it sold out!"

Now she is filling new make into peaty barrels. The open-minded creation of Welsh identity continues.

WELSH WHISKY COMPANY TASTING NOTES

NEW MAKE
Nose: Intense and sweet. Bergamot and fresh citrus-fruit notes. Mint and fir, with perfumed top notes.
Palate: Neat, it is hot and tense, but with water, floral notes, rose, fresh citrus and green fruit, and then a little cereal crunch.
Finish: Fleshy but clean.

PENDERYN MADEIRA 46%
Nose: Clean, sweet oak. Pine and vanilla. Spring leaves/green bark. Light plum at the background.
Palate: Juicy and clean, with lots of apricot nectar and spicy oak relaxing into Lady Grey tea.
Finish: Clean and minty.
Conclusion: The green notes of new make softened and carried forward, along with balanced oak.

Flavor Camp: Fragrant & Floral
Where Next? Glenmorangie Original

PENDERYN SHERRYWOOD, 46%
Nose: Gold. A clear difference to the standard. Bran this time, along with citrus peel, light nuts, and sweet dried fruit (date/fig). With water, some vine flower.
Palate: Has taken the floral notes of new make and deepened them. Similarly juicy, but the fruit is more stewed.
Finish: Figgy and sweet.
Conclusion: Light spirit but balanced here with a complex range of oak-driven flavors. A different take on the new-make character.

Flavor Camp: Rich & Round.
Where Next? The Singleton of Glendullan

France

ELSASS • OBERNAI • WWW.DISTILLERIELEHMANN.COM / HEDGEHOG • AUVERGNE
MENHIRS • WWW.DISTILLERIE.FR/EN/EDDU_SILVER.HTML • OPEN • JULY–AUG, MON–FRI • SEE WEB FOR SHOP
GLANN AR MOR • PLEUBIAN • WWW.GLANNARMOR.COM / MAVELA • CORSICA • WWW.BRASSERIEPIETRA.COM

Just as the diversity of the wines of France reflects not just an earth-bound *terroir* but a philosophical one, so it is with its whiskies: distillates which on first meeting seem like interlopers, weird anomalies in a country whose spiritous map is already quartered into *eaux-de-vie* (east), Calvados (north), Cognac and Armagnac (west), and pastis (south). With those options covered, the question isn't just what is French whisky, but why does France need its own whisky? Maybe this is a reason why its whisky distillers seem to have approached the issue with a profoundly questioning manner.

Making French whisky isn't just a matter of making whisky in France; it is creating a spirit which authentically belongs to France. No surprise, then, that any overview of French whisky takes in a wide range of approaches, of which the examples here are but a taste.

In Corsica, the double act of the Pietra brewery and the winemaker/distillers of Mavela produces some of the world's most extraordinarily scented whiskies, which come across like a barley-based Chartreuse. This is the result of using Holstein stills with their ability to stretch out aromatics, plus a maturation regime that sees the spirit aged first in a mix of ex-Malmsey and Patrimonio Petit Grains de Moscatel casks, before being married in ex-*eaux-de-vie* barrels.

On the evidence of its trio of whiskies—Elsass, Meyer's, and Uberbach—the approach in Alsace is geared towards purity of character: lighter, slightly fruity but understated. While it could be the result of the whiskies being released young, you can't help wondering whether they are also being driven by the *eaux-de-vie* ethos of obtaining the essence of the base ingredient—in this case barley or beer.

Neither is it compulsory to follow a Scottish way of whisky-making. Olivier Perrier in the village of Herisson in the middle of the Auvergne has taken a bourbon base (65 percent corn with malted barley and rye) and distilled it in a Cognac-style alembic before aging for three years in Tronçais oak. The whisky is called

Celtic soul brothers: the Breton coastline is home to a growing number of distilleries.

Hedgehog, after the town. Any thoughts that Perrier is digging deep into his *terroir* can be quickly dismissed: the recipe is one for moonshine extracted from a South Carolina musician.

Terroir was, however, uppermost in former math teacher Guy le Lat's mind when he established his Distillerie des Menhirs in Plomelin, Brittany. Though his family had long made *lambig* (apple brandy), he realized that the distillery only worked for half the year, whereas whisky could be made all year round. His debate centered around what grain to use in order to make it authentically Breton. He chose buckwheat—*blé noir*—though never considered why no one had ever turned Brittany's national cereal into spirit before. He soon found out why: it's almost impossible to mash. Le Lat cracked the problem and his Eddu is a defiantly spicy and complex spirit.

Brittany is home to two other distilleries: Warengheim, which makes the most widely seen whisky, Amorik, and Glann ar Mor ("by the sea"), established in 2005 by former advertising executive Jean Donnay, who also runs the Celtic Whisky Compagnie. Donnay's "crazy dream" is found 400 feet (120m) from the sea on the Presque l'Ile Sauvage.

"I'm a perfectionist," he says, "so I wanted to make a whisky exactly as I like to have it, but I've realized that there's more to making whisky than distilling beer. There's 100,000 ways of doing this recipe. Not all whiskies are equal." His approach is traditionalist: direct fire for feel

The tiny worm tubs outside Jean Donnay's new Glann ar Mor distillery.

and body, wooden washbacks, wild yeast, worm tubs, the effects of a maritime climate, but he is also tuned into the Celtic diaspora. "I'm not making French whisky," says Donnay. "I'm making Breton whisky which has links with wider Celtic whisky and with the sea."

Whiskies made with an uncompromising belief: that's not just French, or Breton, or Celtic; maybe it's whisky's soul.

FRANCE TASTING NOTES

ELSASS, SINGLE MALT 40%

Nose: Fresh, grainy, and sappy with a light felt note. Very light, soft fruit, like diluted fresh fruit juices. Touch of linoleum.
Palate: Sweet and fine with a delicate softness and ripe *poire William*.
Finish: Green malt, then cream.
Conclusion: Fragile but interesting.

Flavor Camp: Fragrant & Floral
Where Next? Mackmyra Special 3

EDDU, MENHIRS 40%

Nose: Very intense and fragrant. Floral: wild rose, elderflower; then white fruit, cinnamon, and nutmeg.
Palate: Mixes fruit honeys with good acidity: heather and lavender. Intense.
Finish: Becomes increasingly spicy.
Conclusion: Brittany's answer to rye whiskey.

Flavor Camp: Spicy Rye
Where Next?: Sazerac Rye

GLANN AR MOR 46%

Nose: Lifted and vinous; apricot. Light, cookie-dough cereal. Robust. With water, there are floral notes, crème caramel, white-chocolate-covered almonds.
Palate: This has weight. Thick but sweet. Yellow fruit. Ripe.
Finish: Soft pear, then spice.
Conclusion: Very young, but already showing complexity.

Flavor Camp: Fruity & Spicy
Where Next?: Glen Elgin-style

GLANN AR MOR, KORNOG PEATED, 57.1%

Nose: Smoky but fragrant. Bean shoots, then nuttiness and briny notes: salt drying on skin, light heather and sage, burning rosemary. With water, samphire.
Palate: Dry, ember-like smoke. Mouth-filling, but the spirit is sweet. Already balanced. White pepper, seashells, rock pools.

Finish: Long. Smoke drifting away. Fresh.
Conclusion: An important new whisky.

Flavor Camp: Smoky & Peaty
Where Next?: Kilchoman

HEDGEHOG 40%

Nose: Fat and oily. Corn and oak with a surprisingly high, crisp, barley note. Strangely like Falernum liqueur.
Palate: Thick sweet/savory notes playing off each other. A little aggressive.
Finish: Oily corn again.
Conclusion: A heavy and highly personal take on whisky.

Flavor Camp: Fragrant & Floral
Where Next? Old Tom Moore

P&M BLEND SUPERIOR 40%

Nose: Hugely scented. Wild herbs: saffron, wormwood, lavender, rosemary oil, wild thyme. Reminiscent of Chartreuse.
Palate: Broad and ripe. Quite fruity. Touch of pepper and camphor, with some honeyed qualities
Finish: Coriander seed, allspice, and a touch of cereal.
Conclusion: Highly individual. Unlike any whisky in the world.

Flavor Camp: Fragrant & Floral
Where Next?: Chartreuse VEP

Netherlands

ZUIDAM • BAARLE-NASSAU • WWW.ZUIDAM.EU • GROUP VISITS BY APPOINTMENT

Based in the village of Baarle-Nassau, the Zuidam distillery was built by *genever* distiller Fred van Zuidam in 2002. *Genever* (wrongly dismissed as simply "Dutch gin") starts as a fermented mash of malted barley, corn, and rye, which in van Zuidam's case, is triple-distilled in a pot still. A percentage of this is then redistilled with botanicals, blended, and then aged. Were it not for the flavoring part this is bourbon! Which leads you to wonder, was bourbon invented by a Dutchman?

Making Millstone single-malt whisky seems therefore to be a logical step for Fred's son, Patrick (now the distiller), to take. "Millstone isn't simply a by-product of *genever*," he warns. "Technically, barley is easy to distill, but it makes a simple spirit. The quality of great Scotch is in the detail. You need to build in character during the [distillation] process, and during aging."

That accretion of character starts with the grain, all of which is ground by windmill to help preserve aromas. This is mashed into a thick porridge, which is then pumped into temperature-controlled fermenters ("It helps create a fruity character), where it ferments with two strains of yeast for five days ("This helps to create esters"). Distillation takes place in Holstein stills with massive copper availability. A key part of Millstone's character comes down to this huge amount of copper.

Patrick's approach to maturation deviates from the Scottish norm as well. "I don't understand the Scottish way of maturation," he says. "Keeping the whisky in the same cask for its entire life doesn't use the full potential of the wood. It's like making a cup of tea. The first tea you make from the tea bag is the best, correct? The Scotch way of maturing is like using the same tea bag every day for years."

Accordingly, Millstone is aged first in new wood and then racked into older casks for the rest of its cycle. A mix of woods (ex-bourbon, new wood casks, French oak, ex-sherry) are used. His latest development is a 100 percent rye whisky.

Sacks of cereal ground by windmill at the Millstone distillery.

"I thought rye is more interesting than bourbon, so I gave it a try," he says nonchalantly. It has been a triumph, and like Millstone's malts, defiantly Dutch.

Holland is also home to the Vallei distillery (which makes Valley single malt), and Us Heit, where distiller Aart van den Linde's Frysk Hynder whisky is bottled at three years from a mix of different casks.

ZUIDAM TASTING NOTES

MILLSTONE 5YO 40%

Nose: Light gold. Green apples in a bed of sweet hay. Pineapple and green plum. Clean, sweet, and fresh. In time it gets more bready, with banana skin and wet green leaves.
Palate: Sweet, smooth, and clean, with custard notes. Rich middle palate.
Finish: Fruit dusted with nutmeg.
Conclusion: Fresh and clean. Well-balanced.

Flavor Camp: **Fruity & Spicy**
Where Next? Arran-style

MILLSTONE 8YO 43%

Nose: Deep amber. Scented, with cinnamon. Light, dried fruit and black cherry. Good oak extract. Reminiscent of a manzanilla amontillado.
Palate: Rounded and fruity, with good depth.
Finish: Tingling citric spiciness.
Conclusion: Evidence that, even at 8yo, this is a serious contender.

Flavor Camp: **Rich & Round**
Where Next? Edradour 1977

MILLSTONE RYE 5YO 40%

Nose: Rich amber. Scented, like beeswax, along with rye sourdough starter, then come ginger, cumin, and coriander cooking in butter, some light suede and vanilla.
Palate: Controlled, smooth, and clean with orange pulp and peel, then a slow release of rye spice at the end.
Finish: Tart but not too acidic.
Conclusion: There's none of the dustiness you get with American rye.

Flavor Camp: **Spicy Rye**
Where Next? Russells Reserve Rye 6yo

Belgium

OWL • GRÂCE-HOLLOGNE • WWW.BELGIANWHISKY.COM / RADERMACHER • RAEREN • WWW.DISTILLERIE.BIZ

Home to the world's most diverse range of premium beers and repository of much brewing knowledge, why wouldn't Belgium become part of the whisky family? One of its handful of distilleries, Het Anker, took this logical step some years back, distilling its Gouden Carols Tripel into a similarly named whisky, aged for four years. The firm has now moved to a purpose-built site in Blaasveld, near Antwerp.

A different approach has been taken by Radermacher in Raeren in the east. The distillery, which has been producing *genever* and other distillates for 175 years, started making whisky over a decade ago. Its oldest expression is a 10yo grain whisky.

Meanwhile, in Grâce-Hollonge, on the outskirts of Liege, distiller Etienne Bouillon and two partners, farmer Pierre Roberti and financier Luc Foubert, set up the somewhat scattered Owl Distillery (originally Pur-E) in 2004. "We wanted to give greater diversification to what the Hesbaye farms produced," says Bouillon, "and to get a fair price for farmers." In some ways this is not far from the motivation of early distillers across Scotland and America, who soon realized that distilled spirit makes more than a bushel of grain.

The whisky-making process is made a little more complex by the fact that the Sebastian barley is malted in Belhou, mashed close by at Roberti's farm before finally being finished at the distillery. The stills themselves also hark back to an old tradition: the ambulatory alembics, which used to go from farm to farm around Europe. Bouillon uses a nineteenth-century Swiss model for this whisky.

Although he is a distiller, Bouillon had no whisky-making experience, so he headed off to learn from Jim McEwan at Bruichladdich. Maybe that sweet, honeyed character in the new make is a homage to his mentor. "We think we have a special spirit," he says, "which is based on the local *terroir*. If you grow the same grape in different regions, then you get different results. Why won't it be the same with barley? Combine that with fermentation and distillation and the whisky will have specificity of flavor." Aged in first-fill American oak casks, the first batch of Belgian Owl was released at a precocious four years.

"We make whisky according to EU rules," says Bouillon, "but we try to make it as Belgian as possible."

The rolling hills around Liege are becoming a center of distilling activity.

BELGIUM TASTING NOTES

THE BELGIAN OWL UNAGED SPIRIT, 46%

Nose: Sweet and slightly honeyed, with peach pit, green apricot. Peach blossom and barley.
Palate: Clean and light, with that honeyed quality coming through. Peach skin now.
Finish: Mixing flowers and cereal.
Conclusion: Already soft and well-balanced

THE BELGIAN OWL 46%

Nose: Pale gold. Instant sweet oak and light wood phenols. New make has been fleshed out and integrated with the oak. Mango and peach with a hint of tarragon. Creamy. With water, green almonds.
Palate: Very sweet. Fudge. It becomes crisp in the center, where again the barley and the oak pull things together. Balanced and very sunny.
Finish: Sweetly fruity. Clean.
Conclusion: Balanced and clean, with room for further development.

Flavor Camp: Fruity & Spicy
Where Next: Bruichladdich 2002, 40 Creek

RADERMACHER, LAMBERTUS 10YO
GRAIN, 40%

Nose: Floor polish and banana. Estery and firm, with a little (pink) marshmallow.
Palate: Very sweet and perfumed. Fruit cordial. Strawberry and banana.
Finish: Sweet.
Conclusion: A simple grain.

Flavor Camp: Fragrant & Floral
Where Next: Elsass

Just like whisky's raw material, the new European whisky-making industry is coming to life.

Central Europe

BLAUE MAUS • EGGOLSHEIM-NEUSES, FRANKEN, GERMANY • WWW.FLEISCHMANN-WHISKY.DE • OPEN ALL YEAR • SEE WEB

SLOUPISTI • SCHLEPZIG, GERMANY • WWW.SPREEWALDBRAUEREI.DE • OPEN ALL YEAR • HOTEL & BREWERY

SLYRS • SCHLIERSEE, BAVARIA, GERMANY • WWW.SLYRS.DE • OPEN ALL YEAR • SEE WEB FOR DETAILS

The countries at the heart of Europe—Switzerland, Austria, and Germany—have a long heritage of distilling, albeit predominantly fruit spirits. Recent times have seen the arrival of a whisky boom, illustrated by the fact that it is now possible to buy nearly 30 different German whiskies, and five to ten from both Switzerland and Austria, plus the famous Golden Cock from the (currently mothballed) Tesetice distillery in the Czech Republic. Several reasons account for their sudden appearance.

Fruit spirits may be the traditional distillation of choice, but this is a tough business: the fruit is delicate, mostly wild, hand-picked, and its quality is dependent on the weather. Whisky, by comparison, is relatively simple. In addition, brewers are now also making whisky.

Although there are many new arrivals, the pioneers have a longer history, with distilleries like Blaue Maus ("Blue Mouse") dating back to the early 1980s. There's no compulsion to stick to a "Scottish" template. Some producers are making whisky from rye, spelt, and wheat, and brewing techniques are being put to use. While some are experimenting with maturing in the Alps at high altitude, others are maturing in ex-wine casks. It will be interesting to see how things have developed in a few years, when both experience and knowledge will have matured.

It is no surprise that the pioneer of German whisky lives in Franconia, northern Bavaria, where beer production has always been strong. Robert Fleischmann founded the Blaue Maus distillery in 1983 in the tiny village of Neuses, south of Bamberg. Since he had little knowledge of maturation he had to fall back on trial and error. He used new, small (so they'd fit in his cellar), uncharred (no one told him about charring) oak casks. This uncharred maturation is now his signature style. Currently he offers seven different whiskies, including a grain expression.

If you drive further south into the picture-postcard Oberbayern area of Bavaria, you will reach the Schliersee, where in 1999 Florian Stetter started distilling Slyrs in an old fruit spirit still. In 2007, a new whisky distillery was built, with custom-shaped pot stills. Part of the malt is kilned over birchwood and matured in new, custom-made American oak barriques.

The Spreewald in east Germany, famed for its pickled cucumbers, and its UNESCO-designated biosphere status, is home to the eighteenth-century brewery owned by Dr. Torsten Römer. Made from a mix of three beer malts—Wiener, Münchener, and Pilsner—Römer launched his Sloupisti whisky in 2007. Distilled in a 159-gallon (600-liter) Holstein still, it is matured in 59-gallon (225-liter) ex-Silvaner wine casks and German oak barriques.

In the future the tiny Principality of Liechtenstein may be known not only for its alleged ability to hide money, but also to produce whisky, following the launch in 2009 of the first release from the Telser distillery. Telsington is a triple-distilled, 3yo single-cask release (from ex-Pinot Noir barriques) that sells at the price of €160 ($201) per 50cl bottle. That's Liechtenstein for you!

There are also distillers in Austria. The Rabenbräu brewery's distillery is located in an old customs and excise building south of Vienna, close to the Hungarian border. It produces two different 5yo whiskies: Old Raven aged in ex-bourbon and ex-Scotch casks

What was once beer and fruit spirit country is now becoming whisky territory as well.

and Old Raven Smoky, the latter matured in an "Islay PX Sherry cask."

If you travel further north to a village called Roggenreith, you will find Austria's first whisky distiller, Johann Haider, who started producing in 1995. His Waldviertler Roggenhof is made in two 119-gallon (450-liter) Holstein stills and comes in a wide variety of styles, the most popular being a rye with a mashbill of 60% rye to 40% malt. There is also a 100 percent malted whisky, which is also available in a "dark rye" version. Finally, two single malts are made: one with lightly malted barley; the other, Karamell, with roasted barley.

With many more distilleries openng up, the central European innovations seem set to grow exponentially over the next few years.

The Holstein still at the Blaue Maus distillery.

SLYRS 2006 43%

Nose: Fresh-cut apples mixed with wood shavings. Some resin.

Palate: A mix of sweet and sour with chewy oak tannins and pencil shavings.

Finish: A more herbal and dry finish. Again, sap-like.

Conclusion: Still young. A lighter, summery whisky, though wood is not yet integrated.

Flavor Camp: **Fragrant & Floral**
Where Next?: Teaninich 12yo, Mackmyra

SLOUPISTI 2008 65.6%

Nose: Pungent, herbal attack, followed by a mixed bag of Asian spices, then some winey notes.

Palate: Dark, sweet, sugary notes and a lot of wood. Again, the wine cask breaks through. Lightly sour fruit.

Finish: Long, lingering mixture of burnt sugar and a herbal bitterness, with some underlying red and black fruits.

Conclusion: A pleasant, if not complex dram. Needs dilution!

Flavor Camp: **Rich & Round**
Where Next?: P&M, Lark

BLAUE MAUS 1989, CASK NO. 1 40%

Nose: Starts with linseed and waxy notes, hints of flowers, and a mix of fresh herbs.

Palate: Oily extracts, exotic scented oak mixed with creamy vanilla.

Finish: Quite a long, herbal finish; some dark chocolate emerges from the woods.

Conclusion: Pleasantly creamy in the mouth.

Flavor Camp: **Fragrant & Floral**
Where Next? Elsass, Speyside 12yo

Scandinavia

BRAUNSTEIN • COPENHAGEN, DENMARK • WWW.BRAUNSTEIN.DK • SEE WEB FOR WHISKY SCHOOL & TASTINGS
MACKMYRA • VALBO, SWEDEN • WWW.MACKMYRA.COM • OPEN TO VISITORS • FRI–SAT • BOOKING ESSENTIAL
TEERENPELI • LAHTI, FINLAND • WWW.TEERENPELI.COM/ENGLISH_BREWERY • TOURS BY APPOINTMENT

There is a certain inevitability about the single-malt distilling boom taking root in Scandinavia. This is a region, after all, with the highest concentration of single-malt whisky clubs in the world, the world's largest beer and whisky festival (in Stockholm), and regular malt-whisky cruises around the Baltic. Distilling whisky is a logical extension of this rise in interest among a new generation.

At the time of writing, there are a dozen distilleries either operational (some just so) or planned. The granddaddy of them all is now a decade old. Mackmyra was founded in 1999 by a group of university friends, who, unknown to each other had all developed a taste for single-malt Scotch. "The idea of starting a distillery has popped up in hundreds of Swedish heads over the past 20 years," says Mackmyra's Lars Lindberger. "The difference was our eight founders acted on the dream."

The group used to meet every winter to go skiing and always took a bottle of spirits for the bar. In 1998 they all turned up with single malt and the idea of a Swedish distillery began to form. A year later, the distillery, 90 miles north of Stockholm, was operational.

Matured in a disused mine, the Mackmyra style is resolutely not "Scotch." Locally grown barley is smoked over peat and juniper branches, and a percentage of the final assemblage is matured in new Swedish-oak casks, which are high in fruit and wood oils.

The whisky itself seems to float above these potentially bold flavorings. There is a slighly distant, cool, ethereal, fir-like quality to Mackmyra, which can seem a little gawky when young, but after slightly longer in the firm's small casks, whiskies such as the recent First Edition begin to show the development of secondary aromas: ginseng, orange, and ginger. A complex, very different (and valid) style of single malt is emerging from the mines.

The runaway success of the brand is now triggering further expansion. A second distillery is being built as part of the Mackmyra Whisky Village, a visitor attraction which will allow people to participate in the production process. With its opening planned for 2012, it will double capacity. Mackmyra is here to stay.

One of the newest distilleries to take up the Mackmyra lead (its whiskies are not yet on the market) is found on the island of Hven, between Sweden and Denmark. From the outset, founder Henric Molin wanted to create an encapsulation of his location. "I wanted to craft a whisky that also reflected the surroundings of the distillery: the meadows, flowers, and the barley fields entangled with the sea/ocean beaches, the seaweed, and the harbor, the stone fruit gardens and the citric notes from the rapeseed flowers," he says. "I had an absolute vision of the final result, which was also a necessity when incorporating the design of the distillery. Then again, nothing becomes absolutely the way you figured it to be. It is a never-ending learning curve."

Barley from the island is given a long fermentation with—and here's a significant difference to Scotland—a selection of yeasts. This estery wash is then distilled in a way to promote extended copper conversation. "The most imperative factor in our flavor profile, however, is the wood policy," says Molin. "We only work with the absolute best air-dried oaks from the best locations around the world." The end result? "A malt which you might love (or not) but that's the point. There should be a reaction! I want my products to be exhibitionists. You could sell a product once to the consumer as a 'new, small, different origin' whisky, but if it tastes like the generic whisky produced elsewhere, the consumer will not return."

Finland's Teerenpeli distillery in Lahti has been operational for six years. Originally a brewery, now the beer side is augmented by a stillhouse with a pair of classic Scottish pots with boil bulbs. Its clean spirit is the maltiest of this early Nordic grouping.

Another pipe-dream distillery (this time triggered by fly-fishing trips to the Spey), Copenhagen's harbor-front Braunstein distillery has been operational for four years, although the plans were in the Poulsen brothers' heads for considerably longer. "We started our application the same time as Mackmyra," says Michael Poulsen. "They were up-and-running in a year while we were still fighting red tape." The Danish authorities insisted that the brothers first proved their capabilities as potential distillers by running a microbrewery for two years before finally granting them their license in 2005–6.

To the best of my knowledge, Braunstein is the only distillery whose water source happens to be melted icebergs from the Greenland ice cap. The barley used is organic, while the authorities' insistence on the microbrewing side has paid dividends in the isolation of the correct yeast types. "Very few people seem to know how important fermentation is," says Poulsen.

The Holstein still produces two spirits: an unpeated fruity make that's aged in sherry casks (Michael's preferred whisky style) and a heavily peated (his brother's). This is the polar (pardon the pun) opposite of Mackmyra's lightness of touch. Here there are big but balanced flavors built in for long-term maturation. "I'm a big fan of diversity," says Poulsen, "and believe that everyone should do their own thing. We're not trying to compete with Scotland; we're not going the Mackmyra route. This is small-scale, traditional craftsmanship and people are now taking us seriously. We've grown out of being the two crazy kids on the harbor." This diversity is key to the future development of the Scandinavian whisky: less a unified style and more a wide range of possibilities in tune with their surroundings.

Sweden's fertile southern plains (here near Malmö) are providing the ingredients for a burgeoning whisky industry.

It may be small and new but Mackmyra has built up a cult following globally.

SCANDINAVIA TASTING NOTES

BRAUNSTEIN E:1 SINGLE SHERRY CASK, 62.1%

Nose: Tight to start. Sweet and soft. Scented. Chestnut flour and blueberry. Cooked fruits.

Palate: Concentrated, with masses of jammy fruitiness. Then come the dusty cereal and dried fruit. Toffee. Good acidity. Balanced. Polished oak.

Finish: Spicy and fragrant. An exotic element.

Conclusion: An identically aged single cask has more intense mintiness with an appetizing, intriguing wormwood note.

Flavor Camp: Fruity & Spicy
Where Next: Benromach-style

MACKMYRA, SWEDISH OAK RESERVE 2006 55%

Nose: Ruby. Intense and cherry-like, with masses of wood oil and a real concentrated range of aromatics. Shifts onto strawberry, nutmeg, fruit, and balsam.

Palate: Grippy oak. Lots of sweet tannins and caramelized notes. Heavy toffee and light astringency, but has the Mackmyra delicacy of touch that allows the spirit to shake free of the oak.

Finish: Oily oak.

Conclusion: A new range of oak aromatics appears.

Flavor Camp: Fruity & Spicy
Where Next: Nant, Hanyu

MACKMYRA, SPECIAL 03 48.2%

Nose: Straw. Light, mirabelle fruitiness. Cool and restrained with fir-like freshness and sweet rye bread. Leafy, with touches of char/smoke from the oak.

Palate: Balanced and sweet. Fresh fruit, wild herbs. Clean and light.

Finish: Soft and gentle.

Conclusion: Balanced, clean, and a good introduction to the Mackmyra style.

Flavor Camp: Fragrant & Floral
Where Next: Glentauchers

MACKMYRA, 1ST EDITION 45%

Nose: Straw. Similar to Special 03, but with more intense citric notes. Ginseng, ginger, Mandarine Napoleon, light smoke but still very controlled.

Palate: Clean and light-bodied, but the ginger and citrus fruit dominate the palate. Light hazelnut underneath.

Finish: Gently smoky.

Conclusion: Light but intense. Balanced.

Flavor Camp: Fragrant & Floral
Where Next: Braeval

TEERENPELI 6YO 43%

Nose: Bran. Roasted and nutty. Clean and light oiliness behind that moves into dry grass and flaked almonds.

Palate: Very nutty/hazelnuts. Young and feisty, with some hyacinth.

Finish: Wheat germ.

Conclusion: Clean and fresh. Balanced and nutty.

Flavor Camp: Malty & Dry
Where Next: Auchroisk-style

Spain

LIBER • GRANADA • WWW.DESTILERIASLIBER.COM • OPEN ALL YEAR • MON–FRI

For many years, Spain was Scotch whisky's golden market, the country that proved to doubters that young people could enjoy whisky. This era, when brands such as J&B, Ballantine's, and Cutty Sark flowed like water—huge measures poured into ice-filled glasses and topped up with cola—seemed to offer a new way to talk about and drink Scotch. Spain liberated the drink from its book-lined study: it made blended whisky relevant once more. The factors that led to the Spanish explosion are many and complex, and go beyond just fashion, or even flavor. Blended Scotch was a signifier for the new post-Franco Spain; it was a drink which said, "We are democratic, we are European, we reject the old ways."

In the protectionist Franco era, imported whisky was expensive (Franco himself was alleged to have a penchant for Johnnie Walker) and out of the reach of ordinary Spaniards. If they can't get Scotch, thought Nicomedes García Gomez, why don't we make whisky here? Already running an anisette business (anise-flavored liqueur), in 1958–9 Garcia acted on his vision and built a massive, multifunctional distillery in Palazuelos de Eresma, Segovia, which encompassed maltings, a grain plant, and a six-still malt site. In 1963, DYC (Destilerias y Crianzas) was launched. Demand was such that, in 1973, the firm bought the Lochside distillery in Montrose to supply fillings, although that venture ended in 1992 when the Scottish distillery was closed.

DYC (now part of Beam Global) has remained a multi-nation vatting of Spanish and "Euro" (i.e. Scottish) whiskies, although in the past year, 50 years after the first spirit ran from its pot stills, a 100 percent Spanish single malt was launched.

It wasn't Spain's first single malt, however. That honor goes to Embrujo, which is distilled at Destilerias Liber in Padul near Granada. Using snow-melt water from the Sierra Nevada, distillation is in two unusual flat-bottomed copper stills, while aging is in, logically enough, ex-sherry casks made from American oak. The brainchild

of Fran Peregrino, the whisky is a fusing of Scottish technique with Spanish influence. "I took decisions which would influence how the whisky would taste: the design of the stills, the choice of the barrels for aging," says Peregrino. "But there are other elements which you cannot do anything about, like the water and the climate. Here, we alternate between freezing winters and hot summers, which gives our whisky its own character and personality."

The market for Scotch blends in Spain is now crashing as a new generation moves to rum, but the sales of single malts are on the rise. Maybe once again, Spanish distillers are in the right place at the right time.

The Sierra Nevada is the backdrop to Spain's newest whisky distillery, Liber.

LIBER TASTING NOTES

EMBRUJO 40%

Nose: Youthful and almost grassy freshness matched by rich, nutty sherry notes. Amontillado-style. Green walnut, madrono (aromatic fruit related to the mangosteen), then cereal. With water, some malted milk and toffee.

Palate: Roasted malty notes add interest to the dried fruit and nut notes from the oak. The effect is of elements coming together. Clean spirit.

Finish: Light, then a final squeeze of raisin juice.

Conclusion: Still young, but has the guts to develop in the long term.

Flavor Camp: Rich & Round
Where Next?: Macallan 10yo Sherry Oak

SOUTH AFRICA

JAMES SEDGWICK DISTILLERY • WELLINGTON • WWW.DISTELL.CO.ZA
DRAYMAN'S • PRETORIA • WWW.DRAYMANS.COM

For some inexplicable reason, some countries have a strange tendency to look down on their own native spirit. Cognac sells more in export than in France; vodka is Scotland's top-selling spirit; rum outsells brandy in Spain. Overlooking the domestic in favor of the allure of the imported also results in many consumers never realizing the quality of the spirits being made in their own backyard. South Africa is a case in point.

Although South Africa is a hot whisky market, thanks to the adoption of blended Scotch by the "Black Diamonds"—those who make up democratic South Africa's emergent black middle class—South Africans have tended to be rather dismissive of their own whiskies.

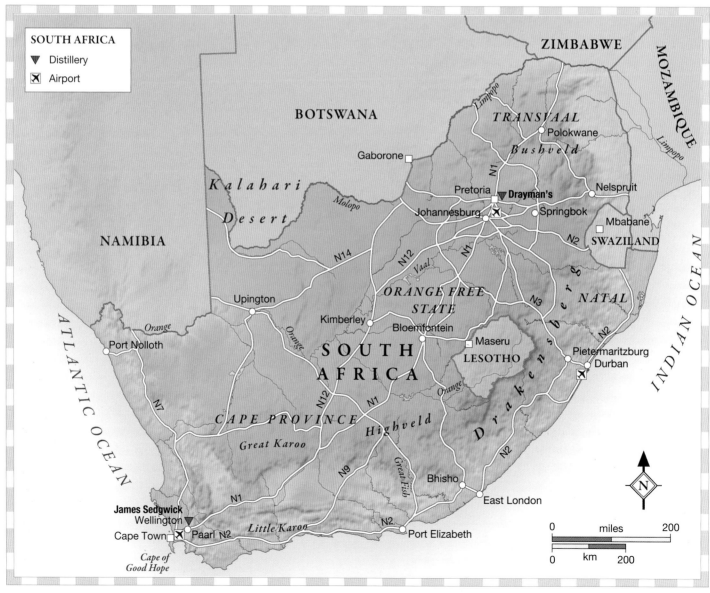

SOUTH AFRICA
▼ Distillery
☒ Airport

Grand visions. After many false starts, South Africa's whisky industry (here at the James Sedgwick distillery) is now on the move.

While best-known for its brandy production, whisky has been made here since the late nineteenth century. A certain A. H. Nellmapius began distilling at his Hetherly farm west of Pretoria, although production was stopped by the second Boer War. It wasn't until 1952 that whisky was made once more, but the pioneering Tops distillery foundered as a result of the preferential treatment given to brandy: whisky was taxed at a 200 percent higher rate.

South Africa's first modern brand, Three Ships, was launched by owner Distell in 1977. It was a blend of local grain spirit and Scotch, sourced from Morrison Bowmore. Today, distiller Andy Watts oversees not only a larger distillery, the James Sedgwick plant in Wellington, but uses local grain and malt for the blend.

Although "international blends" are still produced, Watts has been slowly and quietly introducing 100 percent South African whiskies, such as the limited release of a single malt into the Three Ships range—and picking up international awards with the results.

Watts' newest creation, Bain's Cape Mountain Grain, is specifically aimed at the new whisky-drinking market. "There are many more female and black consumers trying whisky," he says. "They naturally have a slightly sweeter taste profile: hence the idea to release a single grain." Given double maturation in first-fill American oak, it's a lush drink.

"This is the start of Cape Mountain whisky," says Watts, "and we feel that the fact that it is a different style gives it the possibility to appeal to a far wider audience of potential first-time whisky-drinkers. In the past, we've suffered from a perception that whisky (or at least good whisky) can't be made in South Africa. Fortunately, through the help of international tastings and the hugely successful *Whisky Live!* shows in South Africa, the public are becoming more educated, and the perceptions are slowly being changed." Certainly, anyone who has witnessed the exuberant delights of the consumer fairs (at the time of writing the largest such events in the world) can have little doubt of the new South Africa's thirst for whisky in all its forms.

Another distiller has joined Watts in his drive to appeal to the new whisky consumer. In 2007, Moritz Kallmeyer, who ran the successful Drayman's microbrewery in Pretoria, branched out into distilling. His approach to whisky production is both analytical and idiosyncratic, a fusing of brewing techniques: thick mash, beer yeasts, temperature-controlled fermentations, followed by distillation in a remarkable still he designed and built from scrap. The results are aged in small casks and show remarkable quality even at this early stage in their evolution. No doubt promising times ahead.

SOUTH AFRICA TASTING NOTES

BAIN'S CAPE MOUNTAIN GRAIN WHISKY, 46%

Nose: Rich gold. Very sweet with a light, grassy back note. Fudge, mashed banana, and butterscotch with a piney twang.

Palate: Light but succulently sweet. Quite chewy. Ice cream, soft fruit in the middle, then a blast of citrus fruit.

Finish: Cinnamon.

Conclusion: Balanced and characterful. Will appeal to a new (and older) consumer.

Flavor Camp: **Fruity & Spicy**
Where Next: Nikka Coffey Grain

DRAYMANS 2007, CASK NO. 4 CASK SAMPLE

Nose: Spicy and clean. Touches of cardamom, coriander, and straw but also a concentrated persimmon jelly note in the background.

Palate: Very scented and lifted. Rose petal before light cereal comes through.

Finish: Clean and perfumed.

Conclusion: All of the whiskies are clean and scented, showing yet another intriguing development of the whisky palette.

Flavor Camp: **Fragrant & Floral**
Where Next: Aalt-a-Bhainne, Lark LD116

INDIA & THE FAR EAST

The Asian market has long been a fertile ground for the Scotch industry. Here, as in other countries, whisky has acquired a certain cachet as a drink that indicates success, one that gives the drinker a degree of status. In Taiwan, for example, blended Scotch—especially top-end blended Scotch—has long been the drink of choice in what is referred to as the "traditional on-trade": the restaurants and hostess bars frequented by older businessmen. In the past decade, however, consumption has changed significantly in Taiwan with the emergence of the "modern on-trade": Western-style bars frequented by younger people of both sexes.

When this generational shift occurs in most markets, the dominant spirit goes into steep decline, witness the fall of blended Scotch in Spain (or, indeed, Scotland), for example. Taiwan, however, moved in a wholly unexpected direction. The new generation of drinkers didn't just take up vodka, they turned to malt whisky, both vatted malts such as Famous Grouse and single malts. And while there have been some dramatic shifts in the fortunes of individual brands, the predicted volatility of the market has not occurred. Malt whisky has become cool.

It is little surprise then that Taiwan now has its own whisky distillery and a brand, Kavalan, whose precociousness at a young age, thanks to the effects of tropical aging, is winning plaudits around the world.

The generational shift towards whisky seen in Taiwan on paper seems to be replicated in China, where sales are booming. It is not surprising that brand owners are excited by China. Here is a previously untapped market of 1.3 billion people, where there are 11 cities with populations over two million and 23 cities with populations between one and two million. It is the potential of China (and the other Brazil, Russia, and India markets) that prompted the building of Diageo's Roseisle distillery (*see* p.94).

The success enjoyed by Diageo in China is not necessarily replicated across the board. The growth in Scotch whisky has come from the only two players who can afford to build premium

The hills around Bangalore are home to India's best-known single malt: Amrut.

brands in what is a huge and vastly expensive market: Diageo (through Johnnie Walker) and Chivas Brothers (primarily through Chivas Regal). Meanwhile, in American whiskey, only Jack Daniel's is spending significantly in China, although it cannot be long before Beam does the same. Although other brands can see the potential that lies within China, the cost of entry is currently too high.

If, however, whisky does emerge as a genuinely mass-market spirit category in these countries, then it can only be a matter of time before there are Chinese whiskies being made.

Elsewhere in Asia, Korea remains the premium blended-Scotch market par excellence, while Vietnam and Thailand (the former a new and exciting market, the other an established one) are both showing growth. We could well see domestic whiskies from all.

The market with the greatest potential is India, where, as we will see, imported whisky's progress has been stalled because of legal and taxation issues. India is a whisky-drinking market and a whisky producer. It, too, has begun to attract critical praise for the quality of its single malt, particularly in the export-oriented brand Amrut, which was launched in the UK before it appeared in India. Like Kavalan, the benefits of tropical aging allow this to reach full maturity at a young age—another piece of the increasingly complex world whisky jigsaw.

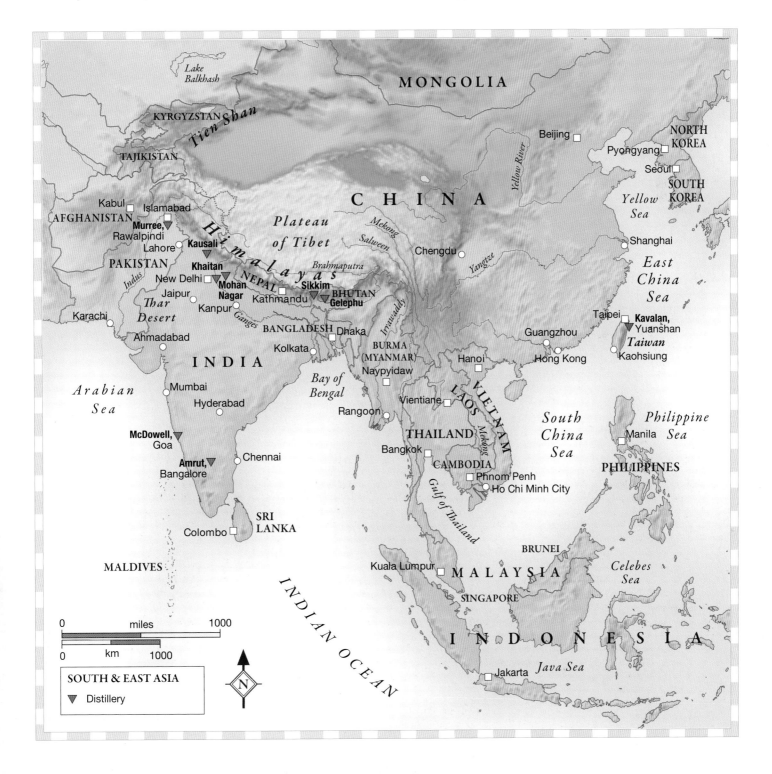

India

AMRUT • BANGALORE • WWW.AMRUTDISTILLERIES.COM

India is a whisky-drinking nation, but most of its domestic brands are a mix of molasses-based spirit and Scotch. The refusal of the world to recognize molasses-based spirit as whisky has hardened the Indian government's line on levying high taxes on imported spirits. Although this rate has dropped significantly recently, each state within India has the power to raise its own taxes, so the tariff has just been collected by another revenue office. The result? Scotch's biggest potential market is effectively closed off, and while both sides feel that a settlement can be reached, negotiations are moving as quickly as a Himalayan glacier.

India does make real whisky, however, as does Pakistan's Murree distillery, claimed to be the only distillery in a Muslim country. High in the foothills of the Himalayas is Mohan Meakin's Kasauli distillery, while the same firm operates the Mohan Nagar plant in the state of Uttar Pradesh, also home to Radico Khaitan's Rampur plant. All are plants making molasses and grain spirit. There are also two dedicated malt sites: McDowell's in Ponda, Goa, and the Indian single malt that is best-known internationally, Bangalore's Amrut.

Here's a single malt that is a perfect case study in how location influences character. Amrut's unpeated barley comes from Rajasthan (any peated component is Scottish), and while distillation is standard—although in stills whose pinched waists make them seem like tightly corseted Victorian ladies—it is what happens when the whisky is placed in a mix of new and first-fill American oak casks that sets Amrut apart from all the rest.

Although Bangalore is situated at 3,000 feet (915m), its summer temperatures range between 68–97°F (20–36°C) and winter is between 63–81°F (17–27°C), while the monsoon season also has an impact. The effect is seen first in the rate of evaporation. In Scotland, the "angels" receive on average 2 percent per annum in volume; in Bangalore up to 16 percent of the volume of the cask will disappear into the ether every year. This tropical aging means that the whole maturation

Amrut has established itself in export before launching on its home market.

process is speeded up, resulting in the oily, saffron, and corn-accented new make becoming mead-like within two years and with integrated coconut and even leather (a classic mature note) characters at five years.

Speed is one thing; achieving balance is the key. It is here, by holding excessive oakiness at bay while also allowing immature edginess to be smoothed away, that Amrut's success lies. It has rapidly (what else?) become an international talking point. Maybe its success may persuade the warring parties that Indian all-malt whisky does, in fact, have a future.

AMRUT TASTING NOTES

NEW MAKE

Nose: Sweet mash, linseed oil, saffron, lightly earthy with a corn note and powdered chalk.
Palate: Oily and thick, with some red fruit, a sweet pepperiness, and a touch of hyssop and violet. Angular.
Finish: Tight.

FUSION 50%

Nose: Integrated oak notes of mocha, coconut, light vanilla bean, nutmeg, toasted hazelnut, macadamia, and a little ginger. A very distant touch of fragrant wood smoke (sandalwood incense?).
Palate: The fruit on the new make is now plump and starting to be stewed. Cacao and that supple (mature) leathery note. Balanced and lightly smoked.
Finish: Paprika and citrus fruit.
Conclusion: Maximum five years of age and perfectly balanced.

Flavor Camp: **Fruity & Spicy**
Where Next? Balblair 1990

Taiwan

KAVALAN • YUANSHAN TOWNSHIP, YILAN COUNTY • WWW.KAVALANWHISKY.COM

The effects of tropical aging are also seen to great effect in Taiwan, the newest member of the global whisky family. The reasons for building Kavalan, Taiwan's first dedicated whisky distillery, in this spot are pretty obvious when you consider that Taiwan is currently the sixth-largest market for Scotch whisky in the world—and that the market itself is changing significantly over the past decade as a new generation of drinkers have adopted Scotch single malt.

Construction of the distillery, which is owned by food and beverage conglomerate King Car, started in April 2005 with commissioning (inevitably) by Forsyth's of Rothes, which got it up and running by March 11, 2006, "At 3:30pm!" says blender Yu-Lan "Ian" Chang.

"The site was chosen for two reasons," he says: "the natural reservoir of spring water from the Shue-Shan mountains which lies underneath the distillery and the fact that about 75 percent of the land in I-Lan is mountainous, giving clean air which is perfect for the maturation of the spirits."

Chang had a clear flavor line in his mind from the outset, triggered initially by the mix of yeasts pitched into the fermenters. "They're a mix of commercially available and our own, and help create the fruity character—mango, green apple, and cherry—which is the signature of Kavalan new-make spirit."

After double distillation, that fruity new make is aged in a complex mix of woods chosen by the man Chang refers to as his mentor, Dr Jim Swan. "It's he who guides me to source and set up our complicated but necessary wood policy, which I'd say is the real secret of success behind Kavalan," says Chang. "I personally believe that with the subtropical climate of Taiwan, plus a multi-variety wood policy, we can achieve something that is unique to us."

The proof is in the bottle. Under Taiwanese law, whisky can be released as such after a period of merely two years, although the first Kavalan brands did have an extra year on them. All show the

The waters of Sun Moon lake may be tranquil but Kavalan whisky is already making waves internationally.

effects of tropical aging in their characters—which is significantly different to forced rapid maturation. The oak is integrated and balanced with the spirit, and the range of cask types allows Chang to be able to play many riffs on his central theme.

KAVALAN TASTING NOTES

SINGLE MALT 40%
Nose: Orange and ginseng tea, with honeycomb and a lightly tarry note. With water, becomes fruity: cherry and some anise.
Palate: Thick and sweet, with lots of mulberry jam notes, black cherry, and a little charcoal. Nuts behind. Tannins provide some grip.
Finish: Tight and nutty.
Conclusion: Fresh but rich. A lot going on in this mix.

Flavor Camp: Rich & Round
Where Next? Arran 1996

PORT CASK FINISH 40%
Nose: Blueberries and rich oak. Has the balance of Solist but the tropical fruit has been taken in a different direction by the use of the port casks which add a jammy but juicy note. Rosehip and *crème de mures*.
Palate: Very sweet, with the black-cherry note seen on the standard Kavalan re-emerging. Thick and liquorous.
Finish: Sloe berry. Sweet.
Conclusion: It's full-on but works.

Flavor Camp: Rich & Round
Where Next? Glenfiddich 15yo

SOLIST SINGLE CASK, EX-BOURBON 58.8%
Nose: Sweet and pure, with corn syrup and soft fruits: mango, melon, and guava cut with ginger and kumquat. Touch of peanut and sandalwood. A hit of sweet sawdust suggests youth.
Palate: Sweet and fruity spirit that's been balanced by classic American oak flavors of ice cream, *crème brûlée*, and spice.
Finish: Custard-like, with canned pineapple.
Conclusion: Sweet and sassy. New malt personified.

Flavor Camp: Fruity & Spicy
Where Next? Glen Moray-style

AUSTRALIA

BAKERY HILL • NORTH BALWYN, VICTORIA • WWW.BAKERYHILLDISTILLERY.COM.AU • COURSES BY ARRANGEMENT
GREAT SOUTHERN • ALBANY, WA • WWW.DISTILLERY.COM.AU • OPEN ALL YEAR • CELLAR DOOR & COFFEE LOUNGE
LARK • HOBART, TASMANIA • WWW.LARKDISTILLERY.COM.AU • ESCORTED TOURS BY ARRANGEMENT
THE NANT • BOTHWELL, TASMANIA • WWW.NANTDISTILLERY.COM.AU • OPEN ALL YEAR • BY ARRANGEMENT
SULLIVAN'S COVE • CAMBRIDGE, TASMANIA • WWW.TASMANIADISTILLERY.COM

The most surprising thing about the Australian whisky boom is that it has taken so long to happen. This, after all, is a country which was widely settled by ex-Scots, is rich in malting barley, and culturally is known to like a drink. In typical Aussie style, however, now that the single-malt distilling boom has started, it has rapidly achieved the same momentum that the nation's modern wine industry had in the 1980s.

Legislation might have had something to do with the lack of legal small-scale whisky production, as Bill Lark, the pioneer of the new single-malt industry discovered. The permanently optimistic Lark is based in Tasmania, Australia's whisky-making center, and his whisky-making story starts like so many of the small distillers around the world: over a bottle of single-malt Scotch while fishing.

Inspired after one such fishing trip, he bought a small still, studied distilling at Roseworthy College, and then tried to get a license. "Bugger me," he recalls, "the guy pulled out the *Licensing Act* of 1901 and told me that stills had to be a minimum of 713 gallons (2,700 liters)." Nothing if not determined, he lobbied the whisky-loving minister of agriculture and got the law changed. His small still was fired up in 1992.

As with all the Aussie distillers, the grounding principle is local. The whisky is made from Franklin brewing barley, bred to suit Tasmania's climate, which gives an added oiliness to the spirit. He then peats some of it—with Tasmanian peat. Because peat is decomposed vegetation, its composition changes depending on

The sands of Albany may soon be the setting for Limeburners' beach barbecues.

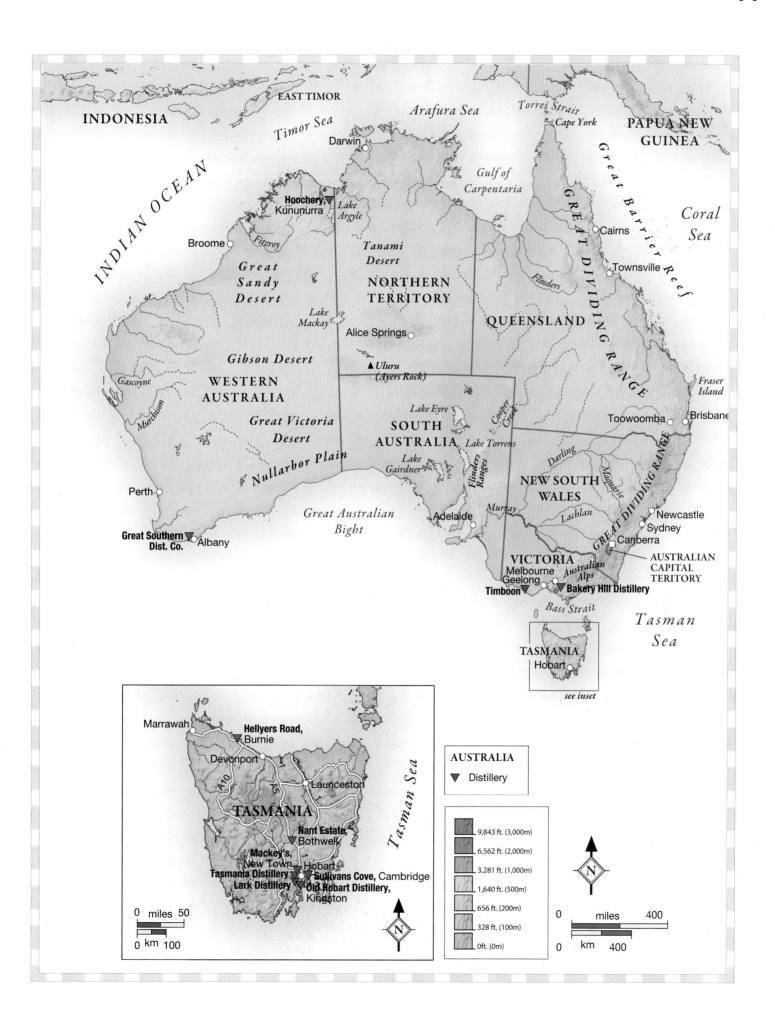

INDONESIA

EAST TIMOR

Timor Sea

Arafura Sea

Torres Strait

Cape York

PAPUA NEW
GUINEA

Darwin

Hoochery,
Kununurra ▼
*Lake
Argyle*

*Coral
Sea*

Cairns

INDIAN OCEAN

Broome

Fitzroy

*Great
Sandy
Desert*

*Tanami
Desert*

NORTHERN
TERRITORY

Flinders

*Gulf of
Carpentaria*

GREAT DIVIDING RANGE

Townsville

Great Barrier Reef

Gascoyne

Gibson Desert

WESTERN
AUSTRALIA

*Lake
Mackay*

Alice Springs

QUEENSLAND

Murchison

*Great Victoria
Desert*

▲*Uluru
(Ayers Rock)*

*Fraser
Island*

Lake Eyre

Cooper Creek

Toowoomba

Brisbane

SOUTH
AUSTRALIA

Lake Torrens

*Lake
Gairdner*

*Flinders
Ranges*

Darling

Macquarie

NEW SOUTH
WALES

Lachlan

Nullarbor Plain

Perth

*Great Australian
Bight*

Adelaide

Murray

GREAT DIVIDING RANGE

Newcastle
Sydney
Canberra

**Great Southern
Dist. Co.** ▼ Albany

VICTORIA

*Australian
Alps*

AUSTRALIAN
CAPITAL
TERRITORY

Melbourne
Geelong

Timboon ▼

▼ **Bakery Hill Distillery**

Bass Strait

*Tasman
Sea*

TASMANIA

Hobart

see inset

Marrawah

Hellyers Road,
Burnie ▼

Devonport

Launceston

A10

A5

TASMANIA

Nant Estate,
Bothwell ▼

Tasman Sea

Mackey's,
New Town
Tasmania Distillery ▼
Lark Distillery ▼

Hobart
▼ **Sullivans Cove,** Cambridge
▼ **Old Hobart Distillery,**
Kingston

AUSTRALIA

▼ Distillery

	9,843 ft. (3,000m)
	6,562 ft. (2,000m)
	3,281 ft. (1,000m)
	1,640 ft. (500m)
	656 ft. (200m)
	328 ft. (100m)
	0ft. (0m)

0 miles 50

0 km 100

N

0 miles 400

0 km 400

N

what grew in the region in the past—Tasmania's is high in eucalyptus and other unique microflora. This, Lark feels, is what gives it such an intense, fragrant aroma: juniper, moss, and gum-tree oil. The yeasts, after years of trialing, are a mix of a Nottingham ale yeast and a distiller's strain.

The whisky itself—oily and floral as an unpeated new make, more scented with the smoke added—is double-distilled in his own pot design. It is released as single-barrel bottlings from a mix of small ex-Australian "port" and "sherry" casks. For all Lark's happy-go-lucky demeanor, he and his daughter, Kirsty, are serious distillers with a focus on quality.

Patrick Maguire, head of Hobart's Sullivan's Cove distillery, is a former alumnus of Lark's. He started at Sullivan's Cove in 1999, and when in 2003 the second set of owners pulled out, Maguire joined with his business partners to take over the business. Here, distillation takes place in a (Tasmanian-built) French brandy still design and produces a very floral, sweet, and full-flavored spirit with notes of lime blossom and allspice. There's no chill-filtering, no caramel, and aging takes place in ex-bourbon and some ex-port French oak.

"The soils our barley is grown in contribute subtle unique flavors," says Maguire. "Also the water takes on the flavors of the rainforest so the flavors of the Australian bush come through, especially since there is no peat in our whisky."

The focus here is solely on whisky-making. One of Maguire's first acts was to close the visitors' center. "We have taken a different approach. We had to," he says. "We are a very small company with no money, producing a product in a country not known for producing whisky. We understand potential consumers will be skeptical, so we have tried to produce the best spirit we could."

Visitor numbers are, however, vital to Keith Batt's vision for his Nant distillery in Bothwell, high in Tasmania's Highlands. Batt bought the old country estate, complete with convict flour mill, in 2004; just like in Scotland, where there's a mill, there's a way to make whisky.

"We thought it could be a worthwhile venture provided we could combine it with a tourism operation to take us through to when the whisky was ready for bottling," says Batt. Former

brewer Chris Condon is the distiller and uses malt sourced from the local Cascade brewery, although Batt's vision is to become self-sufficient. "I guess in the same way that the early settlers came to Nant, we wanted to produce a whisky that was developed with that same pioneering spirit." The whisky is rich and sweet, with a deep, black-fruit character and that lift of aromatics that seems to link these whiskies at an early stage in their lives.

Mark Littler, based at Burnie in Tasmania's northwest, runs what is currently Australia's largest single-malt operation, Hellyer's Road, which is located on the site of an old dairy facility. Again, local barley and peat are used, while maturation is in American oak.

AUSTRALIA TASTING NOTES

BAKERY HILL, DOUBLE WOOD 46%

Nose: Amber. Fruitcake and nutmeg. Lemons and scented oak. Sherried. Young spirit with a good, fresh delivery and the beginnings of an interesting integrated character.

Palate: Plenty of wood extract. Creamy and banana-like, then white raisins. Sweet underneath it all. Has the weight to cope with wood.

Finish: Clean and young.

Conclusion: Balanced and clean.

Flavor Camp: Fruity & Spicy
Where Next? Glen Garioch-style

GREAT SOUTHERN, LIMEBURNERS BARREL 43 43%

Nose: Light amber. Young and fresh, with cereal and a suet-like note. Touch of wax and raisin and sweet ginger.

Palate: The suet pudding continues, then sweet persimmon. Clean and, again, well-made. Dry and crisp.

Finish: Vibrant and fresh.

Conclusion: Young, direct but coming together.

Flavor Camp: Malty & Dry
Where Next? Aultmore-style

LARK SINGLE CASK LD 126 43%

Nose: Old gold. Clean oak. Initially some fresh grist, then a lifted floral, aromatic quality followed by vanilla and black fruit. Grows more complex with time and water and picks up the lily note from the new make.

Palate: Masses of creamy wood. Still fragrant and clean, with the Lark thickness anchoring the flavors, but now given a light grip from oak.

Finish: Fresh and clean.

Conclusion: Well-distilled. One to watch.

Flavor Camp: Fragrant & Floral
Where Next? Hazelburn CV

Working with tall stills to help capture light, fragrant esters he sees his whisky as the result of scientific rigor allied to an element of mystery. "From the very beginning, I've had a mental picture of what I was looking for," Baker explains. "For every step in putting together my distillery there seems to have been an unseen internal force that has been quietly and persistently directing my actions. From that very first decision that I really wanted to make bloody fine malt, the driving force has been to do things differently—not to end up as another 'me too.'"

The whisky-making bug has also spread to the cool maritime climate of Albany, Western Australia, where the Great Southern distillery's Limeburners brand is distilled. Great Southern was started in 2004 by lawyer Cameron Syme, who spent four years searching for the right site. "I found it here," he says: "abundant limestone water from deep local aquifers, peat bogs in the nearby Porongurup Mountain Range, and some of the world's best malting barley." The malt used is a pale brewing malt from Kirin's malting plant in Perth.

"It's a beer malt instead of a distilling malt," says Syme. "While our yield is not as high, we believe that this translates into the fantastic flavor profiles in our whisky." The stills look remarkably like some in a distillery close to Craigellachie in Scotland. Although tiny, they are set up here to produce a light, sweet, and floral new make—with Albany peat. Maturation takes place in a mix of woods: ex-bourbon, ex-Australian sherry and port (cut down to 26 and 53 gallons/100 and 200 liters), and ex-wine barrels which have been decharred and recharred.

In these early days, is it possible to say that an Australian style is emerging? "It would seem that the philosophy of the Australian distilleries is to focus on quality, not quantity," says Nant's Batt. "The climate is a big factor. Faster maturations are possible due to the higher temperatures and greater daily fluctuations. As more distilleries start to use native peat, and necessity forces innovative use of different casks, more local character will evolve."

If these early releases are an indication of the future, then Australia is going to be a new whisky country to watch closely.

If Tasmania is setting itself up as the lodestone of the new Australian industry, there are a growing number of distilleries on the mainland, such as Bakery Hill in Bayswater on the Dadenong foothills of Victoria, which was started by David Baker in 1999.

"I got into single malts because I was just so sick to death of all the Scotch whisky distillers and their marketers telling me and the rest of the world that 'The only place that can ever make good malt whisky is Scotland,'" he says. "From the very beginning I was not out to make yet another Scotch whisky style. Surely it's time for a truly regional malt whisky that reflects all the character and differences from its place of origin within Australia."

NANT, 1ST RELEASE 45.5%

Nose: Ruby. Oak-driven. Quite oily. Highly polished oak, new leather (expensive shoe store). Clean spirit. Sweet. Moves into marmalade. Lots of powerful wood. Candied cherry and nut.

Palate: Big extract. Quite grippy. Black cherry and some chocolate. Full and sweet and needs water. Quite grippy but sweet and citric. Chunky spirit.

Finish: Lightly bitter.

Conclusion: Precocious, thanks to an active cask. Good spirit.

Flavor Camp: Rich & Round
Where Next? Balmenach-style

SULLIVAN'S COVE, HH0104, BOURBON CASK 60%

Nose: Sawdust with a light earthiness, wood sap. Develops well with water, with plenty of vanilla ice cream, lime blossom, privet hedge. Firm spirit.

Palate: Sweet and direct. The spirit at cask strength is forceful but has an inherent sweet character: light-brown sugar, allspice, berries, and pepper.

Finish: Firm.

Conclusion: Fresh and characterful.

Flavor Camp: Fruity & Spicy
Where Next? Hazelburn-style

FLAVOR CAMP LISTS

As you have seen, each of the whiskies tasted (except new makes) have been allocated a Flavor Camp rating, allowing you to browse happily within the style or styles of drams you particularly enjoy. By looking through these, you can also see how the influence of oak and time can shift a distillery from one camp into another. Obviously there are variations within these camps, but all the whiskies in each share a dominant commonality of flavor. *See also* p.26 for more detail and the Flavor Map™ on pp.28–9 in the What is Whisky? section at the front of the book.

FRUITY & SPICY

The fruit we are talking about here is ripe orchard fruit such as peach and apricot, maybe even something more exotic like mango. These whiskies will also show the vanilla, coconut, custard-like aromas of American oak. The spiciness is found on the finish and tends to be sweet—like cinnamon or nutmeg.

Scotland *Single malt*
Aberfeldy 12yo
Aberfeldy 21yo
Arran 10yo
Auchentoshan 21yo
Balblair 1990
Balblair 1975
Balmenach 1993
Balmenach 1979
Balvenie 12yo Signature
Balvenie 12yo Double Wood
Balvenie 21yo PortWood
Balvenie 30yo
Ben Nevis 10yo
Ben Nevis 15yo
BenRiach 12yo
BenRiach 16yo
BenRiach 21yo
Benromach 10yo
Benromach 25yo
Bruichladdich 2002
Bruichladdich 16yo
Cardhu 12yo
Craigellachie 14yo
Craigellachie 1994
Clynelish 14yo
Clynelish 1997, Manager's Choice
Dalmore 12yo
Dalwhinnie 15yo
Dalwhinnie Distiller's Edition
Dalwhinnie 1992 Manager's Choice
Dalwhinnie 1986, 20yo Special Rel.
Deanston 12yo

Deanston 28yo
Edradour 1996 Oloroso Finish
Glencadam 15yo
Glendullan 12yo
The Singleton of Glendullan 12yo
Glen Elgin 12yo
Glenfiddich 21yo
Glen Garioch 12yo
Glengoyne 10yo
Glenkinchie Distiller's Edition
The Glenlivet 15yo
The Glenlivet 1972 Cellar
    Collection
Glenmorangie The Original 10yo
Glenmorangie 18yo
Glenmorangie 25yo
Glen Moray Classic NAS
Glen Moray 12yo
Glen Moray 16yo
Glen Moray 30yo
Glenrothes Select Reserve NAS
Hazelburn 12yo
Inchgower 14yo
Kilkerran 2004
Loch Lomond, 1966 Stills
Longmorn 10yo
Longmorn 16yo
Longmorn 1977
Longmorn 33yo
Macallan 10yo Fine Oak
Macallan 15yo Fine Oak
Macallan 18yo Fine Oak
Macallan 25yo Fine Oak

Mannochmore 18yo
    Special Release
Oban 14yo
Old Pulteney 12yo
Old Pulteney 17yo
Old Pulteney 30yo
Old Pulteney 40yo
Royal Brackla 25yo
Royal Lochnagar 12yo
Scapa 16yo
Scapa 1979
Strathisla 18yo
Tamdhu 32yo
Tomatin 1980
Tormore 12yo

Scotland *Blend*
Chivas Regal 18yo
Dewar's White Label
Dewar's 12yo
Dewar's Signature
Grant's Family Reserve

Ireland *Blend*
Jameson 12yo
Kilbeggan 15yo
Power's 12yo

Japan *Malt*
Hanyu Mizunara
Miyagikyo 15yo
Miyagikyo 1990 18yo
Yamazaki 12yo

Japan *Grain*
Miyagikyo, 6 Nikka Single Cask
    Coffey Malt

Japan *Blend*
Hibiki 12yo
Hibiki 17yo
Nikka, From the Barrel

Rest of the World *Malt*
Amrut Fusion *India*
Bakery Hill Double Wood *Australia*
The Belgian Owl *Belgium*
Brauenstein e:1 *Denmark*
Glann ar Mor *France*
Kavalan Solist Single Cask *Taiwan*
Mackmyra Swedish Oak Reserve
    2006 *Sweden*
Millstone 5yo *Holland*
St. George Californian Single
    Malt *USA*
Stranahan's Colorado Straight Single
    Malt *USA*
Sullivan's Cove HH0104 *Australia*

Rest of the World *Grain*
Bain's Cape Mountain *South Africa*

Rest of the World *Blend*
Kittling Ridge, Forty Creek Premium
    Barrel Select *Canada*

FRAGRANT & FLORAL

The aromas found in these whiskies bring to mind fresh-cut flowers, fruit blossom, cut grass, and light green fruit. On the palate they are light, slightly sweet, and often show a fresh acidity.

Scotland *Single malt*
Allt-a-Bhainne 1991
Ardmore 1977, 30yo
anCnoc 16yo
Aultmore 12yo
Bladnoch 8yo

Bladnoch 17yo
Braeval 8yo
Glenburgie 12yo
Glenburgie 15yo
Glencadam 10yo
Glendullan 12yo

Glenfiddich 12yo
Glenglassaugh 1983
Glen Grant 10yo
Glen Grant 1992 Cellar Reserve
Glenkinchie 12yo
Glenkinchie 1992, Manager's Ch.

The Glenlivet 12yo
Glenlossie 1999 Manager's Choice
Glentauchers 1991
Glenturret 10yo
Hazelburn CV
Linkwood 12yo

Loch Lomond 29yo
Mannochmore 12yo
Miltonduff 18yo
Miltonduff 1976
Royal Brackla 15yo
Speyburn 10yo
Speyside 15yo
Strathisla 12yo
Strathmill 12yo
Teaninich 10yo
Tomatin 1997
Tomatin 1990
Tomintoul 14yo
Tormore 1996
Tullibardine 2004, Aged Oak

Scotland *Blend*
Chivas Regal 12yo
Johnnie Walker Red Label

Ireland *Malt*
Bushmills 10yo

Ireland *Blend*
Bushmills Original
Jameson Original

Japan *Malt*
Chichibu 2008 Newborn
Fuji Sanroku 18yo
Fuji-Gotemba 18yo

Hakushu 12yo
Hakushu 18yo
Yamazaki 10yo

Japan *Blend*
Nikka Super

Rest of the World *Malt*
Blaue Maus 1989 *Germany*
Drayman's Cask 2007 *South Africa*
Elsasser *France*
The English Whisky Co, Chapter 6
   England
Hedgehog *France*
Lark Single Cask LD 126 *Australia*

Mackmyra Special 03 *Sweden*
Mackmyra 1st Edition *Sweden*
P&M Superior *France/Corsica*
Penderyn Madeira *Wales*
Slyrs 2006 *Germany*

Rest of the World *Blend*
Valleyfield, VO Gold *Canada*

Rest of the World *Grain*
Radermacher, Lambertus 10yo

RICH & ROUND

There is fruit here as well, but now it is dried: raisins, figs, dates, and white raisins. This shows the use of European oak ex-sherry casks. You might detect a slightly finer feel; that's the tannin from the oak. These are deep whiskies, sometimes sweet, sometimes meaty.

Scotland *Single malt*
Aberlour 10yo
Aberlour 16yo
Aberlour 1990
Aberlour 25yo
Aberlour a'bunadh
Arran 5yo
Arran 1996 Single Cask
Aultmore 16yo, Dewar Rattray
Balvenie 17yo Madeira Cask
Ben Nevis 25yo
Benrinnes 15yo
Benrinnes 23yo
Benromach 1981
Blair Athol 12yo
Bunnahabhain 16yo
Bunnahabhain 34yo
Cragganmore 12yo
Cragganmore 1997, Manager's Ch.
Dalmore 15yo
Dalmore 1981 Matusalem
Dailuaine 16yo
Dalmore, Candela 50yo
The Singleton of Dufftown 12yo
Edradour 1997

Fettercairn 16yo
Fettercairn 21yo
Fettercairn 30yo
Glenallachie 18yo
Glencadam 1978
GlenDronach 12yo
GlenDronach 15yo
GlenDronach 1989
Glenfarclas 10yo
Glenfarclas 15yo
Glenfarclas 30yo
Glenfiddich 15yo
Glenfiddich 18yo
Glenfiddich 30yo
Glenfiddich 40yo
Glengoyne 17yo
Glengoyne 21yo
Glen Grant 25yo
The Glenlivet 18yo
The Singleton of Glen Ord 12yo
Glenrothes 1991
Glenrothes 1978
Highland Park 18yo
Highland Park 25yo
Jura 16yo

Jura 21yo
Macallan 10yo Sherry Oak
Macallan 18yo Sherry Oak
Macallan 25yo Sherry Oak
Mortlach 16yo
Royal Lochnagar Selected Reserve
Speyburn 21yo
Springbank 15yo
Springbank 18yo
Strathisla 25yo
Tamdhu 18yo
Tamnavulin 1973
Tamnavulin 1966
Tobermory 15yo
Tobermory 32yo
Tomintoul 33yo
Tullibardine 1988 John Black

Scotland *Blend*
Grant's 25yo
Johnnie Walker Black Label
Johnnie Walker Blue Label

Ireland *Malt/Pot still*
Bushmills 16yo

Bushmills 21yo
Redbreast 12yo
Redbreast 15yo
Tyrconnell 10yo Madeira

Ireland *Blend*
Black Bush
Bushmills
Jameson 18yo

Japan *Malt*
Hakushu 25yo
Karuizawa 1985
Karuizawa 1995 Noh Series
Yamazaki 18yo

Rest of the World
Sloupisti 2008 *Germany*
Liber, Embrujo *Spain*
Kavalan Single Malt *Taiwan*
Kavalan Port Cask Finish *Taiwan*
Millstone 8yo *Holland*
Nant 1st Release *Australia*
Penderyn Sherrywood *Wales*

SMOKY & PEATY

These offer a whole range of different aromas, from soot to lapsang souchong tea, tar, kippers, smoked bacon, burning heather, and wood smoke. Often sightly oily in texture, all peaty whiskies must have a balancing sweet spot.

Scotland *Malt*
Ardbeg 10yo
Ardbeg Airigh nam Beist 1990
Ardbeg Lord of the Isles 25yo
Ardmore Traditional Cask

Ardmore 25yo
BenRiach Curiositas 10yo
Bowmore Legend
Bowmore 12yo
Bowmore 15yo Darkest

Bruichladdich, Octomore 5yo
Bruichladdich, Port Charlotte PC8
Caol Ila 12yo
Caol Ila 18yo
Glen Scotia 12yo

Highland Park 12yo
Highland Park 40yo
Kilchoman Inaugural Release 3yo
Lagavulin 12yo
Lagavulin 16yo

Lagavulin Manager's Choice
Lagavulin Distiller's Edition
Laphroaig 10yo
Laphroaig 18yo
Laphroaig 25yo
Longrow 14yo
Longrow CV
Springbank 10yo

Talisker 10yo
Talisker 18yo
Talisker 25yo
Talisker 1994 Manager's
  Choice

Ireland *Malt*
Connemara 12yo

Japan *Malt*
Chichibu 2008 Newborn
The Cask of Hakushu
Yoichi 10yo
Yoichi 12yo
Yoichi 15yo
Yoichi 20yo
Yoichi 1986 22yo

Rest of the World *Malt*
Clear Creek, McCarthy's Oregon
  Single Malt *USA*
Glann ar Mor, Kornog *France*

MALTY & DRY

These whiskies are drier on the nose. Crisp, cookie-like, and sometimes dusty with aromas that remind you
of flour, breakfast cereal, and nuts. The palate is also dry, but normally balanced by sweet oak.

Scotland *Single Malt*
Auchentoshan Classic
Auchentoshan 12yo
Auchroisk 10yo
Dufftown 1997, Manager's Ch.
Glen Garioch Founder's Reserve

Glen Spey 12yo
Knockando 12yo
Loch Lomond, Inchmurrin 12yo
Loch Lomond Single Malt
Macduff 1984
Speyside 12yo

Tamdhu 10yo
Tamnavulin 12yo
Tomintoul 10yo

Rest of the World *Malt*
Canadian Mist *Canada*

Glenora, Glen Breton 10yo Ice
  Canada
Great Southern, Limeburners Barrel
  43 *Australia*
Hudson Single Malt, Tuthilltown *USA*
Teerenpeli 6yo *Finland*

BOURBON & CANADA

Different production processes and different grains mean that different Flavor Camps have been created
for North American/North American-style whiskeys. The whiskeys below are all from Kentucky or Tennessee
unless otherwise specified. Where a whiskey is part of the distillery family, e.g. Jack Daniel's Black Label, the
distillery name comes first. Where the whiskey is made by a specific distillery, e.g. Buffalo Trace produces
Blanton's Single Barrel, the distillery name follows the whiskey name.

SOFT CORN

The main cereal used in bourbon
and Canadian whisky yields a
sweet nose and a fat, buttery,
and juicy quality on the palate.

Blanton's Single Barrel, Buffalo Trace
Buffalo Trace
Early Times
Evan Williams 1999, Heaven Hill
George Dickel Old No.12
Jack Daniel's Black Label
Jack Daniel's Gentleman Jack
Jack Daniel's Single Barrel
Jim Beam Black Label
Jim Beam White Label
Hudson Baby Bourbon, Tuthilltown
Hudson New York Corn, Tuthilltown

SWEET WHEAT

Wheat is occasionally used
by bourbon distillers in place
of rye. This adds a gentle,
mellow sweetness to the bourbon.

Bernheim Original Wheat,
  Heaven Hill
Highwood, Centennial 10yo
  Canada
Maker's Mark
W. L. Weller, Buffalo Trace

RICH & OAKY

The whiskey picks up all of those rich
vanilla-accented aromas from its time
spent in barrel, along with coconut,
pine, cherry, and sweet spice.
This richness of extract becomes
increasingly powerful the longer
the bourbon is in cask, leading to
flavors like tobacco and leather.

Booker's, Jim Beam
Black Velvet, Danfield Reserve 21yo
  Canada
Eagle Rare 10yo, Single Barrel,
  Buffalo Trace
Elijah Craig 10yo, Heaven Hill
Highwood Century Reserve 21yo
  Canada
Knob Creek 9yo, Jim Beam
Pappy Van Winkle Family Reserve
  20yo, Buffalo Trace
Ridgemont Reserve 1792 8yo,
  Tom Moore
Russell's Reserve 10yo, Wild Turkey
Wild Turkey 101
Wild Turkey Rare Breed
Wiser's 18yo, Hiram Walker
  Canada

SPICY RYE

Rye can often be picked up on the
nose in the shape of intense, slightly
perfumed, and sometimes slightly
dusty aromas—or an aroma akin to
freshly baked rye bread. It appears
late in the palate (after the fat corn)
and adds an acidic, spiced zestiness
that wakes the palate up.

Alberta Springs 10yo *Canada*
Barton Very Old Tom Moore
Canadian Club Reserve 10yo,
  Hiram Walker *Canada*
Crown Royal Ltd Edition, Gimli
  Canada
Eddu, Menhirs *France*
Four Roses Barrel Strength 15yo
Four Roses 120th Anniversary 12yo
Four Roses Mariage Collection 2009
Four Roses Single Barrel, 2009
Millstone Rye 5yo *Holland*
Rittenhouse Rye, Heaven Hill
Russell's Reserve Rye 6yo,
  Wild Turkey
Sazerac Rye, *Buffalo Trace*
Sazerac 18yo, *Buffalo Trace*
Tom Moore 4yo
Woodford Reserve Distiller's Select
Very Old Barton 6yo, Tom Moore

GLOSSARY

Entries in SMALL CAPS are cross-references within the Glossary.

Age statement An age on the label refers to the youngest component. Remember that age is not necessarily a determinant of quality.

Abv (alcohol by volume) The alcoholic content of a whisky expressed as a percentage of the total volume of liquid. By law, Scotch whisky must be 40% ABV or more. *See also* PROOF.

Angel's share As a cask breathes during MATURATION, so some of the alcohol will evaporate. This is known as the "angel's share." In Scotland, it accounts for a 2 percent loss of each cask's volume every year.

Backset *See* SOUR-MASHING.

Barley Barley contains naturally occurring enzymes which, once MALTED, aid in the conversion of starch into fermentable sugars. A percentage of malted barley is therefore added to the MASH of cereals in the production of virtually all types of whisky, while single malt uses 100 percent malted barley.

Barrel Term used to define a 53-gallon (200-liter) American OAK CASK.

Beer (USA) Alcoholic liquid to be distilled, aka WASH.

Beer still (USA) The first still (normally a COLUMN STILL) in DISTILLATION.

Blended whisky A mix of GRAIN WHISKY with MALT (in Scotland) or BOURBON/RYE (America). Ninety-three percent of the Scotch whisky sold globally is blended.

Bourbon American WHISKEY style that must conform to the following rules: be made from a MASH containing at least 51 percent CORN (maize); distilled to a maximum of 80% ABV (160° PROOF); and aged in new CHARRED OAK BARRELS at a strength of no higher than 62.5% ABV (125°) for at least two years.

Butt A 132-gallon (500-liter) ex-sherry CASK used for maturing SCOTCH WHISKY.

Caramel A permitted additive used in many whiskies (but banned in BOURBON production) to adjust the color of the spirit to insure consistency between batches. Heavy use dulls aroma and gives a bitter finish.

Cask All-encompassing term referring to the different types of OAK containers used for maturing whisky.

Charcoal-mellowing This technique, which defines TENNESSEE WHISKEYS, involves passing the new spirit through vats of charcoal prior to aging.

Charring All American BARRELS are charred prior to use, creating a layer of active charcoal that acts as a filter to help remove harshness and other unwanted immature aromas. CHARCOAL-MELLOWING accelerates this process.

Clearic *See* NEW MAKE.

Condensing The final part of DISTILLATION where alcohol vapor is turned back into liquid.

Corn The main cereal used in BOURBON production, corn adds a fat sweetness to the final spirit. Also used in Canada and in the production of GRAIN WHISKY.

Corn whiskey American whiskey style. By law, corn whiskey must be made from a minimum of 80 percent corn. There are no minimum aging requirements.

Dark grains The name for the mix of pot ale (high-protein residue after first DISTILLATION) and DRAFF, which is sold as a nutritious animal feed.

Distillation The process that sets spirits apart from wine or beer. Because alcohol boils at a lower temperature than water, if an alcoholic liquid (BEER/WASH) is heated in a still, the alcohol vapor will be driven off in preference to the water, thereby increasing the alcoholic strength and concentrating the flavors contained within the WASH.

Doubler (USA) The simple POT STILL in which the alcohol from the first DISTILLATION is redistilled to produce the final spirit.

Draff The spent grains left after all the sweet liquid (WORTS) has been extracted from the mash tun. It is sold as animal feed.

Dram Although widely thought of as a Scottish term meaning a drink of whisky, "dram" is of Latin origin and refers to a small measure of any spirit.

Drum maltings The most common method of MALTING BARLEY. These huge plants contain large horizontal drums where the green malt GERMINATES.

Esters Chemical compounds created during FERMENTATION. Typically a floral and intensely fruity aroma.

Feints Final alcohols at the end of the second DISTILLATION (aka tails, after-shots).

Fermentation The process by which sugar-rich WORT is converted into alcohol by the addition of YEAST: vital in the creation of flavor.

First-fill A slightly confusing Scottish/Irish/Japanese term, referring to CASKS. When a distiller refers to a barrel as being "first fill," he means that it is the first time it has been filled with Scotch (or Irish, Japanese, etc.) whisky. Because these industries tend to use secondhand CASKS, it is not, however, the first time it has been filled. *See also* REFILL.

Floor maltings Traditional way of MALTING barley. The damp grain is spread on a floor and left to GERMINATE, periodically being turned by shovels or plows. Today, floor maltings have been mostly replaced by DRUM MALTINGS. *See also* SALADIN BOX.

Foreshots The first spirit to appear in the final DISTILLATION. Foreshots are high in alcohol, contain volatile compounds, and are redistilled with FEINTS and low wines in the next DISTILLATION (aka HEADS).

Germination Process in which the BARLEY's growth is nurtured during MALTING.

Grain whisky Made from a mix of a small percentage of MALTED BARLEY and either CORN or wheat and distilled to under 94.8% ABV in a column still. The Scotch Whisky Act decrees that grain must possess the character of the cereal from which it is made.

Heads *See* FORESHOTS.

High wines (USA) The final spirit produced from the second distillation in the DOUBLER (aka doublings).

Hogshead Type of CASK, mostly made from American OAK, with a capacity of 66 gallons (250 liters), aka hoggies.

Indian whisky A somewhat controversial term, since the Indian industry does not conform to the globally recognized definition of whisky being exclusively a cereal-based spirit and permits "whisky" to be made from molasses.

Irish whiskey Although there are only three distilleries operating in Ireland, each makes its whiskey in a different fashion. Cooley uses double-DISTILLATION and PEAT. Bushmills uses triple-DISTILLATION of unpeated MALTED BARLEY. Irish Distillers produces IRISH POT-STILL whiskey which, although unpeated and triple-distilled, uses a mixture of unmalted and MALTED BARLEY in the MASH BILL.

Lincoln County Process The technique that separates TENNESSEE WHISKEY from BOURBON. This involves passing the new spirit through beds of CHARCOAL to remove harsh elements (aka leaching/mellowing).

Liquor (USA) The hot water used in MASHING.

Lomond still A POT STILL that contains adjustable plates in its neck which increases REFLUX and gives the resulting spirit a characteristic oily/fruity quality.

Lyne arm/lie pipe Aka swan neck. The top part of a POT STILL, which leads from the body of the still to the CONDENSER. The angle of the lyne arm will have an impact on the character. An upwards angle encourages REFLUX and tends to make a lighter spirit; a downward angle tends to produce a heavier spirit.

Malting The process which makes the starch available to the distiller through steeping the dormant BARLEY in water, GERMINATING it to start growth and then arresting the barley's growth by drying it in a kiln. This can be done in FLOOR, DRUM, or SALADIN MALTING plants.

Mashing Process by which cereal starch is converted into fermentable sugars.

Mash bill Term used to describe the mix and percentage of different cereals used in whisky-making.

Maturation The final part of the whisky-making process takes place in CASKS and can provide up to 70 percent of a whisky's final flavor (and its color).

Mothballed Term referring to a distillery that has been closed but has not been decommissioned.

NAS Shorthand for a whisky with No Age Statement on the label.

New make An alternative Scottish term for newly distilled spirit. Aka CLEARIC in Scotland and WHITE DOG in the USA.

Oak Legally, all Scotch, American, Canadian, and Irish whisk(e)y must be aged in oak BARRELS. During MATURATION, the whisky interacts with the aromatic extractives present in the wood. This interplay between spirit and oak adds to a whisky's complexity.

Peat(ing) Peat plays an important role in the aroma of many whiskies. Semi-carbonized vegetation laid down over thousands of years on wet, acidic, boggy ground: peat is cut, dried, and then burned in the kilning process in order to impart a smoky aroma to the final spirit.

Phenols The chemical term for the aromatic compounds given off when PEAT is burned. They are measured in phenolic parts per million (ppm), and the higher the ppm, the smokier the whisky. The ppm measurement refers to the MALTED BARLEY and not the NEW-MAKE spirit. Up to 50 percent of the phenols are lost in the distilling process.

Proof A measurement of alcoholic strength, now only used (on labels) by American distillers. American proof is exactly double the ABV (ALCOHOL BY VOLUME) measurement. i.e. 40% ABV equals 80° USA proof.

Pot still The copper kettle-style stills used in batch DISTILLATION.

Quarter cask Contains 12 gallons (45 liters); its use has been revived recently as a way to inject a large amount of fresh OAK into a young whisky.

Quercus The Latin term for OAK. The most commonly used varieties used in whisky are: *Q. alba*, or American white OAK; *Q. robur*, or European OAK; *Q. ptraea*, or sessile/French OAK, and *Q. mongolica*, or mizunara/Japanese OAK. Each has its own range of aromas, flavors, and structure.

Rackhouse American term for a warehouse.

Rancio Tasting term used to describe the exotic, leathery/musky/fungal notes found in very old whiskies.

Refill Term given to CASKS that have been filled once already with SCOTCH WHISKY.

Reflux Technical term referring to the CONDENSATION of alcoholic vapor within the still (i.e. prior to it reaching the CONDENSING system), which turns back into liquid and is redistilled. Reflux is one way of lightening the spirit and removing unwanted heavy elements. It can be promoted through still shape as well as by the speed of DISTILLATION.

Ricks American term for the wooden supports that whiskey BARRELS lie on during MATURATION. Traditional, tall, metal-sided rackhouses are also called ricked warehouses. Also used to describe the stacks of sugar-maple that are burned to give the active CHARCOAL bed through which TENNESSEE WHISKEY is filtered.

Rye (USA) Cereal used in the production of RYE WHISKEY, BOURBON, and Canadian whisky. Rye gives an acidic, mouth-watering effect, with aromas of sourdough, citrus, and an intense spiciness.

Rye whiskey (USA) Legally, a rye whiskey is one made from a MASH BILL containing a minimum of 51 percent rye, which conforms to the regulations governing (USA) STRAIGHT WHISKEY.

Scotch whisky Must be produced at a distillery in Scotland from MALTED BARLEY (to which other whole cereals can be added), which is then MASHED, converted to a fermentable liquid through the BARLEY'S own enzymes, FERMENTED with YEAST, distilled to less than 94.8% ABV, matured in Scotland in OAK CASKS not exceeding 185 gallons (700 liters) in size for a minimum of three years and bottled at no less than 40% ABV. Nothing other than water and spirit caramel is permitted to be added.

Saladin box A method of MALTING that sits halfway between a traditional FLOOR MALTINGS and a modern DRUM MALTINGS, in which the GERMINATING BARLEY is placed in a large, open-topped box and turned via a screw mechanism.

Single barrel (USA) A slightly confusing term; the whiskey in the bottle comes from a single BARREL, but each batch of a single-BARREL whiskey may comprise more than one BARREL.

Sour mash(ing) (USA) The non-alcoholic liquid residue left at the end of the first DISTILLATION, which is then added to the mash in the fermenter. This can make up to 25 percent or more of the total liquid in the fermenter. Adding this souring agent to the mash eases FERMENTATION. Every BOURBON/TENNESSEE WHISKEY is sour-mashed (aka BACKSET, spent beer, stillage).

Straight whiskey (USA) Any whiskey made from a minimum of 51 percent of any one grain (corn, rye, wheat) distilled to 160° PROOF (80% ABV), aged at no more than 125° PROOF (62.5%) for a minimum of two years in new CHARRED-OAK BARRELS and bottled at a minimum of 80° PROOF (40%). No CARAMEL addition or flavor enhancement is allowed.

Tennessee whiskey Is controlled by the same regulations as BOURBON, but distillers in Tennessee filter the new spirit through beds of maple CHARCOAL (aka the LINCOLN COUNTY PROCESS).

Thumper Another name for a DOUBLER. The thumper is filled with water through which the low wines pass—a process that helps remove some of the heavier alcohols. As it does, it makes a "thumping" sound.

Toasting Involves heating the staves of the CASK over a fire to make them more pliable. The heat also caramelizes the complex wood sugars in the OAK. It is these sugars that interact with the spirit to produce a complex, mature whisky. By varying the level of toasting, distillers can create a wide range of effects.

Uisce beatha/Usquebaugh Scottish/Irish Gaelic terms for whisky; translates as "water of life"—a term that has long been given to distilled spirits. It is widely believed that "uisce" was the root of "whisky."

Vatted malt Archaic term meaning a mix of single malts. *See* BLENDED WHISKY.

Vendome still Type of POT STILL with a rectifying column in the neck.

Wash The fermented liquid (aka BEER) that is distilled into whisky.

Wash still The first still in batch DISTILLATION, where the fermented WASH is DISTILLED.

Wheated bourbon A BOURBON whose MASH BILL contains wheat rather than rye. This gives a generally sweeter character.

Whiskey/whisky By law Scotch, Canadian, and Japanese whisky are spelled without an E, while Irish and American have an E, though not all American whiskeys conform to this.

White dog American term for NEW MAKE.

Worm (tub) The traditional manner of CONDENSING spirit. The "worm" is a coil of copper that is immersed in a vat of cold water. Because of the lower level of copper interaction that takes place in this method, worm-tub whiskies tend to be heavier in character.

Worts The sweet liquid that is drawn off from the mash tun.

Yeast The micro-organisms that convert sugar into alcohol (plus carbon dioxide and heat). Different YEAST strains (types) will have an impact on flavor production.

BIBLIOGRAPHY

Books

Barnard, Alfred. *The Whisky Distilleries of the United Kingdom.* David & Charles, 1969.

Buxton, Ian. *The Enduring Legacy of Dewar's.* Angel's Share, 2010.

Checkland, Olive. *Japanese Whisky, Scottish Blend.* Scottish Cultural Press, 1998.

Dillon, Patrick, *The Much-Lamented Death of Madam Geneva.* Review, 2004.

Kaiser, Roman. *Meaningful Scents Around the World.* Wiley, 2006.

Gibbon, Lewis Grassic *A Scots Quair* Canongate Books, 2008

Gunn, Neil M. *Whisky & Scotland.* Souvenir Press Ltd, 1977.

Hardy, Thomas. *The Return of the Native.* Everyman's Library, 1992.

Hume, John R, and Moss, Michael. *The Making of Scotch Whisky.* Canongate, 2000.

Macdonald, Aeneas. *Whisky.* Canongate Books, 2006.

MacFarlane Robert. *The Wild Places.* Granta, 2007.

MacLean, Charles. *Scotch Whisky: A Liquid History.* Cassell, 2003.

Marcus, Greil. *Invisible Republic: Bob Dylan's Basement Tapes.* Picador, 1997.

McCreary, Alf. *Spirit of the Age, the Story of Old Bushmills.* Blackstaff Press, 1983.

MacDiarmid, Hugh. *Selected Essays.* University of California Press, 1970.

Mulryan, Peter. *The Whiskeys of Ireland.* O'Brien Press, 2002.

Owens, Bill. *Modern Moonshine Techniques.* White Mule Press, 2009.

Owens, Bill; Diktyt, Alan; and Maytag, Fritz. *The Art of Distilling Whiskey and Other Spirits.* Quarry Books, 2009.

Pacult, F. Paul. *A Double Scotch.* John Wiley, 2005.

Penguin Press & Carson, *The Tain,* Penguin Classics, 2008

Regan, Gary, and Regan, Mardee. *The Book of Bourbon.* Chapters, 1995.

Udo, Misako. *The Scotch Whisky Distilleries.* Black & White, 2007.

Waymack, Mark H., and Harris, James F. *The Book of Classic American Whiskeys.* Open Court, 1995.

Wilson, Neil. *The Island Whisky Trail.* Angel's Share, 2003.

Magazines

Whisky Magazine

Malt Advocate

Music

"Copper Kettle", written by Albert Frank Beddoe. Recorded by Bob Dylan on the 1970 album, *Self Portrait.*

Smith, Harry *Anthology of American Folk Music,* various volumes

FURTHER INFORMATION

Keep in touch with whisky matters through the net. The vast majority of producers have their own websites these days. Here is a selection of magazines and blogs giving the whisky-lover a broader perspective.

MAGAZINES

www.maltadvocate.com

www.whatdoesjohnknow.com

www.whiskymag.com

www.whiskymagjapan.com *in Japanese*

WHISKY SITES & BLOGS

www.whiskyfun.com, *Serge Valentin's daily musings on whisky and music.*

www.maltmaniacs.org, *This should be the first stop for all malt lovers.*

www.whiskycast.com, *Mark Gillespie's weekly podcast.*

www.edinburghwhiskyblog.com & http://caskstrength.blogspot.com, Two UK-based blogs. *Both are worth checking regularly.*

http://chuckcowdery.blogspot.com, *Want to find out what's happening bourbon-wise? Check Chuck!*

http://nonjatta.blogspot.com, *The must-visit blog for lovers of Japanese whisky (in English).*

http://drwhisky.blogspot.com, *Sam Simmons was one of the first bloggers and is still one of the best.*

www.irishwhiskeynotes.com, *As it says, this covers Irish whiskey.*

www.irelandwhiskeytrail.com, *Want a tour around Ireland's whiskey-related sites? Stop here first.*

www.distilling.com & http://blog.distilling.com, *Keep abreast of news from the world of American craft distilling.*

www.drinkology.com, *Bartender community site that is packed with information.*

FESTIVALS

You can guarantee that as you are reading this there will be one or probably more whisky festivals happening somewhere in the world. The largest global franchise is *Whisky Live!* (www.whiskylive.com); *Malt Advocate* also runs America's largest events, so check its website (above) for details. Also, check the Malt Maniacs' calendar of whisky events on its site (*see* above).

REGIONAL FESTIVALS

Spirit of Speyside, www.spiritofspeyside.com
  Usually the first week of May for one week.

Feis Ile, www.theislayfestival.co.uk
  Usually last week of May for one week.

Kentucky Bourbon Festival, www.kybourbonfestival.com
  Mid-September.

INDEX

PICTURE CREDITS

Mitchell Beazley would like to acknowledge and thank all the photographers, and particularly distilleries and their agents, who have so kindly provided images for publication in this book.

Steve Adams 20bl **Alamy** André Jenny 236–7; Andrew Crowhurst 188b; Andrew Woodley 239a; Bon Appétit 135a; Bruce McGowan 124r; Cephas Picture Library 54b, 70b, 104–5, 134b, 167r, 182b, 256–7; Chris Howes/Wild Places Photography 261l; David Gowans 74–5; David Hutt 12–13; David Osborn 68b; Derek Croucher 280–1; Design Pics Inc.164–5; DGB 106–7; DigitalDarrell 232–3; Epicscotland 6; Ian Woolcock 304b; Image Management 294–5; Interfoto 292–3; Jason Ingram 140–1; Jeremy Sutton-Hibbert 26–7; Jim Nicholson 156–7; Jiri Rezac 69a; John Macpherson 60b, 152b; John Peter Photography 36; Design Pics Inc. 164–5; Les Gibbon 20–1; Margaret Welby 168–9; Mary Liz Austin 234–5; Michele Falzone 212–13; Mike Rex 37; nagelestock.com 30–1; nobleIMAGES 144–5; Oaktree Photographic 128–9; Patrick Ward 183a; Paul Bock 62b, 97a; Peter Horree 190, 254b; rabh images 259a; Richard Childs Photography 34–5; Scottish Viewpoint 38–9, 55a; Simon Grosset 152–3; South West Images Scotland 24–5, 146–7; Stuart Black 289c; Stuart Forster India 300; Terrance Klassen 268–9; Tom Kidd 98r; Transient Light 88–9; Wilmar Photography 24 **Alberta Springs Distillery** 276a **Amrut Distilleries Ltd.** 302 **Angus Dundee Distillers plc** 43, 122 **Arcaid** Keith Hunter/architect Austin-Smith:Lord 94b **Ardbeg Distillery** 158, 159b **Austin; Nichols Distilling Co** 242–3 **Beam Global UK Ltd.**/Lime Public Relations 125, 162a, 163b, 250a & bl, 251 **Ben Nevis Distillery** 143b, Alex Gillespie 143a **The BenRiach Distillery Company Ltd.** 92–3, 126 **Bernhard Schäfer** 292, 293a & b **Bladnoch Distillery** 148–9 **Braunstein** 290–1, 296br **Dave Broom** 23, 162b, 163a, 229a **Brown-Forman** 240–1 **Bruichladdich Distillery** 172, 173a & bl **Buffalo Trace Distillery** 248–9 **Burn Stewart Distillers Ltd.** 5, 110, 166, 181 **Canadian Club** 275r **Celtic Whisky Compagnie—Glan ar Mor** 286a, 287 **Charbay Winery & Distillery** 266 **Chichibu Distillery** 225 **Chivas Brothers** 42, 44a, 45b, 60a, 61, 76, 77c; 78r; 91, 99, 101, 187br **Cooley Distillery** 208–9 **Corbis:** Atlantide Phototravel 278–9, Bob Krist 202, Creasource 22 bcl; Fumio Tomita/amanaimages 216–7; Gary Braasch 22bl; Jonathan Andrew 204–5; Keren Su 22br; Kevin R Morris 244b, 250–1, 267a; L Nicoloso/photocuisine 22acc; Macduff Everton 159a, 171a, 207a; Marco Cristofori 7; Michael S Yamashita 214; Patrick Frilet 297bl; Philip Gould 19; Radius Images 272–3; Raymond Gehman 22bcl; Richard T Nowitz 200–1; Sandro Vannini 48b, 58–9; Studio MPM 22 cc **Destilerías Líber SL** 297a & br **Diageo** 46–7, 48a, 49a, 50, 52, 53, 56b, 57, 72a, 73, 77b, 79, 87b, 90, 94a, 95b, 96a, 97b, 116b, 117, 118, 119, 131, 138, 142, 151, 160, 167l, 182a, 183b, 196l, 199l, Bushmills 206, 207b **Diageo Canada Inc.** 277b **The English Whisky Company Ltd.** 284a & b **The Edrington Group** 51, 62a, 63, 114, 186, 187bl & bc, 194, 196r **Fotolia** Jeffrey Studio 22acr; Kavita 22bcr; Mikael Mir 22al; Monkey Business 22ac; Taratorki 22acl; Tomo Jesenicnik 22ar; Vely 22bcr **Four Roses Distillery** 252l **George A. Dickel & Co.** 260a **Getty Images** R Creation 226b; Sven Nackstrand/AFP 296a; Time & Life Pictures 255; Warrick Page 8–9 **Glen Grant Distillery** 80–1, 82, 83 **Glen Moray Distillery** 98l **Glenmorangie plc** 134a, 135b **The Glenrothes** 84–5 **Gordon & MacPhail** 100 **Great Southern Distilling Company** 304a, 307b **Heaven Hill Distilleries Inc.** 244a; 245 **Ian Macleod Distillers Ltd.** 11, 108l **Inver House Distillers** 127, 137b **Irish Distillers Pernod Ricard** 210–11 **Isle of Arran Distillers** 178, 179 **J & G Grant; Glenfarclas** 54a, 55b **Jack Daniel's Distillery** 258, 259b **The James Sedgwick Distillery** 298–9 **Jenny Karlsson** 188–9 **John Dewar & Sons Ltd.** 64, 65, 78l, 102, 112–13, 115, 120–1; 130,195, 198, 199c **John Paul Photography** 44b, 45a, 133a, 246–7, 277a **Karuizawa Distillery** 224 **Kavalan Distillery; Taiwan** 303l **Davin de Kergommeaux** 276b **Kilchoman Distillery** 173br **Kittling Ridge Estates Wines & Spirits** 274b, 275l **Lark Distillery** 306–7 **Loch Lomond Distillers Ltd.** 109, 193a **Mackmyra Svensk Whisky** 296 bl **Maker's Mark Distillery Inc.** 238, 239b **Morrison Bowmore Distillers Ltd.** 124l, 150, 170, 171b **The Nikka Whisky Distilling Company Ltd.** 222–3, 226a, 227a, 229bl **The Owl Distillery SA** 289a & b **Paragraph Publishing Ltd./***Whisky Magazine* 86l, 136a, 227b **Photolibrary:** Bertrand Gardel 286b; Best View Stock 303r; Britain on View/David Norton 32; David Henderson 139r; Klaus Rainer Krieger 154–5; Marco Cristofori 108r; Robert Harding Travel/Robert Francis 230–1 **Will Robb** 2 **Sazerac Company Inc.** 253 **Scope** S Matthews 284c **Signatory Vintage Scotch Whisky Company Ltd.** Edradour Distillery 116a **Speyside Distillers Company Ltd.** 40a & b **Christine Spreiter** 174, 176–7 **Springbank Distillers Ltd.** 190a, 191–2, 193b **St. George Spirits** 264–5 **Suntory Liquors Ltd.** 218–21, 228, 229br **Teerenpeli Distillery & Brewery** 294a **Tullibardine Distillery** 111 **Tuthilltown Spirits** 267b **The Welsh Whisky Company Ltd.** 285 **The Whisky Couple** Hans & Becky Offringa 40c, 56a, 86r, 136b, 137a; 184–5; 197, 252r, 260b, 261r; Robin Brilleman 41, 72, 87r, 95a, 96b **The Whisky Exchange** 77a, 79a, 87a, 139 **Whyte and Mackay Ltd.** 123, 132, 133b, 180 **William Grant & Sons Distillers Ltd.** 66–7; 68a, 69b; 70a, 71, 199r **Wiser's Whisky Distillery** 274a **Zuidam Distillers BV** 288.

ACKNOWLEDGMENTS

Mitchell Beazley To my wonderful editor, Hilary Lumsden: it has been a blast working with you again; sincere thanks for being there at the right time, being understanding when things got tough, and always giving the right guidance; huge thanks to Leanne Bryan and Juliette Norsworthy for keeping a complex job in shape so fantastically; Susanna Forbes for her patient reading and pertinent points; Maria Gibbs for brilliant picture research; Sally Toms for her mapping, and all the other folks at MB, whose efforts under pressure are much appreciated.

Scotland Nick Morgan, Craig Wallace, Douglas Murray, Jim Beveridge, Donald Renwick, Shane Healy, Diageo; Jim Long, Alan Winchester, Sandy Hyslop, Chivas Brothers; Gerry Tosh, George Espie, Gordon Motion, Max MacFarlane, Jason Craig, Ken Grier, Bob Dalgarno, The Edrington Group; David Hume, Brian Kinsman, William Grant & Sons; Stephen 'The Stalker' Marshall, Keith Geddes, John Dewar & Sons; Iain Baxter, Stuart Harvey, Inver House Distillers; Ian MacMillan, Burn Stewart Distillers; Ronnie Cox, David King and Sandy Coutts, Glenrothes; Iain Weir, Iain MacLeod; Gavin Durnin, Loch Lomond Distillers; Frank McHardy, Pete Currie, J & A Mitchell; Euan Mitchell, Arran Distillers; Iain McCallum, Morrison Bowmore Distillers; Jim McEwan, Bruichladdich; Anthony Wills, Kilchoman; Richard Paterson, David Robertson, Whyte & Mackay; Jim Grierson, Maxxium UK; John Campbell, Laphroaig; Des McCagherty, Edradour; George Grant, J & G Grant; Lorne McKillop, Angus Dundee; Billy Walker, Alan McConnochie, Stewart Buchanan, BenRiach/GlenDronach; Francis Cuthbert, Daftmill; Raymond Armstrong, Bladnoch; Alistair Longwell, Ardmore; David Urquhart, Ian Chapman, Gordon & MacPhail; Bill Lumsden, Annabel Meikle, Glenmorangie; Michelle Williams, Lime PR; John Black, James Robertson, Tullibardine; Colin Ross, Ben Nevis; Dennis Malcolm, Glen Grant; Stephen Bremner, Tomatin; Andy Shand, Speyburn; Marko Tayburn, Abhainn Dearg.

Ireland Barry Crockett, Brendan Monks, Billy Leighton, David Quinn, Jayne Murphy, IDL; Colum Egan, Helen Mulholland, Bushmills; Noel Sweeney, Cooley.

Japan Keita Minari, Mike Miyamoto; Shinji Fukuyo, Seiichi Koshimizu, Suntory; Naofumi Kamiguchi, Geraldine Landier, Nikka; Ichiro Akuto, Venture Whisky.

The USA & Canada Chris Morris, Jeff Arnett, Brown-Forman; Jane Conner, Maker's Mark; Larry Kass, Parker Beam, Craig Beam, Heaven Hill, Katie Young, Ernie Lubbers, Jim Beam; Jim Rutledge, Four Roses; Jimmy & Eddie Russell, Wild Turkey; Harlen Wheatley, Angela Traver, Buffalo Trace; Ken Pierce, Old Tom Moore; Jim Boyko, Vincent deSouza, Crown Royal; John Hall, Forty Creek; Bill Owens; Lance Winters, St.George; Steve McCarthy, McCarthy's; Marko Karakasevic, Charbay; Jess Graber, Stranahan's; Rick Wasmund, Copper Fox, Ralph Erenzo, Tuthilltown.

Wales Stephen Davis, Gillian Macdonald, Welsh Whisky Company.

England Andrew Nelstrop, The English Whisky Company.

Globally Jean Donnay; Patrick van Zuidam; Etiene Bouillon; Lars Lindberger; Henric Molin; Anssi Pyysing; Michael Poulsen; Fran Peregrino; Andy Watts; Moritz Kallmeyer, Bill Lark, Patrick Maguire, Keith Batt, Mark Littler, David Baker, Cameron Syme; Ian Chang.

The snappers John Paul, Hans Offringa, Will Robb, Christine Spreiter, Jeremy Sutton-Hibbert, and also to Tim, Arthur & Keir, and Joynson the Fish for stepping in with photos when distillers admitted they didn't have shots of their own products.

Personal Charles MacLean, Neil Wilson, Rob Allanson, Marcin Miller, John Hansell, David Croll, Martin Will; Johanna and Charles, all the Malt Maniacs.

Massive and everlasting thanks to Davin de Kergommeaux, for stepping in when Canada began to look very sticky; Bernhard Schäfer, for doing the same with the central European countries; Chuck Cowdery, for all his help with the truth about Dickel; to Ulf Buxrud, Krishna Nukala, and Craig Daniels, for contacts; to Serge Valentin for samples and constant good humor; Alexandre Vingtier, for samples; Doug McIvor, Ed Bates, and Neil Mathieson, for the same.

My agent, Tom Williams at PFD.

To my lovely and ever-tolerant wife, Jo, and daughter, Rosie, for putting up with a crazed and increasingly hairy Glaswegian (again).

Written with the aid of Oblique Strategies.